TOWER STORIES
AN ORAL HISTORY OF 9/11

by Damon DiMarco

Foreword by Governor George Pataki

Original Foreword by Governor Thomas Kean
Chairman of the 9/11 Commission

Santa Monica Press

SANTA
MONICA
PRESS

Published by: Santa Monica Press LLC
P.O. Box 850
Solana Beach, CA 92075
1-800-784-9553
www.santamonicapress.com
books@santamonicapress.com

Printed in the United States

Santa Monica Press books are available at special quantity discounts when purchased in bulk by corporations, organizations, or groups. Please call our Special Sales department at 1-800-784-9553.

ISBN-13 978-1-59580-102-9

Library of Congress Cataloging-in-Publication Data
Tower stories : an oral history of 9/11 / [edited] by
Damon DiMarco. — [20th Anniversary Commemorative ed.].
p. cm.
ISBN-13: 978-1-59580-102-9
1. September 11 Terrorist Attacks, 2001—Personal
narratives. I. DiMarco, Damon.
HV6432.7.T69 2021
974.7'1044—dc22
2021015199

Cover and interior design and production by Future Studio

*For all those people sung and unsung
who worked to help others in ways large and small
on that day and all the days that followed.*

CONTENTS

Foreword by Governor George Pataki 9

Original Foreword by Governor Thomas Kean 11

Introduction 15

Timeline of Events for September 11, 2001 17

Map 21

At the Towers   Tom Haddad 25

Florence Engoran 49

Nancy Cass 60

Jan Demczur 78

Arlene Charles 94

Gabriel Torres 100

Homicide Detective "Y" 113

Outside the Towers   Anna Bahney 135

Jesse Lunin-Pack 151

Alberto Bonilla 163

Huston Stewart 170

Ellen Shapiro 174

Drew Nederpelt 178

The Turner Family 186

Mike X 198

Dr. Walter Gerasimowicz 204

Nell Mooney 211

"Joseph" Afse 217

Ground Zero and the Volunteers

Nick Gerstle 225
Roger Smyth 233
Salvatore S. Torcivia 246
Nicole Blackman 262
Tony Rasemus 299
Cassandra Medley 309
Antonio "Nino" Vendome 316
Bobbie-Jo Randolph 322
Rick Zottola 337
Mike Potasso 350

The Aftermath

Jessica Murrow 369
Vincent Falivene 379
Patrick Charles Welsh 385
Lauren Albert and Karol Keasler 397
Kevin Killian 405
Christopher Cass 415
Scott Slater 428
Brendan Ryan and Kristin Irvine Ryan . . 430
Mark Lescoezec 442
Omar Metwally 447
Ken Longert and Fred Horne 450
Jean Knee and Michael Carroll 458
John McGrath 465

Retrospectives

Alice Greenwald 473
Tom Haddad 488
Stephen Adly Guirgis 497
Father James Martin 510
Jillian Suarez 524
Glenn Guzi 532

Contributing Photographers 551
With Thanks To 552
And with Special Thanks To 552

Strange is our situation here upon earth. Each of us comes for a short visit, not knowing why, yet sometimes seeming to divine a purpose. From the standpoint of daily life, however, there is one thing I do know: that we are here for the sake of each other, above all, for those upon whose smile and well-being our own happiness depends, and also for the countless unknown souls with whose fate we are connected by a bond of sympathy. Many times a day I realize how much my own outer and inner life is built upon the labors of others, both living and dead, and how earnestly I must exert myself in order to give in return as much as I have received and am still receiving.

—Albert Einstein

FOREWORD

by Governor George Pataki

TWENTY YEARS after the horrible events of September 11, the stories are still fresh in my mind and the minds of many who were there. But for millions who did not have such an immediate experience, the heroism and sacrifice of that day have begun to fade.

People still remember the numbers. Three hundred and forty-three firefighters. Sixty Port Authority and NYPD officers. In total, almost three thousand innocent souls were killed that day. But the story amounts to so much more than numbers, for each of those figures represents the heroism of someone who reacted courageously on that tragic day.

Tower Stories allows these individuals to share their experiences in their own words. There is no better way for us to hear these tales than through the voices of those who were there. The testimonies gathered by Damon DiMarco include people inside the Towers; first responders who charged into the Towers; eyewitnesses and the bereaved; plus the thousands and thousands of volunteers, both from New York and around the country, who responded so courageously and generously on that day and for weeks and months thereafter.

These are stories that must be told. But, to me—more importantly—these stories must endure.

The story of September 11 contains three different plotlines. Yes, it is a story of the tragic loss of so many wonderful people. But it is also the tale of the tremendous courage with which people from every walk of life responded that day, and ultimately, it is the story of how Ground Zero rose from burning ashes to become a vibrant, active memorial and community.

Today, that community is overseen by the Freedom Tower. Soaring 1,776 feet tall, it shows the world that New York and America will not bow down to those who threaten our way of life. It reminds us that we must never forget the tragedy of that day or the vulnerability that people in a free society will always face from those who despise the freedoms we cherish.

Tower Stories is an important book. I urge all those who appreciate courage in the face of terror and strength in the face of horror to read it.

ORIGINAL FOREWORD

by Governor Thomas Kean, Chairman of the 9/11 Commission

IT IS DIFFICULT to remember that day, but we must. Time has its way of dulling the sharp edge of memory. Once the edge has sufficiently blurred, the distorting colors of apocrypha swirl in, smearing the true images of what we once saw and creating a fable. A myth. By whatever name you call it, the picture is false, yet people will believe it. In later years, they will have no choice since a myth is better than nothing.

This book is unique for several reasons, not the least of which is that it allows our American people to speak for themselves regarding the terrorist attacks of September 11. The events of that day are arguably some of the most traumatic to occur on American soil. There is ample evidence to support the need for a record such as this.

After the Great Depression had ravaged the United States through the early part of the twentieth century, President Roosevelt realized that America needed more than an economic kick start; it needed cultural inspiration, as well. He assigned writers and journalists through the Federal Writer's Project to document the experiences of common people living through uncommon circumstances. Roosevelt knew that a culture which cannot remember its past trials and transgressions will doom itself to repeat them.

The memory of slavery was also fast slipping from the American consciousness. In some ways this was a sign of progress; in other ways it was potentially dangerous. The FWP documented the recollections of thousands of former slaves in what would later become the Slave Narrative Collection. Nearly a hundred years later, these narratives are still performed around the country as theatrical events, assigned as required reading for university courses and read for self-edification by curious citizens. They are a part of our cultural body of evidence against what was, and an inspiration toward a brighter future for what might be. Some of our greatest works of literature were born of this need to bear witness. John Steinbeck's *The Grapes of Wrath*. Jack Conroy's *The Disinherited*. Studs Terkel's *The Good War*.

I'm proud and grateful to see this legacy continued.

What you are about to experience is not media spin, a five-second sound bite, or a coldly recycling film reel. It is a living time capsule of our nation's humanity. The interviews contained in this book are seminal to our American history. They were conducted immediately following the attacks on the World Trade Center, before time had been granted a chance to blur the details. Reading these stories, you get the sense that there was just enough time between the Towers' collapse and the click of the recorder for people to catch their breath and plant their feet on firm ground. Then they began to speak—directly and candidly. They spoke from their hearts, and I can't believe they gave a single notion toward the idea that their words would be preserved forever. It was too confusing and painful a time to fumble with the weight of such ideas. Truth rings out in every word.

I hope this book remains in print for a very long time to come, because everyone should read it. Our children should read it. With regard to 9/11, we—as a people—cannot allow a myth to take root. We must ground ourselves in the reality of our pain if we have any hope of moving forward. And move forward we must.

One of the contributors to this book calls 9/11 "a Kennedy moment . . . Everyone knows where they were when John Lennon was killed. Everyone knows where they were when the space shuttle blew. It's a Kennedy moment. A Pearl Harbor moment." What a valid observation. Yes, it is common for human beings to remember sorrow, difficulty, pain, and loss. But only to inspire us toward higher goals and better times.

And so, I invite you this instant to clear your mind and think back for a moment. Where were you that day?

Watching the video clips spool over and over again on the television . . . listening to your car radio while driving to work . . . waking up to a household exploding with confusion and chaos . . . calling friends, calling family . . . inside the Towers . . . outside the Towers . . . on the streets of New York City, or halfway across the world, wondering where your loved ones were. Wondering. Just wondering.

You were scared. You were angry. You were vulnerable. We all were. But after that initial shock passed, what did you do? Perhaps the most important message recorded in Tower Stories is written between the lines:

You made turkey sandwiches for rescue workers rushing down to Ground Zero . . . you donated goods . . . you sent money to relief charities . . . you held a perfect stranger while she cried . . . you walked the streets of Manhattan, looking for someplace, anyplace to help . . . you gathered together in mourning. You prayed. You hung on. You went back to work. You picked up the pieces.

And maybe, like me, you made eye contact with people you didn't know on the streets where you live, and nodded. Only this time, as our glances met, a new door was opened between us and we were able to share in a quiet secret that everyone suddenly knew—that we are all, in our own way, survivors.

Move forward we must. For we are Americans. This is our story.

INTRODUCTION

THIS TWENTIETH-ANNIVERSARY commemorative edition of *Tower Stories* features six new "Retrospectives" interviews that replace the former "Viewpoints" section. In all cases save one, I conducted these interviews by phone or video chat due to the COVID pandemic.

Like 9/11, the virus has challenged our models for personal, political, economic, and civic behavior. It has reminded us what can happen when a crisis greater than almost anyone could have imagined cuts through the blather of our lives to strike at what is important. Most of all, it highlights the choices we make as individuals, communities, nations, and a world.

Making choices is one of the most powerful things any human being can do. Yes, the tragedy of 9/11 is inescapable. Yes, we should continue to study why 9/11 happened. Yes, we must work to avoid similar incidents in the future. But none of this really matters until we examine the root of the problem: the choices we made before, during, and after the terrorist attacks took place.

Having read these accounts again, I am struck by the choices so-called "ordinary" people made when confronting perhaps the most harrowing trial of their lives. By valuing others as highly as they valued themselves, I believe they showed what is best in both American character and humanity.

Long before physicists teased us with notions of quantum entanglement, the poet John Donne wrote:

> "No man is an Island, entire of itself; every man
> is a piece of the Continent, a part of the main."

He was making a point about interdependence. We human beings cannot exist, let alone thrive, without what the nineteenth-century naturalist Pyotr Kropotkin called "mutual aid." The most complex and beautiful ecosystems only develop when various elements put themselves in service to one another. In this way, they maximize what is best in their partners while nurturing that which is best in themselves.

After twenty years of doing this work, I believe that quantum physicists, John Donne, Pyotr Kropotkin, and so many others are all saying the same thing. We are bound to each other in ways our tiny minds may never be able to fathom. In fact, if an ultimate truth exists, it might be that we function as mirrors held up to each other. Endlessly, we reflect one another. And while it may seem contra-logical, we are less defined by ourselves than by the way we treat one another.

I know this is lofty language. I know that committing to certain choices can be harder than I make it sound here.

In earlier editions of this book, I wrote: "The *Tower Stories* project sprang from the disturbing notion that the memory of September 11 might one day quietly fade from world consciousness."

Two decades later, I am less concerned over what we forget and more intrigued by what we remember, and why.

When it comes to 9/11, no one should wear rose-colored glasses. But in my mind, the horrors of that day still pale in comparison to the unity we found. The compassion, fellowship, and empathy. And the love.

Any fool can tell you these are among life's most fleeting powers. But a bigger fool might admit these are also the things worth living for.

I choose to be the bigger fool.

These days, when I think of 9/11, I think we are all in this together.

There is no *them*; there is only *us*.

And here the work begins.

Damon DiMarco
New York City
April 2021

TIMELINE OF EVENTS

Tuesday, September 11, 2001
Note: All times are offered in EDT

The Planes Take Off

7:58 A.M.: American Airlines Flight 11 leaves Boston for Los Angeles.

8:01 A.M.: United Airlines Flight 93 leaves Newark for San Francisco.

8:11 A.M.: American Airlines Flight 77 departs Washington, D.C., for Los Angeles.

8:12 A.M.: United Airlines Flight 175 leaves Boston for Los Angeles.

The Attacks on the Towers

8:45 A.M.: Flight 11 crashes into the North Tower (WTC 1) of the World Trade Center. A burning hole is torn in the building.

9:04 A.M.: Flight 175 crashes into the South Tower (WTC 2) of the World Trade Center. Now both Towers are on fire.

The First Response

9:15 A.M.: President Bush makes his first statement about the attacks from Sarasota, Florida. He says the nation is the victim of an "apparent terrorist attack."

9:18 A.M.: The FAA shuts down all New York area airports.

9:21 A.M.: The Port Authority of New York and New Jersey closes all bridges and tunnels into and out of New York. The NYSE and NASDAQ stock markets close.

9:40 A.M.: The FAA grounds all flights in the United States. This is the first time in U.S. history that all airline operations have been stopped.

The Crisis Continues

9:45 A.M.: Flight 77 crashes into the Pentagon; the White House and Capitol are evacuated.

9:57 A.M.: President Bush takes off from Florida.

10:05 A.M.: The South Tower of the World Trade Center collapses, showering escapees and emergency rescue workers with tons of rubble.

10:09 A.M.: Heavily armed Secret Service agents are deployed around the White House.

10:10 A.M.: A section of the Pentagon collapses from the damage inflicted upon it. Flight 93 crashes in Somerset County, Pennsylvania; cell phone accounts from passengers on board confirm that the plane was hijacked.

10:15 A.M.: Some 11,000 people evacuate the United Nations.

10:25 A.M.: The FAA reroutes all international flights bound for the U.S. to Canada.

10:28 A.M.: The North Tower of the World Trade Center collapses.

Further Chaos . . .

10:44 A.M.: Federal buildings in Washington, D.C., are evacuated.

10:46 A.M.: Secretary of State Colin Powell, in Latin America, makes plans to return to the U.S.

10:53 A.M.: New York primary elections are canceled.

10:54 A.M.: Israel evacuates its diplomatic centers.

11:02 A.M.: New York City Mayor Rudy Giuliani asks residents to stay home; orders evacuation of Manhattan south of Canal Street.

11:15 A.M.: The Center for Disease Control prepares emergency response teams.

A Long Afternoon

12:05 P.M.: Los Angeles International and San Francisco International Airports are evacuated under the logic that they were destination airports of the four crashed planes.

12:17 P.M.:   The Immigration and Naturalization Service places
              U.S. borders with Mexico and Canada on the high alert
              status, but keeps these borders open.

12:18 P.M.:   Major League Baseball cancels all games scheduled for
              that night.

1:05 P.M.:   President Bush addresses the nation from Barksdale
              Air Force Base, Louisiana. He says that security
              measures have been put into place and that the United
              States military is on high alert across the globe. He
              vows to "hunt down and punish those responsible for
              these cowardly acts."

1:43 P.M.:   The Defense Department announces that battleships
              and aircraft carriers are being deployed around New
              York City; Washington, D.C.; and the East Coast.

1:48 P.M.:   President Bush leaves Barksdale Air Force Base and
              flies to a Nebraska military facility.

2:30 P.M.:   The FAA makes an announcement that all commercial
              U.S. air traffic has been canceled.

2:51 P.M.:   In New York City, Mayor Giuliani announces that
              subway and bus services have been partially restored.
              As far as the number of people killed in the attacks,
              Giuliani says, "I don't think we can speculate . . . more
              than any of us can bear."

3:55 P.M.:   Mayor Giuliani notes the number of critically injured in
              New York City as having risen to 200, with 2,100 total
              injuries reported.

4:09 P.M.:   Adjacent to the Twin Towers, 7 World Trade Center is
              reported on fire.

4:25 P.M.:   The New York Stock Exchange, AMEX, and
              NASDAQ announce that they will remain closed.

4:30 P.M.:   The president leaves Nebraska to return to
              Washington, D.C. Fires are still reported burning in the
              Pentagon.

5:20 P.M.:   7 World Trade Center collapses. The forty-seven-story building sustained heavy damages after Towers 1 and 2 fell. Nearby buildings are also on fire.

5:30 P.M.:   U.S. officials announce that the plane that crashed in Shanksville, Pennsylvania, may have been headed on a collision course for the White House, Camp David, or the United States Capitol Building.

A Longer Evening . . .

6:10 P.M.:   Mayor Giuliani asks New York City residents to stay home on Wednesday, September 12.

6:35 P.M.:   At the Pentagon, Defense Secretary Rumsfeld notes that the building is "operational" and hints at getting to work immediately on responding to the attack.

7:17 P.M.:   U.S. Attorney General Ashcroft announces that the FBI is looking for tips on the attacks.

7:45 P.M.:   Reports confirm that at least 78 police officers are missing; 400 firefighters killed.

8:30 P.M.:   President Bush addresses the nation, asking for prayers for the families and friends of the victims. He notes that the U.S. government will make no distinctions between those who commit acts of terrorism and those who harbor terrorists.

9:22 P.M.:   Reports from the nation's capital state that the Pentagon fire is contained, though not under control.

9:53 P.M.:   Mayor Giuliani announces that no more rescue volunteers are needed, adding that he still has hope that people are alive in the rubble of the World Trade Towers.

10:56 P.M.:   New York City police echo the mayor's earlier sentiment that people are alive in the rubble.

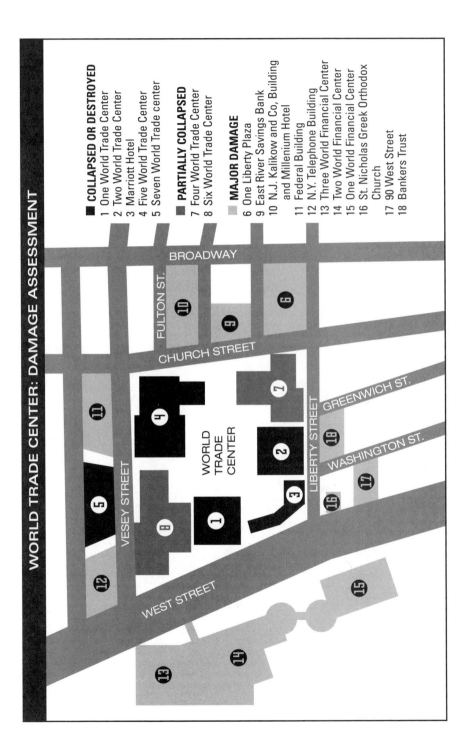

WORLD TRADE CENTER: DAMAGE ASSESSMENT

COLLAPSED OR DESTROYED
1 One World Trade Center
2 Two World Trade Center
3 Marriott Hotel
4 Five World Trade Center
5 Seven World Trade center

PARTIALLY COLLAPSED
7 Four World Trade Center
8 Six World Trade Center

MAJOR DAMAGE
6 One Liberty Plaza
9 East River Savings Bank
10 N.J. Kalikow and Co, Building and Millenium Hotel
11 Federal Building
12 N.Y. Telephone Building
13 Three World Financial Center
14 Two World Financial Center
15 One World Financial Center
16 St. Nicholas Greek Orthodox Church
17 90 West Street
18 Bankers Trust

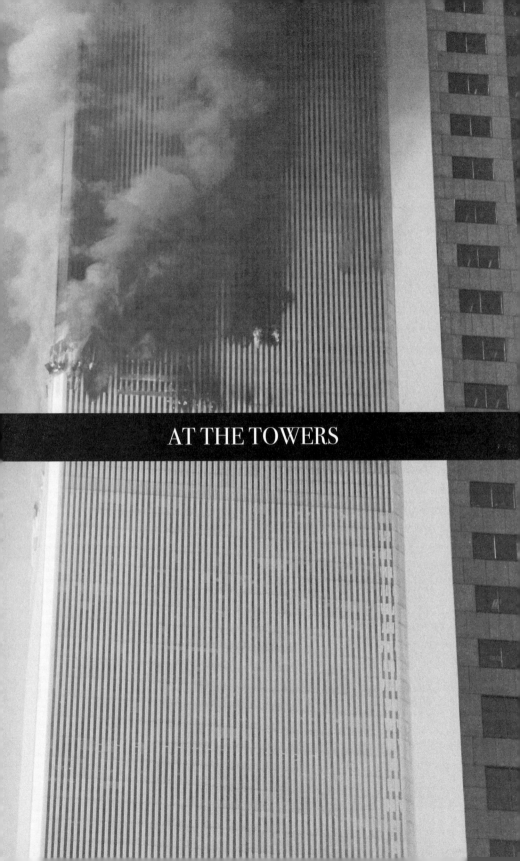

AT THE TOWERS

TOM HADDAD

Tom Haddad, thirty-one, was working in his office, Suite 8901 on the 89th floor of Tower 1, when American Airlines Flight 11 impacted two stories above his head.

FIRST, I HEARD the engine. It was incredibly loud. I'd been in the office late at night during thunderstorms a couple of times. The lightning made the same kind of boom when it hit the river. Then I noticed how the glass in my window had started to vibrate like ripples in water.

Honestly, the order of all this only occurred to me later on. For weeks after the plane hit, I replayed the first thirty to sixty seconds over and over again in my head, trying to make order of it. I couldn't.

Let me start at the beginning.

⫸⫷

I got to work early that day. My company does corporate communications; we do a lot of internal work for banks. JP Morgan had just merged with Chase, so we'd been given a project to educate bank employees on which services were available to them under the new conglomerate.

The client wanted a quick turnaround so I was in the office until about nine at night on the evening of September 10. I got to the office at about 7:30 in the morning on the eleventh, still working on the campaign designs. There were only five people in the office at that point: myself; Lynn, the head copywriter; Sabrina, our receptionist; my friend Evan, who also worked in the art department; and Frances from client services.

I had just completed my designs. Lynn and I were discussing them at my computer. My computer monitor sat in the window well of my office, which faced north. I had a great view from that window.

If I craned my neck about a millimeter to the right, I used to see the Empire State Building off in the distance.

I was seated at my desk and Lynn was passing the threshold to my office, heading out. I thought of another question to ask her, so I got up out of my chair to call her back and look at the designs one more time when we were hit. The impact threw me about three feet, and I hit the wall nearly horizontal. Lynn was thrown a good five feet out my door into the main design department. All the power went out like flipping off a light. The office was plunged into total darkness. Then it erupted into flames. And then the sprinkler system popped on.

When I came to, everything was on fire except for a three-and-a-half-foot path to the door. I was lying in the middle of that path, and so was Lynn. Interestingly enough, Evan, Frances, and Sabrina had all fallen into that same straight line. Later on, after talking about it, we found out how lucky we were. Everything around us had burned.

»»»«««

On a windy day, the Towers would actually sway. You could really feel it move on the higher floors. I could hear the creaking in my office, and sometimes the motion would make the ceiling tiles fall. They'd drop right down on top of you; it was fairly normal.

When we were hit, all of the ceiling tiles dropped on us. And we'd just had construction done on the office to put up walls and so forth, including the wall to my office. One of these inter-office walls fell down.

I stood up, totally stunned. Ahead of me, Lynn got up off the ground and yelled, "Thomas, what are you doing? Run!" She ran toward the front door.

Our office carpeting was that gross kind of indoor-outdoor industrial stuff. If you scraped your feet on it, it would make this sort of *vroooooof!* noise that went right through you. My foot slipped on a piece of ceiling tile and I looked down. Glass was everywhere. That's when I turned and realized that my window had blown in. The columns in the wall had stayed, but nothing else. I was open to the sky eighty-nine stories in the air.

I was stunned at how blue the sky was.

I turned my back to the window, and that's when I noticed the conference room wall had a very interesting pattern of fire running down it. Later I found out it was jet fuel leaking straight down from the ceiling.

>>><<<

I remember how everything was strangely silent except for the constant, high-pitched *whoop whoop whoop* of the fire alarm. Working in the Towers, we'd done fire drills all the time. It was a matter of routine and they'd always played announcements over the intercom system. Nothing now, though.

It seemed like time was moving very, very slowly. I didn't run, I didn't hurry. I just strolled out of the office, absorbing my surroundings.

I got to the front of our office's design department and caught up with Evan. He was as stunned as I was. Together, we walked toward the front reception area. The back wall behind the receptionist's desk was on fire. Sabrina was okay, though. She'd been standing in that same straight line that kept us all safe. But the front doors to the office had blown in. They were on fire, too. And across the hall from our office was a ladies room. The wall was gone and you could see toilets. We were walking on tiles and glass.

Lynn ran through the front door and out into the hallway. We decided to follow her. We were only about six feet out when I looked to my right and realized I couldn't see a thing because of all the black smoke. The entire east side of the building was obscured, and there was no air to breathe.

Evan and Sabrina were with me, and Lynn was in front. But I thought, I don't know where Frances is. So I decided to turn around and go back into the office. At this point, the fire was about six feet high and spreading everywhere. But there was a little spot on the door that wasn't burning, so I put my foot on it and crashed through.

I could hear Frances screaming from the copy room, so that's where I went. I couldn't open the door, though. The filing cabinets in the copy room had all fallen down on top of one another. Frances is tiny; she stands maybe four-eleven. Somehow she'd managed to wiggle in between all those cabinets, which were packed with eleven-by-seventeen reams of paper and lots of hanging files. She was pulling on the door handle, screaming to get out, but it was pointless. She wasn't able to open the door because a filing cabinet had fallen against it. Normally she would have figured this out, but I think she must've panicked.

The cabinets were heavy but I slammed against the door and threw them aside as if they weighed nothing. Pure adrenaline. Evan and Sabrina had followed me, and now they were there, too, raising the rest of the cabinets and debris to clear the door.

When everyone had wriggled out, we bolted through the office again and turned the corner, heading toward the elevators. We could hear Lynn's voice calling to us, "Follow me, follow me!"

We started running.

⟫⟩⟩⟫⟨⟨⟨⟨

It's funny, I found myself remembering stuff I'd been taught in elementary school fire drills. We'd have more air if we got low and crawled along the floor. So I yelled, "Everybody drop! Crawl to her! Crawl to Lynn!"

We crawled right past Kosmo Services, the office next door, which shared a wall with mine. I swear to you, that office looked like nothing had happened even though it was directly under where the plane had flown in. Their power was still on, their phones still worked. Some of the ceiling tiles had fallen and the books were jumbled around a little from the shelves, but it looked as if nothing had happened. I didn't understand it at all.

We crawled into Kosmo and found five people in there including Walter, who owned the company. We tried to catch our breath while Lynn and Walter went out into the hall to see if they could find anybody. They found an elderly gentleman who was yelling, "Somebody please help me!" I don't know his name. I saw him in the elevator every day I went to work but, like a lot of people who worked in the Towers, I never talked much to people I didn't know. Not even a "hello" or "how you doing?" They were just the people in the elevator.

They brought this man back to Kosmo Services. There was nothing wrong with him, he was just scared and in the dark out in the hall. Lynn and Walter reported that they'd discovered all the doors to the stairwells were locked. I don't know why. I've heard that the doors locked automatically during an emergency—some sort of mechanical function. I've also heard that the doors were kept locked intentionally to keep people from smoking in the stairwells.

Each office was apparently equipped with keys, but we didn't know this at the time. I found out later that the keys to the stairwell were in Sabrina's desk at the reception. Which wouldn't have really helped because Sabrina's desk was on fire.

⟫⟪

After Lynn and Walter came back, we closed the door to try to keep the air clean. It was maybe fifteen minutes since we'd left our office and I was still in a daze.

Now this is interesting: in my office, there was a radiator by the window. Every morning, I used to step up on the radiator, into the window well, and put my head against the glass so I could look out and down. From that perspective, you could see everywhere, all of New York City spread out like a carpet. And in the Kosmo office, the first thing I did—by instinct, I guess—was step up onto the radiator, put my head against the glass, and look out.

I wasn't thinking or I might have considered that my own windows had just blown out. Occasionally, flaming pieces of the building would fall and hit the same piece of glass that I was pressing my face against.

Then Walter said, "Hey, you know? I don't think that's such a good idea."

I said, "Okay," and climbed down.

⯈⯈⯈⯇⯇⯇

People started making phone calls. I called my wife, Kim, who works for NBC at Rockefeller Center, but she was still at the gym. She goes there on mornings when I head into work early. I left a message on her voice mail and tried my best to sound even-keeled. I said, "Ah, the building's exploded. Turn the TV on, we're probably on the news."

Then somebody had a great idea and turned on the radio. Simultaneously, Lynn was on the phone talking to a friend who was watching TV. And that's how we learned that a plane had struck the building. Lynn's friend told us.

WNEW radio station was, in my opinion, making light of the situation. They were watching replays of the impact on TV and giving a play-by-play in their broadcast as if it was a sporting event of some kind. Since everyone was freaking out and Frances and Sabrina were crying, I decided that I'd get up and change the station.

That's when the second plane hit. Our building shook, and I was nearly knocked off my feet again.

⯈⯈⯈⯇⯇⯇

We sat on the floor of Kosmo Services. I called my mom, but she wasn't home. I called my wife's machine again and left progressively nervous messages. I later learned there were actually four messages—the fourth message was a hang-up, and I believe it was time-stamped at 9:14 A.M. I hung up on that call because, at that very moment, a guy from Operations came by and opened our office door.

He was dressed in regular office clothes, but he was wearing a hard hat and carried a flashlight. He said that he'd just opened the stairwell and he told us, "Wait a moment, then follow me." But none of us waited. We saw that open stairwell and went for it.

Apparently, there were two Operations guys who came up looking for people. That's what someone told me later on, but I only saw the one. One went down the stairs from our floor and the other guy went up. I assume they were checking to see if they could open more stairwells.

I found out later that the guy who headed downstairs lived. The guy who went upstairs didn't. Later on, I saw a television show on The Learning Channel, and I think I recognized the guy who went up as the Head of Operations, a Port Authority guy.[1]

We started down the stairs. There was nobody on them, it was eerie. There were only eleven of us—five from my office, five from Kosmo, and the elderly guy.

Later on, we were told that everyone else on our floor had been killed.

⋙⋘

We reached the 82nd floor, and someone said that the stairwell was blocked. We'd have to cut across the building and find another pathway down. So we opened the door to the 82nd floor and started walking around, looking for another stairwell.

Eighty-two was completely devastated. The smoke was so thick, you couldn't see your hand in front of your face. And the burning smell . . . I'll still occasionally catch a whiff of it for no apparent reason. Something tangy and pungent, similar to burning rubber. The floor was covered with piles of debris, collapsed plaster walls, and big chunks of metal that looked like beams.

Somebody in our group got the idea to light our way through by turning their cell phone on and off. This little green light would come on in the black smoke and the phone's owner would wave it through the air and around fallen objects so that we could see where they were and crawl through them.

Fire surrounded us everywhere, but you still couldn't see anything. You could only see the fire when you got right on top of it. It was extremely hot. The sprinklers had popped on here, too, so we

---

1 From other accounts in this book, it is likely that this man was Frank DeMartini, an architect employed by the Port Authority of New York and New Jersey who also worked closely with Rick Zottola at Leslie E. Robertson Associates. See Rick Zottola in the "Ground Zero and the Volunteers" section of this book. According to some estimates, DeMartini—along with his Port Authority colleagues Pablo Ortiz, Peter Negron, and Carlos da Costa—saved at least fifty lives in Tower One before perishing when the building collapsed.

were drenched. Fire emergency strobes would flash but we really couldn't see them through the obscurity of debris.

When we got to the next stairwell, we started down again, and now we began to see people. Occasionally, we'd pass somebody going down. We didn't stop for them; we kept to the course and we kept to ourselves. We were tired and scared and very determined.

⇒⟫⟪⟸

When we got to the 78th floor Sky Lobby,[2] we encountered a railing of sorts, a long hallway that allowed us to keep going without actually venturing out onto 78. And at the end of this hallway were two doors, standing side by side. Two guys were standing in front of them and they were yelling at each other.

One door said "EXIT" on it with a sign pointing down, and one man was saying that they should follow that sign, the sign showed the way. But the other man yelled, "No. I've done this before. This other door goes to the bottom. If you take the stairs with the EXIT sign, you'll have to cross the building again."

"I'm following the sign—I'm following the sign!" said the one guy.

And the other guy said: "You do what you want. I'm going this way."

They were very angry and I didn't recognize either of them.

I was in the front of our group at this point. Somehow we'd lost the people from Kosmo Services, so there were just the five from our office and the elderly gentleman. I said, "I'm following this guy if he says this door leads to the ground." Not the guy who followed the sign, but the guy who said, "I've done this before."

And that's the way we went.

⇒⟫⟪⟸

---

2 A Sky Lobby was a sort of dock that increased office space without having to put in more elevators. There were elevator banks at the base of each Tower that would go direct to the Sky Lobbies
on the seventy-eighth or forty-fourth floors. From there, you would take a local elevator to the
floor you worked on.

We entered another stairwell, but this one was flooded. Water was rushing ankle-deep in a constant flow down the stairs from the sprinklers, or maybe from broken pipes. At some points the flow was so heavy, you had to hold on tight to the railing. It was incredibly hot and we were soaking wet.

In the stairwells, you'd see items that had been discarded by fleeing people. A pair of shoes, a tie, a briefcase. As if someone had said, "Screw this, I don't need this tie anymore," and tossed it.

We encountered a lot more people around floor 50. Before that, we'd seen small groups here and there, but there were actual crowds on 50. People were yelling out their floor number as they went down in order to let people know who was evacuating. Not once did we hear any number higher than our floor.

A few people were stopping to drink Cokes, soft drinks, and water from jugs. I heard someone call out, "Does anyone want a Dr. Pepper?" Uh-uh. Were they kidding? We didn't stop for anything or anybody. Actually, that's not true. A couple of elderly women were having trouble getting down the stairs at one point where the water was serious. We helped them get past that area.

We weren't abandoning anyone, but we also weren't allowing how tired we felt to affect our mission, which was to get the five of us the hell out of there.

>>><<<

We'd been walking down the stairwell two by two all along. But this started to break up around the 50th floor since, occasionally, someone would come up the stairs—a building manager or an occasional EMT. When this happened, we had to shuffle ourselves around to make room so they could pass. By the 30th floor, so many people were coming up that we were down to proceeding single file.

And on the 30th floor, we saw the first fireman. He had his full gear on and a hose over his shoulder. I couldn't believe he had the energy to walk up the steps with a load like that. He looked exhausted, ready to drop. He took his helmet off and someone poured water into it. Then he put the helmet back on his head with the water still in it and kept climbing.

It was devastatingly hot.

People weren't panicked on the stairs. No one was pushing. Everyone seemed friendly and calm. I guess we all thought that, by getting to the stairs, we'd be safe. We'd get out. After all, the fire was behind us. It was just a matter of keep walking, keep walking. At that point, we still didn't know what kind of devastation had taken place.

The line was moving slow, but the water was moving fast. As we got lower and lower, you had to hold onto the brackets that held the banister to the wall. The force of the water was that powerful.

⤜⤜⤜

At about the 3rd floor, we found a woman sitting in a chair by the stairwell doorway. She had two firemen by her side and she was in hysterics, saying that she couldn't go any more, she absolutely could not walk anymore.

The firemen were saying to her, "Please. You have to keep walking. You only have three floors to go . . ."

Two regular office guys moved past us carrying a person in a wheelchair via a board slung between the wheels.

A door opened out onto the plaza level. Technically, this was floor two, the courtyard between the two Towers. The Trade Center really had two ground levels: this plaza level and the true ground level at the bottom of the escalators.

I saw that the huge glass windows of the plaza were still

Fish Out of Water by Tom Haddad.
Tom says that none of his drawings have anything to do with his experience on 9/11.

intact, and there was a line of police officers stretching all the way back. The police were shouting to us, "Don't look out the window! Just keep walking! Go!"

And at this point, the five of us got separated. Frances and Sabrina had gotten ahead of us in the stairwell and were lost from sight, but I was still with Lynn and Evan.

❯❯❯❯❮❮❮❮

A guy walked past me and started through the plaza. He was bald and had a massive head wound that stretched all the way over his skull from temple to temple. It was pouring blood onto his white dress shirt.

A cop yelled out to him, "Hey, buddy, are you okay?" and ran forward from the line.

The bald guy had a heavy, matter-of-fact New York accent, and he said, "Yeah. I've had better days."

Then the cops suddenly started yelling, "If you have the energy, run! If you can, you gotta run!"

Lynn took off running down toward the escalator.

I turned my head and looked, just like they'd told us not to. And time stopped dead for me, like it had immediately after the plane's impact. It's tough to describe. I was still walking, but I was completely hypnotized by what I saw going on through the windows in the plaza outside the building.

The Sphere[3] had been smashed. It had a huge dent in it and a piece of the building on top of it. A large chunk of the building façade had landed right outside the window and was blazing fire. And occasionally you'd hear these devastatingly loud thumps. At the time, I thought they came from more falling pieces of the building. It didn't register, but there were hunks and piles of meat all over the ground ... nothing I recognized as body parts. Later on, I found out they were the remains of jumpers.

---

3 Sculpture by artist Fritz Koenig. A huge gold sphere made of steel and bronze, created in 1971 as a monument to world peace through international trade.

Somehow I kept walking and got to the top of the escalator leading down to the concourse level.

The escalator wasn't working; it had stopped. So we climbed down as if it were a flight of stairs. The bottom steps were knee-deep with water. All the glass leading out of the concourse was broken. All the revolving doors? Broken. The floor was covered in glass.

Here, the staggered line of police officers was directing traffic past the PATH[4] station, around a corner by the A train to another escalator up to the plaza level. We exited to the Trade Center campus. I think we were on Church Street, just Lynn, Evan, and myself.

And here there were more police officers, and they were yelling, "Don't look up, just keep going!" Which is, of course, exactly when I decided to look up. I hadn't even thought to do it until they'd said not to. That's when I saw we were standing directly in front of Building 2. I was looking straight up at a gaping hole with fire coming out of it, the same thing you've probably seen on the news.

We decided to walk across the street. In front of an iron gate surrounding a church, Lynn said, "Whatever you guys do, don't leave me. I don't have any money or identification. I left my purse upstairs."[5] She was very nervous. We all were. At this point, Evan hadn't really said anything, but he's a pretty quiet guy.

Then I heard a sound, like a creaking. Almost like when you have an upstairs neighbor and they're walking around, the beams in the ceiling squeak and squeal. Sort of like that, but really, really loud. And then it was thunder. I turned around and saw the building was coming down. We were only a block away.

The three of us ran in different directions.

≫≫≪≪

I ran straight up Dey Street and passed a 4/5/6 subway station. I turned to go in there, thinking I'd be okay underground, but then

---

4 Port Authority Trans-Hudson Corporation. A series of trains connecting points in New Jersey, notably Hoboken, to stations scattered throughout Lower Manhattan.

5 The church mentioned here was probably St. Paul's.

I got confused. Should I go down? Or try to find a building to get into—or a car to crawl under?

In that split second of indecision, the debris cloud engulfed me. It came from the north, south, east, west. It came from above, swirled up from below; it slammed in from every possible direction. I was standing in the middle of the street, there was nowhere to go, and the cloud hit me like a sledgehammer. Since it came from all directions, I didn't fall over.

Total blackness. No air at all. Panic.

Then something hit me on the head and I pulled my shirt up over my head. I couldn't see anyway, so what did it matter? I remember thinking, I can't believe it. After walking down eighty flights of stairs, I'm going to die right here in the street.

I was so tired. My knees hurt. Anytime I stopped moving, my legs would shake. I wanted to just sit down and let it happen.

But you know, it's funny. Just a couple of days before, I'd made a promise to my wife that I'd never leave her alone. How could I do that to her? I said to myself, I love Kim, so I'm gonna keep walking.

And that's what I did.

I remembered there'd been a building right in front of me before the cloud came down. I started toward it, but ended up walking straight into a parked car. I felt my way around the car, kicking for the curb with my foot. Then I got up over the curb and onto the sidewalk. I was walking like Frankenstein with my shirt over my head and my hands out in front of me.

I walked into somebody who grabbed my hands and spun me around and said, "Go this way!" Then they let go and disappeared.

So I did. I walked in the direction that person had pointed me in, toward the left, where I collided with the rough stone wall of a building. And I thought, okay, I'll just keep walking to the left and maybe I'll get to a door.

I kept going, feeling my way inch by inch, and I came to a corner.

Turn the corner, I thought, and follow the line of the building. Eventually there has to be a door.

Fuck it, I thought. I'm gonna walk forward.

And boom! I walked right through a revolving door and into the building.

>>><<<

I pulled my head out from inside my shirt and saw what must've been a thousand screaming people.

I was standing in the building's lobby. Right at my feet, there was a fireman on his hands and knees in his bunker gear. He was throwing up blood all over the floor, and he looked up at me. His eyes were blood red and he looked at me like I was nuts. Then he handed me a Gatorade. He was still on his hands and knees.

I was confused. I couldn't believe I was alive and here was this fireman down on the floor vomiting blood and handing me a bottle of Gatorade.

"Hey, buddy. Are you okay?" Tom Haddad's self-portrait. The line of police officers in the North Tower lobby broke and he saw the bodies of victims lying beyond them in the courtyard.

And he said, "Just fucking drink it."

I had so much soot and ash in my mouth and nose. I took the bottle to take a swig but I hesitated, weird shit going through my head. A stranger hands me a drink after throwing up and I'm worried about germs? I decided to wash my mouth out with the juice rather than drink it. I swirled the Gatorade around and spat it out on the floor and that's when I noticed that the fireman hadn't really been throwing up blood at all. Like me, he'd spat out red Gatorade.

That's also when I noticed I was covered with a layer of ash one inch thick. I'd gotten wet from the sprinklers in the tower and because of that, everything stuck to me, the dirt, the soot, the ash. Everything.

A guy walked up to me, saying, "Hey, are you okay? Are you okay?" He was totally clean. I handed him the bottle of Gatorade.

Then a policeman got on a bullhorn and said, "If there's anyone here with any disability or asthma, follow my hand." And though there were a thousand people in the lobby, I saw this one hand poke up.

I thought, I don't have a disability or asthma, but I'm gonna follow that hand.

So I worked my way through the crowd. People saw me and made a path. The mob split right down the middle, and I went through a back door and into an Au Bon Pain where I found about ten police officers trying to figure out what to do next.

⇶⫷

When I was running from that building, I felt like Carl Lewis. That's the fastest I've ever run in my life. In retrospect, I had no idea where I was. Even now, looking back, I can't pinpoint the location of that building. I haven't wanted to revisit downtown but, after seeing that special on CBS, I think that maybe I'll change my mind.[6] The brothers captured some of the most extraordinary footage ever taken on that day. The film aired on CBS in March of 2002.

I want to find the street again. I want to know how far away I got from the Towers.

In the Au Bon Pain, there was a case of Poland Spring water bottles and I took one of them along with a handful of napkins. I wiped all the debris from my eyes and face. And that's when it hit me like a ton of bricks that I had no idea whether the people I'd escaped with were alive or dead. I've known Evan since our freshman year in

---

6 The Naudet brothers, a pair of French filmmakers, happened to be filming a documentary on the New York Fire Department on 9/11.

college; we were roommates together. And Lynn? She's been such a special friend to me at my job, like a confidante. Where were they now? What had happened to them?

I thought, how could they have survived? I started to panic. Sitting there in the Au Bon Pain with my bottle of water, I started to hyperventilate.

A police officer sat down next to me and took my hand. "It's okay," she said. "Just let it out. You're experiencing post-traumatic stress syndrome."

I thought, post? No way I'm post. I think I'm still in the trauma. But she was very kind to me, very soothing. With a little work on both our parts, I was able to calm down.

Then another officer got on a bullhorn and said, "We're evacuating this building. Please proceed in an orderly fashion toward the door. When you reach the door, an officer there will tell you to walk right or left. Follow the directions you're given."

I got up and started walking. When I reached the door, the police officer told me to exit and walk right, so I did. I started down the street through calf-deep piles of sand-colored building debris. Everything was weirdly quiet, almost as if my brain had shut down from taking in too much information. When the building had fallen, there'd been so much sound, it was almost like having no sound at all. My ears had only registered a white noise, like a drone.

I walked down the street, not knowing where to go, thinking that everybody I'd been with had died. I barely knew who I was, I was dizzy and disoriented, my speech was slurred. Looking back, it makes perfect sense: I'd been hit twice on the head, once in the office and once on the street. The wall of my office had knocked me on my right temple, and whatever hit me in the street had caught my left.

All I wanted to do was get uptown and find my wife. I knew where she worked and I said to myself, I don't care if I have to walk all the way, I'll get there eventually. Just go.

So I started walking.

I heard someone in the street yell, "Hey, these buses are going uptown."

I looked. There were three MTA buses waiting. The first two were jam-packed with people but the third bus was one of those newer jobs, like the type you'd take on a cross-country tour. There was nobody on it, so I got in line—I was maybe the third person. When they opened the door, I looked at the driver and said, "If you're going uptown, that's where I'm going."

I climbed on board and walked to the back and sat down. I was numb. People were filing on. Some were dirty and some were normal-looking. A guy sat down in the seat right in front of mine and slumped down so I couldn't see the top of his head. I figured he was tired. After all that had happened, he had a right to be. But then, suddenly, he sat back up again and started pounding on the window, yelling nonsense at the top of his lungs.

I remember thinking, here we go, this guy's lost it.

Then he slumped down in his seat again and I noticed his reflection in the window glass—the guy was Evan!

I got up, moved to his seat, and sat down next to him. He said, "You've got to be fucking kidding me. After all of this, here you are."

Then I asked him what the commotion had been all about and he said, "This is crazy, but I saw a guy walking past the bus just now with a mustache like yours and the same build. I thought it was you, so I wanted to get his attention."

I said, "Well, you got it." We hugged each other and I said, "Listen. For the rest of the day, we stick together, okay?"

Evan was fine with that. The bus pulled out into the street and headed uptown.

Building 2 fell as we were making the turn off Park Row. We heard the roar and everybody went nuts, and just like that—poof!— the bus was completely consumed in the debris cloud. We had to stop for a while and wait for the cloud to settle. It was bizarre watching it this time from under glass. Like being some kind of fish in a bowl watching the world go by outside. Pretty soon, we were driving again.

We got to the UN[7] and found the street completely blocked by security. The bus couldn't go north anymore so it turned to head cross-town. I looked at Evan and said, "Let's get out here and walk to Rockefeller Center."

>>><<<

When we got to NBC, a security guard looked me over and said, "Who you looking for?"

I said, "My wife." I told the guard her name.

"Well," he said. "They evacuated the building."

I felt like, now what? Where could she possibly be? New York City is huge. And I'd already tried borrowing a cell phone from someone on the bus to call her, but the cell phone wasn't working. I fumbled with it over and over while another guy on the bus insisted on giving everyone an in-depth account of all the people he'd seen jumping from the Towers.

So I was standing there at NBC, completely at a loss. I barely knew who I was, and Evan wasn't much better off. Then I said, "Well, I'd better get to a hospital. I should really have someone take a look at me." And we started walking west, away from Rockefeller Center. I don't really know why.

>>><<<

While we walked, Evan was able to fill in some blanks. When the first Tower collapsed, he hadn't been out in the dust cloud like me, he'd been running down the street. The door to some building had opened and someone had grabbed him and pulled him in just before the impact.

I wanted to know what had happened to Lynn, but he didn't know much. We both fell silent. Later on, we found out that she was alive, too. She told us she hadn't gotten very far when the first Tower fell. The impact of the collapse had thrown her into the gate of the church we'd been standing by and people had trampled her. They ran

---

7 The United Nations, located on 1st Avenue between 41st Street and 42nd Street.

Debris from the planes was later found at remarkable distances from the point of impact.

right over her as if she were a pizza box or something, and the whole left side of her body was a giant bruise. But somehow she managed to survive.

She'd said she'd covered her face against the flying debris and crawled into the lobby of a building, where she tied her shoe and left once everything was over. Then she'd walked all the way across the Williamsburg Bridge to get home.

➤➤➤❮❮❮

Evan and I got to the DoubleTree Hotel[8] and I thought that maybe they'd let us use their phones.

Once we got inside, the people there looked at us as if we were nuts. This was Midtown and we were the only people covered in soot head to toe. We must've looked like space aliens. Little did they know, there were hundreds more people like us. Thousands. But most of them were walking north from the Trade Center. Because of the bus we'd been lucky to board, Evan and I arrived about an hour or so before them.

The receptionist behind the desk at the DoubleTree looked at me

---

8 In Times Square.

and said, "You're dirty." A definite reproach.

Uh huh. Thanks for telling me. "Okay," I said. I remember getting angry. "I was just in the World Trade Center and I need to use your phone."

She just kept looking at me.

"I need. To use. Your phone."

She turned the phone around for me to use without taking her eyes off me. I decided to call Kim's mother in West Caldwell, New Jersey, figuring that, if anyone knew where Kim was, her mother would. I've dialed that number thousands of times. But on that day, I had to make four or five attempts to get it right. First I couldn't remember the number. Then my fingers were shaking so badly.

I finally got through and my mother-in-law answered. She said she'd heard from Kim and knew where to find her.

Kim had been evacuated from NBC but hadn't known where to go after that, or what to do. One of her co-workers had shown up late to work and had no idea what was going on, just that their building was emptying out. And this co-worker had a cousin who worked in a building close by, so they went there. Kim's mom gave me the number where I could reach her.

Apparently, Kim had reasoned that if she went to another office, she'd have multiple phone lines at her disposal. I called at about noon and . . . well, we were happy to hear from one another. About twenty minutes later, she met me at the DoubleTree Hotel and we started figuring out how to find a way home.

>>>><<<<

That's not the end of the story. Not really. I've been keeping to myself lately, spending a lot of time with Kim. We've been married three years, did I tell you that? Three years in May. We met in high school, so what does that make it? We've been together over thirteen years.

Why have I kept to myself? Because I've been an emotional wreck. Not so much in breaking down and crying a lot, it's more like sudden mood changes. I'll flash to anger like never before. I've always had a short fuse, that's nothing new, but I've always been able to keep it in check. Lately it feels like, why bother?

I've also been hideously depressed. I go from normal to extremes, these huge ups and downs. From what I've read, it's post-traumatic stress, but you know what? I refuse to go to any counseling—for multiple reasons. First of all, I don't think that therapists are going to suddenly make me better. It's gonna take time, a lot of talking and a lot of living. Second? I had a horrible experience with the hospital I went to on September 11. My insurance paid for everything, but they kept sending me these astronomical bills. They found out I had a concussion, by the way. Which probably explains why I walked the streets so long like a zombie.

⟫⟪

I say I don't talk to people, and I say that I've pushed a lot of people away. I have. Will that continue? I don't know. But I'll tell you this much: a lot of my friends come to me when they're having hard times and it turns out that I sort of become their counselor. But I felt as if none of them were there for me after the eleventh, when I needed them. Not that anybody could really be a counselor for this. The whole city's in need of counseling right now. I know I'm being selfish.

And I'm truly sorry that my friends are having problems with this and that. One guy I know—his marriage is breaking up and I'm sorry for that, I truly am. But I don't have time for it right now. I keep thinking about the hundreds of bodies I saw. So instead of being an asshole, which I have great potential for right now due to my temperament, I haven't answered phone calls. I haven't responded to emails just so that I don't lash out at people.

I guess it's safe to say that I'm trying to give myself space to take care of my own shit. I don't want to hurt anyone in the process.

I went back to work the week after everything happened. What can I say? They needed stuff done and I thought that it was a way for me to focus on something else. I was driving myself nuts sitting at home. Once I found out that everyone from my office lived, I went back to work. Work sounded like a good idea.

So now I take it day by day. It helps that I've come up with a way of looking at things. For instance, I make a parallel between my situation and the situation of people who've seen combat. My grandfather was on the beach at Normandy, and one time he told me what he witnessed there. It was horrible, of course. But somehow he'd managed to be a part of this horrific event and maintain a normal life. He never allowed that horror to overtake his personality.

So I use that as a motivation. I won't allow this event to redefine me. In all honesty, it has and it hasn't, but I prefer not to think of myself as a victim. I'm a soldier.

UPDATE

Tom Haddad and I caught up with each other in late January 2007, at a diner off Park Avenue South. I admit that I had reservations about seeing Tom again. The man I remembered from our first interview was prone to anger and dark lapses in conversation. Under the circumstances, it was a perfectly understandable reaction. All the same, I wondered how Tom had weathered the past five years. His experience on 9/11 had been dire. How had he managed it since?

My fears evaporated the moment Tom slid into the bench across the table from me. He was smiling ear to ear. We exchanged a few pleasantries and ordered coffee. Then I realized that, miraculously, I was grinning, too. Tom's pleasure was infectious.

"It's funny," he said, looking around and chuckling. "Kim, Evan, and I went to a diner just like this one on West 34th Street on the afternoon of 9/11. Didn't I tell you that? We tried to hop a ferry back to New Jersey but the lines were too long. So we found a diner and walked inside. Evan and I were still covered head to toe in the debris, and we ordered grilled cheese sandwiches. I never ate mine. Guess I had too much on my mind right then."

"How have things been?" I asked.

"Great," he said, shrugging and grinning. "Really. Kim is fine and the kids are great."

"Kids?"

"We've got two sons now," Tom said. "Mitchell, who's three years old, and Malcolm, he's seventeen months." Tom beamed when he reported this, and it was immediately obvious that he was crazy about his boys.

He went on to tell me how he and Kim moved back to their hometown of West Caldwell, New Jersey, and bought a house three blocks from Kim's mother. "I don't know why we did that. Maybe it was the need to return to someplace comfortable. We'd both grown up seeing this old house from the 1930s on the corner, and suddenly there it was, for sale. So we bought it as a fixer-upper and we've been working on it ever since. We'll probably still be patching it up for a few years to come, but—I gotta tell you—I love it. I really do."

Tom's still working for the same company, but a promotion raised him to the level of Creative Director. "9/11 hurt our business a lot," he admitted. "We used to offer full in-house service in all areas, but nowadays we'll partner up and hire out a lot of jobs. Rather than using a staff of full-time employees, we hire freelancers on a per-job basis from outside the state and even outside the country. It's a different model than we used to use, but it's much more suitable to the way we're working right now."

I asked Tom if he ever thought about what happened on 9/11, hoping that the question wouldn't in any way spoil his good mood. But Tom took the question with great equanimity. "Do I think about it?" he asked. His eyes were fixed on the coffee he was stirring into a smooth brown vortex within his cup. "Every day. Yeah, every single day. And I won't lie to you, there've been some really rough times. Here and there I've experienced sudden bouts of panic and anxiety. Do you remember the blackout in August 2003?[9] That really rocked me. But the incidents have been getting less and less frequent."

---

9 Referring to the Northeast blackout of 2003, a massive power outage that became the largest such incident in American history and affected the cities of Cleveland, Toledo, New York City, Albany, Buffalo, Detroit, and parts of New Jersey, Vermont, Connecticut, Long Island, and most of northeastern Canada. Estimates have recorded the affected area at 9,300 square miles. The incident was undeniably serious and incredibly confusing when it happened, not to mention (cont'd)

"Have you ever considered getting professional counseling?" I asked.

Tom shook his head. "No. And I don't mean any disrespect toward mental health practitioners, but I figured, what could anyone really tell me about my experiences that I wouldn't have to figure out on my own? Besides, I found something else that keeps me sane." And with that, he pulled out a sketchbook and started leafing through the pages.

It's difficult to describe what he showed me. A different drawing leaped forward from every page, each stunningly detailed to a professional level. At first I didn't understand what I was looking at, but Tom said:

"My wife bought me my first pad. She thought it would help me work things out. And I had all this time commuting to the city from home, an hour on the bus each way, every day. So I've used the time to draw. I call it my Bus Therapy."

The drawings, quite frankly, were astonishing. In one, a white-collar worker with the head of a bison, in shirtsleeves and a tie, hunched over a computer keyboard, typing with its hooves. In another, a beast with the body of a man and the head of a fish rode a lonely bus from someplace to another, all the while staring out the window at the barren landscape moving past.

In all, Tom has filled countless notebooks with his work. His attic, he said, is full of them. "I can't seem to stop," he grinned. "It's really something. But I should tell you: most of these drawings have nothing to do with my experience on 9/11."

I re-interviewed Tom Haddad in late September 2020. We talked about how he profited from an experimental therapy program designed to treat soldiers with PTSD. You'll find that interview at the back of this edition in the new Retrospectives section.

---

expensive: outage-related financial losses were estimated at $6 billion. However, retrospective analysis shows that cases of looting and civic unrest were much higher in the legendary New York City blackout of 1977. Rumors of terrorism quickly circulated as having been the root of the blackout but these were dispelled within an hour, leaving many people to wonder who was more dangerous, Islamic fundamentalists or the power companies.

FLORENCE ENGORAN

Florence Engoran, thirty-six, worked as a credit analyst at a securities firm on the 55th floor of 2 World Trade Center. She and her husband moved out of Manhattan and into a home in the suburbs six months previous to September 11.

"So many things happened in the spring of 2001," she says. "We had just purchased a house, we moved to New Jersey, and I switched jobs. Then I found out I was pregnant."

Florence was five months into her pregnancy when United Airlines Flight 175 struck her Tower.

AT 8:40 on the morning of September 11, I got a coffee in the World Trade Center lobby and took the elevator up to the 55th floor of Tower 2. Everything seemed normal enough until I got off the elevator and saw everyone standing around, confused. I heard someone say, "A small plane hit the other building."

I wasn't especially upset by the news. We hadn't seen or heard or felt anything. Usually when things like that happen, people stop working and start milling around.[10] So we were like, "What should we do?"

Some people said, "Oh, just sit down, let's keep working, we have to get out some focus reports." They went back to what they were doing.

I went to my office, which was one of five against the far wall. I put my bag down, but something didn't feel right. I walked out onto the floor. Our space on 55 was a big open court with [work] cubes and then a huge window on the other side where you could see the Hudson River. And within a few minutes, we started to see flaming debris falling past the window glass. Then the noise . . .

---

10 The implication here is that it wasn't uncommon for small planes to hit the Towers. During the course of these interviews, subjects offered many supportive anecdotes to this end.

Huge boulders of concrete. Flaming pieces of paper. At first it sounded like it was starting to rain. But then it got so loud . . .

⟫⟪

Now people were really stunned. I still had my coffee in hand. I didn't go back to my office to pick up my bag, I turned right around and ran to the fire steps. This wasn't a conscious thought on my part. I don't even recall wondering, should I go to the elevators? The stairs? Which one? My mind was on autopilot: I went to the stairs.

It was a panic situation. People started running. We had a trading floor attached to a section of our office and the traders were getting up and running to the stairs. I thought, I'm five months pregnant, and now I'm gonna have to walk down fifty-five flights? Evidently, that was the case. I'd have to make the trip with all these guys running past me, pushing to get into the stairs.

The stairway was wide enough for two people across, no more. You either stayed against the wall or held on to the handrail. The woman behind me started to scream, "Go faster! Go faster!"

I screamed back at her, "I'm pregnant, I'm going as fast as I can!" But other people were saying, "Everyone calm down. Relax. Just keep going down. Focus on walking." It took five flights for me to realize I was still holding my cup of coffee. I put it down and kept moving.

⟫⟪

I wasn't exactly in the peak of health. I'd been having morning sickness, and I was thinking, what if I pass out? No one's gonna help me. I'd just switched jobs, so I was pretty new at the office; I didn't know a lot of people. But these two guys I'd gotten to know bumped into me and essentially said, "Oh, there's Florence." One guy's name was Brimley, the other was Brian.

I'd only known them since May. They worked in the accounting department. When I say I knew them, it was more like we said hi in the morning and that was about it. But these two men promised that they were gonna stay with me the whole time down, which they did.

We kept hearing announcements that said, "A small plane has hit the first building. The incident has been contained there, you don't have to go down." Over and over and over again. But in my head, I was not paying attention to this. I was thinking: I'm on my way down, I'm going down. You can tell me later on that everything's okay.

We probably got to floor 20 or thereabouts when the second plane hit our building.

>>><<<

Up until that point, I guess most people were thinking, it's really not so bad, we're not the building that got hit. Let's just get out of here and everything'll be fine. Even though we were nervous and had seen the falling debris and wondered if our building might catch fire higher up, we thought we were safe. But when our building was hit, people started to scream. The impact knocked people right off their feet. I held onto the handrail with everything I had. The building started swaying so badly; it moved six to ten feet, that's what it felt like.

Everybody started calling out, "What's happening?"

"Oh my God, what was that?"

Different people saying, "They're setting off bombs!"

People took out their cell phones and tried to call their families, but other people panicked and said, "No! Stop using the cell phones. Maybe that's what's detonating the bombs as we go down." Crazy things.

And then the lights went out. Concrete dust started wafting up the stairwell—we were breathing it in. People kept screaming but no one was moving. Now I could smell the reek of what I guess was jet fuel; it smelled like gas.

When the building finally settled a bit, people started running down the stairs, pushing to go past. That lasted maybe a minute before people started to scream, "Stop running, we're shaking the stairwell!" And people calmed down again. As bad as things were, no one wanted the staircase to tear itself off the wall.

We covered our faces with napkins someone handed out. Water

bottles were passed around so you could wet your shirt and cover your mouth. There was smoke in the stairwell. It wasn't a thick cloud where you couldn't see your hand in front of your face, but you definitely had trouble breathing.

>>>><<<<

The climb down from the 20th floor lasted an eternity. People were absolutely silent now, where before they'd been laughing, figuring the danger was in the other building. Everyone was more focused and scared, trying to walk down the steps as fast as they could.

I had stopped maybe twice on the way from floor 55 to floor 20 because it was so hot in the stairwell. I was sweating. I needed a breath. Brimley and Brian still accompanied me. They kept saying, "Okay, we're gonna wait with you. When you're ready, we'll start again." But after floor 20, I was more like, "I'm going down now, no more breaks. If I pass out on the way, it's just gonna have to be."

When we reached the bottom of the stairwell, we saw Port Authority workers directing us through a passageway. "Okay!" they shouted. "Make a left, then a quick right!" We followed the route they showed us through an open door, and just like that, we were out on the concourse.

I remember some people asking, "Why are you making us go through the concourse? We could have made a right and gone out to Liberty Street. Why can't we go out those doors?" But no one was answering. Looking back, I guess we didn't go that way because of all the falling debris.

In the concourse, there were police officers and security guards standing at different points. I feel very bad because I think they must have been left in there when the building came down, you know? They got us all out, but they were still in there.

When I saw them, it hit me that this must be something so bad. I mean, usually, what's the protocol in a fire? The authorities tell you, "Everyone calm down, nobody run." But here they were screaming at us, "Run! Get out! Get out! Get out!" Pointing which way to go,

"... when our building was hit people started to scream. The impact knocked people right off their feet. I held onto the handrail with everything I had. The building started swaying so badly; it moved six to ten feet, that's what it felt like."

through the concourse, which, as I said, was a weird way to go around.

We used an escalator that made us go from the Liberty Street PATH train entrance down past the bakery, by the Nine West shoe store, and out. As we got to the top of the stairs by Nine West, there was a cop there directing us, and he said, "Things are falling. I want you to stay under the building, do you understand?"

We nodded and then he said: "Okay, now! Run! Run!"

People ran. I don't remember things falling, though I know they were. I just kept running.

I got across the street by St. Paul's Church, and that's the first time I paused to look around. I'd lost Brimley and Brian, I remember that much. Were they in front of me? Behind me? I didn't want them thinking that I was still back there; I didn't want them going back in after me. Policemen were telling us to keep going, to run across the street, heading north, uptown ...

And that was the point where I turned back and got my first look of the buildings. And I saw something that didn't quite register to my brain. A necktie. On a man. In his suit. Jumping out of the building. I suddenly realized that people were jumping out the windows of the Towers and falling.

I was either on Broadway or Church Street, I don't know, and I started walking up the street, walking north, past a graveyard now, the one by St. Paul's. On the ground in front of me, there was this puddle of blood and . . . it looked like . . . a mass with shoes and clothes in a pile. I looked at it and didn't realize for a moment what it was. A body. It had to be someone from the plane or someone who had jumped.

I said, "Okay," and I kept moving.

⇒≫≪⇐

A little further on, I stood up on the fence of the church graveyard so I could look back. From up high, I spotted Brian and Brimley; they were behind me, coming closer, and I flagged them down. Then the three of us followed the crowd up to City Hall.

But almost at once we all thought, what are we doing by City Hall? What if this is the next target? So we wound through the streets and the next thing we knew, we were at Federal Plaza. But the guards outside the Plaza were telling everyone, "Get away from this building! Get away!" I guess they thought it might be a target, too.

We were on Thomas Street at that point, with Brian walking ahead. We'd pass lines of people on pay phones—maybe thirty people to a pay phone—and hundreds of people fanned out behind them, standing in line, waiting their turns. They were all way too close to the buildings to suit my taste.

We passed a building and some man stepped out of a law firm. Brian asked him, "Can we come in?"

"Sure, sure."

He took us in.

⇒≫≪⇐

They sat us down, gave us water, and let us use the bathroom and their telephones. Everyone was trying to get through on cell phones but all the circuits were dead. I called my father in Long Island to let him know I was okay. I had to try him twice; on the third time, it went through. I probably made ten phone calls, and that's the only one that went through.

I couldn't get my husband. Later on, I learned that when he heard a plane had hit the first building, he went down to the World Trade Center to see if he could see me coming out. He was standing under the building when the second plane hit, trying to call me at work on his cell phone, trying to call anyone. His phone wouldn't work so he went back to his office, which was lucky. He would have been killed when the building came down.

Brimley and Brian told me, "You stay here. We're gonna go to the corner bar and get a drink."

At that time, this made a lot of sense. I was like, "That sounds like a perfectly good idea." And out they went. I guess they needed it so bad, they left the pregnant woman at the lawyer's office. But they didn't even make it to the corner when a police officer came to the door and started evacuating everyone from our building, too.

As we exited the lawyer's office, we saw a building across the street where people were lined up on a huge set of steps, like a bandstand, looking up at the World Trade Center. And all of a sudden they started to scream. "Everyone! We're gonna start to run again! Go up West Street! Get out of here! Now!"

Everyone had been calm in the lawyer's office, the eye of the storm. Now they panicked. I started to run again but I was so dehydrated, I passed out.

>>><<<

Apparently, two guys from the lawyer's office picked me up off the street. They asked the police, "Can we get an ambulance for her?"

The police said, "There's none coming."

One of the guys said, "Wait, I've got my car here."

And the other guy said, "Put her in. Let's drive."

So—one guy in the back with me and the other guy driving. And as we left, the guy with me turned around, looking out the rear window, and he said, "Oh my God, there went the building." It must have been the second Tower. I heard people screaming.

So now, at that point, both buildings were down. And these two guys drove me to St. Vincent's Hospital.

⇾⟫⟪⇽

They had hundreds of beds, rows of empty gurneys four or five deep, lined up outside St. Vincent's with nurses standing around, waiting. I only saw one patient. Already, there were hundreds of people lining up outside the hospital to give blood. Someone had made makeshift signs that said "A," "O," "B," and people were congregating around them.

They put me in a wheelchair and straight on up to the maternity ward. The doctors and nurses were concerned that I needed fluids; they wanted to see how the baby was. They said I was the only pregnant woman brought in from the Trade Center. I looked up and saw twenty nurses milling around the nurses' station, looking at the TV. But no one was coming, do you know what I mean? All these people were waiting, but no one was coming.

As it turns out, I was extremely dehydrated. I'd started a few contractions, but that was from the dehydration and the stress. Once they got fluid in me, everything settled down. The nurses at St. Vincent's kept calling my husband on his cell phone until they finally got in touch with him. He came to the hospital trying to find me, but nobody knew where I was; they hadn't been admitting people properly, so I wasn't in the system. He started walking around trying to find me and eventually got to the maternity ward. It was probably one o'clock in the afternoon when we reunited.

It's funny. All the lawyers in that office, Brimley and Brian, everyone had told me, "Don't worry, your husband's not gonna go to the Tower, he's not gonna come look for you, he'll just walk away."

But I said, "I know my husband. He's gonna look for me." I was worried he'd be standing there at the bottom of the building. When the building collapsed and I didn't know where he was ... let's just say

I didn't feel relieved until I saw him.

>>><<<

Recounting this now, it's almost like normal. Like I'm telling a story. If you'd seen me in the beginning, though, right after it happened, I wouldn't have been able to tell it. I'd have bawled the whole way through. I'm in counseling now. I wouldn't say I'm a hundred percent back to normal. I have trouble going over bridges and through tunnels. But I'm slowly working myself back up. I've been back to the city. That was tough, but I did it.

You tell yourself, I'm a strong person, I'm tough. You never think these things could affect you the way they do.

The baby? She was having a few problems early on, but basically ... she's in there, she's healthy, she's on her way. At St. Vincent's when they were looking at her on the monitor, they said, "Wow, look at that! She's really moving around!" I figured, well, why not? I'd just walked down fifty-five flights and ran for at least a mile, and she was in there through it all, kicking around, moving. Running with me. It's given me a connection to her.

Before, September 11, I wasn't talking to her. I didn't have that connection of, "Okay, little baby. Mommy's running now. Just calm down." Now I do.

I have to admit, a few weeks after the attack I thought, am I out of my mind bringing a child into this world? Especially, too—she was diagnosed with fluid on the brain. I thought, I'm gonna bring this child who's possibly handicapped into this crazy world? What do I tell her? "People in this world will leave you when buildings are about to collapse. They're not gonna help you. You're not gonna be able to get out." Do I tell her that if she comes out unable to walk down a flight of steps on her own? You see, my other source of guilt I have— there were so many handicapped people left in the building. They couldn't get out. No one helped them. And they died. But I'm dealing with that. I'm getting help. I'm working it out.

Now, I definitely feel it's important that my baby's coming. Why should I not have a child? Why let horrible people who only know how to hate fill this world?

Fill the world with good people instead. It's important.

Emily Anne Engoran, the littlest WTC escapee, was born on February 18, 2002, weighing in at 8 pounds 12.5 ounces.

UPDATE

Florence Engoran checked back in with me in December of 2006. She had very good news: Emily Anne now has a new baby sister, Sophia Rose, who recently turned one year old.

Florence observed that her life has changed a lot since September 11. "I try not to reflect on the nightmarish portion," she said. "I don't watch shows with news coverage from that day, for instance. Still can't bring myself to watch it."

Still, Florence noted that 9/11 helped inspire her to quit her job as a credit officer with her firm and go back to school for her master's degree in social work. "I want to work on the issues that really caused 9/11," she said. "Hunger, poverty, and intolerance. War won't change these things, and I wish Bush wouldn't use 9/11 as a reason for the war in Iraq. I think the past elections have let him know how the majority of [the] nation feels about his foreign policy."[11]

Florence also added that the recent movies depicting 9/11—notably Oliver Stone's *World Trade Center*, Paul Greengrass's *United 93*, and ABC Television's *The Path to 9/11*—were productions she was "displeased with." Public sentiment seems divided on this issue.

---

11 Referring to the elections of November 2006, in which all U.S. House of Representatives seats and one third of the seats in the U.S. Senate were contested, as well as thirty-six governorships and many other state and territorial legislatures. The final result of the 2006 elections was a massive tumult in which the House of Representatives, the Senate, and most governorships turned over from the Republican to the Democratic Party. President George W. Bush is a member of the Republican Party, and many political analysts speculated that this sudden shift in the balance of party politics reflected the American people's disillusionment with the current administration's policies.

While *United 93* won Oscar nominations for Best Director and Best Film Editing, the *New York Times* ran a story on September 6, 2006, that effectively recounted the firestorm of negative publicity and upheaval caused by the airing of that particular production.[12]

---

12 The article was named "9/11 Miniseries Is Criticized as Inaccurate and Biased," written by Jesse McKinley.

NANCY CASS

Nancy Cass, forty-three, worked for the New York Society of Security Analysts, Inc., located on the 44th floor of 1 World Trade Center. She was employed there for sixteen years.

8:47 A.M.

There were four of us inside one of the elevators on the east side of the building. I was the last one to step off on the 44th floor. I took four steps to my left, heading toward my office. There was a loud explosion and the building began to shake violently. People began to scatter. I froze in place, not knowing which way to turn.

One man got back into the elevator we'd just stepped off of—he looked frightened. The elevator was dark. I shook my head and told him, "No, don't get back in." He stepped out and ran around the corner. I heard debris falling through the freight elevator. It got louder as it came down the shaft, coming toward us, the sound like a ton of rocks being dropped through a long, long line of coffee cans. Then: a terrific swoosh, which was the freight elevator plummeting past us like a rocket through the shaft.

My first thought was that something had malfunctioned with the electrical systems on one of the higher floors. The passenger elevators on the west side of the building had been out of order for the past five or six weeks, and the elevator company had a crew of men working on the scene. I thought something might have gone wrong up there.

Then white smoke billowed out through the freight elevator doors and flames blasted through the opening.

This all happened in less than fifteen seconds.

>>>«««

When I saw the flames shooting through the elevator doors, I turned and calmly said, "Fire."

The people who'd been in the elevator with me on the way up to 44 had run toward the second bank of elevators that went to the higher floors. Now they figured this wasn't such a great idea, and ran straight for the emergency exit. I followed.

I started down the stairs, moving pretty quickly. People were already moving down in single file, and everyone was calm. But then we came to a bottleneck and had to stop; this must have been somewhere around the 39th floor.

A few hysterical women were screaming. Men in front and in back of me kept calling for people to stay calm and we began to move again, though much more slowly. We had to stop every so often to let people exiting the floors below us file out into the stairwell. And every time we stopped, I heard a woman from above me shout, "Why are we stopped? Why are we stopped?"

»»»«««

We were paused on the 35th floor when the woman called out again, "Why are we stopped?" and this time I heard someone from below answer, "The doors are locked!"

I remember wondering, what doors could possibly be locked going down an emergency exit? A building maintenance worker who was behind me asked the same question out loud. Another maintenance worker said that he had keys and started to go down, pushing his way through people.

I kept thinking, what doors are they talking about? And: Lord, I hope he has the right key.

About five minutes later, I guess they got the problem solved because the line started moving again and we proceeded down once more. At this point, smoke was starting to build up in the stairwell, souring the air with an acidic smell.

A young man two people in front of me took a travel pack of tissues from his shirt pocket. He pulled a tissue out and passed the pack to the guy behind him. I remember thinking, oh please, let him pass me a tissue!

The young man realized I was watching him. He looked at me, then handed me the pack of tissues. I took one, thanked him, and passed the packet back.

>>><<<

We continued down, stopping at every landing. People were still calm. Typical New Yorkers. Nothing much fazes us.

One of the men standing in the landing, three people behind me, said, "I wonder how many thousands of people are in this building."

I answered, "I don't know. Do you work here?"

"Yes."

"Oh. If you didn't, I was going to say, what a day for you to visit."

The men around me laughed politely. Nervously.

>>><<<

At the 33rd floor, two black girls started to panic and broke away from the line somewhere above me. They ran down the steps and through an opened fire exit door, leaving the stairwell and entering the building.

A man standing on the landing hollered, "You shouldn't go there! Stay here!" But the two girls shot through the open door and looked both ways, as if they were crossing the street. Then they ran off to the left and were lost from sight.

The man who'd called out to them muttered, "They shouldn't have done that."

I looked at him and said, "Hey, it's a woman's prerogative to do what they did." I gave him a "what can you do?" shrug with my shoulders.

>>><<<

On the landing of the 33rd floor, people from above us started shouting, "Get to the left! To the left!" We all scooted to one side.

I remember hearing some someone above me calling out, "Which left? Which way is left?" Then, people from below started shouting,

"To the right! To the right!" That was a time of confusion. Left . . . ? Right . . . ?

Someone from below shouted, "The firemen are coming, make way!"

We were all trying to get as close to the railing as possible and I found myself unable to squeeze in so I moved three steps down to the landing, hoping to allow more room for the other people. But that landing was not a good place to be. I remember saying to myself, you'll just be in someone's way. Go back to where you were. And somehow I managed to get back in place just as the people immediately above me started shouting, "Get to the wall. Get against the wall!"

Now that everyone had cleared a path on the stairwell, two, then three guys broke out of the line and started running down. I couldn't believe it, what cowards these men were. I shouted, "Hey! We didn't clear this just for you to come down! Stop it! Stay there."

Then I saw some men walking backwards down the stairs, carrying something from above. These were not emergency workers, just ordinary-looking businessmen, and they were leading a woman, a burn victim.

I'll never forget the look in her eyes, the skin hanging from her burnt face, her arms, her hands. It was as if her skin had been peeled off her body. She was a black woman, but her body showed the wounded pink scars that will be with her for a lifetime. Her eyes were white and opened wide, staring straight ahead. She had that look of total bewilderment. Shock and horror. I stared in disbelief.

When she was right next to me, firemen appeared from below, hustling up the stairs. No one moved. Now we had a gridlock right in front of me. People started maneuvering around as the burn victim was led down the stairs. A split second later, the firemen were dashing past me up the stairs.

They looked so young. Their eyes were frightened. As they passed me, I leaned over the railing and shouted down, "Get a medic, this woman needs a medic!" I was hoping there'd be some emergency medical technicians following close behind who could help the burn victim.

Just then, two older firemen appeared on the landing below. They were totally calm and they assured everyone that the smoke was not as bad below. I immediately assumed they were more experienced because one of them had gray hair and they both seemed as if they'd seen this type of situation a hundred times before. They asked everyone to stay calm, so I did.

I remember thinking, these brave, brave men are going up the stairs. Even then, not knowing what was about to happen, I respected their bravery. They had no idea how bad the fire was, how bad the situation might turn out to be. But they kept climbing up. And the equipment they were carrying: the hoses, the axes, the extinguishers. It was all so heavy. You could hear their breathing coming in ragged gasps. It was extremely painful for me to think they had to go up. But I realized they had a duty to do.

>>><<<

We continued to descend the stairs again, slowly, very slowly. We'd stop for long moments, then descend. Stop and descend. Repeat, repeat.

No one was saying anything. Everyone still appeared relatively calm.

At one landing, a building maintenance worker was holding a roll of paper towels in his hand and ripping off sheets, offering them to people. As I passed him, I told him that it was really nice of him to do that and I took a paper towel because I didn't know what I'd be facing further down. I was holding the towel in my hand and rolling it around nervously in my fingers, crumpling it into a small ball.

I still have that piece of paper towel. It's in the shoulder bag I was carrying that morning.

>>><<<

At another landing, I glanced back at the man standing behind me. He had a gas mask on, covering his face. The gas mask was a vivid blue, not the army green you might imagine. It covered his nose and mouth. I wondered, where had that come from?

I said to him, "Hey, that's a pretty smart thing to have right now."

And he told me how he'd been in the building in 1993 when terrorists had tried to blow it up, how he thought the building officials handled that emergency all wrong. He didn't think they were geared up to manage the situation, so he'd prepared himself to deal with something similar.

I thought that maybe he was taking this notion to the extreme and I didn't say anything more.

At some point during my descent, I heard rumors trickling down the staircase that a plane had hit the building. I was used to seeing commuter planes flying past my office window, so I thought, that could be possible. Something could have happened to the pilot, something could have malfunctioned on the plane.

→»«←

At about the 4th or 5th floor, a fireman told us to start going down one by one. There was an overflow of water cascading down the staircase, and I remember hearing some women mumbling about taking their shoes off. I moved past them, thinking, why are you stopping?

"There were too many people pushing onto the boat—like a bunch of people storming the stage at a rock concert to get an autograph from their favorite musician."

Just go, it's only water.

I grabbed the railing and thought, I'm so close. Now all I have to do is get out of here.

At some point during my descent to the lower floors, the lights had gone out. It was very dark on the last few steps leading to the fire exit, and I stopped, not knowing where to go. Suddenly, I found myself alone, looking around. Where had the men who'd been right in front of me gone? Where did the people go who were in back of me?

I turned my head to the right and noticed a light from outside growing dimmer as a door closed. There! I ran down the hall toward the light with both arms outstretched.

※※※

I pushed on the door lever and stumbled out onto the plaza level. This level was one floor above the lobby or street level of the Trade Center. You could walk outside from here to an enormous courtyard called the Austin J. Tobin Plaza. There was a huge sculpture representing the world in the middle of a fountain. Souvenir vendors used to set up shop out there for tourists to buy trinkets. The plaza had outdoor seating for noonday and evening concerts and sidewalk restaurants where people could enjoy their morning coffee or cigarettes, as I often did. There were cement benches where you could sit and people-watch or just listen to the water as it flowed over the side of the fountain. The Port Authority had spent an enormous amount of money landscaping that plaza. Every month they'd bring in flowers, trees, shrubs, and plants. The landscape of the plaza would actually change to reflect the seasons.

I stood there inside the building, looking out the three-story-high windows on to the plaza. As I watched, huge chunks of glass and twisted beams of black, gray, and red steel that were the size of small cars rained all around me. Scraps of paper flew everywhere, like feathers caught in a breeze. Glass, steel, and metal were scattered everywhere on the ground.

I was stunned by this whole scene. Still under the impression that a commuter plane had hit the building, I thought about the demise of the pilot and his passengers.

I looked at my watch. It was 9:15 A.M.

A voice off to my left brought me back to my senses: "Come this way, come this way!"

A World Trade Center security guard was standing at the far north end of the plaza level. I tried to run toward him, but my knees buckled and I stumbled. I don't exercise regularly. That's what did it. I didn't think the descent down forty-four flights would have had that great an effect on my legs, but it did. I limped toward the guard.

When I reached him, he said, "Go that way," and pointed again to my left toward the west side of the building. He said there was a door that would lead me outside and over to the sky-bridge, the glass-enclosed walkway that used to lead to the World Financial Center.

I walked quickly past the guard and toward the door. I paused to look back. No one was behind me, which completely disoriented me. Where had the people who'd been with me gone?

⤜⤛⤛

Then I saw Daisy, the bookkeeper from my office, and I yelled to her. "Daisy!"

I went to her and took hold of her by both arms. I asked if everyone from our office had gotten out all right and she said that yes, everyone had. But she said she thought that Wayne, our executive director, and Mary, an accountant, had gone to check the offices for other people. She said that Tara, my assistant, Mark, the A/V technician, and Maria, an administrative assistant, were with her when she'd left the office, but they'd all gotten separated while going down the stairs.

"Great," I said. "Everyone's out. Let's go."

She said, "Wait, I've got to put my shoes on."

I thought she was silly to have taken her damn shoes off. They're only shoes. But I stood there, holding her up, while she put them back on her feet.

⟫⟫⟫⟨⟨⟨

As we started for the door, the security guard suddenly shouted, "Stop!"

I turned around and saw a girl coming from around the corner I'd just rounded. She froze and looked up, so I looked up, too.

The glass chandeliers were falling.

I grabbed Daisy and placed my right hand over her head, my left hand over mine. My elbow was on her neck, and I pushed her to the side of the building.

We were so close to the door leading out. I remember thinking, if we can just make it across the sky-bridge to World Trade Center 6! If we stand right up against the outside wall, we'll be okay! I knew of an overhang that had been built to protect pedestrians from rain and snow. I'd often smoke my morning cigarette under it before going inside to work. Now it would protect us from the falling debris. That was my plan, at any rate.

"Daisy, come on. Let's go."

We ran out the door and started across the sky-bridge linking World Trade 6 to Tower 1. I put my right arm over Daisy's shoulder and took hold of her left because she said her legs were unsteady and sore, and she couldn't move fast. I didn't really feel like it either. So we didn't run, we walked. The bridge wasn't crowded. Again, I wondered, where did all the people go?

About halfway across the bridge, I spotted Leslie, a friend whom I'd met while commuting on a bus a few years back. I'd bumped into her about a month back outside the West Street entrance to the Trade Center, where people go to smoke. She had recently started working for Kemper Financial/Insurance on the 36th floor. Leslie was holding on to an older woman the same way I was holding onto Daisy. We both looked at each other and smiled nervously. We kept moving.

On the far side of the sky-bridge, we banged up against the glass wall of Building 6. For a moment, we stood there catching our breath. We were safe, but I wondered for how long. Looking up toward the sky, I saw heavy, flaming debris falling all around us. Paper floated down like someone was throwing a ticker-tape parade.

I looked straight ahead and saw a revolving side door about a hundred feet away from us. I said to Daisy, "Come on, we can make it!" And we ran for it.

We went straight for the revolving doors but Daisy pulled up short and said, "Here! We can go through here." There was an open door right before the revolving doors and we dashed inside.

⫸⫷

The Winter Garden was right in front of us, an indoor atrium that used to house very tall palm trees. You could almost have described it as an indoor version of the Austin J. Tobin Plaza.

Daisy and I were standing at the top of the marble staircase that grandly cascaded down to the main floor. I thought about the many brides I'd seen being photographed from those sweeping steps. It was a beautiful staircase, a beautiful setting.

I heard a voice from below saying, "Go toward the exit! Keep moving down, go toward the far exit!" Now that I was oriented, I knew which way we were heading. The far exit they were talking about would put us on the water side of the World Financial Center.

Daisy and I headed down the marble staircase. I looked to my right and Leslie was there again. She and I gave each other a "here we go again" kind of shrug. We smiled weakly and got on our way. Leslie and the other woman she was leading walked off to the right, toward an escalator; Daisy and I took the stairs. At this point, I lost sight of Leslie.

⫸⫷

Once outside the World Financial Center, Daisy and I stopped, turned around, and looked toward the sky. Both Towers were in flames and smoking.

There were wrought-iron tables and chairs set outside under the trees for patrons of the dockside restaurants at the World Financial Center. I told Daisy, "Let's sit here, we can rest for a while and watch what's going on."

I remembered how, back in '93 when a bomb went off in the underground garage of the Trade Center, I'd walked casually from my office on Broadway to the corner of West and Liberty Streets and stood there watching the chaos of firefighters, policemen, and rescue workers. Now I wanted to watch the Towers and take in history while it happened.

I took a seat and looked through my purse for a cigarette. I pulled one from the pack and looked up, realizing I couldn't see anything because of the trees. I said to Daisy, "Let's move to another table for a better view." Daisy and I moved out from under the trees and looked up.

I said, "My God . . ."

The hole in the Tower was huge. It was only at this point that I realized it couldn't have been a commuter plane that hit; it had to have been something bigger. Now we could see the destruction of it all, the enormous amount of smoke pouring from both Towers.

Leslie appeared beside me and nudged my arm. "There you are," she said. She was relieved.

I looked at her and smiled nervously. Then I introduced Daisy to Leslie. The three of us were standing there, staring, as we watched the first body fall from the sky on the left side of Tower 1.

>>><<<

The body dropped out from the curtain of smoke and tumbled down in a cartwheel motion. I'll never forget that. Cartwheeling down from the sky toward the ground.

I was horrified by the thought that someone was jumping from the Trade Center. Horrified. I said something like, "I can't believe someone would jump."

Leslie looked at me and said, "There's already been ten people. I've seen at least ten."

I looked at her, dumbfounded.

When we looked up at the Towers again, more people were jumping. I don't know how many people I saw . . . but I do remember seeing someone who looked as if he were trying to fly from the right side of 1 World Trade Center to the top of the Marriott Hotel, his arms outstretched like Superman.

The images of those people falling from the sky . . . my God. What about their families?

At some point, a large black woman appeared beside us and joined our little group of silent watchers. Then, suddenly, she spoke out loud to no one in particular. "It was two planes hit the buildings."

I said, "No way."

She repeated defiantly, "It was two planes."

I looked up at the buildings again and thought, this woman is crazy. No way could two planes hit those buildings. One plane must have hit. Maybe the way it impacted Tower 1, high up, it plunged and ricocheted into Tower 2. That made sense to me at the time.

But this woman, whoever she was, said, "It was terrorists."

This time I turned and looked her in the eye. "What? No way."

She screwed her face up. Her eyes got real narrow, as if she were shooting arrows from them. In a very flat and odious voice, she said, "It was terrorists." This gave me a very eerie feeling. It was spooky.

In a soft voice, I said to Daisy and Leslie, "Let's move away from here, we don't need to hear this." I was thinking, why is this woman standing here trying to incite a panic?

The three of us backed away, closer to the edge of the Hudson River.

⇥⇤

We all had cell phones and we started pulling them out to make calls. I wanted to talk to my mom in Florida; we talk every day, but usually in the early evening while I was coming home from work. She was scheduled to fly up to New York that afternoon so she could visit relatives throughout the week and meet with me over the weekend. Now I didn't know if she'd still be coming.

My call didn't go through. Daisy and Leslie couldn't get through to anyone, either. I looked around and saw some men with cell phones held to their ears so I walked over to one and asked, "Are you getting a signal?"

He said, "No."

I asked another. This man also said no.

Leslie stopped in her tracks and said, "Hey, weren't the cell towers on top of 1 World Trade Center?"

Of course they were. That's why our calls weren't getting through.

>>>><<<<

I thought, well, there's no reason to stand around. There's nothing to see that I won't be able to watch on the evening news. And there's no way that anyone's going back to work today, not after this.

I turned around and couldn't believe how close we'd come to the commuter ferryboats going over the Hudson River to New Jersey; we were right next to the railing leading down to the docks. Over to my right, masses of people were pushing their way toward the docks and the boats beyond. I told Daisy and Leslie, "Follow me."

There was an opening at the railing and I thought that, if we just continued to move forward and stayed right where we were next to the railing, we'd be able to board a ship easily. I'm taller than Daisy and Leslie, so I moved them ahead of me so I could keep an eye on them— like a mother duck does to her ducklings when she moves them from one location to another. Miraculously, we slid into the line and onto the dock where a line of people had queued up to buy tickets.

Leslie had no money and this worried her—she said she needed to find an ATM machine. I'd never taken the ferry before, but I said, "There's no way they could possibly be worried about checking tickets today."

There were too many people pushing onto the boat, like a bunch of people storming the stage at a rock concert to get an autograph from their favorite musician. I looked around and saw another boat nearby with hardly anyone on it. Someone in the crowd called out that the empty boat was going to Hoboken, New Jersey. I said, "Let's get on that one."

⟫⟫⟪⟪

As we approached the boat, I asked one of the ferry workers, "To Hoboken . . . right?"

He said, "No, this one's going to Jersey City. The boat across the way is Hoboken."

Thank God I thought to ask. Daisy said she'd take the Jersey City ferry since her daughter lived there; she could stay with her. I said, "Okay, take care." And Daisy left.

Then Leslie and I moved across the dock to the other ferry. Again she said she needed to find an ATM machine. I said, "Look. Don't worry. They're not checking tickets. Let's just get on and go."

⟫⟫⟪⟪

At this point, I started to get a little nervous. The boat was filling up fast in front of us, and I was worried there wouldn't be enough room. Then a ferry worker yelled to the people on board, "Move back, make more room! Move back!" The next thing we knew, we were on board.

Leslie was still in front of me. I wanted to get to the upper outside deck so I could continue watching the Towers, but there were three men blocking the way to the stairs—one standing in front of the stairs and two more sitting on the steps. I thought, why are they just watching all these people push their way in? Why won't they move to allow more people on board?

The man sitting on the highest step held his head in his hands. He looked disheveled, totally consumed by despair. I stood there for a moment looking at him, wanting to ask if he was okay. He was most likely in shock. But I was still being pushed from behind.

Leslie and I made our way toward the back of the boat, where there was a covered section. Wooden benches similar to the pews you see in a church ran three across and down the whole section. Leslie suddenly caught sight of a woman she knew who was sitting in one of the middle rows. "I want to go see her," she said. And off she went.

I went to the very rear of the boat and sat in the last row next to a window. There was a group of five businessmen hanging around there and I couldn't help but overhear their conversation. They were talking about what had happened, and I heard one of them say, "Two planes."

I turned around and asked, "Was it really two planes?"

One of the guys said, "Yes."

I lowered my head and shook it in disbelief. During the whole ride to Hoboken, I kept looking out the window. Both Towers were smoking. That's when I realized how utterly numb I felt. I hadn't had a chance to take stock of it before, but now I was in shock.

⋙⋘

When I got to Hoboken, I hopped a train to Berkeley Heights. I was staying there for the week with my cousin, John, because I had three daytime conferences and three late-evening committee receptions scheduled for the week. Daily commutes to and from my home in upstate New York would have been murderous.

On the train, I found a seat across from a young Indian woman and sat down. We looked at each other and gently smiled "hello." We didn't say anything because words didn't seem necessary.

A young man wearing a yarmulke sat on the aisle facing me. We looked at each other, too. Just a blank stare. I watched him bring out this little prayer book. Again, he looked at me and I blinked my eyes, nodding my head up and down, hoping that he'd get my signal to say whatever he was going to say aloud. He must have understood because he started reciting a prayer in Hebrew. The woman in front of him turned in her seat to listen.

Even though I didn't understand a word he was saying, I knew that it was a prayer for those poor people in the planes and in the Trade Center. And somewhere during his prayer, I started reciting the Lord's Prayer.

He finished. We looked at each other. I smiled a little smile and I knew he understood it for a thank you. I kept reciting the Lord's Prayer for a long time.

⋙⋘

At one point I remember thinking, all of my shoes are gone. See, I never wore good heels to the office. I commuted in comfortable shoes, like penny loafers or sneakers. I kept about fifteen pairs of shoes in one of my desk drawers, blue shoes and red shoes, purple shoes and tan shoes. Beige shoes. Green shoes. I had sandals with big high heels and sandals with low, short heels. I must have had five pairs of black shoes. All gone.

Then I realized how stupid it was for me to think about my shoes. What about all our office equipment? We'd finally gotten a great postage machine and now it was gone. All of our computers; all of our membership records; all the paperwork I'd ever generated in sixteen years. Gone.

Then it hit me. My God. The people.

And that's when I knew. I knew that those brave firemen who'd passed me going up the stairs—never came back down.

And I thought, God bless this country. God bless us all.

UPDATE

On September 11, 2006, Nancy Cass wrote a short essay to her family and friends intended to summarize what 9/11 meant to her five years later. She called this piece "What I Lost and What I Have," and has generously shared excerpts of it for publication:

On that day I lost my secure life. I would lose my job within fifteen months at a company that I had worked at for sixteen years. I lost contact with people who were part of my everyday life. Life goes on, but the memories of that day have not faded. Five years later, and as I write this essay, the anger of what happened to me is still within. I still cry. I still pray. I still fantasize about how my life would have been had bin Laden and his group, al-Qaeda, never crossed our borders. Yes, I am still angry five years later.

I still have visions of the people I saw falling or jumping from the building. This haunts me and I pray that the family members of those that jumped will never know that it was their kin. I have a great appreciation for life.

I have a hatred of radical Muslims that preach death to "the infidels." I fantasize that somehow they will all be eliminated from the face of this earth and a peace-filled universe will come about. I know that this will never happen. I have a greater appreciation of my faith and pray that the Lord continues to give me the patience and strength needed to get through another day of news about what is happening in our country and abroad.

I have continuing sorrow for the men and women who lost their spouses on September 11. Their lives turned upside down in turmoil. Not being able to realize a future with their life partner. I have a greater appreciation for my husband and the future that we can share together.

I have heartfelt sadness for the family members who lost a brother, sister, son, daughter, aunt, uncle, niece, nephew, cousin. Memories of those victims are all that they have. I have a greater love for my family and my ability to reach out to them at any time.

I have a deep sadness for the people who lost their best friend(s), never to be physically seen again. I have so much appreciation for my friends and the hugs that we can share.

I have sadness for those people who were physically scarred by the destruction of that day. The daily reminders when they look in a mirror. I truly appreciate my wrinkles and my physical health.

I have mixed feelings about our government and our news media reporting on the war. I understood about going into Afghanistan to go after the Taliban and bin Laden. I understood about going after Saddam and eliminating the terrorist network that was supported there. What I don't get is [how] our country [has been] divided by what the media reports. Who can you or what can you believe? I have the deepest appreciation and gratitude for the men and women in our military who honorably serve our country.

September 11, 2001, has not gone away. I did lose my life as I once knew it. However, I am alive and I have my health. [I] have my husband. I have my family. I have my friends. I have my faith. I have my home. I have my dog. I am a survivor. I have my life!

I will not forget.

JAN DEMCZUR

Jan Demczur, forty-eight, came to the United States from Poland in 1980 and worked as a window cleaner in the World Trade Center every day for ten and a half years. On September 11, using only his window washing bucket and cleaning tools, Jan helped a group of men escape from a stalled elevator in the North Tower shortly before it collapsed.

Mr. Demczur speaks in a soft Ukrainian accent, which turns words like "squeegee" into "skveegee."

AT MY JOB, I worked 6:00 A.M. to 3:00 in the afternoon, and I had a routine. I knew where to start in the morning since a lot of the floors were closed that early. And I knew a lot of the security guards since I'd worked in the Trade Center so long. They would open the doors with their keys and let me in to do my job.

That morning, I had already finished a couple of floors: the 48th, the 49th, the 50th. Then I went up to the 92nd and 93rd floors, which was all part of my routine. And then I did the 77th.

At a quarter after eight, I decided to break for breakfast and took the elevator from the 78th floor Sky Lobby to the one on the 44th. Then an escalator down to the 43rd floor, to the cafeteria to get some coffee and some Danish.

I was eating and thinking of where I would go next. Usually, by that point in the morning I would start on the upper floors and work my way down. So I decided to go back up to the 70th floor. I finished my breakfast maybe twenty minutes to nine, and went back to work.

>>>><<<<

I rode the escalator back to the 44th floor Sky Lobby and took an express elevator to the 70th floor. There were five gentlemen riding in the car with me. They pushed buttons for their own floors: 68, 73, and 74. I didn't push mine, because someone was standing in front of me.

The door closed. We were going up, but not so fast. Then, I felt something—the building shook a little bit from side to side. It was a little swing, nothing unusual. Still, I felt that something was wrong and I said, "This elevator's going down." Everybody looked at me because I was in uniform.

We hadn't reached the 68th floor and now we were starting to go down. The plane had hit the building, but we didn't know anything about that in the elevator. All we knew is that the elevator was dropping when it should have been going up.

I moved to the panel and hit each button, thinking that maybe the elevator would stop at different floors. But no, it was still going down. Then I hit the emergency intercom button and heard ringing on the other end, but no one answered. And the elevator was still going down.

I screamed to the guy on my right side, "Push the red button!" He just stared at me. I screamed it again and he seemed to snap out of it. He pushed the button. The elevator stopped suddenly.

It was a relief, but we had no idea where we were.

>>><<<

A few minutes went by before a man started talking on the intercom. He said, "What happened there?"

I said, "We're in a car. Something's wrong, we dropped a couple of floors."

"Which floor are you stopped on?"

I said, "I don't know, they don't show it."

At the same time, smoke started coming up from the bottom of the car and I thought, this is bad.

The man on the intercom said, "We have a problem on the 91st floor. That's what I heard. Something hit the building."

And that's when we started yelling to him, "Are you going to send somebody to help us?"

Right then the intercom stopped working and we were on our own.

>>>><<<<

There were six guys in all. One tall guy, George—I knew him. I'd see him two or three times a week in the cafeteria, on a floor, in a Sky Lobby. He started pounding on the roof to open the hatch, like in the movies when you see someone in an elevator try to jump from one car to the next. George was pounding, but he couldn't get it open.

Another guy, John Paczkowski, used his hands to pry open the elevator doors. The doors rolled back and we saw a wall with a big number 50 staring at us.

Then two of the other guys complained because smoke was coming into the car. They said, "Close the doors, close the doors!"

I said, "I don't know if that's a good idea."

We closed the doors but the smoke still came in. And I said, "Look, we have to open the doors because in fifteen minutes we might pass out here on the floor."

So we opened them again. I had my wooden stick with me, it's like a broomstick. I used it to reach higher windows or inside-the-glass partitions. It's about four, four and half feet long, between three-quarters to an inch thick, and it fit exactly between the doors—the perfect size. I wedged the stick between the doors to keep them open.

Then I put one hand on the wall and said, "Wow. This is drywall. That's not gonna be so bad. Usually this is only three-quarters of an inch thick."

So we started kicking it.

>>>><<<<

Two guys kicked but we couldn't break it. I said, "Wait, something is wrong. I can't believe we can't break through sheetrock. Usually, you just cut it with a knife and break it like paper."

I turned back to the group and said, "Does anybody have a knife?" Everybody looked at me. "No, no."

Then I looked in my pocket. I said, "Maybe we can work with the squeegee." I grabbed it and started chopping a hole in the drywall. Just a little hole so we could start to break through. I was trying to figure out how thick the wall was.

I chopped through a layer of sheetrock one inch thick and said, "Look at that. I don't usually see a one-inch thickness." But sometimes they use that in office buildings, I guess. I saw another piece of sheetrock behind the first and I started chopping deeper. We did that second piece of sheetrock, but there was another behind that one. I was surprised at this.

Three guys switched off with one other, each taking a turn with the squeegee, digging deeper. We made a hole maybe two inches wide and one inch high.

Finally, I took the squeegee from the third guy and I start banging it. I felt it break through on the other side and I said, "Wow. That's three layers, each layer's one-inch thick." And we started kicking again but the hole we'd made was too small and the wall was strong; it didn't give up.

⟫⟫⟨⟨

We didn't panic or get scared because we didn't know exactly what had happened. We just got busy digging the hole. It was quiet. We got wet with sweat. There was a lot of smoke, and the wind blew powder from the sheetrock into your mouth and eyes and nose.

The first thing I thought was that our elevator had gone down because of some local building problem. But when the smoke started coming out, I changed my mind a little, though I didn't expect something as big as what I later learned had happened.

We cut the hole wider from side to side, maybe twenty-four inches. On both sides of the sheetrock was a metal channel that held together sheets of drywall. Now the gentleman behind me picked up the squeegee's handle, which I had taken off before, and he started scratching at the wall. He cut through one layer and maybe half of the next.

While I took a turn cutting, my squeegee fell out and dropped onto the other side. I was very upset with myself. The guys behind me didn't know that my squeegee fell down and I didn't tell them. I just

looked at the gentleman scratching with the handle. He was exhausted. I grabbed the handle from him and started to cut through another
layer in the middle of the wall.

I turned back to the group and said, "Gentlemen, two men have
to kick this wall at the same time. Now we should be able to break it."

I had on shoes with rubber soles, not very good to kick with. I
looked at George; he was a tall guy with a size ten or eleven shoe. I
said, "You try to kick. Your shoe is leather, it is better to kick with."

He turned around and supported himself with his arms against
the other side of the elevator. Then he back-kicked like a horse a couple of times, really hard, with John Paczkowski, also, the two men
kicking together.

⇶⇶

After a couple of kicks, George's foot broke through and we all started kicking around the edges to make the hole bigger and bigger while
I grabbed the pieces of sheetrock and pulled them down. Finally, we
made a hole big enough for me to look through. But when I did, I
said, "It's dark."

Behind the wall, there was a space maybe eight to ten inches
deep. And beyond that there was another wall made of corrugated
metal two-by-fours and sheetrock.

I took this new wall to be the inside wall of an office space and
said, "Well, there's usually only one piece for that." So we kicked the
new wall a couple times, and that's all it took. We felt the sheetrock
crack and heard tiles spill out on the other side of the wall. I looked
through the hole we'd made and I could see sinks and toilets. I said,
"This is a men's bathroom."

We made this second hole in the office wall bigger, and a skinny
guy named Alfred said, "Let me get through. Maybe I can get through
first."

I thought, right. You guys have been standing in the back doing
nothing, now you want to go first through the hole. I didn't want to be
mean, but I was tired. I looked at Alfred and said, "Okay. Go ahead."

Alfred went halfway through the hole and came out over a sink in a bathroom. At one point, he got stuck. Half of him was in the elevator and half of him was in the bathroom. He started yelling, "Push me! Push me!"

That's one question I remember someone asking me in an interview.[13] "You weren't scared? You were halfway in the bathroom and halfway in the elevator? That elevator might have moved down and cut you in half."

I don't know. You don't think that way when you're doing something like that.

〉〉〉〈〈〈

We pushed Alfred through and when he was safe on the other side, I said, "There must be another bank of elevators around the corner. Go check them and see that nobody got stuck there."

Alfred said, "Okay, okay," and he left to go into the hallway. I guess he took the elevator down to the 44th floor Sky Lobby, because he returned very soon with a civilian and two firemen.

But by the time they returned, we had already made a bigger hole and everybody had climbed out of the elevator. I took my bucket with me and John Paczkowski had his laptop.

When the firemen approached us, they saw five guys standing around, and they were surprised. They said, "Okay, gentlemen, let's hurry up. We gotta move."

〉〉〉〈〈〈

We were inside that elevator for like, forty-five minutes, I think. When the plane hit, it was a quarter to nine or something? Now it was probably 9:30. It turns out we were on the 50th floor. Our elevator had dropped down that far, almost twenty stories.

Some of the guys from our elevator went for the stairway. And I saw a sign that said not to use the elevator when there's fire or an emergency. But the two firemen hopped back inside an elevator along

---

13 Mr. Demczur was interviewed at length by many news organizations following September 11.

with the gentleman from the building who carried the elevator key, which you have to use in an emergency, since the elevators won't operate without it.

I didn't want to go back inside another elevator; I wanted to use the stairs. But the fireman was yelling at me, "Move it faster!" and I don't know what I was thinking, I jumped in the elevator with them.

They brought us down safe to the 44th floor. I still had water in my bucket and, on the Sky Lobby, there were plants, you know? Lots of flowers. I dumped this water onto the plants because I didn't want to carry it down. I said, "Let them grow."

It was only for one second, a very quick moment. I don't know what I was thinking there, either. I guess I was thinking, who knows? Beautiful flowers. Don't want them to dry out.

⟫⟪

On the 44th floor, I went to the stairway and ran into the rest of the guys from the elevator. We started walking down, and at first, we didn't see anybody on the stairway. Then, two or three floors down, there were a lot of people, so many that you couldn't move. After that, it was going very slow.

I just counted floors and wondered, how long is it gonna be until we get down?

There were people evacuating from the lower floors, that's what was taking so long. It was foggy and wet in the stairwell. I heard two guys talking about how two planes had hit. One gentleman who worked up on the 68th floor said, "Don't worry about what happened now, worry later. We'll find out what happened when we get down."

I wasn't really concerned with what had happened, either. I was thinking that maybe the two planes had hit each other in the air and the parts fell on the building or something.

We walked down the staircase very slowly.

⟫⟪

On the 17th floor—or maybe it was the 15th—somebody was

yelling, "Help! Help!"

The door to that floor was open off the stairwell, and I saw a nice gentleman in a white shirt with a briefcase. I said, "What happened?"

He said, "There's two people over there. I need help." But it was dark and I was scared. I was already tired. I saw two firemen and said to them, "This guy says two people over there need help."

One fireman went over to help. By that point there were a lot of firemen around. As we were going down, a lot of firemen were coming up. And I kept going down.

When I was on the 12th floor, I heard a very loud noise. Unbelievable. Smoke was coming up the stairwell fast. I got oxygen twice from firemen on the stairway. I'd been carrying my bucket all this time and people were telling me, "Leave it! Leave it!" But I said, "I like this bucket. I've had it for nine years. I got this bucket for a purpose."

See, the supervisors at my job always told me, "Have two different buckets, a round bucket and a little rectangular bucket." But before, when I was working with a round bucket, I had to stick both hands down in the water. With this bucket, I just had to stick one hand down. It was very convenient.

All the guys I worked with learned a lesson from me. I told them, "Take this bucket from me and try working with it today. See how easy it is to wet the glass." I wanted to keep that bucket for retirement.

But I saw the smoke coming out the doors and I said, "I guess I have to leave it." So I took the rag from the bucket and the handle from the squeegee and kept going.

>>><<<

Then I heard this loud noise on the 12th floor, and it scared me good. I was thinking maybe a transformer had blown up or something. Some fireman started yelling, "Go back up!" and I found myself running from the 12th floor back up to 15.

The people above me didn't like that. They screamed, "What are you doing?"

And I said, "This guy's yelling to go back up."

They said, "No, no, no! It doesn't matter what happens. Go down! Go down!"

So I turned around and went back down.

It was dark. You couldn't see anything. But then I bumped into a couple of firemen with flashlights who said, "Where is the exit here?" One of them turned to me and said, "You work here, right?"

I said, "I *was* working."

"Do you know where the exit is?"

I said, "Move your flashlight on the wall and I will try to recognize which floor this is."

He started moving the light from one side down to the middle and I said, "Here is the exit." Because I saw the door was open and I recognized the slop sink where I usually dumped the water I washed windows with. We were on the 3rd floor.

We pushed the door open, went through, and kept climbing down to the ground.

➤➤➤◄◄◄

There was powder on the floor maybe two or three inches deep, like snow, and everything was twisted and broken. The big glass walls of the first floor, those large panes that stood sixteen feet high in the lobby, were shattered. There was a lot of falling debris that could hit you on the head. It was crazy. In fact, I only recognized that we were in the lobby after I saw the security gate where we slid our ID cards to enter the building each day.

I turned right. In the front of the building was a big vestibule. The visibility was low because of all the smoke, but I recognized the direction that the West Side Highway was in. I started calling out, "We're supposed to go this way, it's more safe this way. If we go the other way, I think it's too far to the exit."

And we ran from the Towers. I followed two firemen out a revolving door. Another one stood outside and yelled, "Hurry up, hurry up!" There was another fireman there holding a hose who said, "Hey, come over here. Get some water."

I washed my mouth and face. Then a medical assistant grabbed my arm and took me maybe ten feet away. He said, "Sit down," and gave me an oxygen mask to put on.

There were a lot of people sitting there, getting treated. I didn't know what was going on. I lifted my head and looked at the building. It was on fire, and I said, "Wow, that's gonna be bad. The top floors are gonna be burned." But I also thought, they're gonna renew it and we're gonna come back.

Then I started looking for the other Tower. At first I thought maybe I was at a bad angle, maybe it was behind the Tower I was looking at. I asked another guy with an oxygen mask on if he could see it, but he didn't say anything.

So I asked another guy if he could see the South Tower and he said, "The South Tower is down."

I said, "What do you say?"

He repeated, "The building is down."

When he told me, my skin froze. And my hair. I was thinking it was gonna go gray right there on the spot. I couldn't believe it had happened. I still can't. That big, strong building went down. All 110 stories.

⤜⤜⤜⤜

I had only been sitting there a very short time when the firemen started yelling to the medical assistants, "Take those people far from here! More people are coming in from the buildings and we need the space."

I picked myself up and started to move. I saw a big policeman who I knew from the Port Authority. Often, I'd see him in the elevator on the 88th floor, a nice guy. All of a sudden he started yelling like crazy, like someone put a knife in his throat or something. I looked at him and said, "What? What is it? What's going on?"

Then I looked behind me and saw the antenna on the top of the North Tower turning upside down. The whole building started to come down, and I wasn't even two blocks away.

I ran. I didn't know—was the building gonna fall on its side?

"I lifted my head and looked at the building. It was on fire and I said, 'Wow, that's gonna be bad. The top floors are gonna be burned.' But I also thought, they're gonna renew it and we're gonna come back."

Which side? Where should I go? It was crazy. I turned around and tried to keep my eyes on what was going on behind me. To do that, I took off the mask and left the bottle of oxygen in the street. I saw that the building wasn't going over on its side, after all; it was collapsing on itself like a stack of pancakes. I ran faster.

I tried to go as far as I could, maybe I got four blocks. But I was shaking. I couldn't walk. I felt as if something had exploded in my head. Everything—my head, my hands, my legs—was shaking. My voice was breaking and I couldn't talk. Probably . . . definitely, I was in shock.

»»»«««

Then some guy came to me and said, "What's your name?"

I replied, "Jan."

He got closer to me and I said, "What's your name?" He was real familiar-looking.

He said, "George." The same guy who was with me in the elevator.

It turns out he'd gotten out of the Tower a couple minutes earlier than I had, and he told me what he'd heard from firemen and policemen. That one plane had hit one building, another plane the other. One plane had hit the Pentagon. He told me there were four more hijacked planes in the air, and that F-16s had shot a plane down. He was scared.[14]

George had a cell phone with him and he'd called his wife. I said, "Can you call my wife for me?"

I gave him the number but I screwed it up. I must've been in shock. Then he gave me the phone to make the call myself and I held the cell phone to my ear and tried to talk, but I couldn't get through.

George said, "Where are you gonna go?"

I said, "I'm gonna go to my wife. She doesn't know if I am alive or not." She was working on 2nd Avenue between 13th and 14th Streets, not far from where I was.

I'm from New Jersey and so is George. He said, "I heard that ferries are taking people from New York to New Jersey. I'm going there and somebody's gonna come with a car to take me home."

So that was that. He went his way and I went mine.

➤➤➤◄◄◄

I went to my wife's workplace. She had known what was going on because she had tuned into the television and radio. She was happy I was alive, but still very upset.

From the TV, I confirmed all the information I hadn't known before for sure—the two planes, the buildings collapsing, the Pentagon. I was disturbed significantly. The beautiful place where I'd worked for so long had come down. To me, it was a second home. The commute from my house was only twenty-five minutes, and I liked working there because I liked all the friendly people and the many tourists that came to visit.

---

14 Various accounts from this time show that rumors had already begun to spread through the streets of Lower Manhattan. These rumors listed the number of attacks in wildly varying numbers, locations, and degrees of severity.

I would hear so many different languages on any given day. People would come to me and ask, "Can you translate? Do you speak this language?" I speak very good Polish, Ukrainian, Russian, and English, so I could help a lot of people. And if I didn't understand them, I always knew someone who could.

I knew so many people who worked in the Towers. They were my friends. A lot of people were killed, and—at that point—I didn't know who was alive and who was not.

My wife and I took a train and then walked to 12th Avenue, where they were taking people across the Hudson River in ferries to reach New Jersey.

>>><<<

The boat dropped us in Hoboken, and there were a lot of policemen, firemen, and ambulances where we landed. Right then, I started feeling pains in my chest. I was holding my chest and someone asked, "Sir, are you all right?"

I said, "Not really."

He said, "Come here," and this man—whoever he was—put

After the planes' impact, emergency first responders administered oxygen, IV drips, and saline eye washes to office workers fleeing the Towers. Over the following days, similar treatments were applied to exhausted rescue workers working on the pile of rubble which the Towers left after their collapse.

me in a wheelchair. He wheeled me to a stretcher and medics checked my blood pressure. They decided to take me to the hospital.

There were nice people all around me at the hospital who told me that I had low oxygen in my blood. So they put me on oxygen for two and a half hours until my level got normal.

The doctor was laughing with me, saying, "You're going to live."

I said, "Yeah, but I don't know for how long."

I was in bad shape. I was in shock. I didn't feel safe. I was scared. I was freezing. I felt pressure in my head, like something had broken inside. But finally, they said I could go home.

While my wife looked for a taxi, I asked a lady police officer near me, "Were you working at the World Trade Center?"

She said, "No."

Then she asked me where I was from. I said, "I was there."

And she said, "What happened?"

I told her about the elevator and how I got out. Behind her was another man, who was listening as I talked to her. He said, "What's your name?"

I said, "Jan."

"I'm the chief of the medical supplies for the Hoboken Fire Department. Where do you live?"

I said, "In Jersey City."

"That's not far away," he said. "Come on. I'll take you home." A very nice guy. He brought us home and was so happy he could help.

>>><<<

I was home by 9:30 in the evening, and there were a lot of messages on my answering machine. My brother called from Poland after he saw everything happen on television. His message said, "Please call home. We don't know what happened to you."

Long-distance wasn't working until the next day, so I bought a telephone card and got a connection overseas to my mother and father in Poland.

When they first picked up the phone, my father couldn't talk. He was crying. He heard me and handed the phone to my mother. "I'm so happy I've heard you," she said. "I couldn't sleep all night. My pillow was all wet."

Finally, she knew I was alive and the rest of the family called each other with the news.

>>><<<

How am I doing now? I don't know. I'm much better. I went to group counseling with other people who worked at the World Trade Center. Everyone had their own story. But after a while, a lot of people dropped out and went to personal counseling.

I did also. I still go every other week. I also see a psychiatrist once a month and I take pills every day. It helps me.

The first month, I couldn't sleep. Maybe an hour or an hour and a half each night. I was so tired, I couldn't eat. I had no appetite, no energy. Everything was bothering me—like the sounds of ambulances, police, even the sounds of planes in the air. If someone took out their garbage and made a noise with the cans, that would bother me.

Everywhere I looked, I'd see the faces of my friends, who I learned later on had been killed. Three policemen I knew pretty good; a couple guys from my crew. Altogether, we lost twenty-seven people from my union—I didn't know them all, but I knew eight or nine real well. Other businessmen and people I knew from the floors, I saw their faces in some pictures in the newspaper.[15] I try to close my eyes and sleep, but their faces still come out.

Right now, I do not work. When will I go back to work? I don't know. The union is working on it. I hope they find a place for me that's convenient. Not a dangerous place, not after what's happened to me. People understand. The bosses? They know life. I don't need their respect, but they should understand what I've been through.

When will it all get better? As time goes by. For me, it'll probably take the rest of my life. I was there and I saw this. I know what happened. And now we're at war, but this is only the beginning. At any time, something could happen; if not here, then somewhere else, in a different state or a different country. The terrorists have a strong connection and their job is not done, not yet.

This is the blackest day in the history of America.

---

15 The *New York Times* ran a daily section for many weeks called Portraits of Grief, which presented a dignified memorial to the people lost in the Towers. The page shared photos alongside well-written short pieces celebrating the lives and personalities of the deceased.

UPDATE

Not long after he was interviewed for this book, Jan Demczur's story was picked up by nearly every major news agency and broadcast around the world as a story of heroism and perseverance in the face of 9/11's many adversities.

Jan is currently listed on the U.S. Department of State's International Information website as one of the international heroes of 9/11. A year after 9/11, the *New York Times* reported that Jan's squeegee, which saved his life and the lives of his companions, was put on display at the Smithsonian Institute.[16]

Jan was later honored by over 700 of his colleagues.

A year after 9/11, he had not returned to work and, as reported by the *Christian Science Monitor*, he was sometimes overcome with fear and dizziness whenever he ventured outside his home.[17]

"I'll go back," he told the *Ukrainian Weekly*. "But when I do go back, I only want to clean windows that I can get to with a ladder."[18]

---

16 Anthony DePalma, "Jan Demczur; He Is Alive, and What's Left of His Squeegee Is in the Smithsonian," *New York Times*, September 11, 2002.

17 Harry Bruinius, "A Stunning Tale of Escape Traps Its Hero in Replay," *Christian Science Monitor*, September 9, 2002.

18 Andrew Nynka, "World Trade Center Hero: Ukranian with a Squeegee," *Ukranian Weekly*, June 30, 2002.

ARLENE CHARLES

Arlene Charles, forty-six, came to the U.S. from the island of Grenada over thirty years ago. She worked as an elevator starter on the 78th floor of Tower 1, a few floors below where the first plane slammed into the building at 8:45 A.M. on September 11.[19]

Arlene speaks with a lyrical island accent. Occasionally, she exhales a spirited "hooooo!" before plunging into a difficult memory. She gives the impression of a practical and able woman.

I WENT TO WORK at six o'clock that morning on the 78th floor. That wasn't my normal spot, but one of the other ladies called in because she was on vacation and I said I'd take up the slack. My friend, Carmen Griffith, was with me, along with my friend James Rutherford.

Everything was going well until we heard that explosion. *Boooom!* Like everything in the building started shattering. I didn't know what had happened. And I don't know if it was like whiplash or what, but the strength just left my body and I went down, lying down flat on my face. I was scared.

I heard this lady screaming and I thought to myself, damn. Who is that screaming like that?

Then the woman's voice screamed out, "Arlene! Please help me!"

I said, "Who is this?"

She said, "It's Carmen! Can you help me?"

I said, "Carmen, I'm scared. But let's talk to each other. We'll talk to each other and follow each other's voices."

We had to follow each other's voices because we wouldn't have found each other any other way. When I looked up and opened my

---

19 An elevator starter monitors the elevators in a building. If someone gets stuck in a car, the elevator starter tracks where the car has stopped, coordinates the efforts to free anyone trapped inside, and ultimately greets the people once the car doors are finally opened.

eyes, everything around me was black smoke. You couldn't see anything on the 78th floor, not nothing at all. *Hoooooo!*

>>><<<

Now all of us elevator starters have a radio, you know? So while all this was going on, people were calling me on my walkie-talkie from downstairs and all over the place. I couldn't answer at the time because I was so scared, and I guess they thought I was dead because I wasn't responding. But when I finally answered they told me to get out of the building. I told them I was trying to find Carmen and I couldn't leave her. As if I could see anything.

Well, the air began to clear out a little, and then I was able to see that the windows that faced Church Street and West Street had popped open. Shattered. We were open to the air seventy-eight stories up.

Then someone stumbled right into me and she was screaming and bawling. I turned to look and it was Carmen. She was on fire.

Over the walkie-talkie, they told me again to leave the building and I said, "I can't do that, Carmen's on fire."

>>><<<

See, what had happened to her . . . she said she was in the elevator, taking people up to the Windows on the World. The explosion happened at the same time she closed the door. The car couldn't move anywhere; everything was standing still. But she's an elevator operator, so she knows how to take her hand and open the door, and that's when she got burned. She had six people in the car with her, and she turned around to make sure they were okay when a ball of fire flew right up in her face and burned her.

She didn't know what happened to the people in the car. She didn't know whether they got out or not. Everything happened so fast, she said.

She had crawled right over to me, with me calling to her and all and saying, "Follow my voice." Well. She was literally on fire when she

reached me. Her face was all red. Her fingers were peeled back. No
skin left. *Hooooo*, it was awful.

→≫≪←

Now I was so scared. I led Carmen around, and we came upon this
security guard for the floor.

I said to him, "Can you help me with Carmen, please?" But I
think he was scared himself because he just turned around and disappeared, and I don't know which way he went. I don't know if he
made it out of the building or what. I never saw him or heard from
him again. He was a new guy and I didn't really know him.

Then this man came and started helping me with Carmen. He
told us to come to his office. Meanwhile, I'm trying to call downstairs
on my walkie-talkie to find out what's going on and the people on the
radio kept repeating, "Arlene, just get out of the building!"

I said, "Well, I have Carmen here with me and she's not too good,
so I can't get out."

They asked me, "Where's Rutherford?"

Rutherford was on the 106th floor. He had gone to bring some
people up there before the explosion. He didn't make it.

I kept on calling downstairs, but I couldn't get no answer.

Then Carmen told me, "Arlene, I don't want to die like this. Let's
get out of here, please."

And I said, "Okay."

→≫≪←

Right about now, this woman showed up who worked for the Port
Authority on the 88th floor. Her name is Audrey. And I asked her,
"How did you know where we were?"

She said she had just passed Carmen and me on the floor right
before the attack, and she said she'd heard Carmen screaming after
the attack and she didn't want to leave us. She had followed the noise
until she found the office where me and Carmen were.

Well, Carmen kept screaming and screaming that she was

burning and Audrey helped me put water on her skin, but it was all . . . it was all . . . it didn't look good.

Then Audrey helped me get Carmen to the stairs and we climbed all the way down to the 30-something floor. I don't really know which number it was we got down to, but it was a long way, I want to tell you that.

⤚⟫⟪⤙

These two guys passed us in the stairwell—they were going up while we were coming down—and one of them gave me his shirt and wet it with some water. We applied it to Carmen's face and the rest of her. She was still crying out that she was burning—she wanted the water to cool her off. Then some firemen passed us—they were on their way up, as well—and they opened their hose and wet us down.

Then a man saw us, two ladies struggling to help one another down the stairs, and he asked us if we needed help.

I said, "Yes. Thank you. Very much."

They kept calling me on my radio and I kept on telling them what floor we were on. It was ridiculous. At that time, I didn't know a second plane had hit. I didn't even really know about the first plane, I just knew we were in big trouble. We were just trying to get out, that's all.

Finally, we reached the concourse, having walked all the way down from the 78th floor, and I couldn't walk anymore. *Hooooo!* I threw myself down and some lady said, "Oh my God, somebody give her some water."

One of my co-workers, Alan Stephano, came over and gave me some water. He and a guy named Vito picked me up and brought me outside to an ambulance.

They asked me if I wanted to go to a hospital and I said no. All I was thinking was that I wanted to get home to my family, to my kids. They'd been calling me on my cell phone—for some reason it was working, don't ask me why.

My little cousin had been at work and she kept calling me in particular. I said to her, "Alhana, I'm getting out, I'm trying to get out.

Stop calling me. Just go tell my father, my aunt, and everybody that I'm okay."

But she kept calling, wanting to make sure I was out of the building.

I got out of the ambulance and started trying to get home just as Building 2 started crumbling down. I had to start running for my life again. I ran inside a building and I felt like the whole city was falling apart.

I didn't see nobody I knew in there. I saw this guy and I begged him, "Please don't leave me," because I was so scared.

"No," he said. "I'm not leaving you. I'm not leaving you."

»»»«««

It turns out I walked all the way to the Brooklyn Bridge and across. I walked so far, my legs wouldn't work the next day, all the way to Dean Street and 3rd Avenue, which is my neighborhood. *Hooooo!*

I found a phone and called my aunt. She told me to stay where I was and a cousin would come to pick me up. He came all right, but it took him almost an hour what with the traffic and all.

I didn't have my pocketbook on me. I didn't have no money. Everything vanished in the fire. My cousin took me to my aunt's house, and I got a shower. I didn't have a house key—that was gone, too—so I had to wait for my kids to come home.

My thirteen-year-old son, Jamahl, ran away from school when he heard about the Towers. He knew I worked in the building, and he thought I'd died. At lunchtime, he'd left the school and they couldn't find him. The administrators were really worried. They knew I worked in the Trade Center, too.

The school kept on calling my house and they couldn't find me, they couldn't find my son's sister or my stepdaughter, Sharon. She's a cop and had to go in to work. When they finally got hold of me, it was nine o'clock at night. I answered the phone and someone asked to speak to Jamahl.

"Jamahl?" I said. "Who wants to talk to Jamahl? Who's speaking?"

It was the principal at the school. And when I told him who I was he was so happy. They'd been worried about Jamahl since he'd left, knowing why he'd gone, knowing that he thought he'd lost me.

⋙⋘

Sometimes, when I tell people that I made it down from the 78th floor, they can't believe it. And Carmen, the fact that she made it down with me is a miracle.

They took her to Long Island Hospital. Her husband was in the building during the attack, too, and they couldn't find each other during all the confusion. But they eventually transported him to the same hospital, and that's where they found each other. Imagine that.

It was so funny. The same day they moved Carmen's husband to that hospital, the Maury Povich show came and picked me up. They took me to see Carmen. I hadn't seen her since the eleventh, and it was good to see her again.

Right now, I'm on workers' compensation. Our union is helping us out a lot; the company is trying hard to get everybody back to work. A lot of people are back already. We've got good people in our union, a good president and a good vice president, thank God for that. If we didn't have the union, I don't know what I'd be doing right now. We never expected this to happen.

We knew everybody in that building, you know. To us, they were like a family. Since we were in charge of the elevators, we'd say good morning or good night to nearly everyone we came across, and we saw them every day. The people in Cantor Fitzgerald?[20] We saw them every day.

This is something I'll never get over. Never. I came to this country thirty years ago, and I love this country, I really do. But this wasn't what I expected, you know?

---

20 Cantor Fitzgerald, one of the strongest bond trading firms in the world, lost approximately 700 of its 1,000 employees in the attack. By September 19, 2001, the firm's management had made a pledge to distribute 25 percent of the firm's profits each quarter for five years. They further committed themselves to paying for ten years of health care and benefits for those families and loved ones who had lost family in the attack.

GABRIEL TORRES

Gabriel Torres, thirty, is a security officer who manned lobby entrances and various checkpoints throughout the Trade Center complex. Part of his job was to monitor the traffic of office workers passing by. His usual post was in Building 5.

Of the World Trade Center, Gabriel says: "It was a high risk place. We used to get bomb threats all the time. Anytime an anniversary of the 1993 bombing passed, for instance, somebody would call and say they had a bomb."

Gabriel goes on to say that this complacency—the fact that people became somewhat inured to threats that never coalesced—became a factor in how people initially responded to the attacks on September 11. He speaks with a rapid-fire, streetwise cadence when he tells his story.

SEPTEMBER 11 STARTED like a normal day. I used to get to work at 5:00 A.M. for the 5:30 roll call. Then at 6:00, they dispatched me to the concourse level of 5 World Trade.

I saw the people I normally saw and said hi, talked to them. I knew a lot of people by name. Where my post was, they had a news-stand right in front of the E train—they had a Mrs. Fields cookies shop. The lady there used to give me chocolate chip cookies.

The morning went by, and everything was quiet. Then, around 8:45, I was talking to a co-worker and we heard a loud bang, but we didn't pay no mind to it. It wasn't close to us; it was more like a far-away bang. We thought it came from construction outside. You know how they have those big metal plates that cover the ground during road repairs? We thought somebody had dropped one of those.

Seconds later, people came running down the hallways of the concourse and I thought, what the hell's going on? I tried to ask somebody and I could have sworn I heard somebody say, "Gun!" So right then I was thinking that some madman was running around with a weapon in the concourse. I told people, "Come over here! Come over here!"

A couple minutes went by and I still didn't know what was going on. Then I saw one of my co-workers who worked in the lobby of Tower 1 stagger around the corner. He was holding his arm and he was real busted up, bleeding from a wound on the back of his head.

I yelled at him, "What the hell happened?"

And he said, "I don't know, an explosion." So now I thought this was a bomb.

I sat him down and tried to talk to him. I called on my walkie-talkie, but the radio was buzzing with mass confusion. Everybody was calling each other at once, and I heard a lot of screaming.

Someone said, "Get off the radio!" But I said, "No, I got a guard over here that's hurt. He's a mess. I need help." So they sent the EMS.

EMS came quick and my supervisor was with them. She told me, "Look, we gotta start evacuating these people. A plane just hit the building."

⇶✳⇷

While EMS was working on the co-worker of mine from Building 1, he told me this: He'd been at the turnstiles where people swipe their security cards to enter the Towers. Then there'd been a big crash, which we now knew was when the plane had hit the building. When that happened, some elevators must've ripped loose from their cables and shot down their shafts to the main floor, because they broke through the wall he was standing right in front of. The wall exploded and the pieces went flying, hitting his arm and head.

I said, "Oh my God," and I told the people at Mrs. Fields and the newsstand that a plane had hit the building. I started to get them out.

Then I said to myself, hold on, let me run off and call my mom. I'd tried using my cell phone, but that wasn't working, so I went to the pay phones. After a while, I finally got through. I called my mom at her job and said, "Mom. Yo, there's something going on here, a plane hit the building."

She was like, "I know. We're watching it on TV. You gotta be careful. Get outta there."

I said, "Mom, I'm here doin' my job. I gotta do what I gotta do. But God forbid—if I don't make it—call my wife and tell her I love her. Tell my son."

At that point, my mom went crazy on the phone. And then the line went dead.

⧓

Then the F and D20 got on the loudspeaker and, for some reason, told the people in Building 2 that everything was okay. I guess they thought it was just an accident. Hearing that, a lot of people went back up to their offices. Minutes after that, the second plane hit. I didn't hear it, though. I was in the concourse, evacuating people.

Right about then, I saw people coming toward me with skin missing, bleeding, smoke filling up the place, *ba ba ba ba*, you know? And I was like, "Awww, shit." You know what I mean? I started talking to myself, saying, "This is crazy." Thinking it must all be some kind of dream.

Then one of my co-workers, a tall African guy name of Ajalah Godwin, he decided to walk over to Building 2 to evacuate people and see what was what. A lot of my supervisors and coworkers had been in that area before the buildings came down, trying to figure out what was going on. I watched Ajalah go, and right then someone told me that another plane had just hit the Pentagon. So I ran over to Ajalah, told him the news, and said, "Be careful."

He looked at me and said, "What's going on?"

I didn't know, and that's what I told him. Not a clue. I thought about staying with him but instead I ran back to Building 5 and kept evacuating people. Must've been a couple of minutes later . . . that's when Building 2 started coming down.

⧓

It was like something out of a movie, you know? All I heard was the noise: *Whhhhhhoooooooooooouuuuuuu.* Then the wind and the pressure coming for you. From a distance, I could see all the lights in the concourse cutting off, one by one as the darkness rolled toward me. I thought it was another plane coming through the building, right over me.

"Holy shit."

I dove under the pay phones in the concourse. As soon as I did, everything flew past me. People. Debris. A hurricane. I was balled up with my head down, screaming, "Oh my God, what's going on?" It was the wind caused by the pressure of the building coming down, and it was blowing everything and everybody away. Windows blew out from the stores around me. I kept on screaming.

Then? Everything got real quiet. I looked up and saw nothing but smoke and fire, nothing else. I touched myself to make sure. I was okay.

⫸⫷

I heard a female co-worker screaming. It was Sergeant Winters; I recognized her voice. I called out, "Sandra! Is that you?"

She was calling me by my last name, "Torres, Torres! Come get me!"

I said, "Sandra, I can't find you."

She was like, "Follow my voice!"

So I followed her voice and crawled over to her and picked her up. She's a pretty big girl, but I picked her up. I said, "Look, we're gonna have to start walking outta here." We started toward the Building 5 entrance on Vesey Street. Toward that way, there were thirty or forty people all grouped up, trying to figure out what to do.

One girl was hysterical, screaming. This guy was gonna slap her, but I said, "No, no. Y'all gotta calm down. You're gonna get us all killed."

Another co-worker, a good friend of mine, William Fields, was also there. Me and him started talking, and William said, "We gotta get these people outta here." So we told everyone, "Everybody's gotta hold hands and walk slowly."

They were all bunched up because the entrance me and Sandra

had been walking toward, the one they were at, was blocked off. So we backtracked to the entrance of 5 World Trade, where the Warner Brothers chain store was. We all held hands, and little by little we started walking over the debris to the escalators. Once we got there, I had the people go up one by one. The last person was my friend William Fields. He said, "Come on, come on."

But I said, "No, I want to stay and see if there's any more people."

>>><<<

I watched William make it to the top of the escalator, and right then two firefighters came up from the area where the E train was.

They said, "Who are you?"

And I said, "I'm security for the building, I just got some people out. I'm trying to look for more."

One of them told me, "We don't know our way around here. Can you help us?"

I said, "Sure, I know this place like the back of my hand."

He gave me a fire extinguisher and we started looking around. A lot of stuff was on fire, burning rocks and debris. We yelled out, "Hey! Hello! Is anybody here?" But we didn't hear nothing in return.

We got to the part on the concourse where some escalators led down, and one of the firefighters asked, "What's down there?"

I said, "That's the PATH train."

And he said, "You think there's anybody down there?"

"I don't know. We can check to make sure."

We went down to the platform where they had stores. The firemen had two little flashlights, but they weren't doing a whole lot in the dark, what with the smoke and all. I said, "There's a parking area between Building 1 and Building 6. Maybe people are over there."

We kept calling, "Hello? Anybody here?" Still, nobody answered.

It was dark in that parking area; we couldn't see a thing. Mind you, that place was right next to Building 1, and we weren't in there but five minutes when that Tower started coming down. We heard the same noise I'd heard the first time: *Whhhhhhooooooooooouuuuuuu.*

I already knew what it was and I went to dive, not knowing there were doors right in front of me—the underground entrance to Building 1. As I dove forward, the two doors exploded off their hinges. One of them smashed me in the face.

>>><<<

I suddenly had all this stuff on top of me, you know? Debris, the doors, rubble, and dust. The firefighters were a little ways from me, but they didn't get injured because they had their rough suits on. They called out to me, "Are you okay?"

I said, "Yeah. But I got this door on top of me."

I threw the door off. I was down on my knees when they hustled over to me. I said, "All right, it's all right, I'm okay." But when I stood up, I started bleeding from my forehead. "We gotta get outta here," I said. Trust me when I say that, at that point, we all just wanted to leave.

I took off my shirt and held it to my head. We looked for the way out. We tried to make it back the way we'd come down, but it was difficult—the escalators were totally mangled. There was rocks and debris and fires all around. Everything was destroyed. So we tried climbing up the piles of debris, twisting and turning ourselves over anything we could climb. We thought we were headed back to the main concourse where the stores were, but it was so dark and smoky that I guess we didn't really know where we were.

>>><<<

Then we heard a helicopter and looked up. We could see the sky through a big crack in the ceiling. I said, "Wow, we're either outside or in a building with no roof and if we're in a building with no roof, that's dangerous because the building's gonna collapse and we're gonna die." The helicopter kept blowing the smoke around in swirls.

I looked to my left and saw the fountain and the ball they had in the middle of the fountain.

"The Sphere?" I said. "Oh my God, look! That's the fountain.

We're outside." The wind started clearing up, and I saw Buildings 5 and 6. That's when I knew we were in the plaza.

Somehow, we'd managed to climb through a hole and make it outside.

I kept thinking, "I hope these buildings don't collapse." That's all I kept thinking.

We stood there for maybe an hour in the middle of a blasted city block full of twisted metal, cement, rocks, and fire. And we screamed, "Help! Help!"

⫸⫷

I had a hole in my leg and didn't even know it. I must have gotten it when we were down in the concourse, but I guess it didn't register at that point because I was so pumped up on adrenaline. Now that we were stopped, stuck out there in the middle of nowhere sitting on these rocks, I began to actually feel things. I was holding my shirt to my face to stop the blood, and little by little I began to feel this pain in my right shin.

I said, "Damn. What's that? What's going on?"

I looked down and saw a hole in my pants and, through it, a hole in my leg. I could see the bone. So I cut a piece of my undershirt off and wrapped it around my leg to stop the blood.

We were just sitting there, breathing in all this smoke. One of the firefighters gave me a cloth, this thing, like a dickey that he had around his neck. It's an item I guess the firemen use like a hood to protect themselves from the smoke, and he gave me his.

Then the other firefighter said, "Let me try to find a way out." And he climbed up on this mountain of debris and went over to the other side. We couldn't see him anymore, but we kept calling out, "Are you okay?" and he would holler back, "Yeah." But pretty soon he came back to us, because he saw that there was no way to get out—the debris just kept rolling on and on forever, he said.

⫸⫷

As time went by, we heard people moving around in the area, and we yelled, "Help!"

We heard, "Hey! Who's over there?"

And we saw a firefighter in the distance on top of some debris, so we got real happy. Some firefighters said to stay where we were. They went back underground, back into the concourse; it turns out that a part of it was still good. They worked their way up through another hole and called for us. We kept calling, "Here! Here! We're over here!"

A firefighter standing on part of the plaza threw us a rope. We had to climb up this metal thing, and he gave us the rope so we didn't fall. We climbed and he pulled us up. From there, they brought us back down into the concourse through the hole they'd made, and we made our way through the underground again, out through the N/R subway train at Cortlandt Street.

In the station, I remember we had to go down one set of stairs and up the other side, like you would if you were transferring from the downtown to the uptown train. When we finally made it to street level, we came out in front of the Millennium Hotel.

>>><<<

When I got outside and looked around? Unbelievable! Everything was mass destruction. Buildings were on fire, and some were collapsed. People were running back and forth. There was a fire truck and a bus right there, all burned up. The situation was just horrible. I was speechless.

Right then it all hit me, and I laid myself down on the ground. Some people grabbed me and dragged me to the Duane Reade pharmacy store on Broadway, where some medics looked at me. They cut off my pants and wrapped up my leg, my head, and my elbows—I had glass and cuts in my elbows from when I'd been on the ground during the blast, I guess. And the medics said, "Is there anybody we can call for you?"

I said, "Yeah, I need to call my mom. She probably thinks I'm dead."

One of the guys called my mom and told her, "Ma'am, your son is alive. He's a little banged up, but he's alive."

Then he passed me the phone and I spoke to her, started crying on the phone, actually. I said, "Mom, I'm okay. I'm here. Now I just gotta get out."

⫸⫷

I looked up and asked someone, "How do I get outta here?"

They told me, "There's no traffic going in or out of Manhattan. None whatsoever. What you need to do is sit right there and take it easy."

But I said, "Look, I'm not just gonna sit right here, I've got to go home to my wife. My son's at my mom's place, you understand? I gotta leave." I was very persistent.

But they were telling me, "Don't go nowhere." They thought I was delusional or something. "Stay, stay, stay."

Being stubborn, I ignored them and walked right out of the building. Mind you, I had a hole in my leg so I was actually limping right out of the building. I had my uniform on—my skin's all dark from blood and smoke, my face was black from the soot. I walked right out of that whole mess and kept on walking right over the Brooklyn Bridge, 'cause that was the only way for me to get home.

There were very few people on the bridge and the police weren't letting anybody back and forth; they were very busy handling people. They tried to stop me, too, but they took a good look and said, "Okay, if you want to go, go."

I was already stressed out. I said, "Fine, I'm going." And I walked over the bridge, one limp at a time. I must've looked like a monster.

⫸⫷

As I went over the bridge, there happened to be a reporter from the *Daily News*, taking pictures of me like I was a movie star or something. *Click, click.* "Sir! Sir! Over here! Sir?" *Click, click.*

That reporter got me really mad because he was so persistent. He came right up to me and said, "Sir, my name is so-and-so and I'm with the *Daily News.* Are you okay?"

I said, "Yes." But I kept on walking.

He followed me. "Can you tell me in your own words what happened?"

I looked at him. Right then, I wanted to throw him off the bridge. And using whatever little strength I had left, I started going off on him. I mean, the nerve of this guy. Treating what had just happened to me like it was some kind of circus or something. I don't remember exactly what I said, but it wasn't too pleasant.

"No, no!" he said. "Please! I didn't mean it like that."

I said, "Do me a favor? Get away from me."

I continued walking to the other side.

>>><<<

They had a lot of police in that area, like I said, not letting anybody go across. When I got to the other side of the bridge, the Brooklyn side, the cops took one look at me and said, "Hey, are you sure you're okay?"

They sat me down and I went through the whole thing all over again. "Yes, yes," I said. "I just need to go to the 88th Precinct. My mom works there and I need to see her."

One of the cops turned around and said, "That young lady over there works for the 88th."

I looked to where he was looking, at this girl, and I recognized her. She knew me, too. She said, "Oh! You're Lydia's son! Jump in the car. I'll take you to her."

>>><<<

They drove me to the hospital first and took me into the emergency room right away to check me out and see if I had any broken bones, a concussion, or anything like that. Then they started stitching me up. My mom showed up and called my wife and she came down, too.

I don't like hospitals in general, so I was freaking out. And my mom—she wasn't hysterical, but you could see in her face that she was nervous. So I started cracking jokes. Like, my wife said, "Oh, you're hurt." But I said, "Don't worry, baby. The good stuff's still intact."

The nurse and the doctors started laughing, and one nurse asked me, "How can you be cracking jokes when you almost died?"

I said, "Well, I'm here now, so I'd better make the best of it."

≫≪

For the next few days, a lot of stories about me went around. My little sister thought I was in a coma. She thought that part of my head had been removed and all that was left of me was body parts. Everybody was calling her and she told them, "Yeah, he's in a coma," and that got everybody crying. My grandmother in Puerto Rico thought I was dying.

Then there was more confusion because my stepmother—my father's wife—worked in Building 1 and she didn't make it. The confusion came from the fact that my stepmother and my wife have the same name: Vivian. So when my stepbrothers and sisters called my aunt and asked, "Did you talk to Gabriel and see if our mom got out?"—well, my aunt called my mom and said, "How's Vivian?"

My mom, of course, said, "Vivian's here with him. She's fine." Meaning my wife.

My aunt thought she was talking about my stepmother, so she said, "Oh, good, good!" Then she called all my stepmother's kids back and said, "Don't worry, your mom's fine." And of course they were real happy.

But later on, my aunt called again and said, "Vivian's not home yet, where is she? Is she still with you at the hospital?"

My mom said, "Yes, she's still here." Again, she meant my wife.

My aunt said, "Oh, good! I'll tell Pauly and John, they were so worried."

And that's what gave my mother the clue. She said, "Wait, who are you talking about?"

It was all so confusing. See, my father has the same name as me, too: Gabriel. A long time ago, everybody in the family started calling me by my nickname, which is Pepsi. So to clarify, my mom said, "No, no. You want to know about Vivian. I'm talking about Pepsi's Vivian. I thought you meant my son's wife."

My aunt said, "No, I meant the other one."

"You mean she's still missing?"

Now the kids were really depressed. They'd thought their mother was alive, but now they weren't sure.

》》》《《《

Vivian worked for Blue Cross/Blue Shield on the 28th floor of one of the Towers. The people from her office say that she never made it in to work. Judging by the time she left her house on the morning of the eleventh, she should have arrived at the Towers right around when everything started. So I think she was either standing in front of those elevators when they exploded, or she was on one of them. People have said that those elevators fell straight down their shafts like a pea through a straw and smashed down flat to about two inches high. Nobody on them would have had a chance.

It hit me very hard when I found out she was missing. See, when the attack happened, I forgot she worked there. I was running around, trying to help people, thinking about my wife, my son, my mom. So many things.

To this day, I think, if I had remembered, I would have run over to Building 1 to try and help her. But then I probably would have died when the building came down.

It's like I told my wife: "I know it's not my fault. But I feel bad. And I don't want my stepbrothers and stepsisters to hate me because I made it out and their mother didn't."

》》》《《《

My son was baptized on his birthday, September 16, five days after the attack. We had made plans prior to the World Trade Center coming down. I went to the rehearsal on Friday; the baptism was on

Sunday. By then, I was a mass of stitches and I was limping around on a cane.

As I entered the church, the lady who does the rehearsals, Ms. Negron, was addressing the guests, speaking about the people in the World Trade Center. She said, "Let's take a moment to bow our heads down and offer our condolences for the people who lost their lives." I heard this as I was walking closer and closer.

Then Ms. Negron looked up and said, "Oh my. What happened to you?"

I said, "I'm one of the people from the Trade Center."

She turned to the crowd and said, "Look. We have one here!"

People were looking at me with these "oh my God" expressions. Like, "This guy actually made it to church?" I couldn't say nothing right then. I was speechless. I guess it was then that I started to realize how lucky I am.

Baptizing my son was the happiest thing for me. See, this big tragedy happened, but a great event happened afterward. Life goes on. It brightened up my spirit, you know? If I had died, my son wouldn't have known me. Other kids would ask him, "Who's your father?" And he'd have to say, "I don't know. He died when I was one year old."

That's a sad thing to think about, and that's exactly what runs through my mind these days.

HOMICIDE DETECTIVE "Y"

Homicide Detective "Y," thirty-eight, is a member of the New York City Police Department. He works out of an East Side precinct, which covers all investigations south of 59th Street in Manhattan. He keeps his name a secret for reasons related to his work.

Detective "Y" has been on the force for eighteen years; he's served as an undercover narcotics officer for five. Before joining the force, he pulled a three-year stint in the Marine Corps. He is a big, affable man with unstoppable energy, a real New Yorker who talks with his hands and tells you exactly what's on his mind.

I'M ON THE WAGON, I'm drinking water, I gotta lose weight. I gained like, ten, fifteen pounds since the attack. A lot of it has to do with the long hours I'm putting in at the precinct. They bring tons of food into the station house. It's a busy time. If you're not at the Morgue or at the Fresh Kills Landfill or down at Ground Zero, you're sitting in the office, working and eating. For about a week straight when it all first happened, we were on duty all the time.

See, we're officially treating the attack on the Towers as a homicide case. One gigantic homicide case, some 3,000 victims strong. Basically, in a homicide investigation, you try to collect enough evidence to bring to the DA so you can make an arrest. Initially, the First Precinct got assigned, but then, right away, it became a federal jurisdiction. Meaning we were handling the initial investigation, doing the grunt work, and the feds muscled right on in and took over. The FBI. I call them the "Famous, But Incompetent." Or "Forever Bothering Italians," depending on where you grew up. You can quote me on that.

Most NYPD guys feel the same way about them. These feds aren't street people; they're college graduates. They got degrees in accounting. What the fuck does that have to do with the street? It gets in the way. They got no common sense, no street smarts. I mean, I can talk to a person for ten, fifteen minutes and get a sense for what type of person he is. But I've done numerous interviews alongside FBI agents. The way *they* question people? Man, are they missing something.

Picture it: You got some guy from Iowa coming over here to interview people from the streets of Manhattan. It doesn't work. Me? I was born and raised in Brooklyn, I got a sense for this city. These guys? Yeah, you got a few good federal agents. But ask around, you find that the good ones are ex-cops. *They* know how to communicate. But I don't want to get into the feds. Please don't get me started. It's just gonna piss me off.

≫≪

I been on the force eighteen years. I could retire if I want when I get my twenty years in, but I won't. I like the job. What I do now is like being the CEO of a company. To me, homicide is the ultimate crime. Everything else? Not exciting. You steal something from someone, so what? Money, property, whatever—it can all be replaced. But can you replace a life?

In my business, you see bodies, you see killers, you see assholes. If you let a case get to you emotionally, that's when the problems start. You work a child murder or an elderly person is killed? That's when it gets to you. You get a store owner gets killed when somebody holds him up? Any normal person got no business getting whacked? That's the stuff that gets to you.

But if a street person gets killed? No problem. You take that as being part of the street. You're a wise guy, you get whacked? You're a drug dealer and somebody kills you? You're robbing somebody's store and you get shot? Hey, you're in the game and those are the rules.

Like I say, it's the innocent people that get to you, and that's why September 11 was such a giant wake-up call for this country.

≫≪

To me, freedom is not free. A lot of people don't realize that. These liberals! They got this attitude that we shouldn't bother anybody.

"Leave everyone alone." Oh yeah? Well, look what happened to the USS *Cole*.[21] The liberals and Clinton didn't do a goddamned thing about that. And the message we sent was, "You can do whatever you want to this country and we won't do anything back." These are the liberals I'm talking about here, not the working-class people who know what it is to make a living.

What I mean when I say freedom is not free . . . if you get to a checkpoint on the highway and you get stopped? Don't complain about it. Or when you get on a plane now and you're being frisked, you gotta take off your shoes? Don't complain about it. I just got back on a plane from Los Angeles, right? And coming back, the pilot of the plane only showed one ID at the gate. Security wanted two. So they put him through the search like anyone else. The pilot was not too happy about that. You know what? Fuck him. That's for *your* safety. That's for everybody's safety.

A lot of people don't feel that way. And you know where that comes from? Being born in this country and thinking you can do whatever the fuck you want, whenever you want. Civil rights and "you can't touch me." Bullshit. Tell that to the 3,000 victims at the Towers. Or better yet, tell that to the families of the victims.

»»»«««

You know, the same thing goes for when you're working homicide. I mean, say that—Jesus, knock on wood—but say that somebody in your family gets killed. Do you want me worrying so much about how the killer feels about his civil rights when I'm conducting my investigation? Or would you rather I get the job done? God forbid, your brother or your mother or your sister gets killed. You want me

---

21 The USS *Cole* was docked in Aden, Yemen, for a scheduled refueling on October 12, 2000, when a terrorist bomb ripped a huge hole in the hull of this Arleigh-Burke class destroyer, killing seventeen crewmen and seriously injuring thirty-nine others. As part of the official judge advocate general's investigation of the event, Secretary of the Navy Richard Danzig was quoted as saying: "We must account for why seventeen people under our charge died, and why many other people, material, and interests within our responsibility were lost. In the process, we cannot avoid our own responsibility for what the terrorists achieved. We owe it to those who suffer to provide the comfort of explanation, to the best of our abilities."

talking to their murderer in a nice manner, making it easy for them to get away with it? Or do you want results? If I gotta break your balls to get results, I'm gonna do it.

You treat people accordingly, though. I only break balls if I have to. See, if you start out high? You got no place to go from there. You gotta start out here.[22] And then? According to where the conversation goes, you adjust accordingly. If you *earn* the respect, you *get* the respect. If you act like an asshole, you get treated like one.

⇒⟫⟪⟸

A wake-up call, that's what I'm telling you. Liberals? They're the most annoying people on the face of the earth. To me, they're in la-la land. It was a few days after the attack and I'm driving down 42nd Street. There's people out there protesting us bombing Afghanistan.

Now see, I'm at the point now where I'm older; I don't get as uptight like I would've. But those people? They don't look at the big picture. They don't realize that they're able to protest only because they're in this country and they're allowed to. They got these signs out: "Two wrongs don't make a right." What the fuck are you talking about? Are you a mental midget? I got an idea! Why don't we let the terrorists do whatever they want and leave them alone so they can attack us again?

Those people with the damn signs? I guarantee none of them were down there at the World Trade Center when the attack happened. They didn't see the aftereffects. I guarantee no one who was down there turned around and held up a sign saying, "No more war."

You know what I call a conservative? A liberal who got robbed.

⇒⟫⟪⟸

Was I down there that day? Yes, I was. What happened was this:

Homicide detectives work what's called a turnaround tour, meaning we work two four-to-ones—from four in the afternoon to one at night. Then two eight-to-fours, which run eight in the morning to four in the afternoon. When you work your third shift, you get off

---

22 He thumped his gut with an open palm, indicating—I suppose—a reliance on instinct.

at one in the morning and you gotta be back at work by eight. So we sleep at the precinct. That's the turnaround part.

September 11 was the morning we slept over, so we were up and working real early. My partner and I were in the racks.[23] We got up, my partner looked at his beeper and said, "Oh shit. Look at the date. It's 9/11—911, like the emergency code. I wonder if we'll catch a homicide today."

I says to him, "Hey. You never know." And we brushed it off, right? This is eight o'clock in the morning.

We went upstairs and almost immediately got a phone call from our detective bureau to respond down to the World Trade Center. "A plane hit the World Trade Center." When we initially heard that, we thought it was one of those Cessnas that went off course. But then we turned on the TV and said, "Holy shit. Now *there's* a problem."

There were six of us working. We split up, three guys in one car, three guys in another. At any given time, you've got five detectives and a sergeant, so essentially my whole team went down.

I was driving. We took the FDR down, I guess, 'cause I knew it would be easier to go around the Trade Center that way.[24] The second plane hit as we were heading down. We didn't see it, but we heard it. We got near the Brooklyn Bridge and then we saw it. Or what I'm trying to say is you could see what was left of it, the Towers, through the outline of the city. That's when we said to each other, "Holy shit. This is not an accident. We've got problems."

We went down by the Battery Tunnel, went around that loop, and parked the car underneath the overhang just outside the tunnel. I figured, if we had to get outta there fast, that was the best way—there was no way to bring the car up any closer, anyhow. We got out and started walking up West Street, a couple blocks south of the South Tower.

>>><<<

---

23 Precinct bunks.
24 The Franklin Delano Roosevelt Drive runs along the east side of Manhattan.

Christ, it was a mess. There were cops everywhere and fire trucks pulling up. EMS was there, treating people who were injured with cuts. There was glass all over the place, so deep you were afraid to walk. I saw one body on the ground that was already covered. Somebody had put this yellow poncho over it.

We had our shields out on the lapels of our suit jackets, but nobody cared, it was mayhem.[25] We were trying to tell people, "Get the hell out! Get the hell out!" but some people just weren't getting it. I don't know if you want to call it shock or stupidity; people were just sitting there. They were strolling along as if they were going to see a play. I was like, "Let's get going! What are you doing? We *have* to be here, you folks don't. Get the fuck outta here! Move your asses!" Nobody really paid attention.

So three of us stuck together. We made a pact that when we got down there, that we would stay with each other because it was total mayhem. But I says to my guys, "You know, this'll sound funny, but I gotta go to the bathroom in the worst way." I'd had two cups of coffee that morning, which I normally wouldn't have, and it was running right through me. Bad timing.

As it turns out, I do a part-time job further south of the Towers on Trinity Street. So I knew the area, and I said to my guys, "Hey, you know what? Why don't we go over there to my job, and I'll use the bathroom. We can get on the phone to find out where all the detectives are gonna be."

See, we didn't know where everyone was. Turns out all the detectives had been sent to the north side of the Towers; we were the only morons on the south side. So we started walking down Greenwich Street, straight south.

We got to Thames Street when we heard a rumble. Sounded like an explosion. We looked up and there it was, the building was starting to come down. We broke into a run, and as we're going, this thick cloud comes down and covers us. It was like being in a wind tunnel, everything turned black. We were literally blown off our feet, this

---

25 Badges.

hurricane picked us up off our feet and threw us.

We landed and none of us could breathe. The smoke and the concrete dust was so thick, it burned our eyes.

➤➤➤◄◄◄

Now, I always carry a hanky. Always.[26] So what I did was, I kept passing it back and forth so we could all breathe through it. I knew where we were in terms of the geography, and I knew we had to head south in order to get away from everything. South was where the water was, and I figured it'd be a little easier to breathe down there. So we held onto each other's belts and I basically led the way.

One of the guys with us—not my partner but the other guy—he couldn't breathe at all on account of his asthma, and we were getting a little nervous for him. I wanted to pick him up and carry him outta there but he didn't want that, he absolutely wouldn't let me, you know? Personally, I can understand that. He's a man. Getting carried around like some little baby isn't the way a man wants to feel.

Still, we weren't in too great a situation. It was like walking around at midnight. Couldn't see your hand in front of your face. You know those little street carts where you get your cup of coffee sometimes? We didn't see one of these things until we walked right into it. It was totally deserted so we went into it, got bottles of water, and poured water onto the hanky. We took a few bottles with us for backup and kept passing the hanky back and forth. Like that, we kept moving.

➤➤➤◄◄◄

Then, outta nowhere, this guy appears, walking next to us like a ghost in the smoke. And he says, "'Scuse me. Am I all right? Hey. Am I all right?"

He had this big, nasty-looking cut running across his forehead over his right eyebrow. A middle-aged man in his late fifties.

I said, "Listen. You're all right. You just got a bad cut. You're going to need stitches." Plus a whole lot of antibiotic, because the cut was

---

26 He gestured to the pressed white handkerchief in the breast pocket of his suit jacket.

covered in filth.

We rinsed his wound out with our water bottles. I wasn't gonna give him the hanky, I hate to say it, that was all we had. Instead, I said, "Listen. Put something against your head to stop the bleeding and follow us."

At this point, we'd made it a couple of blocks further south and our eyes were starting to see things a little better. Now we could make out the hazy forms of people running around us. But we didn't want to run yet ourselves because visibility still wasn't good enough, and we were worried we'd run into something again.

Then a female hooked up with us, too. I guess she saw our shields. And she said, "Do you mind if I come with you guys?"

"No. Go right ahead. We're just gonna try to get to the water."

So that's what we did. We kept walking toward the water and, little by little, the air started to clear.

>>><<<

I'd remembered to call my wife on my cell phone when I first got down to the Trade Center. This was about ten, fifteen minutes before the South Tower collapsed. And I'd told her, "I'm right underneath the South Tower. It's mayhem down here. I can't talk to you but I want you to know I'm okay."

She wanted me to find her brother, who works on Barclay Street, very close by. At that point, he'd been on his way to work and nobody could get hold of him. She gave me his cell phone number and, of course, I couldn't get through.

I'd just spoken to her and told her where I was, and she told me she was watching all this on TV. Then the building fell; she thought I was killed in the collapse. I didn't realize this until I finally got through to her four hours later. She was hysterical.

I been married fifteen years. We got an eleven-year-old daughter at home. When I finally talked to my wife, I made her go to my daughter's school right away. I said, "I don't care what you gotta do, pull her outta there." She's in a Catholic school in Staten Island.

Does that sound paranoid to you? Hell, maybe it was. But, you know? When I saw this happen, I didn't know what was gonna happen next. What other kinds of attacks would there be? Schools? Bridges? I knew we were in a lot of fucking trouble, and I knew it wasn't over. So I took precautions for my own family.

See, what was going through my head during all of this was, we're in for a lot of shit. We—meaning the country—are in for a lot of shit. Because if they attacked here? If they could bring the Towers down? Jesus. We didn't even know about the Pentagon at that point, or the other plane in Pennsylvania. We didn't have radios. We didn't know what was happening.

But I said to myself, one thing's for sure. Life, as we know it, has totally changed.

»»«««

I'm getting a little ahead of myself. We walked all the way down to Water Street and Battery Park, where we met up with a lieutenant I know from the detective bureau and a chief I know who just happened to be there, directing people to walk up the FDR Drive.

They told us to get to work. "See this building on the corner? This building's gotta be evacuated, there's still a lot of people in it."

So we tried to get everyone out, but people were saying things like, "Well, the building personnel told us we should just stay where we are." It was the most frustrating, aggravating thing, like being in a comic strip. You just couldn't understand what the fuck these people were thinking—I mean, these are educated people, they have white-collar jobs. You'd figure they'd have a little common sense.

I said, "Listen, the Towers just fell. Manhattan is obviously a major target. I don't think they're gonna attack Brooklyn, know what I mean? So get the fuck outta here." We tried to get them to walk over the Brooklyn Bridge—just get them outta the buildings! We didn't want anyone in buildings.

At that point, my partner panicked because he heard a jet overhead. I said, "Take it easy, that's one of ours."

"How the fuck do *you* know?" he says.

"I spent three fuckin' years in the Marine Corps. I know what the hell a fighter jet sounds like. Trust me."

"What if you're wrong?"

"If I'm wrong and the terrorists got hold of a fighter jet, we ain't got a prayer in hell anyway, so don't worry about it."

I wasn't really thinking then. Logic tells you that, if they'd had fighter jets, they wouldn't have used commercial planes. They would've attacked with missiles or something else.

⸕⸎⸏

Then we started walking up Water Street, 'cause we were told there was a temporary police headquarters set up by Pike and South over by the Pathmark grocery store. We learned about it through a radio one of the guys had, so we started walking toward there.

We didn't realize how bad we looked. We were covered head to toe in soot and dust. People walking by stared at us. And the weird thing was . . . we'd look at each other, but we never really thought, I must look like that, too. I guess we must have been in shock a little. Plus there was this instinct of "let's get to where we gotta go so we can start doing something." I wanted to get in the game. Up until then it was like, okay, this is a fight. Now it was time to take a swing at someone.

We got all the way up to Pike? Cherry? One of those streets over there. We were walking underneath the bridge when this uniformed guy started screaming, "Get back! The bridge is gonna blow! Get back! Get *back!*"

Well, we started running for our lives. Again. My shoe went flying off, and I got a cramp in my leg. My partners were ahead of me and felt me slow down, so they turned around and started screaming at me, "Come on! Come on!" It was insane.

I said, "Go! Don't worry, go!"

"We're not leaving you!"

Turned out somebody had left a truck on the bridge and just

walked off. The uniforms assumed it was a truck filled with explosives. Nobody was gonna get close enough to it to try and figure it out.

>>><<<

We got to the temporary headquarters. At that point, all the cops there were in uniform. Except us, of course. We looked like we'd walked straight outta hell.

They said, "Listen, there's a decontamination unit set up behind the Pathmark." So we went, and they literally hosed us down from head to toe with our suits still on. They washed out our eyes with solution and our eyes looked like demons' eyes, they were so red.

But we finally relaxed and were able to get something to drink. And we finally got hold of one of our supervisors, who told us that everybody was gonna muster at Church Street. So we start to walk, now from the East Side back over to the West Side.

We walked right through Chinatown, sopping wet in our soaked suits. And Chinatown was going about its business as if nothing happened, selling fish heads and fucking rice. You could look into the backdrop of the skyline, and all you saw was this plume of smoke. But in Chinatown, it was like being in a different world where nobody cared.

Me and the guys looked at each other like, what the fuck is going on here? Are we in a different city? I mean, not to degrade the Chinese. But I was a little offended. I was a little pissed, to be honest with you. I said, "What the fuck is wrong with you people? Do you realize what's going on?"

>>><<<

We didn't realize that the three of us were among the officers reported missing from the NYPD. Our partners thought we were dead. But we all reunited at Church Street and when they saw us, everybody hugged. "Are you all right?"

"Huh? Yeah, we're all right."

Meanwhile, they'd all gone through the same type of deal over on the north side of the Towers. For instance, one of the sergeants from the detective bureau got his leg run over by a van. He dove beneath the van when the Towers fell and I guess somebody got into it, started it up, and ran him over. He ended up spending about a month in a Jersey hospital. They took him there with a harbor launch and he's doing real good now, thank God.

>>><<<

All that stuff that happened afterwards? Maybe that was the worst. At my daughter's school, they lost six parents. Three firemen, plus a woman and two men who worked in the Trade Center. That's a big nut when you consider it's a small school, only two grades per class.

That night, going home . . . I remember it being so eerie going across the Verrazzano Bridge. Everything was quiet. All the toll-booths were up. No lights—it was all black. We'd gone to the hospital to get treated, and I had to be back at work by four the next morning.

I got home at twelve midnight. When I walked in, both my wife and my daughter were up. They gave me a big hug and a kiss. It was good to be home, but I wanted to get back to work.

My daughter actually understands what's going on. Not because she's my daughter do I say this, but she's very intelligent. Her attitude is, "What do they want, these people? Why don't we just give them what they want so they'll leave us alone?"

I asked her, "What do you think they want?"

And she says, "It can't be that important for us not to give it to them."

She doesn't have a mean streak in her.

>>><<<

I broke down one night later on. We had a party at my house and I'd been drinking. Nobody there was a cop, but everybody was talking about the World Trade Center, whether the information we receive is accurate, and I didn't want to hear it.

I was like, "You people don't know what the fuck you're talking about. I'm in the middle of this shit. I know what's being found, I know what's not being found. I'm at the morgue every day, I see what's going on."

I drank myself into oblivion. After everybody left, I went upstairs.

A good friend of mine was killed in the Towers. We were partners in Narcotics from '92 to '96. He'd been in the Marine Corps the same time I was in, we just didn't know each other at the time. We were very close. I found out he was missing that second day, September 12, and I knew that anyone missing by that point was dead. Every day I've checked the morgue to see if they've found him. Not yet.

So I broke down. My wife came upstairs because she heard me sobbing. My daughter started to come in the room but I turned over and my wife said, "No, it's okay, honey. Daddy doesn't feel good."

My little girl knew something was up. You think kids don't know. But they do.

My daughter didn't really see me too much and that's good, because I never want her to see me upset. To me, it shows weakness. And I never want her to see weakness in me. I don't want her to ever worry that I'm not there to protect her. She always says she wants her mother, but when something big happens, who does she call for? Daddy.

I never want her to see me vulnerable and think that Daddy won't be there.

⟫⟪

Like I said, the attack on the Towers is technically a homicide, and right away our office started working on tips coming in. Stuff like, "I know this Arab who said he wasn't going to work on September 11 and he wouldn't tell me why."

We didn't have a homicide in the city for a week following the eleventh. We didn't have a homicide in Manhattan South for almost a *month* after the attack. I guess people had other things on their minds. So our job was to track down these leads.

Now this is where my problem with the FBI comes in. We'd go out on a tip and find out that two FBI agents had already been there.

It's like, "Let me ask you a question, what the fuck's going on here? Either we're gonna work together or not work together. But don't waste my fucking time."

The leads coming in were being filtered into a command center, then they were being filtered back out again. If a lead had something to do with Manhattan South, we went out on it. If it was something that took place in Brooklyn, the Brooklyn detectives went out. But all these leads went through the command center, see, where the FBI analyzed them and, if they felt like doing it, took first dibs.

On one tip, there was this Egyptian pilot staying in a Midtown hotel. Someone called in to say he'd overheard this guy saying, "The skyline's gonna change," or words to that effect. The fact that he's Egyptian and a pilot made someone suspicious, so we paid him a visit. That's when we found out the FBI had already been there.

I said, "Lemme call this FBI agent." I had his number. I got him on the phone and said, "Did you talk to this guy?"

He says, "Yeah."

"Well, what did he tell you?"

"Not much."

"Well, how'd you talk to him? What'd you say to him? How'd you question him?"

This guy starts to get an attitude with me. He says, "Well . . . you know . . ."

"No," I said. "I guess maybe I don't."

I went back upstairs to question the pilot myself. He didn't understand the point to our investigation. "Why are you bothering me?" he says. "Leave me alone. I don't bother nobody and I really don't have time for this, I'm going to brunch with my friends."

That's when I got a little hefty with him. Apparently the FBI guy hadn't gone that way with him, 'cause as soon as I got a little heated, this pilot kinda understood that we weren't fucking around. I said, "I'm gonna throw you out the fuckin' window in about two seconds if you don't shut the fuck up and answer my questions. You think I'm playing? You try me. I'm in no fuckin' mood for your shit today, okay?"

At that point, we thought there were 5,000 people dead from the Towers. So I said, "You think I'm gonna listen to your bullshit today? I'll throw you out that fuckin' window so fast, your head'll spin."

What can I say? He came around. He sat down, shut the fuck up, and answered my questions.

But you know, the FBI didn't do that. It's not in their playbook, what I did. That's a street thing. I don't mean to be mean. But you gotta show people you're not playing games.

>>><<<

Turns out that the whole lead was a joke, a get-even thing.

See, the Egyptian went through it all, where he was and what he'd been doing on the eleventh. And during all that, I could tell by looking at him that he might have been homosexual. So I says, "Are you gay? Were you with any lovers recently? What's the story?"

I'm not shocked by anything like that. You gotta be an asshole if you're shocked by that sort of thing, especially if you're a detective in New York City. I mean, if the guy thought he was gonna shock me by telling me he was gay, well . . . you'd better get yourself some Rice Krispies and have a good breakfast, 'cause it's not gonna bother me. I seen it all. I told him that.

He told me he'd gone out to a few clubs and been with a few different lovers in one night. I said, "All right, fine, no problem, no big deal. I just need to know all this." Then I said, "Do you know all these guys' names?"

He says, "No, I don't." And I knew he didn't. In that community, that's a lifestyle that happens a lot. We've worked plenty of homicides with gay individuals that sleep with three, four men a night and don't even know their names. You know what? If I could do that with women, I'd do it. I mean, that's a great lifestyle if you can do it.

So when the guy told me he didn't know the guys' names, I believed him. But I don't think the FBI would have believed him. They never even got to that fuckin' point! Again, I don't mean to throw a blanket over all FBI agents. But the majority of these guys couldn't find their asses if they had a map in their back pockets, know what I mean?

As it turns out, the Egyptian *was* homosexual and a jilted lover of his was trying to get even with him by giving us a bogus tip. We wound up getting a lot of those early on. And the fact that the feds were going out on these leads before we got them meant that they were trying to upstage us. It's frustrating. The right hand don't know what the left hand's doing. And when we ended up telling our bosses what was going on, they pulled us from the cases. They said, "Well, if this is what's going on, there's no reason for us to waste our manpower."

Now look: I know nothin' about al-Qaeda cells.[27] I'm no expert on terrorism. But you know what? I learn pretty quick. I know how to get information. That's my job. I'm good at what I do, and everybody I work with is good at what they do. You don't want to tell me what's going on? Fine. Then tell me who to interview and tell me what you want to know, and I'll talk to them. I can contribute.

But the feds took everything over. And we went back to work on the active homicides we had prior to the attack.

⤜⤛⤛

We also pulled duty at the Fresh Kills Landfill, sifting through the debris from the Trade Center, hoping to find body parts, identification, and the black boxes, which are actually orange.[28] In the beginning, we found lots of body parts.

The area was set up like a military camp. We had tents set up with designations—Body Parts, Bones, Identification, Papers—all of them in separate spots so you could drop off whatever you found and

---

27 Early reporting from various sources suggested that the al-Qaeda organization was not a set body, but a clandestine cell system. By this level of management, various groups of people, known as cells, function with little or no directive from a centralized structure or leadership. This is done to ensure each cell's secrecy, autonomy, and security. Cells can be difficult to penetrate by outside influencers, such as opposing intelligence services. The nineteen hijackers of the planes used as weapons on 9/11 were all considered members of an al-Qaeda cell with the dedicated purpose of causing mayhem on that day.

28 An airplane's supposedly indestructible Flight Data Recorder (FDR) and Cockpit Voice Recorder (CVR) are useful tools that aid airline disaster investigations. The boxes cost from (*cont'd*)

it could be analyzed. Some of the stuff we found that we thought was human flesh wound up being meat from a refrigerator. And some stuff that we thought was meat from a refrigerator wound up being human flesh. They had scientists up there who could tell the difference.

We'd bring the stuff over in buckets. We were dressed up in the Tyvek suits with the gas masks. You can't appreciate that type of work until you do it.

And then we were assigned to the morgue, on 1st Avenue and 30th Street. As the bodies and body parts came in, each thing had to go to a different area. If you had an arm, it went to the area where the arms were. If you had a leg, it went to the leg area. Torsos went into refrigerated trailer trucks. They had teams of detectives escorting body parts to wherever they had to go, just to make sure everything was done in a proficient manner. It's a pretty good system.

If a fireman or a cop's remains came in, there'd be a ceremony. We'd all line up. A flag would be draped over whatever was found, then somebody would fold the flag in the right manner. The remains would be saluted, and then the body would be taken in. Most of the time, there really wasn't much of a body, but it's something for the family, at any rate.

To describe the way the bodies are? You can't. When you see some of the homicides I've seen, you see accidents, all kinds of different deaths, horrible things being done to people's persons. None of it prepared me for the destruction of the bodies I saw coming from the World Trade Center. What happened with those people . . . it lives with me every day. We homicide detectives don't leave it. We're always around it. Cops and firemen are still right in the middle of this shit.

>>><<<

$10,000 to $15,000 each and can reveal events that immediately precede in-flight disasters. Boxes use magnetic tape or solid-state memory boards to record data that is then dumped into a Crash-Survivable Memory Unit (CSMU), which can store up to two hours of CVR audio data and up to twenty-five hours of FDR information. Solid-state FDRs can track up to 700 flight parameters in larger, modern aircraft; this includes data pertaining to acceleration, airspeed, altitude, flap settings, outside temperature, cabin temperature and pressure, and engine performance. Both boxes are generally stored in the rear section of an airplane.

When you walk into that morgue, the smell hits you. If you've ever smelled bad meat? Multiply that by a hundred—that's the only way I can really describe it. If you've never smelled it before, once you do, you'll never forget. And once you know it, if you walk into a room and you get hit with that smell, you know there's a body in the room.

Every dead body is different; it depends on the temperature, the time of year, ventilation. But it's essentially the same goddamned smell, just at different levels. When you get a guy that's been dead for two weeks in an apartment that's a hundred degrees in August . . . *that's* got a certain smell to it, let me tell you. It's hard to explain.

⫸⫷

I don't think I have much of a story. A lot of people went through a lot more, people who got injured, hit with glass, people who got cut.

When we went back the next day to get our car, it was destroyed. What would have happened if we'd still been in it? Or standing next to it? We'd be dead, that's what. We escaped narrowly with our lives. All because I had to go to the bathroom.

I believe that if your time's up, your time's up. I was always kind of a believer in that. But after the attack, I knew it. And knowing that? Personally, it makes life a little easier.

I used to think that I had a destiny when I went into a firefight or knocked on a door. But I have an attitude now where I'm always careful. I always do my tactics. When my time's up, it's up, and there's nothing gonna change that. But there's no need to hurry it along, either.

You say to yourself, what if I *didn't* have to go to the bathroom? What if I *hadn't* had somewhere to go downtown? What if I *didn't* go to the Towers that day? A lot of what-ifs.

We laugh about it. Things happen for a reason.

⫸⫷

As far as the way people treated the cops after the attack? In my eighteen years, I've never seen that kind of admiration. The hellos on the street. People coming up to us—kids coming up with pictures they'd drawn, pictures of the Trade Center with captions that read, "We love you, New York City Police" and "Thank you so much for what you're doing." They're handing these to us. Heartbreaking. It was just heartbreaking.

See, everybody loves firemen and everybody hates cops, that's what it boils down to. Firemen don't give you a summons. Firemen don't lock you up. But I seen this guy on an interview who was down at the Trade Center that day, working in one of the firms. He said, "I used to walk by the police all the time and I took them for granted. I don't do that no more."

What this city turned into after the attack happened was the most beautiful thing I've ever seen. I was shocked. For a while, everybody was, "Hey, how are ya?" Concerned about each other—what we used to call esprit de corps in the Marines. A camaraderie.

But things are back to normal now. People are back to being assholes. Now everybody's back to, "Fuck you, get out of my way, I got business to attend to."

»»»««««

I'm offended by that viewing ramp they built.[29] Handing tickets out to people, whatever the fuck it is. I'm offended seeing tourists down there snapping pictures. Maybe I'm being a little sensitive, but to me, that's a giant tomb. A gravesite. I take offense to these fucking European scumbags coming here taking photos like it's a fucking circus attraction. A carnival. How would a family member feel knowing people are taking pictures of a loved one who's not home yet?

I want to say to them: "What are you folks taking a picture of? Do you have any idea what you're looking at?"

But what are you gonna do? People are gonna be people. That's human nature. The asshole factor's always out there.

---

29 To accommodate the growing number of tourists interested in visiting Ground Zero, the city built a viewing ramp overlooking the site.

OUTSIDE THE TOWERS

ANNA BAHNEY

Anna Bahney, twenty-six, works at the New York Times. *Anna had a peculiar experience on September 11. While most of Lower Manhattan was fighting like mad to get out of the city, she was fighting like mad to get back in.*

I LIVE IN WILLIAMSBURG, Brooklyn. My alarm went off at 8:30 A.M. and I was listening to NPR on the radio. I opened my eyes, turned over in bed and looked out the window. I remember thinking, this is an alarmingly beautiful day.

The radio said that there was a fire up on top of one of the World Trade Towers and my response was, time to make the donuts. Meaning: today was going to be a big news day.

I was actually scheduled to work on news at the National desk that day. A building fire would technically be a Metro story, but the way the desks worked, I knew that a story like that would eventually trickle down to National. So I wasn't tearing out the door. I figured I had a little time.

I got up and went through my morning routine. I had the radio on in the shower. When I got out of the shower they were already interviewing an eyewitness, who said she saw a plane kind of veering off toward Brooklyn, as if it wanted to go towards the airport. But then she saw it fly into the building. So we knew then that it was an attack.

I turned on the television. You could see smoke coming out from the one building. And then there was this moment—like one of those subliminal clips they put in movies to make you buy Fritos or something. You saw this dark, shadowy object coming toward the front Tower. You could see it, but you almost couldn't consciously see it, do you understand? It was so shocking. And then my whole TV went black.

That's when I knew this was serious.

>>>*<<<

I didn't freak out. I just kept saying to myself, "This is serious. This is serious." I knew this was a deliberate attack.

The TV came back on, and I continued to watch and eat my cereal. They cut to a split screen where they had "New York" and "Washington." I had this sudden image of eighteen cities up there. New York, Washington, Chicago, Boston, San Francisco, Los Angeles. All of them. I was afraid somebody was gonna come on and say, "These places have been hit, too, and they're taking over."

Then the pieces started falling into place: two airplanes in New York, another one at the Pentagon. I knew I had to get to the office. But by this time, they were saying that the bridges in New York had been shut down, as well as the subway systems. No traffic in or out of Manhattan. And I'm thinking, I have to get to Manhattan. I have to get to the *Times* office.

My boss, Erika, called and said, "Hey, have you heard about this?"

"Yeah, I've heard about this."

"Are you gonna make it in?"

I could just imagine the frenetic energy in the *Times* office, how they would need people. A lot of people who work at the paper live in the suburbs and even more remote areas. No prayer for them to get into the city.

"Yeah," I said. "I'm leaving now. The bridges are closed and the subway is down. But I'll do what I can."

>>>*<<<

The *Times* building is near 42nd and Broadway. Normally, I take the L train to 14th Street, then the N/R up to Times Square, but none of those trains were running. The only access into Manhattan from Brooklyn was the Williamsburg Bridge, which is on Delancey Street, forty-plus blocks away to the south.

I had on blue jeans, a white T-shirt, and sandals. Since I didn't know what I was getting myself into, I changed into walking shoes. I got my backpack and put in a big bottle of water. I was very, very calm.

Like thinking, I'm packing for destruction. Okay. I put in an extra shirt, which I thought I might need to cover my face. And I packed some bagels, a notebook, and some pens.

I set off walking down the street.

There weren't that many people on the streets. I got the feeling that they didn't know. That they either weren't listening to the news or they weren't understanding it. Or maybe they didn't care. No one looked terrified. But then, I guess I was really stressed out, too, and I didn't think that I looked terrified. Maybe they were looking at me the same way.

⟫⟪

This drunk was standing on the street, talking to himself. I remember thinking, he doesn't know what's going on. I wonder when he's going to figure it out.

I continued walking. There were radios on in the delis and some cars on the streets. I'm hearing things as I'm walking: "The second Tower has fallen." "Children will be held in school." "President Bush is crisscrossing the country in a plane."

I tried to call the *Times*, but my cell phone was dead. I kept walking.

I got to the train station and there was mild chaos there because people were still trying to get to work. They didn't understand the severity of the situation. "Where are the trains? What's going on?"

Around the train station, Williamsburg is a very artsy, urban hipster area. The kids who couldn't get to work had sat down in the cafés. Like I said, it was a beautiful day.

I went to see if I could walk over the Williamsburg Bridge.

⟫⟪

I walked through a Puerto Rican area, and the news from the radio became all Spanish. But I could hear "Giuliani," and I could hear "American Airlines." I could hear "World Trade Towers" and I could hear "President Bush." There were many more people on the streets in this neighborhood. There was a lot more chatter in this area.

Finally, I got to the bridge. By this time, I'd met lots of people who were asking, "Is the train closed?"

I said, "Yeah, it is."

"What should we do?"

"Well, I'm gonna walk to the bridge."

So now there's more people moving with me in that same direction.

⧓

I got to the bridge and there was a footpath, a pedway that went up. There's a white sawhorse barricade across it with three policemen there and about a hundred people gathered at the foot of it. People were petitioning the cops.

"My child is over there."

"My father is over there."

"I live just on the other side."

"I just need to get across."

The police were saying, "No, no, no, no, no." One policeman was Hasidic, one was Latino, and one was Polish, and they were saying no to people in various languages.

I'm looking for a way to bypass them and get across.

There were lots of people trying to use their phones. One person would get a connection, then eight people would try to use that cell phone. There were offers to exchange money—this man held out $5, saying, "Please, let me use the cell phone. Please." But no one was charging anything. A woman saying, "No. Here. I'm finished. Use this."

It was an incredible rumbling going on, all these people trying to get across, trying to communicate. And then this tall black man ran out of the crowd and right up to the policemen. He said something to them and he showed them a card. He was allowed to step onto the bridge and cross.

I asked some people who were closer to the front what had

happened. They said: "The only people allowed to pass are members of the press and hospital workers."

I had my *Times* ID card, so I showed it.

"Look," I said, "I have to get there, I have to get to work."

There was no question after that. The police just said, "Go ahead."

Meanwhile there were torrents of people coming down off the bridge from Manhattan. On the Manhattan side, they were letting people start across the bridge in heats. A group would come across, then there would be nobody for a while. Then another group. Then no one.

A bunch of people had just come across as I was allowed to pass through. It was like walking through a mob. But once I got past them, I took off running.

⤜⬥⤛

I ran up the ramp and up the stairs and started across the bridge. There were hundreds and hundreds of people walking toward me. Businessmen. Storekeepers and their families. Old people. It was if the whole island of Manhattan had been tipped on its side and dumped out onto the bridge.

As I'm running, this guy shouted, "You're going the wrong way!" But I kept going. By the time I reached the middle of the road, this next group had thinned out and I was alone again on the bridge.

At that point, I could actually see what I was running to. I saw the two distinct columns of smoke and the . . . nothing. The Towers just . . . weren't there. I ran harder for what seemed like a long time.

⤜⬥⤛

When I got to the other side, there was a policeman standing guard before you hit the off-ramp down to the streets of Manhattan. When he saw me, he kind of bolstered himself up.

Just the two of us on this bridge. A doughy sort of cop. A middle-aged man gone sort of round in the middle, balding, with a mustache. He looked terrified and alone.

At first, he postured himself like, you're going the wrong way, what's your reason for crossing? I showed him my card and he completely changed. He looked so vulnerable.

There was a moment of silence and he said, "What do you know?"

I didn't know anything. I was clueless myself. But I told him what I'd heard on the radio, having walked as far as I had. "Vice President Cheney holds office while the president is moving to a safe location."

He said, "Oh." And he looked down. We were both quiet for a minute.

And then? I don't know why I did this. I'm not a religious person, I'm not Catholic. But what I really wanted to do was cross myself, though I have no spiritual, traditional reason to do that. So I touched my hand to my forehead. I offered the man a salute. A benediction, I guess. A gesture of respect I wanted to give to him. Something. Because I appreciated him standing on that bridge so much, being vulnerable.

And I said, "God bless you."

And he said, "God bless you."

I ran down the stairs.

>>><<<

At the bottom of the stairs there was another barricade and thousands of people waiting to go up and cross. The crowd spread from the very start of the pedestrian bridge way back down Delancey Street, which was shut down across all four lanes of traffic. All the way back past Essex, past the streets of the East Village whose names I don't know. Plus traffic from all the cars on the tributaries to the Williamsburg Bridge. Lots of trucks backed up in a gridlock. Lots of people in cars, stuck there, nobody moving. Everyone had their radio on.

I had made it into Manhattan. But what now?

I tried to use my cell phone again, and I called into the office. This time it worked. I talked to Erika and said, "Look. I'm in Manhattan. I'm down here. Does the Metro desk need anything?"

She said, "Hang on, I'm gonna transfer you."

I talked to an editor at Metro and repeated, "I'm down here on Delancey Street, do you need anything?"

And they said, "Oh, yeah."

It's a pretty tight ship at the *Times*. They had already dispatched a lot of reporters, and they had things covered for the most part. But the sort of over-arching things that they would need—the sights, the sounds. They wanted to know about the ad-hoc crisis centers that were being set up. They wanted interviews with people who had actually seen and/or participated in rescues. They were very specific about all that, and I said, "Okay."

>>><<<

Right where you come down from the Williamsburg Bridge, there's a firehouse, which you can see from the top of the bridge. I backtracked to there. A woman there was hooked up to some sort of oxygen mask. She was dressed in business attire with her purse at her side, and she was covered in dust. Her purse was black leather but the dust had turned it white. She was sitting there by herself, breathing into this mask.

Three firemen were standing nearby and I talked to them. I said, "Are you with this house?"

They said, "No, we're from Queens. The firemen from this house have been sent out already, we were brought in to cover them." They had their trucks and their ladders with them, the idea being that they would rotate out when the house came back in.

These guys knew what was going on. They had seen the pictures on TV, same as all of us. And they were waiting in that firehouse, knowing they had to go down there when and if these men came back.

The lid was on. They were so nervous. They were pacing back and forth, and there was a *rat-tat-tat* rhythm to their conversation. They just had to keep talking, keep talking. They told me, "Yup, we've been here, we know this is what's happening, we know these people are coming back, we're waiting, we don't really know what's going on."

They didn't have much information. They just had this raw-nerve energy.

I took some notes and kept walking.

>>><<<

I saw a group of businesspeople coming toward me with cloths over their faces, and I said, "Where were you?" They'd been in a building near one of the Towers and were covered in debris.

I walked down toward Chinatown. No cars. All the streets are shut down. It was a pedestrian free-for-all with everybody heading north and east, away from where I was going. I was still heading in the wrong direction.

There was this young blonde woman crying on the street corner. She was with another young blonde woman, who was trying to console her. The crying woman had all these keys in her hand, as if she'd just run out of her house. The two women were standing there when all of a sudden this police car, covered in debris like snow, swerved up and came to a screeching halt in front of them.

A policeman jumped out. He was covered in debris, too; there was dust all over his hair. He ran to the crying woman and embraced her, lifted her off the ground and spun her around while the other woman stared.

The couple pressed their foreheads against each other and talked, saying private words. Then the officer got back in his police car and drove away.

I asked the woman, "Is that your husband?"

The crying woman could barely talk, she was sobbing so hard. "No," she said. "That's my boyfriend. He was working down there and he has to go back."

I took more notes and kept walking.

>>><<<

Most places I passed were shut, but I found some delis open with their radios on and people gathered around, listening. Some places had telephones, water, and toilets, and if they had these three things, they put up signs that said "Telephone, Water, and Toilets." These were the beginnings of my makeshift crisis centers. Several churches had these signs out front, and people were going into the buildings. Along the Bowery, methadone clinics and halfway houses were taking people in.

I kept walking faster toward the traverse of the Manhattan Bridge. It was still a free-for-all, with people walking in all different directions. This big crowd passed me and suddenly, right before me, stood one of my co-workers, Jesse, this guy that I sit next to every day who also works in Culture. We saw each other and stopped. Then we gave each other a big hug.

This is a person I work with; I certainly wouldn't under normal circumstances go up to him and give him a hug on the street. I had seen more people in that one morning than I had probably seen during my whole time in New York, masses of humanity. But in all that, I had been anonymous. Jesse was the first person I'd run into that I knew from my life before the attack. And even though we were all—everyone in New York—witnessing what was happening together, even though there was a bond, a friendship of sorts, it was almost not validated for me because they hadn't been there yesterday. They hadn't been part of my life, my routine.

Seeing Jesse was like validating that this wasn't a dream, this was my life. I was here. There. Right where it was all happening.

Jesse had been dispatched down to the scene to gather information. We exchanged brief words of, "I'm doing this, I'm doing that." He was going off to Brooklyn to visit churches that were serving people who'd fled the city.

We said goodbye, and he went along his way.

≫≪

I ended up walking through Chinatown, and I got as far as Canal Street before I was stopped at a checkpoint of barricades. The authorities had a bunch of emergency vehicles lined up. Policemen all over the street. I could not pass. There was no getting into the zone we now call Ground Zero.

I circled around for a bit. Eventually, I ended up sitting on a curb in front of a firehouse in Chinatown. It was still a beautiful day. And in Chinatown, I watched workmen continue construction on a shop. Men were painting the doorjamb and the doors. Other shops were open for business, and kids were playing ball on the sidewalk.

I sat in front of this firehouse, waiting for the fire teams to come back so I could interview them. Waiting. And waiting. And waiting.

>>><<<

Eventually, some firemen returned to the house. Some of them were from Westchester County, and I found out that different teams who'd come into the city from the outlying regions to volunteer were brought to a command center up in Harlem, then dispatched down to individual houses throughout Manhattan on a rotation plan.[30] These Westchester men had that same nervous energy I'd seen in the guys from Queens.

Finally, the team I was talking to loaded up and headed out. I remember seeing them climb onto the fire truck. They didn't know where they were going. But they smiled and waved and everyone on that street cheered them as they drove off.

By now it was almost three o'clock in the afternoon, and I figured I'd be needed more in the office. I had a long walk ahead of me, so I decided to start.

Was I tired? I don't know. I had sat down for a while. I hadn't really eaten anything. But I was charged. Charged, but calm. Fully cognizant. Everything was very clear.

---

30 Westchester County lies in the heart of the Hudson River Valley, directly north of New York City. It can be reached within minutes by train from Grand Central Station in Manhattan. The county's southernmost tip, which includes towns like Yonkers and Mount Vernon, touches the northern border of the Bronx. Westchester is filled with historic sites, rolling acreage, golf courses, parks, beaches, and quaint towns. It is a popular, upscale suburb for people who work in Manhattan.

≫≫≪≪

I was walking north on 3rd Avenue when I saw this man walking ahead of me in jeans and a T-shirt. On his left leg, from about the middle of the thigh down, his jeans were ripped. Gone. He had a big bandage across his leg above his knee and blood was seeping through it.

I asked him, "Can I talk to you for a moment?" He said, "Sure," and I found out what happened.

He was a livery driver who delivered supplies for the mayor's office. He'd been at City Hall; his truck had been out on Broadway when the planes went into the Towers. He'd watched them. People had started screaming and running as the buildings fell. He ran with them. But the power of the falling buildings had caused all the windows along Broadway—around John Street and Church Street—to explode.

Somebody had screamed, "Everybody get down!" And everybody had. Then the shrapnel and smoke washed over them. The driver said it was like a flood of water, but it wasn't like water falling down, more like water falling up, seeping up toward everyone on the streets.

After the major stress of the impact passed, the driver said that people started checking each other out. There was an elderly couple near him, so he started helping the old woman, who thought she'd hurt a bone in her hip. The elderly man was helping his wife when, suddenly, the old man looked at the driver and said, "Your leg. Are you okay?"

The driver looked down at this huge gash in his leg. He hadn't known what caused it. Glass? Or metal? Something. The wound had torn his jeans leg off and right through the flesh so you could see his bone. Here he was, helping these other people out. Now someone was telling him, "No, you need to get in the ambulance first. You're bleeding."

They got him in an ambulance and he went directly over to St. Vincent's Hospital. I was trying to get a gauge on how the hospital was treating the severity of incoming victims, so I asked this driver if he'd been treated immediately.

He said, "Yes. I went right in and they put twenty-two stitches in my leg." Four hours later, here he was, walking down the street.

Under normal circumstances, you know, if there had been an accidental fire or an explosion and someone had sustained that sort of injury—they would have been kept in the hospital. But apparently no one had the facilities and the resources to do that. The driver's injury was deemed "walkable," which is all that anyone could do at the time. There were no cabs or trains running.

And that's what a lot of the crisis centers I saw were about. People had these injuries that weren't completely life-threatening, so they left them to recover in relative quiet.

This driver . . . he was walking down the street, kind of in a daze but laughing as he told me his story.

I said, "Well, where are you going now?"

He had no clue. He lived in Brooklyn but he had no idea how he was going to get home.

>>><<<

At 8th Street, I found that the N/R subway lines were running so long as you were headed north. I boarded a train, took it up to 42nd Street, and went to the *Times* office. The energy at the paper was palpable as I walked in.

The old warhorses at the *Times* always bemoan that nowadays the place is so placid and tranquil. They don't have the *rat-tat-tat* of typewriters anymore; you don't have to yell into your telephone in a noisy newsroom. They pine for those days that have been replaced by computers and soft, digital phones. But that day, I got a feeling for what it must have been like in earlier years. People were yelling for copy. The noise level was pitched way above the norm. There were maps spread out and everyone was so focused, directing each other. People from the Metro desk were debriefing people like me. Now *this* was a news agency in full swing.

Before I headed up to the office, I had called in my interviews. Usually they have one news assistant on the Metro desk who answers the phones and handles copy. That day, there were eleven of them manning the phones, tracking the reporters, taking transcriptions from staff who called in. Similarly, the National desk usually has one news assistant. That day, they had eight.

It was "rally the troops and carry on now, no matter what." Everyone was there. Management had even called in people who used to work at the *Times* six months previous. Reporters from Culture—people like my friend Jesse—had been dispatched to the Trade Center site to cover stories.

In all, I thought it was an amazingly generous performance on behalf of the paper.

⋙⋘

For the next two weeks, I was in the office from nine in the morning until nine at night or beyond. They brought in food, and thus began my "*Times* diet." We were given three meals a day. Bagels in the morning, sandwiches for lunch. Greek salad and cookies and some sort of chicken thing for dinner—all catered. In the end, it became a kind of joke. Most of the employees at the *Times* are stockholders in the company, so two and a half weeks into this feeding plan, people were like, "As a stockholder in the company, I think we can cut out the free catering now."

But that first week, it was necessary. So many places weren't open, and people were too busy to get something to eat on their own. I think there was also an emotional component. Everything was in such an uproar, you had to stop once in a while and have someone tell you, "Okay. It's lunchtime now." You needed to have consistency.

There's a hard core to journalists who've worked their way up the ladder to write for the *New York Times*. These people live for their work. Things like food and sleep kind of fall by the wayside during times like the attack. People became very tight. You're working together, spending twelve hours a day together, eating your meals with each other. And so much information is passing back and forth. In the following days, documents would come in containing sixteen

The days that followed the Towers' collapse saw Lower Manhattan papered with homemade posters and flyers begging for information that would lead to the whereabouts of missing persons.

terrorists' names. Another document came in with nineteen more.

Meanwhile, I was working on the National desk. That first week, flights weren't going anywhere. The breaking stories in Florida were on a national scale. We were calling our reporters in Atlanta and Houston and telling them, "Just get in your car and drive. We don't know where you're going yet, just drive in the direction of Florida. That's where the story is."

We were trying to coordinate information from the FBI and other sources, trying to figure out who these terrorists were and what their connections were to each other, to the organizations who may have endowed them.[31] Meanwhile, we were also trying to figure out who'd been killed in the attacks.

The advent of all the posters and missing flyers that were seen all over the city? I'd been dispatched one day to go down to the Armory and collect as many of those flyers as possible so that we could start a list of the missing.

31 In the days that followed September 11, many terrorists involved with the hijacking of the four airliners were traced to Florida flight schools and other locations in the state where they had planned their tactics and trained themselves.

≫≫⫸⫷≪≪

I'd been holding myself together, maintaining objectivity, trying to do two jobs at once. Then, one day in the newsroom, all at once I just . . . stopped.

I looked down. In one hand, I had a fax listing the bank account numbers, the addresses, the frequent flyer numbers, and the social security numbers of nineteen dead terrorists. In the other, I had the photographs, job descriptions, names, and family breakdowns of eight dead civilians. It was overwhelming.

I walked away for a little bit. I didn't cry—and I do that, I cry a lot. That wouldn't have been unusual. I just didn't have any tears at that moment. I was beyond them, I think.

≫≫⫸⫷≪≪

This whole thing has stripped this country down to its fundamental operating procedures. The terrorist attack happened, and we found ourselves asking new questions. Do baseball games need to happen? No, we can do without. Football games? No. The stock market? No. Do we need the flag? No. Transportation? Not so much. Not so much as we'd thought, at any rate.

Do we need a president? Yes. Do we need firemen? Yes. Policemen? Yes. We needed to hear from Rudy Giuliani. We need direction.

But the attacks also stripped us down on an individual level, relegating us to a personalized basic operating procedure. Emotions, for instance. Do I need them right now? No. Do I need to get this work done? Yeah. Do I need to talk to people? Yeah. Do I need to eat food? Yeah. Sleep? A little, yes. When I can.

I realized so much about myself through this process by having all the extraneous layers stripped away, all the social formalities, all the fears. All of the luxuries of life that we take for granted. They were suddenly gone.

In some ways, I really don't miss them.

UPDATE

After seven years with the *New York Times*, Anna began writing for a host of other outlets including *Forbes*, the *Fiscal Times*, the *Washington Post*, and *USA Today*. She attended Columbia University's Graduate School of Journalism, where she concentrated on business and economics and served as a fellow at the *Columbia Journalism Review*. She is currently a finance and investments reporter for CNN Business specializing in real estate, investments, and cryptocurrency markets.

JESSE LUNIN-PACK

Jesse Lunin-Pack, twenty-eight, is a native New Yorker. He works for an investment banking firm that used to be based in the World Financial Center, just west of the World Trade Center. He witnessed the attacks and the mass exodus from downtown Manhattan mere minutes after the first plane hit the North Tower.

I USED TO WORK across West Street and I loved working downtown; it made you feel like you were in the middle of everything. I could look out my office window, and right there was the World Trade Center.

My apartment's in Midtown, so every morning I'd take the E train to the World Trade Center station, then walk from the station into the mall underneath. I'd either head out onto the plaza or walk through the lobby of the North Tower—up an escalator to the bridge, which took you to the World Financial Center. My standard morning commute.

I was running a little late on September 11 and I was very annoyed that someone had moved my polling place without bothering to tell me.[32] When I got to my initial polling place, the voter registration people told me, "Sorry, you can't vote here" and sent me to the new place. Aggravating. But I got my vote in and hopped the train and made it down to the World Trade Center subway station.

I got off the train and walked through the turnstiles. There was a row of glass doors at the south end of the station which let you into the underground mall, do you remember? And as I was approaching those doors, every one of them opened at the same instant and a wall of people came streaming out with everyone talking loudly about a bomb.

---

32 September 11 was the mayoral primary in New York City. Following the attack, the primary was postponed.

They were rushing—I wouldn't say it was abject panic with people running for their lives, but they were certainly moving with purpose and if I didn't move with them, I might have gotten trampled.

»»«««

I've lived in New York City my entire life, lived through bomb threats and scares. I've worked for Jewish agencies and organizations where we had to evacuate our buildings. So it wasn't the first time I'd confronted a situation like that.

I remained calm, thinking, every other time [someone's talked about a bomb], it's been a false alarm. I'm sure it's a false alarm this time, too. See? There's enough people moving in one direction. I'll just move along with them.

I didn't want to get trapped underground if something bad was really going on. As I turned and moved away from those doors, I saw the first possible exit over to my left: a staircase up to the street. I moved toward it.

Everyone was being helpful to one another. There was a woman with a baby carriage who was struggling, so two people grabbed the front of her carriage with the baby inside and helped lift it up. I'm sure if anyone knew what was actually going on, we would have told her to take the kid and leave the carriage. But nobody knew yet.

»»«««

The reality of the situation hit me while I was on that staircase. We were moving slowly and there were a lot of people crowding behind me. But when each person ahead of me got to the top of the stairs, they started screaming. Not good.

Some of us started urging people, "Keep moving. Please. Don't stop when you get to the top. We all need to get outta here." Having no idea of what was at the top of the stairs, we prepared ourselves to run for cover.

I got to the top of the stairs and looked up. I don't remember if I screamed or not, but I know I had that same sentiment, the feeling of wanting to scream.

I saw the North Tower on fire. And then I saw the confetti—for lack of a better word—falling down all over the place, a blizzard of paper.

Then I looked closer and saw that larger things were falling, too, and it became clear pretty quickly that these were people jumping. Or falling.

⤞⟫⟪⟫⟪⟪

I moved away from the staircase and headed east, toward the corner. Came up on Vesey Street, which ran along the northern edge of the World Trade Center plaza. I don't know how far down the block I was, but I was closer to Church Street.

My thoughts went right back to '93. Okay, I thought, a bomb caused this. But the damage I'd seen was so high up on the tower, it had to have been a really big bomb.

I moved to the corner and found a colleague of mine, who was looking up in disbelief. We conferred. Near to us, there was a pay

". . . I asked, 'What kind of airplane?' The guy in line for the phone said, 'A little corporate jet.' Right, I thought. A little corporate jet that must've been packed with explosives to make a hole that big."

phone with a long line of people waiting to use it, and I overheard one of the people say, "No, no. It wasn't a bomb, it was an airplane."

Which didn't make sense to me. I remembered that an airplane had once hit the Empire State Building, but that had been in the middle of a storm. So I asked, "What kind of airplane?"

The guy in line for the phone said, "A little corporate jet."

Right, I thought. A little corporate jet that must've been packed with explosives to make a hole that big.

But the man kept talking and said he'd seen the tail of the plane as it entered the building, and I accepted this. It made sense enough at the time.

⤞⟫⟪⤝

We stood there watching more and more people fall. Luckily, my view of the plaza itself was blocked by 7 World Trade, so I didn't see the bodies hit the ground. A friend of mine from business school, who had been in 7 World Trade, later described walking out of that building like this: "It was like a meat truck had overturned on the street because there was hamburger everywhere."

The people falling was a horrible thing to see, but it didn't affect me much at the time. I was already in shock and besides, I'd worked on an ambulance corps for four years in college. You teach yourself to become immune. I think that instinct must have kicked in.

⤞⟫⟪⤝

My colleague and I still maintained this fantasy of getting back to our office, but at that point we decided to move away because the first fire trucks were beginning to arrive.

It's odd. I remember still being able to rationalize: Okay, there's a big fire up there and that's horrible. But we've all seen building fires before and the fire department is here and they'll take care of it.

I'm saying that the situation had not yet progressed to something none of us could fathom.

We started walking north. We were walking in the middle of the street because there were a lot of other people moving north, too. We didn't get very far, maybe not even one or two blocks up Church Street, when there was an explosion behind us. I turned around and saw a fireball coming out at me.

That's the image that I haven't been able to get rid of, more so than the people jumping: the image of the second Tower getting hit. You've seen the video footage of the plane going into the South Tower? I'm sure you have. That's what I'm talking about.

The plane was traveling from south to north when it hit and I was just north of the building, so all the debris and plume from that explosion shot out over where I was standing. The exit wound of the building, for lack of a better word.

If there was ever a moment of utter pandemonium, that was it. Everyone started running. No one knew what was going on.

To give you an idea of how close I was, I felt the heat on my face from the fireball coming at us. At first, I thought, there's no way I could've felt that heat. It's too far away. But my colleague mentioned the same thing later on. It was real.

I started to run. Didn't know where I was going, mind you, but I knew I wanted to move away. A piece of concrete larger than a cinder block hit the ground about ten feet in front of me, big enough that, if it had hit me, I wouldn't be talking to you right now.

I started feeling, one, angry at myself for standing around looking at things for so long and not moving away. Two, pretty sure there was a good chance I'd get hit by something, some piece of falling debris, and die. And three, pretty sure that dying was really going to hurt. I wasn't thinking noble thoughts, like thoughts about my family or anything. It was, I'm about to die and it's really going to hurt. Now how do I keep that from happening?

I saw a car parked on the street, so I crawled under it. It was an old American car, something really big and really heavy like a Chevy Monte Carlo. I tried to get the engine block over my head because I figured that a big hunk of steel like that would protect me.

⤜⤜⤛⤛

No, I don't know if that was the smartest thing to do or not. I was panicked, I wasn't thinking right. I'll tell you one thing, though: there's a lot less room underneath a car than I'd thought. I really had to flatten myself against the ground to fit under there.

I saw other people crawling under things, too. Some hit the ground and covered their heads. From under the car, I watched pieces of debris hit the street in front of me. I waited for a bit. I don't know how long I stayed, but eventually I decided to come out and put some more distance between me and the Towers.

I slid out from under the car as a fine white dust began to fall. I helped one person up to their feet and they started running. I went after him. Just then, the colleague I'd been walking with came around the corner suddenly. I'm sure he thought I was dead or severely injured, since one minute I was running next to him and the next I disappeared. But I joined him around the corner and we regrouped for a moment, noticing only then how people were filing into the lobbies of buildings to get off the street.

A woman came running over and pressed herself up against the building next to us. I'll never forget her face. I said to her, "Are you okay?" She had really wide eyes and she just nodded but didn't say anything. I said, "Let's all try to move north, away from here." She just nodded again and we took off at a dead run.

⤜⤜⤛⤛

Somehow I wound up a block east of Church Street; I have no idea how I got there, I just know I was moving north and that's where I ended up. My colleague and I ran into another person we knew, and she joined us. We had our own little group going now.

Off-duty emergency services people started showing up. An off-duty fireman was directing traffic, and I asked him if anyone had evacuated the World Financial Center yet. At that time, my stepfather also worked in the World Financial Center, and I began to worry about him. The fireman said he had no idea what was going on, so we

"From under the car, I watched pieces of debris hit the street in front of me. I waited for a bit. I don't know how long I stayed, but eventually I decided to come out and put some more distance between me and the Towers."

kept moving north.

Further on, I asked a cop the same question: Had anyone evacuated the World Financial Center? She said, "I don't know what's going on. Here, you find out." And she handed me her two-way radio. I still can't believe she did that. She was too busy to listen for what was going on and direct traffic at the same time. She said, "If you hear anything, let me know."

I sort of listened to the radio for thirty seconds and said, "Thanks, but I'm going to get out of the area."

No, I don't remember what I heard on the radio. Thank God I don't remember the cop's name, she'd probably get into a lot of trouble for doing that.

⇶⇷

I made a decision to go to the offices of a competing investment bank where I have friends: Solomon Smith Barney at 388 Greenwich Street. My cell phone wasn't working, but at that point I felt I had to get word to my family that I was okay. I figured my friends at

Solomon would let me into their office to use the phone and internet. But when we got there, we found out they'd already evacuated.

So I started moving north again and decided that this time I would go to the Stern School of Business at NYU, where I'd graduated a year before. It was going to take me a lot less time to get there than to walk home to Midtown. I also knew there were phones and internet connections at Stern.

At some point, I stopped next to someone who had their car radio turned up, and I learned that the Pentagon had been attacked. Then I heard the radio announcer scream, "Oh my God," and I heard the people around me scream, too. I turned and saw the South Tower collapsing.

I see that image of the Tower collapsing still. Vividly. I was pretty close, but not so close that I was in danger this time. My first thought was that I'd just watched 10,000 people die. And then I thought that I probably watched half of the New York City Fire Department die—I'd seen the fire trucks and I know how those guys work. They go in, they go up, they fight fire. That was a very sobering thought.

Now I was really concerned for my colleagues and stepdad. What if they'd decided not to move away? What if they'd been told not to?

I kept moving north.

⧫⧫⧫

I knocked on someone's door, and a young couple with a little baby opened it.

I said, "I worked down there. I gotta get word to my family. Can I use your telephone?"

They invited me in but their phone line was dead. They had their video camera on until the first Tower collapsed and then they just went inside, shut the door, and didn't want to think about it anymore. They wished me luck and I kept moving north.

Then we heard another jet engine, and people started to get scared again. I recognized the sound, though—not a commercial aircraft but a fighter jet. Suddenly I was able to put things into context again. I thought, okay, we're at war. The military is here to defend us.

While I was under the car I'd had a moment to think and question. How could a fire in one Tower cause an explosion in the other Tower, and cause it to fall apart? It didn't make any sense. I'd voiced that opinion out loud, and someone near me said, "No, no, it wasn't the one plane, it was another airplane."

I couldn't believe that. I thought, cruise missiles look like airplanes. We must be under attack by cruise missiles. At that moment, each person I talked to tried to rationalize what was going on, to put it into a context they could understand. But it started to dawn on all of us that this wasn't an accident. We didn't know what it was, but an accident? No.

I kept moving on. When I crossed 6th Avenue east to get to school, the North Tower was still standing and I stopped to look at it. But not for long. When I got to NYU, I walked along the south side of Washington Square Park, past the Catholic Center. They had just put a piece of paper up, saying, "The Catholic Center Is Open for Quiet Prayer and Contemplation."

It reminded me of stories I'd heard when *Apollo 13* was in trouble.[33] The churches opened their doors for people to pray.

>>><<<

I got to the business school and they had a lot of televisions turned on and tuned in, with everyone crowding around the screens. I'd lost my eyeglasses when I was crawling around under the car—I'd realized it at the time, but didn't go back for them. At any rate, I couldn't make out much of what I was seeing on the TVs.

I looked a mess. I was covered with dirt from when I'd laid down.

The dean of the school, who'd been a professor of mine, saw me in the lobby and came right over to shake my hand. He asked how I was doing. Stern Business School has a lot of connections to Wall Street

---

33 The *Apollo 13* lunar landing experienced an equipment malfunction in April of 1970, which placed the lives of astronauts James A. Lovell, John Swigert Jr., and Fred Haise Jr. in severe jeopardy, forcing them to return to Earth before reaching the moon.

and the Trade Center, so he was trying to take stock of the situation.

We chatted for a minute and I asked him if the phones were working. He said, "Sometimes yes, sometimes no. Let yourself into any office and do what you need to do."

It took me a few tries, but I finally managed to get through to my mother's secretary and I left a message that I was okay. I also told her that I'd meet her later on at her apartment along with the rest of the family. My mother, father, stepmother, stepfather, brother—all my relatives work in the city. Later on, when we compared stories, it turned out that my stepfather, father, and I had all been within three blocks of each other.

I knew my brother had a two-way internet pager, and I knew they were still working because I'd seen other people using them. I sent him an email. Then I started running into colleagues of mine from school, people who I'd graduated with. Like I told my mother later, "We all had the same idea—to go back to school. There were phone lines and internet, and we could maximize the communications."

But my mother balked at this. "Bullshit," she said. "When you're under stress, you go somewhere you feel safe. Like a small community."

I spent at least two hours there. The school ordered pizzas and said we could stay as long as we wanted. And later on, a guy came in who'd been on the 69th floor of the South Tower. He was totally covered in white dust and said that he'd run down all sixty-nine floors. He'd barely made it across the street when the building came tumbling down behind him. He was . . . well, psychologically I think he was a mess.

I decided to go home.

>>>«««

Against my family's advice, I went back to my apartment alone for the first night. I felt a strong need to return all the phone calls I knew would be waiting on my answering machine. I was useless for the first two or three days after that.

The first time I felt normal was when I got a phone call from the office. I knew I still had a job, but there was no place for us to work. So I tried to volunteer. I registered with the Red Cross and city agencies, but they didn't need me. And because of some recent international travel, I wasn't able to give blood. There wasn't anything I was able to do, so I spent time with friends and company.

As it turns out, that was very important.

>>><<<

When I finally went back to work, it wasn't to do my original job. I got a call from my company to go to New Jersey to unload trucks of computer equipment.

A colleague said something to me that was very inspiring. He said, "Jesse, I'm not a doctor, I couldn't rush to the hospital to put people back together. I'm not a construction worker, so I couldn't dig. I tried to give blood, but the line was four hours long; they said to come back tomorrow. So the way I fight back is to make sure our company is not affected. I can do whatever it takes. And if that means moving boxes from here to there, well, that's what I'll do."

I think those of us who are recovering well have taken that to

According to the 9/11 Commission Report, each tower collapsed in approximately ten seconds.

heart.

It's tough. I've been to funerals. I have a very close friend who lost her father, a remarkable man. Another colleague of mine broke her collarbone in the evacuation when she got trampled in a crowd.

But we gotta keep going. If you let the attack affect you as minimally as possible, that's the best way to fight back.

»»»«««

Look, I grew up in this city. Those Towers were a part of my life.

I remember my fourth-grade class took a field trip to the observation deck when we were studying the island of Manhattan. I used to go dancing at the Greatest Bar on Earth up near the top floor. I remember. And I take this personally.

When your city gets attacked, it's like you've been attacked. Physically hurt. Those buildings came down and a part of us was lost, too. A part of each one of us.

The rest of the world thinks of New York City as a terrible, tough place. But when you live here, you know. New Yorkers are wonderful people, helpful people. Have you seen the way we pulled together? I think that's what the rest of the world has learned from all this: what it means to be a New Yorker.

ALBERTO BONILLA

Originally from Honduras, Alberto Bonilla, twenty-eight, moved to Jersey City from Tempe, Arizona, to study acting in New York. He is a brightly energetic man.

I GOT A CALL from *All My Children*, and the casting director said they had a role for me and that it would tape on the eleventh. I was told to bring a bunch of different clothing for costume options. So I had the eleventh down on my calendar as a day I'd be acting in a soap opera. Imagine that?

>>>＜＜＜

Normally I left the house at 7:30 A.M., but that day I ended up leaving at 8:00. From my apartment, I took a bus to the PATH station at Grove Street in Jersey City, which shot me directly into the World Trade Center. From there, I'd hop a subway to Midtown, where I temped at Morgan Stanley.

Well, the day started off bad. The bus was twenty-five minutes late. I was furious and worried. I was carrying four changes of clothing, which was awkward and heavy, so my back hurt. I remember I kept looking at my watch because I was so concerned about the time; I had to get to work early so I could take time off for the *All My Children* shoot. I couldn't afford to lose my temp job.

Finally, the bus came at 8:15. Late, late, late.

I got to the PATH station and it was mobbed. There were two trains running, one to 33rd Street in Manhattan and one to the World Trade Center. Either one would have got me where I was going, but I took the Trade Center one because I was into this routine where I'd get my breakfast at a smoothie place in the mall underneath the Towers. I'd buy the $3.45 smoothie. So I took the train for the WTC.

Well, we made it to the Trade Center. It was 8:42—like I said, I was dead sure because I kept checking my watch. There were hordes of people in the mall, and I got into this huge line to get a smoothie. Looking back on it all now, I'm a little ashamed. I think: How self-involved am I? I don't remember a single face from anyone standing in that line of people. Not one of them.

It's 8:44 or 8:45. I'm still standing in line, I'm frustrated, it's taking forever. Then I look in my wallet and . . . I don't have any money. That's how it is when you're an actor. Sometimes you have money, sometimes you don't. That week had been financially rough for me. I was literally a starving artist.

So now I'm really pissed off and I'm going over my options in my head. I can find an ATM in the middle of the mall, or I can go without breakfast. Getting out of line to find an ATM meant having to get back into line, which would waste even more time. Going without breakfast meant being miserable and hungry all morning.

I got depressed. That can happen when you don't have money to eat. So I figure, okay, this morning I just won't have breakfast. And I hightailed it out of the mall.

⋙⋘

I went to catch the E train uptown, and the oddest thing happened. There was nobody waiting on the platform. It went from being utterly crowded to nobody. Maybe this was all after the first plane hit, I don't know. Like I said, I was really into myself that morning. Did I miss people running? I don't know how it makes sense now. I know I sat down on the train and I sat there and I sat there. It wasn't moving.

There were only two other people on board. One was a teenaged Oriental rave girl with headphones, a hip black outfit, and a silver purse; she was all the way at the end of the car. And sitting right next to the door was this older black lady wearing a dress who was knitting and humming to herself. An empty car in the World Trade Center transit hub, at rush hour on a weekday morning? Even then it didn't dawn on me.

We waited. And we waited. And we waited. Nobody came. The

station stayed empty, and I was a mess. My backpack's falling off my shoulder, I'm holding on to my clothes. If I didn't have enough money for a smoothie, I certainly didn't have enough money for a suit bag, so my clothes were all on hangers in dry cleaners' plastic. And I'm so involved with my own drama that I'm shouting at myself in my head: Why the hell isn't this train moving? I'm gonna be late!

Then all of a sudden, the doors closed and the train started to go. Still nobody else on board but us three. And that's when I thought, is the train operator crazy? Why is he leaving? There's nobody on board.

>>>><<<<

I work for the Data Integrity group at Morgan Stanley on 47th and Broadway, so I got off the train at Times Square and started running. I got to my work building and took the elevator up to the 37th floor, thinking, I'm late, I'm late, I'm late! Ran to the bathroom, dying to use it. I ran back out, and . . . everybody's gone. Again. The whole cubicle section is empty.

And again, I'm thinking, what the hell is going on?

That's when I noticed all the computer screens in my department.

Almost immediately following the tragedy, many of the buildings flanking Times Square sprouted flags, banners, and homemade signs.

They were all logged on to CNN.com, and they were all showing this picture of the World Trade Center with fire coming out of it. Every single computer. Now I'm thinking, what? *What?* I mean, I'd just come from there.

I ran to the windows at the corner of the building. Looking downtown, I could see it now, clear as day. Both Towers burning. From the altitude I was at, they looked really close. I could see the fire and the yellow, the red, the black smoke. A few co-workers appeared and came up beside me. Nobody said a word. The TV was turned on but nobody was watching. I remember hearing someone crying hysterically. A sound I'd never heard in an office environment.

You know, as an actor, I study things so that, later on, I can re-create emotions and behavior. I have no idea how to describe what I'm going to say next. But that sound of someone weeping in the office? It was as if God was crying. I looked around to see if somebody else had heard it, but everybody was staring out the window. Then I checked to see if the person crying was me, but it wasn't.

Over the intercom we heard, "Everybody leave." And just like that, they evacuated our building.

⤙⤚

After that, I walked through Times Square and saw all these people who didn't seem to know what was going on. People were laughing. Some tourists were taking pictures of the TKTS booth.[34]

And then it hit all at once, like a wave. This energy.

Suddenly, everybody started popping their cell phones on. Suddenly, everyone got frantic. Suddenly, the information rolled over everyone—don't ask me how, but you could see the effect it had on every person standing in Times Square. All at once, everyone was in on this terrible secret. The look on everyone's face changed all in one moment.

I grabbed my cell phone, too, and called my best friend Rex in Arizona. He was crying on the other end of the line, crying from all the way on the other side of the country. "Oh my God, it's falling," he said.

---

34 An outlet for discount theater tickets.

I didn't know what he was talking about. Later on, I learned he'd been watching the whole thing on the TV. "Alberto!" he yelled. "It's falling!"

Standing in the middle of the street, I yelled, "The Tower? The Tower's falling!" And everyone within fifty yards stopped and looked at me, even the people on their phones. The whole world stopped.

Right then, my phone died. Everyone's did. I ran into a New York Sports Club and watched on a video monitor as the second Tower fell.

Not long after that, the whole city locked down.

> ⟫⟪

A little later on, I called a friend, Nancy, who lives on the Upper West Side. She invited me up to her place on West 75th Street. I started walking, and around 70th Street, I saw people running to the Red Cross to give blood right away. It was a fine idea but, as it turned out, of no use whatsoever.

I got to Nancy's place and she asked me, "Are you hungry?" I realized, yeah, I'm starving.

Then I called ABC Studios—this is the actor in me not wanting to lose my job. And I asked them, "Uh, are we still booked for today?"

Normally gridlocked with pedestrian and automobile traffic, Times Square became eerily quiet and empty in the days following September 11, 2001.

The guy on the other end says, "Yeah. Why wouldn't we be?"

I said, "Because we're being attacked by terrorists?"

He said, "Oh. Okay. I'll call you back."

I got a page a little later and called in. A different person, very somber, said, "We've canceled."

>>>⫷⫸<<<

Nancy and I went out to a Greek place for a late breakfast and I kept asking myself, "Why am I so hungry?"

I sat down and the waiter brought our food. Which is when I realized: Holy shit. I'm hungry because I didn't have enough money to buy breakfast. And because of that, I didn't have to wait on line. And because of that, I wasn't directly under the Tower when the first plane hit. And all those people, those faces I can't remember . . . I wasn't with them when it happened. Did some of them die?

And I'd missed everything because I didn't have $3.45 to my name.

That was the best breakfast I never had.

Shortly thereafter, this feeling started to set in, and it took me a few days to realize what it was. Guilt. The guilt of being alive.

The waiter brought me a mimosa and I downed it quick. Then I drank Nancy's, too. I was happy to be an artist that day. I think my life was spared because I didn't have any money.

>>>⫷⫸<<<

Walking away from the restaurant, I ran into another friend, Katie. She saw me and burst into tears. Then she hugged me and told me this: Katie had an estranged sister whom she hadn't talked to in years. The sister had just sent her an email that said, "I don't know where you are. Please contact me. Let me know you're okay. I'm sorry for everything. I'm so sorry."

I looked at Katie and said, "A lot of people lost their sisters today. But aren't you lucky? You got yours back."

UPDATE

Alberto Bonilla has been working hard since last we talked. Apart from logging television appearances on *Law & Order: Criminal Intent* and *The Sopranos*, he wrote a play, *Walking to America*, which garnered critical acclaim for its 2005 debut. *Walking to America* dramatizes the true story of Oscar, a young boy from Honduras who one day leaves his village and literally walks 2,400 miles to the United States in search of the American dream.

Apart from the impact Oscar's story made on Alberto, the two young men shared other connections: both grew up in the same village, and both saw immigration to the United States as their only means of survival in a world whose cruelty and lack of opportunity increased exponentially with each passing day.

Oscar's journey didn't end as well as Alberto's. Once he crossed the U.S. border, he was apprehended as an illegal immigrant and thrown in a Texas prison. When Alberto decided to write a play about Oscar, he contacted the immigration lawyer who'd handled Oscar's case, hoping to speak with Oscar himself. The lawyer responded, "Why do you want to interview Oscar? If you go down to the border, you will find hundreds of Oscars, and those are the lucky ones that actually made it to America. There are so many more that never make it that far. And the ones who do are usually sent right back to where they started."[35]

"The point I am making [with *Walking to America*]," said Alberto, "is . . . how amazing a country [this is] that has that kind of technology, how blessed we are that we can have a choice. [And yet] how disturbing is it that there are millions of children around the world dying . . . from starvation and lack of attention? We are a nation that has infinite possibilities, but it is where we put our values that I question."

---

35 Author uncited, "An Interview with Alberto Bonilla—Walking to America," the New York Theatre Experience website, 2005.

HUSTON STEWART

Huston Stewart, twenty-four, hails from Jacksonville, Florida, and went to school at the University of Alabama, Tuscaloosa. After receiving a job offer in New York City, Huston (pronounced like the Texas city) made plans to move to Manhattan in the fall of 2001.

Huston's experience of September 11 was one that many people around the country and around the world shared: the tension of waiting for news of a loved one who worked in the Towers.

I WAS IN New York from August 15 to August 30 of 2001 to apartment-sit for friends of my parents. These folks were going back to Jacksonville to vacation for two weeks, and it worked out perfectly. I had two interviews right away with Doyle Dane Bernbach, one of the largest advertising firms in the world. Then, on my third day in Manhattan, I interviewed with Opal Financial. They offered me a job on the spot and it wound up being perfect for me—a transfer into finance, which is what I'd always dreamed of.

Opal asked me to start work on September 17, so that left me with two weeks to vacation. I wound up meeting this girl, Hobby, while I was in New York. We started dating and fell in love.

She was like, "So you're gonna move up, huh?"

"Yeah."

Can you believe it? Suddenly, I had everything in the world going for me.

I went back home to Jacksonville on August 30. My plan was to fly to New York from Jacksonville on September 12. Right after that, I'd move into an apartment.

Bad timing, as it turns out. I had all this stuff set up for the day after September 11.

❯❯❯❮❮❮

On the morning of the eleventh, I turned on the computer at about 8:30 at my parent's house in Jacksonville. Walked over, turned on the TV, put on CNN like I do every morning to follow the economy and check the news. The first Tower had already been hit. I thought it was some kind of freak accident.

I immediately called my girlfriend, who was on the way to her job at Sotheby's auction house. I told her what had happened but she didn't get it, she hadn't realized the magnitude yet. She was in the stairwell of her building and she said, "I'll call you later."

So I sat down at the computer and logged on. I'm still watching the TV. All of a sudden I see the silhouette of a plane fly behind the second building and *boom!* Just like that, the second Tower exploded.

The first thing that went through my head was, "I'm not going up there. I don't have a job anymore."

◆◆◆

Of course, the next thought that went through my mind . . . I started immediately frettin' about my best friend, Whit. He was working in the Towers at the time. We grew up six houses down from each other in Jacksonville. He'd been home to Jacksonville two days before the eleventh, and we'd gone out deep-sea fishing. Man, all I could think about was his parents, how strung out they must have been. But I didn't want to go down to their place because I guess I didn't really want to know.

I sat on my couch in shock until around noon. Finally, I went down the street. It turned out Whit's dad, Dr. Athey, was alone at the house; Whit's mom was in Connecticut visiting his sister. A few close family friends had gathered, and I was welcome, of course. But the front of the house is all glass—you can look right into the living room. As I approached, the first person I saw was a priest, and I flipped.

See, I was 50/50 on Whit's chances before I got there. I saw that priest and I was like, "Oh, shit."

I got inside, and they all said, "We're waiting to hear," which was sort of a relief. No news is good news, right? But then I thought, they hadn't heard anything for four hours. That can't be good.

I don't know how long I hung out there. An hour? It seemed like a long fucking time. Then the phone rang. I don't remember who called, but Whit's dad picked up the phone and just listened for a second. Whoever was on the other end must have just said, "He's okay."

Dr. Athey fell down on the couch and buried his face in his hands, crying tears of joy and relief.

>>><<<

When I visited New York that August, I'd contacted an old fraternity brother of mine. He showed me his apartment and offered for me to move in. It was a beautiful place. Huge, with bay windows that over-looked the Trade Center.

After the attack, I emailed him to see if he was okay. Hell, to see if he was alive.

He said, "I'm fine, thanks. You're still coming up, right? You're more than welcome to."

So I did. It went perfect. Searching for an apartment in New York City is insanity, but here I got this place with no broker's fee, no lease. Of course, when I moved in, those Towers were gone. But it made sense. I was paying cheap for a huge apartment that didn't have a great view anymore.

We were alive, though, that's something to think about. And I didn't lose any friends in the attack, so I figure, what the hell have I got to complain about?

>>><<<

On Thursday, September 13, I called Opal Financial to see if I still had a job, and they said, "Well, just come up and see what happens."

So I moved to New York exactly seven days after the eleventh. The economy was a mess right then. The stock market had re-opened, but no one knew what was going to happen in the long term. It was a scary time. Whole companies had been wiped off the face of the earth.

The guys at Opal advised me to start sending out resumes, but I was patient. A funny thing—there was this guy who was supposed to start the same day as me? He got really impatient and they told him to back off. His impatience reflected poorly on him.

I started working at Opal three weeks later. So did the other guy. But after a month, the other guy was asked to leave.

⟫✕⟪

I let September 11 be a testament to the fact that I was coming to New York regardless of what happened. I was ready to do something with my life, to pursue something. I met a girl worth enough to make me move, which is a big step for me. I'd made the commitment to go way before September 11.

Everyone tried to talk me out of it. They didn't think that, being the Southern boy that I am, New York would be the place for me. I took that into consideration. But I've done pretty well since. And I've never been happier, and I'll never regret it.

ELLEN SHAPIRO

Ellen Shapiro, thirty-two, owns and operates the burgeoning gourmet shop New World Catering, located in the affluent metropolitan suburb of Maplewood, New Jersey.

AROUND THE CORNER from me, on James Street and Main, they arrested this Iranian guy for burning his wife. The morning of the eleventh, he put out prayer mats, and the police came and arrested him about two days later. Strange.

He owned a bookshop called Prints of Peace. The place is closed down now.

He didn't kill her; he burned her. I don't know how he did it, or why, or what he used to do it. But on the eleventh he set her on fire at the end of my street in South Orange, New Jersey.

I knew this guy. His name was Mohammad. I used to buy cigarettes from his store. He drove around in a Mercedes-Benz with New York plates.

So the police took him away and now he's gone, don't ask me where.

There were some other people living with him. But after this happened, they all just . . . went away.

I think the wife must've known something. In fact, that's what everyone in my neighborhood thinks.

We're so close to New York. You never know who lives next door to you.

>>><<<

My friend, Mark, had just landed a new job working in the World Trade Center.[36] He's an insurance agent for a big insurance company.[37]

---

36 Not his actual name.
37 Actual name of the firm withheld.

He'd literally just started his job a couple weeks [before September 11]. His wife just had a baby, three months old. Mark's . . . let me see. I'm thirty-two, so that makes him . . . thirty-four? Yes, that's right. Thirty-four.

Anyway, this is what he told me. He was going to work that day, and he walked into the building and pressed the button for the elevator. He was standing there, waiting for the elevator doors to open, when he heard this loud crash. It was the plane hitting the first Tower. So he turned around and went outside along with many others. He looked up, and he saw the crash. He said he was standing there, looking at this great big burning hole in his building when he realized that everyone was running away. So he ran, too.

Mark told me he got three blocks before he turned around to watch what was going on. At that point, he noticed there were a lot of people rushing past him, going toward the building to see what they could do to help, you know? Then the second plane hit the other Tower. He was watching the whole thing. And right at that point, everyone that ran past him to help? They all died. There was a rain of fuel and debris and bodies.

And Mark said there was one guy who fell . . . "flew," he called it. A guy who flew out of the second Tower.

Now, I don't really know if their eyes met or what happened. All I know is what Mark tried to describe to me. But Mark is convinced that he made a connection with this gentleman, this falling guy.

He said he might've been fifty yards away from the building, said he saw maybe fifty people fall from the building. Maybe seventy-five people in all died right there in front of him.

And he's telling me he definitely can't sleep. He doesn't want to come into the city to work anymore. His psychiatrist told him not to.

Basically, my friend is a mess.

>>><<<

I'll tell you why I think this is important.

I saw Mark yesterday, on the twenty-third of September. So it's been, what? A week and a half since the attack. My boyfriend and I were invited over to visit with the new baby and drink beers.

When we arrived, Mark was outside. He's a big, handy man. His place is rural; he's got two acres of land covered with thick trees. And the first thing we saw, he'd put up a forty-foot flagpole in the front yard with this huge American flag.

Okay, I thought. That's a bit unusual. Patriotic. But unusual.

So we went inside, he's laughing and joking and everything seemed normal. Too normal. Then Mark got a videotape and said, "Get a load of this." He popped in the tape.

It was a video of his baby, his three-month-old little girl trying to say hello. Real cute. And then it switched to something else. This—he had filmed this. On a tree in his yard, he had tied a noose with twelve knots. He had one of those Anatomical Annie dummies from CPR classes, a big plastic doll with a chest cavity. He'd wound a black-and-white scarf onto the dummy's head in a turban, and he'd hung it on this noose. Next to it was a sign painted on a big piece of plywood that said "BIN LADEN MUST DIE."

It was dark outside on the tape. But Mark had put spotlights out. So here's this video of a body hanging by a noose in a spotlight, a body that didn't have any legs from the waist down, which was eerie in itself. And the spotlight fell on the American flag, too; it was very dramatic.

I sat there, watching the tape, stupefied.

This is one of my best friends. He's generally a pretty calm guy. But this behavior. Um. He's been married for five years, and now he's got this little girl. This was a little scary.

>>>«««

Mark's company moved, and now he's actually working at an office in Parsippany [New Jersey]. He said he got a phone call from his wife during the week, because she wanted to make sure it was okay to take the doll down. The cops had come to visit her, and they said, "We don't have a problem with what you're doing. It is your freedom of speech. But there are three or four school buses that go by here every day, and this is not something for kids to see."

So she said, "I want to make sure it's okay with my husband." She hadn't wanted to hang the doll up in the first place.

So Mark said, "Take it down." But he still has the dummy in his garage.

I had no idea what to say to him as he showed me this video and told me all this. And I can't even comment on what it must have been like for him to have gone through what he did. What can you say to seeing a hundred people die right in front of you?

I consider myself lucky to not have witnessed what he did.

DREW NEDERPELT

Drew Nederpelt, thirty-four, went downtown to help his girlfriend—a noted television reporter—cover the news shortly after the second plane hit.

They arrived at a distance three blocks from the North Tower as it began to fall.

I SCREAMED AT her to move, but she just stood there. I'm not sure if she was just in awe or what—it was an unreal sight, this huge gray mountain just falling in on itself. Or maybe she couldn't process what was happening. Whatever. It didn't matter. We were only three blocks away. If we didn't move, we'd be toast. That's the only thought that was running through my mind.

I grabbed her hand and we ran about forty yards down the street, where we rounded a corner and I threw her into a doorway on Murray. I guess I expected the debris to file nicely along the avenues and streets, like water pouring into the cubicles of an ice tray. But instead it came crashing overtop the thirty-story building we were hiding behind. The sound was incredible—just a great big unbelievable *swooooosh*—and suddenly, everything was pitch-black. I mean totally, unbelievably black.

I screwed my eyes shut, but when I opened them again, there was no difference. Everything was black with them closed and black with them open. Then I started to cough. Breathing was nearly impossible. Which got me angry. I thought, I'm not just going to sit here and die in some dingy doorway. So I backed up and started kicking at the door we were standing next to, which was made of metal and glass. It was an outer door to an apartment building, I think, and not very strong.

On the fourth kick the latch just popped out and the door flung open with a crash. We both ran inside, thinking we were clear. But there was another door in front of us, a large, sturdy solid metal thing with a thick glass window. And of course, in the blink of an eye, all the debris that was outside just whooshed in after us and there we were, in the same predicament, choking in this tiny, confined space. And I remember thinking, so this is it, huh?

>>><<<

I really didn't have a choice. I believed that if we wanted to live we had to get out of the debris. I had no idea how long the cloud was going to last, but I wasn't going to wait around to find out. There was no way I was going to break down that inner door, it was too solid. So I started on the interior glass.

I kicked it, but I had on a pair of rubber-soled sandals and my feet just kept bouncing off. I remember this all very vividly—knowing that my leg was eventually going to punch through that glass and shred my entire calf, being absolutely sure about it. And I've run marathons, I'm a runner; my legs are important to me. But I couldn't have cared less. I kept kicking. It was one of those things where you figure a shredded leg is a small price to pay for being alive. So I just kept it up. Kick, kick, kick.

We were both starting to choke pretty badly from the debris, and I was blindly wailing away on this door—fifteen, maybe sixteen kicks into it, now. Then, slowly, the glass began to tear away from the sides and the whole pane just folded down, leaving a hole in the bottom half of the door, which we crawled through.

We found ourselves in a small anteroom, staring at an elevator. I hit the button and the elevator door opened with a cheerful *bing*—like it was saying, "I'm ready for you, thanks, today is business as usual."

I looked inside. It was a bright, clean elevator. Thinking back, I can hear peaceful elevator music but I know that isn't possible. I think it just seemed so far removed from what was happening outside—so surreal—that my mind was playing tricks on me.

I made the decision that we weren't going into an elevator in a war zone. So instead I threw up on the floor.

>>><<<

Then we heard banging.

I looked down the antechamber we'd come through and saw the shadow of a person outside the first door. And I hate to say this, but I looked at this guy and my first thought was, you know what? We have our air and we had to fight for it. If I open that door again it'll let all that stuff back in here.

But then, you know, you remember that's a human being out there.

So I ducked through the hole I'd kicked in the second door and opened the latch on the outer door, and this cop staggered in. He was completely covered with the soot, like we were. He came in and just stood there, panting.

I asked, "Are you okay?"

He didn't say a word, he just barely nodded. He was completely stunned. He stood there in a daze with his shoulders slouched, ghost-white from the debris—which was interesting because he was African American. You could see the word "POLICE" stenciled on his vest.

Then there was another banging. This time, my girlfriend opened the door. Another man crawled in and he didn't say a word either, he just stood in the corner, grabbed a hanky from his pocket and began wiping himself off in silence.

This second guy was covered from head to foot in an inch of crap, and he was dusting himself off with a little checkered handkerchief. It was absurd. He reminded me of Lady Macbeth trying to scrub off the "damned spot"—like he was in shock, or denial. He didn't realize he couldn't make a dent in his appearance with his little hanky.

As it turns out, he was a plainclothes policeman.

I always carry my digital camera with me, and I took a few pictures.

After four or five minutes, it looked as if things were getting clearer outside. So we all stepped out and went our separate ways without saying a word. The cops, I guess, went and did what they had to do, and we went to report the news.

⋙✕⋘

Every minute or so, you heard an explosion from somewhere close by. I thought at the time that they were bombs, but I later found out they were cars exploding from the heat of the fires.

I remember hearing that the Pentagon had been hit. At the time, there were all these rumors: the Sears Tower was in flames; the UN had been hit. And I remember thinking very clearly as these explosions were going off around me that, if the news feeds were reporting buildings across the country going up in flames, this must be what it's like to feel under siege. Like London in 1941, or Dresden. To feel like everything that is near and familiar and yours is being destroyed by people who don't know you and don't appreciate you, who don't care what you do or who you are.

I wanted to grab hold of whoever was responsible for all this and shout, "Don't you understand? You've got the wrong place, the wrong people! There's been some misunderstanding!"

I think that most of history's conflicts have really been about misunderstandings.

⋙✕⋘

Later that night, my girlfriend used her media clout and convinced a couple of cops from NYPD intelligence to drive us through Ground Zero.

I'll never forget it. The jagged shards of the Towers loomed up into the sky like fangs sprouting from the ground, fangs that were lit by hundreds of spotlights as thousands of firemen and rescue workers climbed over them, picking through what had already become known as the Pile.

We were the only car on the streets. As we trolled along, the driver gave little bleeps on his horn to move the Hazmat units out of the way.

I was bothered that we were disrupting the rescue efforts to indulge in our personal guided tour of the area. But my girlfriend made a bargain. These cops were with intel and wanted to know more about what had happened just before the attacks. So my girlfriend promised to put out a call over the airwaves for any video that had been shot in the hours before the attacks. That's what she bartered to get us into Ground Zero.

The media exists for quid pro quo.

⟫⟪

At one point, a cop with a gas mask banged on the window of our car and yelled, "What the hell are you doing?" He peered in at the two of us in the backseat while our driver rolled the window down.

"We're with Intel," the driver said, and showed him a badge.

The cop looked at the badge, looked at the driver, and said, "You're a fucking asshole." And he walked off.

We didn't turn back, I guess because my girlfriend didn't offer and these cops felt they owed her—a deal was a deal. But not one minute later, another cop ran up to our car. I mean this literally when I say that we were the only vehicle moving on the streets. Everything else had been pulled off to the side of the road and here we were cruising around in a white Crown Victoria in the middle of Ground Zero at nine o'clock on the night of the eleventh.

This second cop started banging on the window, screaming, "What the fuck are you doing?"

Our driver rolled his window down again and started to explain: "We're with Intel, and . . ."

But this new cop screamed at the top of his lungs, "I don't care who the fuck you are! Turn this fucking thing around and get the fuck out of here! Now!"

So we did a six-point turn in the middle of the road, which sent all the poor rescue workers who we'd just beeped with the siren scrambling for the sidewalks again. And we left Ground Zero.

My girlfriend managed to do a live phone report on network television. She called what she had just seen "the face of hell."

⟫⟪

Here's my bottom-line assessment:

In a lot of ways, the media did some great things that day. They provided a lot of value, and often acted heroically. But there was a lot of terrible stuff, too.

For instance, several journalists we know managed to "acquire" some hazmat suits and helmets, and they snuck into Ground Zero and videotaped everything going on for hours. Thankfully, our network didn't use any of the footage. They knew they'd have to answer for how their reporters had managed to get footage from inside Ground Zero.

I remember another incident where my girlfriend and the host from a very popular network morning show got into a screaming match about using some ex-NYPD bigwig for a guided tour of the Pile. They went toe-to-toe, if you can imagine it, right there in front of 200 people, tearing at each other about who had the right to tell the story, while 300 yards away, thousands of missing people lay buried.

And there were assistant producers crawling all over the place who'd been dispatched to help out their TV stations. Without many exceptions, assistant producers in TV are all young twenty-some-things trying to get their start in the business. On 9/11 and the days after, their idea of getting an interview with a rescue worker was to walk out from the bullpen where reporters were kept tethered, grab a subject, and literally hang onto their sleeves, physically dragging them to the sidelines. It was really unbelievable.

I remember seeing dozens of firemen shaking their arms while these APs hung off them like rabid schnauzers. All these girls and boys who'd never been out of a studio in their professional lives and whose idea of convincing someone to do an interview was to scour Lower Manhattan for anyone in uniform and forcefully yank them aside. It was sad.

And more than a few on-camera reporters who'd been caught under the debris refused to have anyone brush them off. On September 11, my girlfriend physically fought off a dozen people—producers, friends, bystanders, anyone who walked up to her and tried to dust her off. She was proud of the fact that she'd been there from the beginning. That debris was her badge of courage.

I remember seeing tape of one news anchor who'd been under the North Tower when it collapsed. Reporting from the studio two hours later, he still had the dust in his hair and all over his shoulders. The makeup department must have gone to extremes to do his face without disturbing the soot that covered him.

>>><<<

But there were bright spots, too.

I remember two cops who asked me to take a picture of them. They were smiling and so proud to be together, to have survived, to be helping. I saw so many examples of utter selflessness, a level of human compassion that was staggering, just staggering.

The owners of The Square diner opened their doors to everyone and gave out all their food for free. They literally refused to take any money—even from the expense account-laden media. I managed to hide twenty bucks under a cake stand on my way out that they hopefully found long after we'd all gone.

And I befriended a firefighter from Connecticut; a few months later, I was able to get some media for a 100-mile bike rally he was planning to Ground Zero to benefit the victims.

I became very close with the camera and the sound guy I'd worked with at Ground Zero. When I ran into them unexpectedly several months later, I was so happy to see them, we hugged. It was great. They told me they still worked as a team. In many ways, the event had brought them together.

In retrospect, when I think back to all that happened, I prefer to remember these other things. These bright spots. I think they tell me so much about what that day could potentially mean for our future.

>>><<<

It was quite a day. I don't know how else to say it. It was flat-out on the go, from the moment I got up that morning and went for a run in the park until I hitched a ride home on the back of a fire truck after midnight. I went all day on a Powerbar. Food was nothing. Food was a joke.

I remember I didn't cry that day, but I think I shook for most of the morning. I didn't cry until I was standing in my shower at 1:00 A.M. on September 12. All alone in the silence, I watched the black and the soot and the God-knows-what stream off my body and swirl down the drain.

UPDATE

Drew Nederpelt and his girlfriend broke up shortly after the events of September 11, 2001. Sensing that his talents were better suited to a different field, Drew switched careers and founded his own publishing company, Sterling & Ross, "a commercial trade publisher of current affairs, celebrity, pop culture, and other media-centric, compelling books for mass consumption."

Drew's publishing philosophy holds that "the literary wasteland is populated with great and valuable books that died on the vine because they were not given the proper publicity to achieve success." Sterling & Ross takes on ambitious book projects that deserve a wide readership and works closely with its authors in ways that larger publishing companies can't.

Some of Sterling & Ross's titles include *Scout's Honor: The Bravest Way to Build a Winning Team* by Atlanta Braves TV host Bill Shanks and *Beneath the Pleasuredome: Designing the Playboy Mystique* by Ron Dirsmith.

THE TURNER FAMILY

The Turner family: Jake, forty-eight; his wife, Sean, forty-five; their daughter, Madeline, eleven; and their new boy, James, eighteen months.

By sheer luck, the Turners moved from an apartment on Warren Street to a space further away on Greenwich Street on September 1, 2001.[38] *The shift in location spared them from being directly beneath the Towers and the collapse of the buildings during the attack.*

Jake: THE GREENWICH STREET location was an empty warehouse when we bought it. The renovation took over two years of planning. We gutted the place and converted it to livable quarters from scratch. We had to install everything: heating, ventilation, plumbing, electricity, the works.

The byzantine city bureaucracy held us up for a long time. We had to get permits and papers; there were codes and statutes. We'd already moved into the space by the eleventh, but it was far from finished. We still had workmen going full tilt every day.

I was shaving in the bathroom when one of the Chinese workmen came in. He couldn't speak much English but he said, "Come out here. Come, come, come!" He took me out into the street, and together we looked up at this big, gaping hole in the Tower.

The first thought I had was, well. We can fix that. You know? That can be fixed.

$$\text{\Rightarrow\!\!\!\Rightarrow\!\!\!\Leftarrow\!\!\!\Leftarrow}$$

Jake: I keep going over the sequence of events because I want to remember everything. I think in my old age I'm going to forget the minutia.

Sean: I knew right away. I said, "That's terrorism."

---

38 The Turners' former address on Warren Street was three blocks from the Trade Center.

Jake: Sean yelled, "Go get the camera." And there I was, standing out there in the street videotaping this gaping hole . . . and that's when the second plane hit. The explosion shot out fire that covered several blocks, which is when I dropped the camera and said, "Shit. This is terrorism. I'd better go get Madeline." She was at her school, which is about two blocks north of the Towers.

Sean: It was her fourth day at a brand-new school in Battery Park. She's at IS 89,[39] which is right next to Stuyvesant High School. She'd just started middle school, sixth grade.

Jake: We'd actually gone through this whole process because in New York, to enroll a child in a city school, you have to go through an interview. You have to pick your school location, and you have to be accepted at the school. Some of her friends went to a place over on the East Side, but we thought, well, we're in this new neighborhood and IS 89 is a brand-new school. It's a beautiful facility, and she can walk there.

So after the second plane hit, I grabbed my bicycle and jumped on. I rode down West Street, heading south. Meanwhile, people were streaming in the opposite direction, running, walking—it was hard to ride the bike, there were so many people coming at me head on. Plus sirens were wailing and trucks were going south.

I get to the school and was surprised to find everything was very calm. I didn't have a clue as to where Madeline was—she was new there, so I didn't know her homeroom or anything. I ran through the school, sprinting up floors, looking in doors. Finally I ran into a teacher, who said, "They're all down in the cafeteria."

>>><<<

Jake: I went back downstairs, found the cafeteria, and sure enough, the students were massing. They didn't know what was going on. Some of them had heard the explosions, but none of them had actually seen them, I don't think.

---

39 In the New York City public school system, "IS" stands for "Intermediate School."

I found Madeline and grabbed her. She said, "What's going on?"

And this is where it started to fall apart for me because I said, "Oh. Well . . ." And I didn't know what to tell her. I just looked at her.

All I could think was, I'm so sorry you have to experience this. I'm so sorry I have to tell you what's going on. I mean, I had never experienced this. Nobody'd ever experienced this. And there she was, eleven years old and about to go through it, fumbling and terrified like the rest of us.

I think I said something like, "It's okay, honey. A plane's run into the World Trade Center, that's all. Come on." And we went outside.

>>><<<

Jake: Her school's right there. When we walked out the door, we looked up and saw the blizzard coming down, the people jumping out the windows, everything. I don't think she actually saw any of the bodies because there was paper and debris flying everywhere. I hope she didn't see anything.

We walked north. By this time it was too crowded to even consider using the bicycle. There was this van parked in the middle of the street with its doors wide open and the radio blaring. The president was on, and he was telling the nation about what's going on in New York City, describing for the whole country what was going on right where we were, and that was surreal. This huge crowd of people had massed around this van and was standing quietly, trying to listen, trying to figure out what happened while this chaos was exploding all around us.

To me, it was one of those moments in history you only read about. That's when I realized this was big. This was huge.

>>><<<

Jake: We got home, and I picked up the camera again. I was standing out on the street, filming, when the first building collapsed.

Sean: On Greenwich Street, we're fifteen blocks away. You could see everything.

Jake: The first building collapsed and I thought back to '93; we were here in the city when that first bomb went off. Nobody expected a collapse to happen then, and nobody expected one to happen now. But a little while later, the second Tower came down. I don't now how to describe that to you.

Our apartment is on the street level, so we watched this steady crowd of people stream right past our windows. Then, suddenly, this guy who was totally covered in dust pressed himself against the glass of our living room pane. He was all white from the dust; you could only make out his eyes. He pressed a badge up against the window and shouted out that he was from the FBI. I wouldn't know an FBI badge from anything, but I let the guy in.

He wanted to use our bathroom to wash off, and we said, "Sure. It's over there."

As he was walking toward the bathroom, he said, "This is the saddest day in American history." He went into the bathroom and closed the door.

We were waiting out here for him to finish up. He took a long time. We stood here and listened while he started weeping in our bathroom.

»»»«««

Jake: There were lots of FBI guys in town that day for some sort of UN conference. When the guy came out of the bathroom, I said, "Do you want to use the phone? I don't think it's working but you're welcome to try."

He looked at me and said, "My office was in the Tower. It's gone. It's all gone. I don't know who to call."

The poor guy didn't know what to do. And he was, you know, a federal officer. Eventually he decided to go back to his hotel, which was someplace in Midtown, I think. He said, "I guess I'll just go back to the hotel and see who shows up." He didn't know what had happened to his colleagues. He had no idea what became of them.

➤➤➤◄◄◄

Jake: Sean's a real estate broker, and later that afternoon, she walked down towards the Towers for an apartment showing, thinking that her clients would keep their time slot.

Sean: I was supposed to be closing an apartment at one o'clock on Broadway and Warren. The eleventh was supposed to be our final walk-through before signing the papers. When Jake left to get Madeline, I started heading down Greenwich to make the appointment.

When you walk down Greenwich, the first thing you come to is the Smith Barney Travelers building. That's the tall building about three blocks down, with the neon umbrella logo. Everyone who worked in that building had spilled out on the street, a herd of people whose median age was thirty or forty years old. Every ear had a cell phone jammed in it, and every head had turned in the direction of the Towers. Everyone was talking. And I thought, oh my God. They're talking to people who are up in the buildings, their friends who work there and got trapped.

It was frightening.

I cut over to Hudson Street. These are blocks that I walk every day of my life, but this was so different from any other day. I don't know if anyone else you've interviewed described this to you, but you'd be walking along, things would seem normal. Then, all of a sudden, for some unexplained reason a group of people would panic and start running, even though nothing new had happened. You felt an electric fear that worked itself through whole crowds on a whim.

Jake: Right. For instance, at 5:30 that afternoon, when 7 World Trade collapsed, there was all this panic. People were screaming, "The building's collapsing! The building's collapsing!" We were sitting here, having watched the Towers collapse, thinking, why are you panicking *now?* I think people react in different ways.

Sean: We weren't filled with panic when we saw the planes hit. I guess we just thought, okay, life is gonna go on. Those Towers are gonna burn, but life is gonna go on.

Anyway, as I walked closer and closer to the scene, I started feeling those little pockets of panic hit. And when I got down to the building on Warren Street where I was supposed to show the apartment, the superintendent was there sweeping out the lobby as if it were any other day.

I didn't see my client anywhere and I thought, well, she may not show. I'd better go up and check the apartment so that, at the closing, I can vouch for the fact that it was in good shape. This is how you're thinking!

So I went up to the apartment and everything looked fine, everything worked. I lowered the shades to hide the view. Then I went back down and waited a bit longer, but the client didn't show. So I thought, I'd better go find a phone. But every pay phone had huge lines of people snaking away from it.

That's when I felt the air change. I felt little particles. Then I heard a roar. I looked down Broadway and saw that brown cloud you've seen in all the reels, with people running full tilt up the street in front of it. My first thought was bio-terrorism because of the brown quality of the air.

When I first heard the noise, I thought the terrorists had hit something else, like the Woolworth Building. I was surrounded by so many buildings directly in front of me, I couldn't see the Trade Center.

Jake: On the videotape I shot, I have the aftermath of walking down there. There was like a . . . snow everywhere. Army vehicles drove by. People covered their faces with handkerchiefs, napkins, shirts, anything. When the Towers collapsed, everything was like living in a dream, a dream where you kept thinking, we're going to wake up. Any moment now, we're going to wake up. But of course we never did.

>>>«<<

Sean: I decided to head north and get back home. My biggest concern, strangely enough, was that I didn't want to get trampled to death by the mob. I went down a side street to get away from everyone and I thought, I know this area really well, I used to live here. I'll be smarter than them, I'll go down Thomas Street. No one's gonna go down Thomas. Which is when I saw the McDonald's.

There were two sets of workers: the workers outside and the workers inside. The workers outside were hollering, "Come on! Go!" Like they were in the path of a bomb or something. And the workers inside were just as adamant. "We can't leave, we can't just leave!"

Their friends outside screamed, "Get out of there!" But these few guys inside hung in, they wanted to stay. I guess they were going to work that day no matter what.

Jake: That was just like the guys who were here working on our place. They're Chinese and they don't speak any English. Lew, their Taiwanese foreman, was crying. They were all in such shock.

We all huddled in this empty room where we had a TV and nothing else. We sat on the bare floor.

Sean: Yeah, how come our cable continued to work? We never lost our cable throughout the whole thing.

Jake: I don't know, ask the cable company. But we all sat in there and Sean went out to get sandwiches.

Sean: I thought, the only thing I can do for people is feed them. So I took Lew with me to this cruddy little deli a block away and said, "We'd better get supplies." We loaded up with anything I could think of. Things we might have to eat for the next three or four days.

Jake: We didn't know what was going to happen next, you know? For a long time, part of the stress was wondering, when is the other shoe going to drop? So we stocked up and there we were, all of us in that room. Five or six Chinese guys—

Sean: No. More than that.

Jake: Maybe. Five, six guys and Lew—who spoke a little English, the only one of all of them who did, really. Everybody was stunned. As it turns out, they didn't eat anything.

Sean: They only ate potato chips.

Jake: They didn't want to eat. We all watched the news. Nobody knew what to do.

Sean: We were getting ready to have them stay with us, if that was what needed to happen. For all we knew, they would live with us. We didn't know where people would go.

Jake: That was sort of an error in translation. For a while, they thought they had to stay. Those guys are so used to their jobs. Eventually, we just told them to go home. We weren't kicking them out, you understand. But we made it clear to them, "You certainly don't have to work today. Go home to your families. Make sure everyone's okay."

Sean: For our old neighbor, Marcella, September 11 was a double whammy. She'd just found out she had brain cancer. Being so close to the Towers on Warren Street, they were eventually displaced from their home. So she had to deal with brain cancer and being a refugee.

Jake: What are the chances of that?

Sean: Their skylight had begun to leak a day before the World Trade Center. By the time they found anyone to fix it, like a month later, their whole floor was warped. Everything was ruined. Water just came pouring in.

She had surgery, she's fine now. But . . . wow.

Jake: We took Marcella and her husband, Foster, in right after the attack. They needed a place to stay. Foster's suffering from severe colon cancer. While they were staying with us, he had to walk north nearly every day to get his chemo treatments. The military stopped him every time he passed the checkpoint, and he had to keep explaining to the authorities who he was, where he was staying, why he was staying there, and what he was going to do. Talk about determination, the poor guy.

Jake and Sean's eleven-year-old daughter, Madeline, entered the room and added her recollections to the conversation.

Madeline: When I first heard the noise, it was a loud boom and there was a whirling sound outside my math class. The windows faced out toward the West Side highway. We couldn't see the Towers, but we saw people running with their hands over their heads. Then teachers started running into the classroom and shouting things.

The first teacher said that a car had hit the World Trade Center, but we all thought that was strange. A car had made all that noise? Uh-uh. Then another teacher came in and said that no, it was a plane that had hit. That seemed a little weird, too, but it seemed . . . I don't know. More right. Finally, our principal's voice came on the overhead loudspeaker. She said we should all stay calm.

Our teacher tried to get us back to work on adding, subtracting, multiplying, and dividing fractions. It was a really easy assignment because it was only the fourth day of school. But then parents started running into the classroom. The gym teacher came on over the loud-speaker and told everyone to go down to the cafeteria. So we did.

Everyone was just waiting for their parents to come. A lot of kids couldn't get in touch with their parents at their offices, so they went home with friends and their friends' parents. My dad was already in the cafeteria when we got there, and he took me home.

When we got back to my house and were standing in the door, I saw my old fifth-grade teacher walk by with some of the students from her class. She was holding onto their little hands and walking north.

I said, "Hi," and she said, "Hi," but she kept walking. I guess she had a lot on her mind.

>>>><<<<

Jake: Were you scared?

Madeline: [*pause*] Yeah.

Jake: You were?

Madeline: Yeah.

Jake: What do you think about the move to the new school, to where you are now?

Madeline: [*shrugs*] I was only in the other school for four days, anyway. We didn't really get used to it. It's still my school at the new place because the building's not the school, the people are, and they're all the same. The teachers and the students. Except that some students never came back. Like this one kid got so scared, he never came back.

Jake: But all of your textbooks are still in the old school, right?

Madeline: Except for the math ones. We had those with us when we left.

Jake: They've been working on Spanish without textbooks.

Madeline: Some kids that day had stuffed things into their lockers for the afternoon. Like, our lunches were in there. I heard that they broke open our lockers to get the lunches out.

Sean: I hope so.

Madeline: I had one of my favorite books in there, too. I had my writing notebook, which I'd decorated nicely. But then I had to use another one that they gave us. Some of my friends had cell phones in their lockers, but the cell phone company gave them new ones.

Sean: Do you guys talk about all this much at school now?

Madeline: No. But things are a little different. We got to go see a free performance of *Beauty and the Beast*, and we got to go see a lot of old silent films where a live band plays along with the film. We used to go to Chelsea Piers Amusement Park about every week and a half to do rock climbing, soccer, basketball, and the batting cages. I don't think about it much anymore.

⟫⟪

Jake: From what I've seen, two camps of people, parents, and teachers have formed in the neighborhood. There's the people who want to move ahead and the people who want to dwell on the incident.

A lot of people want to get back in the school, get back into things, get back into living life. Other people are panicked for any number of reasons. They focus on the schools not being safe, because the air quality's not good. As far as that goes, I have to think, well, this is New York City. How good was the air quality before all this happened?

I mean, look—you can worry about the air quality. There's an argument there. But at the same time, during this crisis, people were sitting around watching other things happen to our children which were just as detrimental. Sean and I feel that it's more important, psychologically, for people—certainly for the kids—to get back into some sort of normal routine.

Obviously, you want to acknowledge what happened. You have to—how can you not? But at the same time, why dwell on it? Because really, in the end, what can you do?

Madeline: I do want to go back to my school, because the school we're at is scary. We're sharing space with teenagers and high schoolers, and some kids were mugged across the street in a park just the other day. Plus, I play the clarinet. Right now in music class we have to be taught alongside the saxophones and flutes. The class is split in half, so we only get twenty minutes to work on something. When we go back, we'll be able to have our own time.

Jake: When do you go back?

Sean: The twenty-second of January.[40]

Madeline: We missed a lot of school days the week after the attack happened. And while they're moving stuff back into the school, we're going to miss another, like, three days. That's what they tell us. I don't know whether we're going to make up the time at the end or what.

Sean: I'm sure they'll figure something out.

Jake: Maybe they'll just say, "Okay. We can forget about it." Would that be all right with you?

Sean: [*smiling*] Yeah.

---

40 2002.

UPDATE

When I caught up with the Turner Family, Jake Turner told me this:

In the fall of 2006, Madeline and the family hosted an exchange student from Argentina. The exchange student wanted to take in some sights, especially the legendary views from the top of the Empire State Building. Even though Madeline had grown up in New York (or perhaps because of it), she had never been to the Empire State Building. So, mere days after the fifth anniversary of September 11, the two girls made an excursion to 350 5th Avenue.

The trip ended badly. Shortly after making it to the top, Madeline experienced a severe, uncharacteristic panic attack and became so incapacitated that help had to be summoned. She was escorted back to ground level, where her condition stabilized very quickly. Shortly thereafter, somewhat embarrassed, Madeline called Sean to report the incident. Sean, in turn, called Jake, who found the situation unfortunately logical.

"She'd never been up in a building that high," he said simply. He thought about it for a long moment, and then added: "I still think about that day. About what happened, sure, and everything that followed. To the people above and the people below. Not long after 9/11, I went out and bought bio/chem attack suits for everyone in the family. For protection, you know? Just in case. They were awfully expensive, but I didn't want to be caught unprepared the next time around.

"Mostly, whenever I think of the eleventh, I think of Madeline. She was so young when it happened, and it was such a shame that she had to see it. That day was the death of her innocence. No parent wants to watch that die in their child.

"When the innocence goes away, what else is left? Where do you go from there?"

MIKE X

Mike X refuses to give his last name. He says he's worked on the floor of the New York Stock Exchange for fifteen years, and he was in the World Trade Center immediately before the attack on September 11. From the Towers, he walked to work at the Exchange in a state of shock and witnessed the shutdown of the American economy.

This interview was conducted in a popular Wall Street area bar.

MY NAME'S MIKE. No, I'm not giving you my fucking last name. That's it. Just Mike. All right?

I'm a trader on the Exchange floor. I'm not going to tell you what company I work for and what sector I handle. Suffice it to say, we're the two-dollar broker on the floor of the New York Stock Exchange, all right?

You know what? Turn that thing off till I get good and drunk.

⤛⤜

I live in Jersey, and I'd take the PATH train into the Trade Center every day. I'd walk through all the stores and the galleries underground. And every day I went into the Trinity Church cemetery, walking my regular route from the Trade Center to the Stock Exchange.

So. This day, the eleventh. I heard a noise and looked up. Couldn't see what was going on 'cause of all the buildings on Broadway. Thought maybe it was just another transformer blew.[41] So I kept walking.

I came down Wall Street. Saw people pointing up, so I looked up. Said, "Holy shit." There's this big plume of smoke, and I was like, "What the hell's goin' on now?"

Kept walkin' down Wall Street. Now the plume's getting closer. I'm on Broad and Wall. Turned around, and paper started comin'

---

41 Mike did not bother to qualify this, so I asked, "How often did you hear transformers blow downtown?" He looked at me with open hostility and said, "They blow, man. They blow."

down outta the air. You know, papers from the World Trade Center, papers like woulda been on somebody's desk. Spit out of computers. They're all burned 'round the edges.

Again, I think, holy shit. This ain't . . . ya know. This ain't normal.

Three minutes. Three fucking minutes earlier, I would have been right under it all.

⟫⟪

Everybody ran into the Exchange. I get in there, and the first thing I hear is some guy sayin', "Yeah, some twin-engine plane hit the Trade Center."

Everybody's gathering around the TVs we got on the trading floor. I'm, like, "No. That's not a twin-engine plane. A Cessna would have just bounced off those buildings."

Jesus Christ. Confusion. Mayhem and confusion. The market never opened that day. The head of the Exchange announced, "Trading will be delayed until we can figure out what's going on." Then, as things developed, he said, "We're not opening at all."

I'm on my floor, got nothing to do, so I call my parents and friends. Everybody. Tell 'em I'm all right. Then the first Tower came down.

⟫⟪

The Exchange building started shaking. There's these huge glass windows all around the Stock Exchange, and they started rattling. Lights started flickering. That's when I thought, wow. This is it. They got us, too.

Everybody tried running out but that was stupid, you couldn't get out. No matter how many fire drills you have. Nobody could get out.

The foreign markets had opened. England was open, Europe was still open. But after the second plane hit, all the news services stopped broadcasting. A lot of them were headquartered in the Trade Center, right?

After that, we got all our news from the TVs on the floor. We got our financial information, all our information from the networks just like the rest of yous.

>>><<<

That whole week, we didn't open. There wasn't a lot . . . nothing to . . . you know? No work. So you sit at home with all this news. The TV was always on in my apartment. Phone was ringing. I got the damage report little by little from friends. Not about damage to the Towers, that stuff was pretty obvious—you could see the smoke plume real clear from my place in Hoboken. And not damage to the nation—who cares about that?

I don't mean it like that.

What I mean is—as it turns out—I lost six buddies in all. Six good buddies. They were in there when the buildings came down. That, to me, is damage.

That whole week. Fuck it.

Where's the bartender?

>>><<<

We went back to work the first day of trading, which was last Monday, September 17, 2001. It was . . . I don't know. Somber. You know?

Usually you feel this great rush of adrenaline being in the Exchange. Now nobody wanted to be there.

All sell orders that day. It was expected.

I'm a phone clerk. I take orders from the outside customers, give them to a broker to execute. That day? Ninety percent sell orders. And anything that had to do with recreation got crushed: Disney. Kodak. Travel stocks. Crushed. It made sense to me. The airlines? Jesus, who wants to fly after what happened? Who wants to take a cruise? Hotel stocks? Crushed.

The second day went pretty much the same as the first. So did the third day. And the fourth. That whole week, we all just watched. Numb. The market plummeted. Then it held. Plummeted again. Rallied a little. Plummeted further, and rallied once more. But it was definitely a downward slide. It just kept slipping down. Fighting like a wounded animal. But we handled it.

Give you a good example. I got this chain email circulated on October 2, 2001. Pretty much said it all, you know?

It said:

"If you bought $1,000 worth of Nortel stock one year ago, it would now be worth $49.

"If you bought $1,000 worth of Budweiser (the beer, not the stock) one year ago, drank all the beer, and traded in the cans for the nickel deposit, you would have $79.

"It's time to start drinking heavily."

>>>><<<<

It turned around first time last Friday. It tried to rally serious. That's what we wanted. Rallied 'em a little bit. Then this week. We rallied 'em up 400 points. Down about 16 percent overall by then, but hey— only 16 percent. I mean, *only* 16 percent. Come on. Let's give ourselves a little hand, huh?

These experts on the news . . . they call themselves experts. I got other names for them. They're saying this is the worst slip since the Depression. Well, yes and no.

A lot of stocks are undervalued right now, shouldn't be tradin' where they are, but nobody has the confidence to step up and buy 'em. Middle America isn't going to do it. Not yet. No, no.

As a point of perspective? I saw the crash of '87. Let me tell you: '87 was a panic. This was [a] lot more orderly. Unless you work down there, I don't know how to explain it to you. People were just more . . . prepared.

For instance, we didn't have the computers, the electronic capability back in '87 that we have nowadays. Nowadays, the computers stop the market before it slips down too far. Cooler heads prevail. You don't want a mob mentality out there on the floor, let me tell you.

You gotta let people digest the news, you know? Disseminate the news. Cooler heads. That's what happened this time. In my opinion, the Exchange acted exactly perfect.

≫≫≪≪

Sure, trading'll be back up. I know it will. How long will it take? Shit, if I knew that I'd be a billionaire. It's all about consumer confidence. And if I knew what that was, I'd be a billionaire. Right now, I wouldn't say it's business as usual. It's still very tough.

Hey, grab that guy, wouldja? I want another beer.

≫≫≪≪

I saw a lot of people lose their shit that day. Old guys on the Exchange with their heads in their hands, crying. I got scared.

And now? I don't take the PATH train no more. I take the ferry out from Hoboken. Still.

Twice a day I gotta walk past those Towers. Sorry. That place. The Towers are gone. Twice a day. It'll never be business as usual again. And it's sickening. Seeing what happened. Sickening.

I personally lost six buddies, I tell you that? Maybe another thirty people I knew from, "Hey, how you doin'?"

You deal with that. You go on. Do what you can do. Like, I'm a big New York sports fan, so I got Rangers season tickets, Giants season tickets. I go to all the games. Try to live my life as much as normal.

But no, I won't ever forget this and I don't want to. You forget and you know what happens? It happens again.

UPDATE

The September 11 attacks made a significant economic impact on the United States economy. The Federal Reserve temporarily reduced its contact with banks due to the failure of switching equipment in the lower New York financial district.[42]

The stock markets re-opened on September 17, 2001, after the longest closure since the Great Depression in 1929. On that day, the Dow Jones Industrial Average stock market index plummeted 684

---

42 See the interview with Kevin Killian of Verizon.

points, or 7.1 percent, to 8,920, its largest-ever one-day point de-
cline. By the end of the week—at close of business on September
21, 2001—the Dow Jones had fallen a total of 1,369.7 points (14.3
percent), making it the largest one-week point drop in history. U.S.
stocks lost $1.2 trillion in value for the week.

As of 2005, Wall and Broad Streets near the New York Stock
Exchange remained barricaded and guarded to prevent a physical attack upon the building.

On February 14, 2007, the Dow Jones hit a new high of 12,700.

DR. WALTER GERASIMOWICZ

Dr. Walter Gerasimowicz, forty-nine, worked as the director of advisory services for Lehman Brothers beginning in the autumn of 1995.

I HAVE A bone disease called Albright's syndrome, which is also called polyostotic fibrous dysplasia. It's a very rare condition which most physicians never see; as a matter of fact, it's so rare that it's not even funded as an orphaned disease by the government for research purposes.

What Albright's amounts to, is that I have portions of normal bone and portions of bone which are somewhat fibrous, non-crystalline. They bend, they deform, they break. I'm most impacted on my left side, particularly in my left femur, hip, and back. I'm permanently on crutches.

On that morning, I went into my office, which is on the 28th floor of 1 World Financial Center, directly across the street from the World Trade Center. My office faces West Street, with a direct view of the Towers. I'd say the distance is fifty meters at most, probably closer to thirty.

I heard the first impact, and people started to rush toward the east side of our building to watch the Towers burn. Initially, we were uncertain as to what had happened, whether it was a bomb or some other explosion. Then we were told, by word of mouth, that a plane had struck the building. We were told by security people to stay put. At this point, there were quite a few people in the offices watching what was occurring. In addition, some of us had televisions in our offices, on which we'd watch the financial news networks. We used these to grab the news as it broke.

I was surprised because there was a great deal of chaos in my office. People running, people screaming, people horrified. No one knew exactly what had occurred—I think that many people thought that perhaps a pilot had gotten sick or had a heart attack. But we were all watching this . . . and then the real horror began as people began to leap from the Towers to their deaths. You could see them as they climbed out of the windows and onto the ledges. Then—falling or leaping. It wasn't one or two, it was scores of people. I was literally in a state of shock for the next two weeks.

⫸⫷

I got on the phone to one of my colleagues, Doreen Benson. She was traveling in Florida. I told her to turn on the television and she did, so we were speaking and watching the coverage on the television simultaneously.

She said, "Walter, leave. Leave now!"

And I immediately did. People were screaming and running past my office in tears. Then we saw the next plane fly in and hit, exploding. At that point, we knew this was no accident. Total pandemonium broke loose with everyone heading for the stairwells. The situation was obviously too dangerous to get on elevators and we didn't know, by the way, if our own building was under attack.

⫸⫷

Now, as I said, I'm on crutches. And as I started to head toward the stairwell, I was filled with mixed emotions. Should I wait? There were hundreds of people trying to run past me. Should I hold them up or should I begin the long, tedious process of getting down those stairs? I value my self-preservation, but I wondered how that would impact a greater number of people.

As it turns out, when I got to the stairwell, people came to me with assistance. I'll give you their names, because it's something I'll never forget: Mark Stevenson, Steve Campbell, Richard Feldman, Richard Cuomo, Alan Reichman.

These men. Despite that no one knew what was going on and we could all be in grave, immediate danger, they refused to leave me at any point.

I said, "Go. I'll get down. I'll be all right. Just go."

But they refused.

I was using one crutch and the banister of the stairwell to descend. I gave my other crutch to another colleague who was headed past us down the steps. His name is Mark Soloman. I told him, "Just leave it at the bottom of the staircase, I'll retrieve it when I get there."

>>><<<

So there I was with these men, going down the steps with people rushing past us. We were trying to tell everyone, "Go around! Go around!" Obviously, it was taking me a lot longer to use the stairs than anyone else.

Again and again, I told the men who were with me to go ahead. Again, they refused.

When we got to the main level—the street level—there were two paths to take, two stairwells. The gentleman who'd taken my second crutch had taken one of those paths but no one knew which way he'd gone. So we just chose one, and we never found the crutch that day. We must've chosen the stairwell that Mark didn't. Thus, I ended up with one stick.

What's kind of interesting about that crutch—the one that I'd given up to Mark—it was used to hold the door open in the other stairwell. It allowed everyone who passed that way to run right out of the building. My colleagues found it there three weeks later when they were allowed back into the building to inspect the damages. It was still propping open that door. So it served a noble purpose, I think.

>>><<<

Once we got down to the street level, I put my arm on the shoulder of Mark Stevenson. Mark is the manager for the New York office. So I had my crutch under my left shoulder and Mark under my right. We turned and headed west toward the Hudson River, passing the Gateway building. We were basically between 2 World and 1 World.

We'd walked about a hundred meters or so to where there were some benches and I sat down temporarily—I had to, I was exhausted.

Pandemonium ensued all around us: emergency people were rushing in; thousands of office workers were rushing out. Boats swooped in from the Hudson River to dock at rescue stops.

We were only two to three hundred yards west of the Towers, facing them, watching both burn. At the same time, we saw more and more people jumping from both Towers. Time was more or less surreal.

And at some point the first Tower went down. It just . . . it went down. It was absolutely horrible.

Everyone started running but in my case, with my mobility so limited, I continued walking toward the river. Alan and the others flagged down emergency personnel, who pulled up in this sort of golf cart—like a flatbed electric cart. Alan and Richard Cuomo and I got in. We were taken down to the Hudson River, where the boats were waiting. The other men who'd been in my company left the area immediately on foot.

⋙⋘

The boat landing was pandemonium as well, because many boats were using makeshift docks and, in many cases, the boat decks didn't come up level to the ground. People were so desperate to get on board that they tried jumping onto the decks from the dockside. Some broke their legs as they landed. Some fell into the water.

I didn't know how I would be able to get aboard, but luckily one boat had a platform that folded out from the back and became flush with the ground. With Alan's help, I was able to begin boarding.

At this point, Rich Cuomo turned around and went back to find our colleagues. He wanted to tell them there were boats available to take them to safety. Unbeknownst to any of us, the rest of the men from my company had begun to head north, walking up the West Side in order to get away from the disaster.

⟫⟫⟫⟪⟪⟪

As the boat I was boarding opened up that back platform, hundreds of people tried to stampede aboard. Alan stood more or less in front of me, acting as a buffer, and I held onto the rail with all my might; I would have been knocked down otherwise. We waited for everyone to pass.

There were people covered from head to foot with ash, many were in a state of shock. People were crying, running, panicking. Others filed past with absolutely no expression, as if in a trance.

After the melee had passed me, Alan helped me onto the main body of the boat, to a place where I could sit down. And as I sat there, facing the boat's aft, facing the Towers, I saw the second one go down. It happened so fast. Within seconds, all of us and all of Lower Manhattan were consumed by an opaque black cloud of ash, dust, and soot. You couldn't see the Battery at all.[43]

One of the rescue workers on the boat was standing next to me, crying. He said, "My God. I'm here trying to help everyone else, and my family is down there. I live there."

We all tried to call our loved ones on our cell phones but, of course, we couldn't get through for hours.

⟫⟫⟫⟪⟪⟪

Ultimately, our rescue boat left and crossed the river. It was like a war zone evacuation. The people of Lower Manhattan were ferried across the river and dumped in different places. In my case, we ended up in Hoboken. Alan Reichman was still with me, and he helped me off the boat; now I was using him as my crutch.

We ended up getting on a train that took us to the most northerly

---

43 An area at the base of Manhattan below the Financial District, now the site of Battery Park, which is visited by thousands of people daily. The Battery gets its name from the fort that was built there during the War of 1812, later named Castle Clinton in 1817 after DeWitt Clinton, who was mayor of New York City at that time. After the army left the site, it served as an entertainment center, an opera house, and an immigration landing depot. It even served as the NYC Aquarium until the site was closed in 1941. The Battery currently serves as a dock site for boats to Ellis Island and the Statue of Liberty.

point in New Jersey, and then we crossed over into New York State, where Alan's home is. From there, we were able to grab a taxi. I live in Manhattan, but there was no way for me to get back into New York City for a number of days. All the bridges, the tunnels, everything was shut down. So I stayed with Alan's family.

Alan brought me back into New York once the George Washington Bridge opened and delivered me to my home on the Upper East Side. I received hundreds of phone calls from family and friends, people from around the world, a huge outpouring of concern and support. It was all very moving.

⇛⇚

In the days after it all happened, a friend called and we talked about the state that the city was in.

He said, "Walter, we've got to do something about this. We can't just sit back and do nothing."

I agreed, so we went out to some of the local pet stores and bought up all the dog food and supplies we could find. We thought that so many items had been donated for humans, food and so forth, but no one had really thought about the rescue dogs who were being used to sniff for survivors at Ground Zero.

We loaded up the car with everything it could carry and I drove. We made it all the way downtown,

"We thought that so many items had been donated for humans, food and so forth, but no one had really thought about the rescue dogs who were being used to sniff for survivors at Ground Zero."

stopping here and there at various checkpoints. For the most part, the officers pulling security duty would wave us on when they saw that we were carrying supplies. We basically made it to the base of the site, which, by that point, had been sealed off rather heavily.

I suppose we were allowed to get down that far because the food we were carrying was sorely needed, as were the dog "shoes" that we had. Many of the rescue animals had gravely injured their paws by walking over shrapnel and debris to look for people.

»»»«««

One thing I'd like to point out: New Yorkers became a far gentler group of people in their behavior toward one another during and following the time of the attack. Unfortunately, it didn't last long. I wonder if it ever does. Sooner or later, we all seem to go back to our ways.

Those men who stayed with me? They did so at the risk of their own life and limb. These people have families themselves. I think that's what I'll always remember the most. How they willingly put themselves at risk on my behalf.

I'd like to get those men together and take a snapshot of all of us together as a remembrance. Just a simple shot with all of us together in one picture. I will never forget what they did for me that day, and I'd like to keep a photo like that as a reminder.

NELL MOONEY

*Nell Mooney, twenty-three, lives in Astoria, Queens. Picture a strawber-
ry-blonde spitfire with a pixie grin as big as the moon. She sometimes gets
so involved in what she's saying that she hops up and down in her seat.*

I HATED MY temp job on Wall Street! I worked in the check processing department of a major firm with a woman who was the most
miserable human being on the face of the planet. Don't get me wrong,
all the other women I worked with were great—I loved them. My
boss, for instance, was fantastic. She was the Buddha, one of those
strong women who have their college degrees and their master's, but
was perfectly happy to spend her days in the check processing department of a major firm. But that one woman made it hell.

She would come to work in the morning and everyone would say
in a sing-songy voice: "Good mooooorrrrnnnnnning, Rosaria!"

And Rosaria'd say, "Hrrrum! What's good about it?" And she was
serious.

She suffered from diabetes, but she'd bring in Krispy Kreme donuts and Italian pastries. God only knows what kind of see-sawing
was going on with her glucose levels. I'm telling you, she was not a
happy woman. Rosaria was the epitome of unhappy. The devil was
her playmate. And on that job, we weren't at desks, we were all in
bullpens.[44] And, naturally, I had to share my bullpen with—guess
who? You got it. Rosaria.

See, some temp jobs are perfectly fine, but that Wall Street job
was a temp job where I actually had to work, which I found unaccept-
able. Jot that down as a historical note on the state of the economy
in 2001. Dear People of the Future: at the start of the twenty-first
century, it was common for major corporations to employ boatloads

---

44 Office cubicles.

of people who'd do nothing but hang around all day and get paid to do nothing while waiting for other pursuits in their lives to take root.

When somebody from the temp agency called and said, "We have a different job for you, if you want to nix the Wall Street job," I said, "Fine! Yes! I'll take it!"

I left Wall Street on a Friday and started a new job on Monday, September 10. To this day, I wonder how many artists pulling day gigs as temp workers had the dumb luck to get stuck in the Towers that day.

⇶⫷

My new job was at *Reader's Digest* on 35th and 5th. I was hired to help them move office locations. This was also kind of a lousy job, but at least there was no Rosaria.

I actually saw the first Tower on fire as I took the subway into Manhattan from Queens on the morning of the eleventh. Nobody knew what had happened, but everybody kept saying things like, "What stupid ass set the World Trade Center on fire?" Nobody knew it was a plane. Nobody knew it was terrorism.

As everybody on the train stared out the windows and talked about what we were seeing, the usual boundaries between people fell away in an instant. Very soon, we had our own little train car community going, and everyone had a hypothesis.

"Must've been a kitchen fire in Windows on the World. What jerk could have done that?"

My mom called just before the train went into the tunnel and said, "Are you all right?"[45]

I said, "I'm fine. How are you?"

She said, "Nell, the World Trade Center's on fire."

"I know, I can see it."

Then she said, "A plane flew into it."

I got off my cell phone and looked at everyone in the subway car

---

45 Many subway trains that run to the outer boroughs do so above ground at certain intervals, which makes cell phone reception possible.

and said out loud, "A plane flew into the Tower!"

Everyone was like, "Oh my God."

And the train went into the tunnel.

>>><<<

I got to work at about 9:30 A.M. and watched the second plane hit the second Tower. I watched the first Tower fall as it was happening on the office TV. Next thought: Forget this, I'm getting out of here.

That day, I hung around Manhattan longer than most because I was waiting for my boyfriend. He was working a temp job, too, at 47th and Madison. We met on a street corner and he took the time to go get the new Bob Dylan album, which had just come out that day. I remember telling him, "The world is crumbling, the world is in fetters, and you're buying the new Bob Dylan album? Okay. That makes sense."

Afterwards, he was guilt-ridden over that. "I can't believe that the world was dying and I had to go get Bob."

>>><<<

The subways weren't working, so we walked along the streets all afternoon. People were on their cell phones, and we'd stop and ask them to give us news.

"The second Tower has fallen," they said. "There are still planes in the air. They bombed the Pentagon."

And then a bunch of other things. Rumors. "The Capitol was hit. The Supreme Court, too." By this time, we could see the F-16s raking the sky overhead. You could hear their screech as they tore through the air, and there was mad panic in the streets.

My boyfriend and I live in Queens, and it seemed that the only way we'd be able to get there was to walk over the 59th Street Bridge. So we started out for it. Along the way, we saw many strange things. One man gave another guy $100 to take him home on his motorbike. It was nothing unusual, though. We were seeing things like this all over the place.

⟫⟫⟪⟪

It was a long hike, but we finally got to the bridge. At this point, we didn't know whether we were trapped in Manhattan or not, whether authorities would actually allow us to cross over to Queens.

I said, "Okay, if we're trapped, we're gonna go get a late brunch in style with champagne. 'Cause if we're gonna die, I'm gonna get drunk. Either that, or we'll have sex in an alley." But the bridge was open. So we started walking across.

It was really hot, I remember. And there was this mass exodus of people. It looked like the New York Marathon, where the 59th Street Bridge is littered with people—so many that they look like a colorful torrent of ants. There was one lane open for cars going back to Queens, and one lane for pedestrians. No cars were allowed into the city.

We kept seeing dump trucks rolling by, full of people. The truck drivers were evidently letting people climb up and ride. There was an empty one cruising past us, and this guy walking about two or three lengths ahead of us called out in this heavy New York accent, "Hey! Why wonchoo let us on?"

The truck had some lumber and debris in it, but it stopped. I made a run for it, jumping the lane island, while my boyfriend was like, "Ah . . . sweetheart? Ah . . . I don't think we should do that . . ."

Well. We hopped in the back of that dump truck. And I swear to you, inside it was like the demographic from *The Stand*.[46]

It could have been a Showtime movie. *Back to Queens: The Long Walk Home*. There was a social rainbow of escapees from Manhattan. We had the nice white couple. A little Korean girl. The driver of the truck was Latino. There was this black woman, a construction worker who must have been the size of Hulk Hogan, who reached down and lifted a skinny Chinese man into the truck's payload compartment. I

---

46 A novel by Stephen King. In the story, the government accidentally releases a biochemical weapon that destroys most of the earth's population save for a small group of survivors, who come from all walks of life and who begin a final battle with one another to survive.

remember the construction lady laughed and said, "You guys just aren't used to this, are you?" Meaning the dirty conditions of the truck. We were all in our business casual outfits. By way of comparison, I was wearing a skirt; she was wearing heavy-duty overalls.

The construction worker woman was massively strong. She reached down and lifted everyone into the back of the truck and we all sat there, huddled together, this motley crew, getting bounced around on top of each other, dirty and crazy while the truck rumbled across the Queens Borough Bridge. We talked here and there about what had happened, and I guess we were trying to convince each other to believe it all. The normal boundaries that would have existed between blacks and whites, Asians and Hispanics, economic distinctions, gender distinctions . . . they fell away and disappeared. Between us, there stood nothing but what we had seen and what we hoped it all meant.

❯❯❯❮❮❮

We got off the truck at the end of the bridge. My boyfriend and I live at least five miles from that point in Astoria Park. Geographically, Astoria runs parallel to the beginning of the Bronx. So, if you think about that, we walked from 34th Street in Manhattan, drove over the bridge, and then we hiked all the way up to the Bronx. People had their radios on outside as we walked along the streets, and we'd stop every once in a while to listen. It was a pretty amazing day.

The whole journey took us about four hours. We got home around 2:00 P.M. We ended up listening to that Bob Dylan album all day long while watching the news. I don't think I'll ever listen to it again.

I know how awful it is, what happened. But what upset me the most is the thought that there were artists temping in the World Trade Center that day, people who weren't there doing the thing they loved, they were there working to finance it. And they died. All that sacrifice they'd made for their art . . . it came to naught. The whole incident disturbs me, of course, but that aspect strikes me as a special tragedy.

I think any type of huge upheaval makes you re-evaluate what you're doing with your life and how you're living it. So I decided right then that there were other ways, other jobs I could work to support myself financially without having to compromise my artistic integrity.

When my temp job ended with *Reader's Digest*, I went on unemployment. I haven't been back to the temp office. But then, wouldn't you know? I landed this great job. I'm training to be a certified teacher of ballroom dancing in the New York public school system. I love to dance, and the job leaves me just enough time to audition for acting roles. And it pays well.

I'm just training right now. I haven't been in to teach a class yet, and the thought terrifies me! But at least now I'm doing something for a living that doesn't suck my soul.

"JOSEPH" AFSE

"Joseph" Afse, thirty-six, from Bombay, India, says he's proud to be an American citizen after immigrating to the United States twenty-six years ago.

His parents have owned and operated a small luggage and leather goods outlet called India Bazaar on Church Street for many years.[47]

Joseph has worked there nearly every day of his life, greeting customers and getting to know the unique menagerie of people who worked, ate, shopped, and thrived in this vital district four blocks under the massive shadow cast by the Towers.

Now those Towers are gone. When I spoke to Joseph in 2002, India Bazaar was still in operation. But the neighborhood, he noted back then, had changed forever.

Note: Joseph's English is quite good. Nonetheless, he'll occasionally mix up verb tenses, idioms, and so forth. Additionally, it should be noted that "Joseph," while not Mr. Afse's given name, is the nickname he now uses here in the U.S.

THE BUSINESS IS dead now. Dead. September 10 was a great day. I earned a whole month's rent on a Monday! Then the eleventh came, and now everything is gone.

⇶⫷

September 11, I saw on the news that everything was gonna be sunshine. So I came to the store early, opened up like 7:30 A.M., and fixed everything up real nice. It was a beautiful day, a lot of people walking

---

47 Joseph's shop is typical of many small industries in that district. Backpacks and suitcases are laid out on display in front of the shop. You can walk inside the tiny store to view more wares: wallets, belts, handbags, and the like. Joseph will greet you with an instant hello and a warm smile, beaming from the dusky moon of his face. He speaks with the frankness and honesty of a merchant who spends his life talking to people and getting to know them for who they are rather than who he wants them to be.

around.

Then, at 8:45, I heard too much sound, like a plane was landing right here in the street.

When I look up, it was a plane, all right. I could see it coming through the sky. It hit the building. I saw the flames, the windows shatter, everything. All the people walking here thought it was an accident. A lot of us thought that the pilot is a drunk.

Then the ambulances coming, police running. People are scared, watching the Twin Towers like we was all in a movie theater. Two news people from Channel 7 came out fast and set up a movie camera right here, taking pictures.

Then? After fifteen minutes, I hear the next one. *Boom!* That looked like a big bomb. There was smoke.

The police came by and told all the merchants on this street, "Close up, close up, close up!"

I called 911 and said, "This looks like an attack on the United States. This is like a war is starting!"

⇛⇚

So I'm trying to close up. Almost, I'm done. I put the shutter down over the storefront, I put the lock on. I am putting on the second lock when I saw this thing, like a hurricane coming. Darkness. Suddenly, you can't see nothing. Everything is gone.

Smoke gets in your eyes, your hair. I am like a blind person, can't see nothing. I try to run, but on Warren Street, everything is a dark cloud.

When I was running, I hit the fire bumper since I couldn't see, and I fell down.[48] And this is a natural, human thing: when I fall down, I put out both hands. See what happens to both hands? I rip it up. Knees, too. Rip it up.[49]

I thought maybe I was gone. I thought maybe I should just lie

---

48 He means the curb.

49 Joseph shows his hands, the palms of which have been ground up into raw purple wounds. He shows his knees, which are the same.

down and go to sleep. Then I thought of my wife, my daughters, my sons. I have seven children. My mother is too old to have me die. At that time, I called God and said, "I don't want to die now. If I'm going to die, my mother is going to die too from a heart attack."

I stood up after two or three minutes—too much pain, but I had no choice. And I walked up to the Municipal Building.

※※※

I saw a lot of fire officers, police officers, and they put me in an ambulance. I told them I had too much pain in my foot, so they cut my pants off, and checked. The doctor is expert, so he moved my leg and said it was good, not broken. Then he looked at my hands.

This one? He said it had too much crystals in the wound. Like dirt and glass and whatever. He washed them out.

The doctors dropped me off at my house and told my wife what medicine I should take. They gave me tablets, capsules, liquid medicines. Too much medicine.

See how they are now? The skin has come back seven times and they still look like this. It hurts. The blood comes back in, and the skin cracks open again. But it's still much better than it was.

※※※

My business! My business was covered in dirt. And I lost a lot of merchandise. I tried to clean it off but some of it is ruined. A lot of business I lost.

You know, 90 percent of my business was from the Twin Towers. A lot of my customers worked there, coming in from all over New York, Connecticut, Long Island, New Jersey, Brooklyn, Queens. They all died. Their bodies burned inside the Towers. Or they're missing. Or they don't want to come around here now.

No one buys my merchandise now.

※※※

The Red Cross people! God bless these Red Cross people! The

Salvation Army. FEMA. Safe Horizons. They have helped with my home apartment rent.

I went to Pier 94 on October 1. So many people there—so many people were affected. I saw store owners, limousine drivers, taxi drivers . . . everyone who suffered stood all in a line, and they were being helped. All of them.

The agencies gave out coupons according to how many family members you have. They take down everybody's social security number so they can find out how much help the person needs, how much food they need—and they write a coupon.

Safe Horizons gave everybody a two-week paycheck. At that time, I made $200 a week; they gave me a check for $440. Some woman standing in front of me in line worked in a bank in the World Trade Center, and she made $750 a week after taxes. I saw them give her a check for $1,500. If you made $500 a week, you got $1,000. I tell you! The Red Cross is number one!

The government—all agencies. Trying to help those people who are injured. Suffered. Big problems. Lose business. They helped me and many people in this neighborhood. I have many Chinese friends with stores along Canal Street. They're getting help, too. Anybody! Everybody who needs it.

»»«««

Are things getting back to normal? No. Business has picked up to only 20 percent of previous earnings. But a lot of people have no jobs. There's no money to spend, so how are they gonna go shopping?

We try to keep the store. We're talking with the landlord and we tell him, "This is not a tragedy, this is a war," you know? I tell the landlord, "We need your support."

He says he's thinking about giving a break to everybody on this row. Even for the people who live in the apartments above the store. He owns this building, a nice gentleman. He came personally to every store and every apartment; he talked to everybody. He's gonna give us a break for January, February, and March of 2002. Then he says,

"After that, let's see how the business picks up."

He comes by every two weeks to check for himself. When things get back to normal, everybody will pay what they used to pay.

>>><<<

See this restaurant next door? It used to be open twenty-four hours. Now they close at 6:30 every night. No customers.

Before? On this street? Too much traffic! You come out here at two o'clock in the morning, four o'clock in the morning? It looked like daytime, at twelve o'clock. People walking everywhere. Limousine drivers, yellow cab drivers parking all over the place, waiting to pick people up. All for the World Trade Center, which was open twenty-four hours.

They had a lot of big companies there. Lots of international banks. They had a Hilton Hotel inside, you know that? A lot of restaurants. The shopping mall underneath. It was a good life.

Now, there's nothing. It's all gone. Now it's . . . how do you call that? Too much "headache."

>>><<<

One thing I saw, this announcement two weeks ago on Channel 7. The government asked, "Who lost their loved ones?"

In Washington, D.C., the director of this charity office says he will give $1.5 million to people who lost their loved ones. And this is a good thing. Because you know, loved ones cannot come back. You lose a son, who in turn has a daughter four or five years old; it affects everyone, everyone in the family.

Money should go to help these families, because that son helped the whole family with what he earned, you see?

GROUND ZERO AND THE VOLUNTEERS

NICK GERSTLE

Nick Gerstle, twenty-four, worked for Verizon as a construction techni-cian and splicer.[50] On September 11, he saw a rare opportunity to make a very important contribution.

I WAS AT WORK in Brooklyn when we heard about the attacks over the radio. Our foreman called us up and told us to go to one of our COs—the central offices where huge computer networks handle the telephone switching. There are dozens of COs around the city— that's how the telephone network is built in New York. Cables con-nect your home or business to central offices, then the central offices connect to other central offices, like tentacles of nerve fiber going in and out of a massive brain.

When I pulled into our central office, I asked my foreman if there was any kind of volunteer effort being organized within our company. He said, "It's too early, it just happened a few hours ago. Watch the TV, and if they need you for the Red Cross, you can volunteer that way."

Well, that wasn't enough for me.

⇾≫⋘⇽

I just went down there. I didn't know if the trains would still run to the Trade Center or if I'd even be allowed to help. But my company's certified me every year in CPR and first aid—that's one of the things that motivated me to act. And I'm a pretty big guy. I knew they'd need people who were used to working with their hands and could move things, especially people with the knowledge that I have and the training Verizon provided me. Even if they had me just handing out cups of water, I'd have still done it to make a difference.

---

50 Phone cables run on poles or underground. A splicer climbs to the top of a pole or crawls be-neath a manhole cover to gain access to a problematic line. He locates trouble in a cable, which might contain a bundle of up to 1,200 wires, and repairs it by hand.

I took the N/R subway and had to change trains a couple times to make it into Manhattan. The train ran above ground into the city as we headed in from Brooklyn, and as we went over the bridge, we could see the smoke billowing out from the Towers. It was horrifying. People were looking at it in awe and crying. Mothers were crying because they knew their families—their kin—were in the buildings.

The first stop that let off in the city was Canal Street. As soon as I got out, I got a sense that nothing was as it was supposed to be. Basically, it was like Lower Manhattan had turned into some kind of war zone. From Canal Street down to the Trade Center, I had to find "holes" in the police barricades where I could convince authorities to say, "You can go through with that pass."

I kept showing my ID and telling them I was first-aid certified. Some cops would let me through, some wouldn't. If they wouldn't let me past, I'd walk a block away and try another police officer. Like that, I worked my way closer and closer downtown.

Finally, I made it to a temporary triage center by a college near the Brooklyn Bridge. When I went in, there was no power, just emergency workers who'd gotten injured. I asked for gloves and the people in charge gave me a little mask—not the type that would stop anything serious, but it still helped.

I knew that in order for me to go into the zone, I needed protective gear. I scrounged around and picked up a firefighter jacket from a Burger King down on Church Street near the Trade Center; someone had made it into, like, a temporary rescue center headquarters. I also got some heavy-duty gloves. I needed all this because otherwise, I just had the shirt on my back.

—»›‹«—

As I walked down Church Street . . . I can't even begin to describe it. Three inches of layered soot on the street. The surrounding area was wet from fire hoses. It was like the war zone you see in that film *Terminator 2.*

There I was on Church Street, waiting with hundreds of

firefighters and a small group of volunteers. There were marines standing next to us; they were suiting up and getting ready to go into the debris field.

The area wasn't organized at all. It wasn't like someone was in charge and giving orders, like, "You, you, and you! Go there!" It was more like, "Okay . . . hell. I'm going in." Whatever you could find, whoever you could get to go in with you, you just did it.

I remember some of the guys who were preparing to go in. There was a volunteer fireman from Maryland who told me he'd heard what had happened, put a siren on his car, and driven from Maryland to New York in an hour and a half. That trip usually takes four hours, so I gotta imagine he was doing a hundred miles an hour the whole way.

I remember another volunteer, a Hispanic guy from Long Island. He didn't go into the rubble with us, he knew his fire company was responding and he was going to wait for his equipment to arrive.

Half an hour later, when I finally got into the debris myself, I found that group of marines again and linked up with them. This was a good thing. They needed all the help they could get, because they'd found two Port Authority cops who were trapped fifteen feet under the rubble.

⇶⥅

You could see one cop's hand sticking out of the debris. The hand was alive and wiggling. The cop called up to us and said that his partner was down there with him and wasn't doing so well.

There were three marines with me, and we tried talking to them. "Hey guys. Don't worry."

I remember one of the

"I kept showing my ID and telling them I was first-aid certified. Some cops would let me through, some wouldn't. If they wouldn't let me past, I'd walk a block away and try another police officer. Like that, I worked my way closer and closer downtown."

marines saying, "By this time tomorrow, you'll be somewhere on a beach, sipping a drink."

We started digging. We didn't have any tools, so we used our hands to dig away at the rubble.

I looked down into the hole at the two men and said, "Anybody order pizza?" I was trying to lighten up the mood, you know?

I'm glad I had the fireman's jacket and gloves. Some parts of the rubble were very hot. Some of the I-beams sticking up out of the rubble were glowing, even. I was scared but at the same time, there was so much camaraderie you didn't feel the fear. We were right there on the rubble, under it sometimes, and we heard these guys saying, "Don't let us die! Please! Don't let us die!" That keeps you motivated.

And I thought while I was working, don't worry, guys, I'm right down here with you. I won't let you go, because if you go, we all go.

⋙⋘

Like I said, the hole those cops were in went down about fifteen feet. It was a small hole with a huge I-beam sitting on top, holding up the concrete and rubble so it wouldn't collapse in on them. We formed a line from the rubble pile to the street and began bringing tools in. It was an unbelievable landscape, you gotta picture it. Amidst the smoke and rubble and darkness, flickers of light from fires all around.

When the professionals finally arrived, I told them I was a volunteer, and they ordered me out. They said they needed space to get the trained emergency personnel in. I said, "Okay, I'll go," but I stayed next to the hole.

Then I started to feel nauseous. I couldn't breathe. I suddenly felt like I was only able to use 50 percent of my lungs. It was around twelve o'clock noon.

A fire lieutenant asked me if I was fine. I said, "Yeah. Yeah." But ten or fifteen minutes later, he saw me again. This time I was gasping for air, down on one knee, and he said, "Hey guy. You gotta get out of here."

I wanted to stay there as long as I could, but I'm glad he told me to go.

The core fires under the colossal pile of debris left on the World Trade Center site by the Towers' collapse would burn for more than five months. The intense heat of this inferno resisted any attempts by firefighting crews to extinguish it.

When I was evacuated, they still didn't have the two cops out. They were just starting to bring them up.

⟫⟫⟪⟪

I started stumbling out of the rubble, gasping for air. I swear to you, I couldn't fill my lungs. If it wasn't for the line of firefighters giving me air from their oxygen tanks on two occasions, I don't think I would have made it back out of the debris field.

It was a long way back; the rubble was a mammoth field of smoking hills. The hole where the cops were was in the middle of the Trade Center area. And all the way out, I had to jump over fallen I-beams and climb over things. If it wasn't for the thick gloves they gave me, my hands would have been burned. You had to be careful not to step in holes, too, because you didn't know what was down there. A lot of times, I looked down and all I saw was glowing red fires.

The firemen's air tanks were so heavy, and I was so weak that I dropped it the second time I was being given oxygen. I was so exhausted.

There was one last hill before me. When I got to the apex of it, I could see firemen below moving everywhere. It was like looking down from a plane and seeing these little ants. And it was a great feeling when I saw it. Home free. Almost.

Once I got down the hill, they had gurneys ready. Firemen helped me, giving me their shoulders to lean on. I collapsed on the gurney and two doctors started working on me as they hustled the gurney out at about fifteen miles per hour, heading toward a triage area.

I was exhausted, but I was amazed. I'm a pretty heavy guy. At times, they had to lift me up to get me over the debris, but they did it. They moved me like I weighed nothing.

⯈⯈⯈◀◀◀

I checked into the hospital later on, and that's when I heard about those two cops on the TV news. They got them out just fine and man, that felt good to hear.

At the hospital, I was treated for smoke inhalation. Apparently, I'd burned my lungs and throat pretty badly. They gave me some steroids to reduce the swelling.

They'd torn my shirt off when I was admitted, and I needed a new one before they'd let me out. I didn't want to wait, but they told me, "No, no. You have to wait."

I said, "Okay," and sat down for forty minutes.

They finally gave me a clean shirt and I was about to leave when Mayor Giuliani walked in. One of his aides saw my fireman's jacket and said, "Wait right here. Mayor Giuliani wants to see you."

The mayor'd come to console injured firemen, and here I was, a telephone worker who looked like a fireman. I guess I had some explaining to do.

Giuliani was really nice, with a smile that made you feel like he was your dad. He looked at me for a couple seconds, shook my hand, and said, "Tell me what happened."

I told him my story. That I was a volunteer who worked for Verizon and how I was part of the group that helped rescue the two Port

Authority cops. He started pumping my hand, saying, "Wow, you're a really great person."

The NYPD and FDNY commissioners were there, too, and they both congratulated me.[51] I guess it's true that the NYPD commissioner doesn't smile at all. He had this stern look on him the whole time. I'm sure he had a lot on his mind that day.

I told him that, and I remember what he said to me. He said, "What's your name again?"

I said, "Nick Gerstle."

"One more time?"

"Nick Gerstle."

Now I know why he asked that. A day later, he had a meeting with Verizon Vice Chairman Larry Babbio and told him that he'd met me, and that I was a hero. That's the story I heard through the corporation, at any rate.

Remember, I'd taken off work without leave, so I called my foreman and said, "Hey, I'm over here at the hospital and my lungs are messed up."

He said, "The whole company already knows about it. I've got VP's calling me about you. Don't worry about it."

✦》》《《✦

I was discharged around nine that night, and I went to my sister's house in Queens. We watched the rescue efforts from there. But I thought, I can't be here, what am I doing here? I want to go back and help.

So Wednesday night I left at six, took a train, and got to Ground Zero around eight o'clock. I stayed there till six or seven the next day. The fireman's jacket helped me get downtown through the barricades again. While I was walking past Canal, I saw a police van going to the site and I waved him down. They thought I was a fireman, and that's all it took for me to zip through all the blockades.

By Wednesday, things were much more organized. We weren't

---

51 Bernard Kerik and Thomas Von Essen, respectively.

inside the smoke this time, we were outside the rubble. They didn't want anyone going in because it was too dangerous.

After that second adventure, I went home, fell asleep, and didn't wake up for a long time.

>>><<<

Right now, it's December [2001] and I'm back at work repairing special circuits, the lines that go to stockbrokers and businesses. We've set up a temporary facility we call "Verizon City" where we've been working since virtually the day after the attacks—it's a camp downtown in an old parking lot that our company's real estate people came upon and said, "Hey, we need this space."

Our company's built construction trailers and a garage for service vehicles and tools. A lot of lines are down, and we're working to make sure data gets through. A lot of translation problems in the lines have to be re-programmed. It's tedious work, a lot of paperwork. We estimate that the whole restoration will take most of 2003.

Me? I'm just happy to be here and helping.

>>><<<

There weren't that many people pulled from the rubble; I think only four people were rescued that way of all the thousands who were killed. Such a tragedy. And that makes it an even better feeling for me that I was able to help rescue those men.

Before? I was just another person. Now, I'm a good person. If something happens, I know I have the guts to jump in there and help.

What did I take away from this experience? That's easy. Do whatever you can do to help. Don't think. Don't wait for approval. Just go do it.

ROGER SMYTH

Roger Smyth, thirty-five, moved from Belfast, Ireland, to New York City in order to work as a 911 paramedic.[52] *"The job suits me," he says. "It's never predictable." When he speaks, his voice rolls out in a clear, lyrical northern Irish drawl.*

September 11 was supposed to be Roger's day off. This is how he spent it.

IT WAS LIKE Vietnam going over the Brooklyn Bridge. You saw all these refugees spilling over the bridge, the smoke billowing out behind them. And then I heard . . . you know how you're driving near an airport? That sound? *Hwwwwaaaaaaaaaaaaahhhhh!* It was the sound jets will make when they land.

I remember thinking, wait a minute, that's too low.

But let me backtrack a bit.

>>><<<

My girlfriend woke me up about a quarter to nine. She said, "The Trade Tower's been hit by a plane."

We went up to my rooftop in Brooklyn, and you could see the Tower smoking. I took pictures of it.

Back in the apartment, we heard a call come over the television set for anyone who could help, people with skills that'd be useful in a state of emergency. I work at NYU Downtown Hospital, so I figured,

---

52 A paramedic's job covers all the basics of emergency care: oxygen, splinting, long boarding. They give the same emergency care in the field as would be given in an ER. They carry drugs, intubate, perform cardiac procedure, and administer IVs. The City system (911 dispatcher) is under the jurisdiction of the New York Fire Department. Calls from dispatch are routed to independent hospitals and paramedic staffs. A common shift for Roger lasts eight, twelve, or sixteen hours maximum. How many calls come in on a sixteen-hour shift in New York City? "One," says Roger. "Or twenty. You just don't know. There's no such thing as a typical day. You might treat some kid for asthma, or you might have three cardiac arrests, a couple of shootings, a few very bad car accidents . . . or the World Trade Center."

not only am I a paramedic, but I knew the area well. Ten minutes after I got up, I was driving into Manhattan.[53]

I took my car because it's equipped with lights and sirens. It was pandemonium running through Park Slope, Brooklyn. There was an orchestra of sirens goin' off.

The first plane had already hit and, like I said, I was driving over the Brooklyn Bridge when I heard the second plane come in. *Hwww-wwaaaaaaaaaaaahhhhhh!* I couldn't see it hit, but I saw the explosion. I marked the time at 9:03 A.M.

My first thought? Oh shit. That's another one. The people on the bridge heard the plane and they seen it, too, I think, 'cause before, the crowd had some sense of calmness. They'd been walking over the bridge. Now they started running. Suddenly a big cloud of smoke covered the Brooklyn Bridge, totally engulfed it. And here I was, driving right into it.

⟫⟫⟪⟪

Despite the confusion, the police had everything cordoned off well, so I made it from my home to work, door to door, in literally ten minutes. Police respected the fact that I was in uniform, driving an official car with sirens.

I went to NYU first off and picked up an ambulance, then I grabbed my bags. A paramedic ambulance carries two main bags, a trauma bag, and a medical bag. In the trauma bag you've got an intubation kit, fluids, IV setups, drip administration, trauma bandages, that kind of thing. We'll also carry some equipment for crichs, in case you encounter a crushed airway and have to cut into the neck.[54] In the medical bag, we carry about sixty different drugs for cardiac arrests, diabetic and respiratory emergencies. Morphine, Valium, Versed, Ativan, and Narcan, which is a reversal agent for heroin overdose. Vasopressin. Benadryl. Lasix, for removing fluid from the lungs.

---

53 Three blocks from the World Trade Center, at 170 William Street.
54 "Crich" is short for Needle Cricothyrotomy, a procedure that involves puncturing the cricothyroid membrane and creating an airway tube. It's a similar procedure to a tracheotomy.

Adrenaline. Lidocaine. Atropine. Magnesium sulfate. Sodium bicar-
bonate. Different types of cardiac drugs. Calcium channel blockers.
For cardiogenic shock, we carry dopamine.

There's a whole slew of other drugs, too, but what's the point?
None of that came in handy on September 11. Neither did my training, for the most part.

⁕⁕⁕

My partner and I parked at the base of the World Trade Center while
the Towers were still standing. How can I describe it? Pandemonium.
Bits of bodies, office furniture, luggage, shoes, handbags, mementos,
and personal items had scattered everywhere from the impact and
the explosion. Bodies were falling out of the sky, and people scattered
in every direction while emergency workers were trying to get people
out.

This was not a structured call like you'd get on a regular day over
the radio dispatch. You can't imagine what it was like. Thinking back

"This guy you see here in this photo? That's Ronnie. I told you I'd teamed up with
another girl who had lost her partner, right? Well, that's him showing up five hours
later. If you see us smiling, it's not because we were having a good time. It's because
we thought he was dead."

on it, it's hard to comprehend the amount of people swirling around.

Our first patient was a young girl approximately twenty-five years of age who had third-degree burns across her entire body, head to toe. Some people ran toward us, calling, "You've got to help this girl, she's badly burned," and they thrust her toward us.

We intubated her—passed a tube down past her vocal cords to her lungs so she could breathe. That way, she could receive oxygen and medications. And we took her straight to NYU Downtown, along with a couple of walking wounded, where she was stabilized before we brought her up to Cornell Burn Center.

In the midst of all the confusion, I lost my partner. I teamed up with a girl I knew, a fire department EMT from Brooklyn who'd lost her partner, too, and we headed back into the thick of it.

On our way back down the FDR, the South Tower crumbled right in front of us as we were driving. That was at 9:50 A.M.

Nobody believed . . . you know, you used to hear so much hype about those buildings. You didn't think they were ever gonna fall, and you never in a million years imagined you'd be under them when they did. But when the first one came down, we pretty much knew that the other was gonna go, too.

»»«««

At that stage, the visibility was down to around ten feet from the debris. Flames were everywhere. It was like a nuclear snow. Hard to believe it was New York City.

We got to within a couple hundred yards from the base of the Towers, quite close, and set up a triage area. There'd been a few ambulances positioned closer than us, but we soon learned that they'd been wiped out in the collapse of the first building.

We were starting to dispense treatment to people who were collapsing all around us when everyone started shouting, "Look out! It's gonna collapse! It's gonna collapse!" And everyone scattered. Concrete started falling everywhere, and we ran under an overhang. And then this huge engulfing cloud of smoke blew in. I looked at my watch. It was 10:29 in the morning.

As soon as the cloud settled, you could hear voices screaming and shouting from people not knowing what direction was what because the smoke was so dense. Then—this was peculiar. You heard all these high-pitched, whining electrical screams. *Reeeeee. Reeeeee. Reeeeee. Reeeeee.* At first I didn't know what it was all about. But then I remembered that the fire department guys wear motion trackers programmed to go off if they stand still for more than thirty seconds. The whines were the sound of the boys who'd been trapped in the rubble.

As soon as the smoke started to clear, I saw people getting up and going toward the rubble to get whoever they could find out of there.

⫸⫷

We stayed there the rest of the day, administering treatment to emergency and fire personnel. But after the buildings came down, it became clear there were no survivors.

One guy in particular we helped was a firefighter in his early to mid-forties who'd been burned around the sides of his neck, head,

In the FDNY, ladder companies' primary function is to conduct rescues while engine companies focus on extinguishing fires.

and back. Could have been caused by hot metal hitting him, fuel, burning debris, I honestly didn't know. His blood pressure was very low, and we tried to get an IV started. And while we were treating him, he started wrestling with me to get back up and get back into the rubble. I said, "No, no, man. It's over for you, now. Your job's done."

And he said, "My whole company's in there, my whole battalion. I need to get back in."

I ended up literally having to wrestle this guy back down so we could treat him. I couldn't even take him into the ambulance, he was just sitting on the edge off the back. And then he disappeared when my back was turned. He just got up and left.

I told him not to go, but what can you do? If I were in his position? If I'd come out with maybe fourteen of my buddies still in there? I probably would've gone back in, too. There was a camaraderie and a selflessness right when it all happened that I'd never experienced before.

⇒⇒⇒⟵⟵⟵

This guy you see here in this photo? That's Ronnie. I told you I'd teamed up with another girl who had lost her partner, right? Well, that's him showing up five hours later. If you see us smiling, it's not because we were having a good time. It's because we thought he was dead.

You'd bump into different people down there throughout the day. You didn't know who'd come down and who hadn't made it out. There were a lot of different rumors floating around, too, about who was missing and who wasn't. Nothing was verified. You just worked and worked and hoped for the best.

⇒⇒⇒⟵⟵⟵

After the second Tower came down, we didn't transport any more patients to the hospital. Instead, we treated people for smoke inhalation, respiratory heat emergencies, and a lot of irrigation of the eyes.

You see in some of the photos I took where the fire department

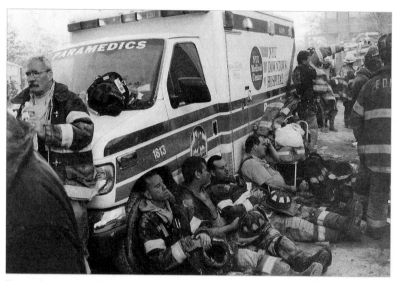

"Around noon, these firemen you see here came out of the rubble and just threw themselves down against my ambulance. Wrecked. Dog tired. They fought their way in and had fought their way out."

guys are sucking on the oxygen. Those particle masks people were using? The kind made for painters? They didn't work, so I didn't use one. We kept wet cloths over our faces instead. Breathing the air was pretty horrible. You weren't suffocating, but just the force of the blast coming toward you was enough to make you gag. And you didn't know what had gotten into the air.

One thing I seen, it was a bit bizarre. It looked like a Halloween mask lying on the ground but it was somebody's skull with all the skin fried off it. It looked like a joke mask, you know? Like one you'd see in a window that doesn't look real? But it was.

The body parts. It was hard to see anything clearly. If you got a big lump of meat and threw it on the ground, covered it with dirt and rolled it around . . . is that a body part? Is it not? Obviously, if it was a torso or an arm . . . we'd go up to it. Look at it. Ooop. Yes, it is. But we didn't do anything about it. It wasn't our concern. At that point, cleaning up body parts wasn't anybody's priority. At that point, we were all still looking for survivors.

There were a lot of people down there who weren't part of any special structure. For instance, there was a cop from New Jersey who'd just come down with his search dog. I guess his thought process was like: Right. I've got a dog. I'm ready to go. What do you need?

There'd been an initial organization in response to the planes hitting the buildings, but it all got wiped out when the Towers came down. So you had a lot of fire crews and paramedic crews who were freelancing, going in, search and rescue. There was no tabs on any of them. And a lot of boys were very emotional, you know? They'd lost friends and brothers, so you knew they weren't going to listen to reason. If you're my boss and you tell me to stay put when I've just lost two of my best pals in a flaming pit of ash, I'm gonna go, "Fuck you," and go back in. I mean, you can see from these photographs. These boys are really fried.

Around noon, these firemen you see here came out of the rubble and just threw themselves down against my ambulance. Wrecked. Dog-tired. They fought their way in, and had fought their way out. There's another photo of an ambulance that was parked at the foot of the Towers when they collapsed. See? Crushed.

Our ambulance was right beside those boys who were raising the flag.[55] There was smoldering rubble everywhere. Smoke and chaos. We were all waiting for something to do. So I seen these three fire

---

55 Firemen Dan McWilliams, George Johnson, and Billy Eisengrein raised a U.S. flag amid the rubble of Ground Zero on the afternoon of 9/11. The act created an instant media sensation, a moment of inspiration in the wake of the attack. Many people couldn't help but notice a similarity between the image of the three firemen and the one depicted in the United States Marine Memorial, commonly referred to as the Iwo Jima Memorial, near Arlington National Cemetery. The incident eventually sparked controversy, however. A bronze memorial statue was commissioned from photographs of the firemen raising the flag. McWilliams, Johnson, and Eisengrein—all white men—were replaced in the sculpture by a white man, an African American man, and a Hispanic man. New York Fire Department spokesman Frank Gribbon stated that, "given that those who died were of all races and ethnicities, and that the statue was to be symbolic of those sacrifices, ultimately a decision was made to honor no one in particular." Opponents to the statue claimed that politics should play no part in a historic memorial.

department guys climbing up on top one of those broken buildings near Vesey Street and the West Side Highway with a flag post they'd set up. You could see the Stars and Stripes come out as they started to raise the banner.

I'm not into any form of patriotism, but I was very moved by what was going on, this symbol of defiance in the midst all the rubble. It was very reminiscent of Iwo Jima; even as I took the photo, I was struck by that. And there was total silence.

"You might think, looking at the pictures, that there was this massive noise and chaos going on all around. But they were raising that flag in this very eerie silence."

You might think, looking at the pictures, that there was this massive noise and chaos going on all around. But they were raising that flag in this very eerie silence.

⫸⫷

I didn't come down emotionally until I got home that night. I'd gotten to Ground Zero at around 9:00 A.M.; I got back to my apartment around one in the morning. I came back with two friends from the site, Robbie and Trin, and we met with a couple of friends who live downstairs from me—a Scottish couple, Mark and Tara, who set us up with a couple beers. We sat down to chat, but no words came out. We all just sat there with the thousand-yard stare.

It's . . . I felt something but I couldn't describe it. There was a numbness going on in my body. We were still very hyped up when we got back, not quite sure what to think. And then we put on the news.

And we hadn't seen it, you know? We hadn't seen the media coverage. So all of a sudden, we're looking at the destruction through a camera lens, the buildings, the chaos . . . and we're going, "Jesus Christ."

Then one of the fire department guys came 'round and picked up Robbie and Trin. I was sitting with Mark and Tara, watching the news, when I felt this well of emotion brewing inside and I broke down. I couldn't contain myself. I cried like a baby for twenty minutes. Uncontrollable sobbing.

Our spirits had held up while we'd been down there all that day. We were working and joking with each other a bit to keep morale up. But the enormity . . . when I actually came home and sat down, away from the work area, I realized what had actually happened. And then the emotion set in.

⇛⤛

If the Towers hadn't have fallen, we'd have been busy, busy, busy. But they fell and they crushed everybody and that was it, that's the long and short of it. If 110 stories of concrete and steel is coming down, what's it gonna do to you? I mean, you're only human.

The thing I had the most problem with was finding the personal stuff. A shoe. A handbag. That sort of stuff still sticks in my head, not the body parts.

A shoe would turn your imagination around a little bit. "Well, where did that shoe come from? Where did that person go? Is that from luggage? Is that from a person on the plane, or is that from a person that fell? Was that person burned?" Whereas if you look at a body or a body part, it's like, "Well, that's a body part, and that's it, that person's dead."

Maybe it's the paramedic viewpoint. We're so used to seeing the gore that our interest gravitates more toward the intimate things.

⇛⤛

I treated this firefighter guy, Sal. He works for Ladder 7, Engine 16, and I met him on the first day. He was suffering from heat exhaustion.

He was badly dehydrated, with muscle cramping, feeling a bit dizzy. We started a couple of IVs for him, to give him fluid therapy and get him going again.

I kept bumping into Sal on that first day and I thought, you know, it's quite uncanny that, in the midst of all this, I keep bumping into the same person.

Then on the fourth day, September 15, we did Search and Rescue and I kept bumping into Sal again. And I thought, there must be something in this.

I told Sal, "Wherever you guys go today, I'm going, too. I'll be your paramedic." I was down there on me own time, wasn't getting paid for it. I had my trauma bag and all me equipment. So I went Search and Rescue with their company, right into the rubble of the Towers.

>>><<<

After thirteen hours of searching, all we found was a rag doll and a bag with a journal in it.

The journal? It was a little notepad and it had these words written in it: "Flirting is just an innocent way of getting to know somebody." I found it in the rubble and I remember thinking, huh? That weird sense of, did he write that just before it happened? I believe the writer was a he. There were bills in the bag with a man's name on them. Personal stuff. Damp and wet. I didn't bother flicking through. I picked it up and thought, well, that's somebody's personal stuff.

After I checked the journal, I put it back in the bag and handed it back. That was the procedure we followed if we found any personal items: we passed them back down the line to where people were collecting them. Probably the Red Cross, the fire department, somebody like that. There was so many agencies there, I really don't know who was doing what.

A couple other things I seen. There was a big glass paperweight, a solid ball paperweight that had sat on somebody's office desk, I guess. I didn't know where it came from and I certainly didn't know how it didn't shatter during the collapse of the building. But there it was, lying atop the wreckage as if somebody'd placed it there after all was said and done.

There was an unbelievable amount of paper lying around, too; paper and luggage from the fuselage of the plane. All the bags were charred and broken, but intact. Everything was there in every possible stage. And there was such an influx of the senses, too; your sense of smell, what you were taking in with your eyes . . . it was demoralizing. Overwhelming.

⫸⫷

The day I found the journal and the rag doll was the day the president came, September 15. The rubble of the Towers was still smoking very badly, and—you know where the gold ball was?[56] We were like, twenty feet away from that.

I found myself looking around and, in some strange way, it was like being on a movie set. The surroundings didn't seem real. I was waiting for somebody to holler, "Cut! That's it! Action!" But maybe that was just a coping mechanism.

Then the next thing we heard was the *whhooooopp, whhooooopp, whhooooopp* of the big Chinooks coming toward us, two big helicopters. Then, out of the smoke, the Tomcat jets banking in, making that awful screeching sound we'd heard before it had all happened: *hwwwwwwwaaaaaaaaaaaaahhh*. And I was standing there in the rubble of the World Trade Center, in the middle of New York City, watching these war planes swoop down on us. It was too surreal. You know that scene from *The Terminator*, when those big robots come in and start blasting everything from the sky? A postapocalyptic nightmare, that's what it reminded me of, and I was standing right there in the middle of it all.

⫸⫷

Eventually, I realized that, as a skilled paramedic, there was nothing

---

56 *The Sphere* by Fritz Koenig, a sculpture in the plaza at the base of the Towers.

more for me to do. I was just an extra set of hands down there. If I stayed on, all I'd be doing was collecting rubble. So I left.

I was probably down there about seventy hours total. About thirteen or fourteen hours the first day; seven hours on the second. Third day? Maybe seven or eight. I had my normal shifts at the hospital and I went to those as well, but in-between I'd go down to help. I couldn't sleep anyway.

After the fifteenth, I didn't go down anymore. My skills as a paramedic could be utilized elsewhere. People were still having heart attacks in other areas of the city. People still slipped and fell and needed attention. The world moves on, after all.

In all, fourteen EMS workers were lost on 9/11. For that, I felt this mix of emotions, part of me saying, "Shit, I'm glad to be alive." But another part of me feeling a tremendous guilt and saying, "How come them, and not me? How come there's guys in the rubble who have families and here I am, a single guy with basically no ties?"

I understand that's a normal grief reaction. Survivor guilt. To be able to identify with that? It's a normal grief to have.

⋙⋘

When I was walking around in the rubble, I bumped into this fireman who took one look at me and said, "Are you fuckin' kidding me?"

I said, "What?"

He said, "Take a look at your shield number."

My number is 9110. A strange number to wear at Ground Zero.

The coincidence of it. I feel that, in some strange way, when I was given that shield number, I was meant to be there.

SALVATORE S. TORCIVIA

Salvatore S. Torcivia, thirty-five, is a New York City firefighter.

Sal served as a New York City police officer for nine and a half years before switching to the NYFD. "I wound up with the fire department because it was more of a brotherhood," he says. "And I was slotted to work the September 10/11 Monday night shift, a twenty-four-hour overtime tour from 6:00 P.M. to 9:00 A.M. But I gave it up to George Cain, may he rest in peace."

A total of nine firefighters were lost from Sal's ladder company.

Sal coughs frequently as he talks, turning his head to one side and hacking from deep within his chest. But his incredible attitude and buoyant good humor is infectious.

I DROPPED MY sons off to school that morning and took my daughter to the YMCA for her first preschool class. One of my best friends was there because he had his son in the same school class. He took me aside and said, "Sal, I just heard a plane hit the Twin Towers."

I was thinking he meant a two-seater plane, you know? One of those little jobs. So I said, "Do you know what size?" He said no.

I figured it was nothing, so I got in my pickup truck and headed for home. I had Q104 on, and I heard the announcer say that another plane just hit. That's when I said to myself, what do you mean, "another one hit?"

At home, I put the TV on, and there I was looking at everything that was happening, totally in shock now. I called my father and told him, "Dad, I just want to let you know, I'm heading into work. If you don't hear from me, don't worry. They might need me."

My father told me he was on the phone with my sister, who was, at that moment, standing outside the Towers; she works in one of the banks opposite the complex. "She says people are jumping, Sal,"

he said. "Things are falling. Thank God you didn't go to work today."
I said, "Tell her to get out of there right now."

⟫⟫⟫⟫⟪⟪⟪⟪

From home, I went back to the YMCA. I wanted to tell my wife, Adrienne, that I was leaving; she was waiting for my daughter to get out of class. I searched the whole place but I couldn't find her. I didn't want to leave without telling her, but I had no choice. So I told my friends, "Tell Adrienne I had to go into work." Then I grabbed some clothes since I knew I'd be down there a while. I could tell that just by seeing the devastation on the TV. Hell, I packed enough clothes to last me a week, and started driving.

My truck's got four-way flashers on it, which allowed me to tuck in right behind a police escort while I was still on Staten Island. I wasn't worried about breaking the law or nothing. Those police weren't about to do any car stops; they obviously had to get someplace fast, and I wasn't causing any problems. We ducked in and out of empty streets. Everything was a ghost town. They took me right up to the Verrazzano Bridge, where somebody checked my ID and let me through.

Everything was going well until I got to the Battery Tunnel. That's where the police stopped me and said, "Everything's closed off.

"That night, around midnight, we found our truck. . . . It was abandoned, parked a few blocks away from the Trade Center, covered in filth, and totally empty, like it was waiting for the guys who'd rode her down. . . ."

No getting in or out of the city."

>>><<<

There was a bunch of firemen waiting in their trucks, getting ready to get through the tunnel. They'd set up a temporary command post; I think they were Battalion 32 from Red Hook, Brooklyn. Since I had nothing else to do but wait, I started looking around, seeing what I could do to help, and that's when I ran into a police captain from the 76th Precinct—also in Red Hook—who used to be my captain from the 60th Precinct when I was a cop in Brooklyn.

We shook hands and he said to me, "Sal, I could really use you right now. Help me get people out of the tunnel."

He meant civilians who'd run from the Trade Towers and fled through the Battery Tunnel on foot. They were everywhere. So we corralled them as they came out the mouth, took them aside, gave them water, and soaked their faces. We checked everyone to make sure they were okay and pointed out ambulances to anybody we thought needed them.

After doing that for about a half an hour or so, someone told me that the Brooklyn Bridge was open. So I hopped back in my truck, grabbed another off-duty fireman, and drove him to his firehouse in Manhattan at 24 Truck on the West Side. Then I went back to my own firehouse, which is 16 Engine, 7 Truck—on 29th Street between 2nd and 3rd—where I proceeded to get into my gear. The captain of my engine was there, plus the lieutenant from my truck.

We loaded up my pickup truck with guys and equipment and also commandeered one of the fire department's Chevy Suburbans; we loaded that up, too. Then we drove down to the Trade Center.

>>><<<

The fire department had told everyone to stay at their firehouses and wait to be called, but we knew both our companies were down there already and weren't going to sit around on our hands. We didn't have any fire apparatuses on us, but we didn't care. We just wanted to get there and help.

We drove as close to the Trade Center as we could; I'd say we parked about six blocks away from the Towers off the West Side Highway. From there, we got out and walked the rest of the way down.

Sure, we'd heard the Towers had collapsed. But I was still, in my mind, thinking that just the top part had come down or something, the upper stories where the planes had hit. I couldn't believe, you know? I couldn't have it make sense that the whole building came down. Both buildings.

We were walking through this disaster area, trying to find where the new temporary headquarters for the fire department was. We couldn't believe the amount of rubble there. I kept looking up, but there were no Towers standing. Either one. Which put me in a state of shock. We all were.

We saw one of the battalion chiefs and approached him, asking, "What do you want us to do?"

He said, "Find whatever tools you can and start digging."

➤➤➤◄◄◄

We found an area and started working. Digging, just like he'd said. And we searched the rubble that first day, trying to find survivors, anybody. But just looking at the Pile, my first opinion was, "No one could have survived."

They told us where the command post had been situated: off the West Side Highway by Battery Park City. We figured that'd be the place where we'd have the best chance of finding survivors. Uh-uh.

We kept coming up with bodies of the deceased and body parts. It was awful.

➤➤➤◄◄◄

At one point later in the day, they pulled us off the main Pile when they thought another section of the building was coming down. We all pulled out and waited, but nothing happened. So we moved back in and started digging again. This time, we found more and more civilian bodies.

I remember losing my bearings a lot on the Pile; it was hard to keep track of where you were. With all the geography gone, I couldn't remember what street I was on, what building used to stand where, nothing. Everything started to look like a big pile of rubble.

I'd say I started helping out that morning at 9:30 on the Brooklyn side of the tunnel. By the time I got down to the Trade Center itself, it had to be around 10:30. And I worked in the Pit from 10:30 to 6:00 at night. But then I had to stop.

I did as much as I could until I became dehydrated and started cramping up real bad. I said, "Let me go to one of the ambulances to get an IV, something for the cramping." I hoped to pull in, get patched up, head back out, and continue working. I ran into a gentleman named Roger Smyth, a paramedic from NYU Downtown hospital who hooked me up with a couple IVs, gave me a few bananas, and got me back on my feet enough for me to continue until 11:30 at night.

That first day while I was getting the IV, another building, a hotel, started rumbling and everyone started running because they thought it was another collapse. It was scary. I was still so cramped, I couldn't

On 9/11, 343 firefighters and paramedics, 23 NYPD officers, and 37 Port Authority officers were killed.

get the needle out of my arm. Another fireman from my house had to help me pull it out as we ran for cover. We watched the building come down, just barely out of range.[57] After that, I guess the higher-ups decided they didn't really know what they were dealing with, so they moved everyone out.

It was probably a good move. I'd heard nothing but explosions all day, like bombs going off. It makes sense, looking back. The fires from the planes' jet fuel was still burning. Air conditioning and refrigerator units in the nearby buildings were going off like firecrackers, exploding from the super heat. Also, I believe the Secret Service had their armory in one of the Towers. Someone later told me that all the explosions we heard was actually ordnance going off deep beneath the rubble, but I never got the long or short of that.

⟫⟪

Late in the evening, the [fire] department called off any worker who'd been on the Pile all day. They said, "Take a break. We'll get a night crew in here. Come back in the morning."

They'd already tried that a number of times. Most of the time, we ignored them. But by the end of that day, a lot of guys were physically spent. Me? I felt like I'd had the wind knocked out of me. By that point, I figured I'd be no good to anyone if I kept on working. And anyway, we had a fresh bunch of guys waiting, so me and a few others figured, "Let them jump in and we'll be back in a few hours."

That night, around midnight, we found our truck from Ladder 7. It was abandoned, parked a few blocks away from the Trade Center, covered in filth and totally empty, like it was waiting for the guys who'd rode her down to come back and head for home.

That was a sad time. I went back to pick up my own truck, and a few other guys drove our fire truck back to the house. We started cleaning the debris off her; it took us until around five in the morning.

---

57 Here Sal is probably referring to 7 World Trade, a building which was part of the Trade Center complex that collapsed early in the evening of September 11 from damage sustained by the crumbling Towers. Thankfully, the building had been evacuated much earlier as people fled the initial attack, so no one was reported injured or killed when 7 World Trade came down.

That truck was covered from head to toe with pieces of cement, paper, lots of dust, lots of rubble. We moved fourteen full bags of garbage off that rig. She's a tower ladder truck with a bucket that three guys can stand in at once to operate a nozzle and control a fire, or get to a window for a rescue maneuver. The collapse of the Towers had damaged the ladder controls, and the truck's radiator was clogged up good with about two inches of soot and garbage. Other than that, she was still running.

※»※«

A friend of mine who has a business in Coney Island told me something interesting later on. He said, "Papers from the Trade Center were falling like snowflakes by my store. You get that? As far away as Coney Island they came! When I saw them, I thought, ho boy! The buildings in Coney Island have started to burn."

They found inches and inches of soot on cars all over Brooklyn.

What I'm saying is, Coney Island's a nice distance from Manhattan, maybe fifteen miles or so. So, yeah, I kind of consider that unbelievable. Debris from the Towers landed all over the city. Imagine that.

※»※«

When the Trade Center collapsed, the fire department initiated what we call a recall. Anyone off-duty, on vacation, or out sick had to report into work, no matter what their condition was. We needed manpower, and we needed it badly. We lost so many guys.

That first day, we worked around the clock. The second day, too—so that was forty-eight hours straight combined. Then they broke us into two shifts. You work a twenty-four, you're off twenty-four.

For days, the fires were out of control. You kept dousing water on the blazes, hoping you could keep them at bay. One of the buildings we covered had to be thirty stories tall, and I'd say 90 percent of the floors were on fire. We didn't know if it was going to come down on us or not. On that one, the fire burned for a day and a half, but the building was left standing after all was said and done. It was strange.

"Our fellow members of the fire department, close friends, were missing. We were doing whatever we thought it would take to find them, very often putting ourselves in harm's way."

So I guess I'm trying to say that, while we were working to pull bodies out of the rubble, we had all this other stuff going on around us.

How do you fight a fire like that? You just keep trying and hope for the best. By that point, we were all in reaction mode, automatic pilot. Our fellow members of the fire department, close friends, were missing. We were doing whatever we thought it would take to find them, very often putting ourselves in harm's way. But the camaraderie—I can't even describe it.

Myself and this other fireman from my house, Jerry Bonner, we stayed together almost the whole two weeks. A lot of guys were doing the bucket brigade—Jerry and I did that in our downtime.[58]

But most of the time, we searched the voids and tunnels of the debris field, hoping to find some sign of life. It was such a large area and we didn't have enough radios to go around, so you couldn't, for instance, report in, "Okay, I'm searching over here or over there . . ."

---

58 During the first few days after the collapse of the Towers, rescue workers and volunteers formed lines going into the debris field. The man at the head of the line scooped debris into plastic buckets and passed the buckets back for dumping. Some of these lines reportedly ran as long as fifty people.

All we had was a can of spray paint.

We'd mark wherever we went, over the rubble and under it. If we found something that looked promising—a space that looked big enough for someone to hide in—we'd start digging ourselves and send someone out to start a bucket brigade. But we never pulled anyone out alive.

We found a cop who was later identified as part of the police academy photo unit this way. Half his torso and one of his legs was missing.

※※※

At times, you knew there were remains where you were digging—the smell was unmistakable. But you couldn't find anything. The bodies were totally crushed, plus they'd been ground up into the dirt and the rubble. That's what we were smelling.

I was a cop for ten years, and I saw a lot. Sometimes we'd get a DOA call and get to the location—an apartment, let's say—and the body's been sitting for two or three weeks because the deceased had no family. The body's decomposed, but you had to wait until the medical examiner got there to remove it.

But this? This was like nothing I'd ever experienced, and nothing prepared me for it. Even when we found someone's remains, nothing was recognizable. And that was so very sad. How many thousands of people were we talking about, all there in one place, decomposing?

The smell got to everyone after awhile. By the second or third day, it was raw down there. I was gagging. If we uncovered anything that resembled a body or a body part, we'd shovel it into a body bag—there was no other way to pick up what we found. We hoped they'd be able to ID the remains through DNA testing down at the medical examiners' office.

※※※

On the fourth day, I started finding intact bodies, but everyone was naked. I was like, why don't these people have any clothes on?

I talked to other firemen who were down there that first day when the buildings crumbled, and discovered an answer of sorts. They said that, as the Towers came down, firemen ran from the area but the force of the blast created a wind tunnel effect powerful enough to rip their bottles—the packs we wear for breathing—right off their backs. It lifted their jackets up and threw them aside like dolls.

What I'm saying is, this stuff we wear is heavy equipment and it's strapped onto us tight. So if the blast could rip off our gear, business suits and regular clothes would be like nothing, like tissue paper. Like blowing bubbles away.

→⟫⟪←

We couldn't find any glass, or office furniture. No office equipment, either. I think there was so much steel and cement coming down in the collapse that everything was pulverized into powder from the force.

Everyone was asking, "Where did all this dirt come from?" Simple. Everything was destroyed from the force of all that heavy steel and cement collapsing. In the section of the Pit where I was working, the largest piece of cement I found I could pick up with one hand. Everything else was powder.

You had every type of material in the powder that you could imagine. A lot of crushed glass. Plus a lot of chemicals, which really gets me worried.

Both Towers had transformers, which carried PCBs to keep them cool. [59] That stuff causes cancer. We lost quite a few firemen back in the '70s in a telephone building fire—they were exposed to PCBs when the transformers in that building burned and the men weren't wearing the proper equipment to protect themselves. The first year after that job, numerous guys died from cancer. Over the next five to twenty years, all the guys who'd responded to that fire died, all from cancer. The majority of them went within the first ten years.

I continued going back down to Ground Zero every day for two weeks straight until they called us off.

---

59 PCBs are polychlorinated biphenyls, chemical liquids used as insulation in electrical equipment until they were banned in the 1970s for being highly toxic.

⊷⟫⟪⊶

There's gonna be a lot of people sick from this. And not just firemen.

I wasn't wearing a mask the whole time I was down at the Pit. They issued us these paper masks that workmen use for painting, but they don't stop anything. So I wore the hood that we wear around our heads when we go into fires. It reminds me of the headgear a knight would wear to protect himself in battle; it keeps the heat from our head. When we have our face piece on, it seals our forehead down to our chin and ears and keeps us from getting burned.

So that was my respirator, that's what I found worked the best. I used it to cover my nose and I tucked it into my shirt. I didn't feel like I was getting exposed to the dust in the air . . . but the way that I feel now, I don't think that measure offered much protection. At the time, it kept me going. I guess that's what's most important.

⊷⟫⟪⊶

From day one, everyone was complaining of the cough and the sore throats. We thought it was from inhaling the dust; we didn't think of contaminants. But the second day or third day, I was getting told by private test groups at the site that the contaminants in the air were off the charts, so high they couldn't register them. But we were also being told by the city and the state that everything was within a safe range, no one could be harmed. Looking back, that just wasn't so—it wasn't possible.

I'm not laying blame. Deep down, we knew that stuff was gonna harm us. But we were out there to find our brothers and civilian survivors. That's what we get paid for, and that's what we wanted to do. We wanted to bring our family home.

But as time went on, the sore throats and the coughing got worse. I noticed it around three weeks after September 11: I was getting winded very easily.

⊷⟫⟪⊶

Two weeks after the Trade Center happened, the department wouldn't let anyone from the first, third, or eleventh divisions go back down. Two-thirds of the men we lost were from those divisions; we were all working on our days off to compensate for the holes in our ranks.

Then, going out on the normal runs, we noticed that a lot of us were getting tired very quickly. Some guys less, some guys more. On regular walk-ups, where I never had a problem before, I suddenly felt like I was gonna have a heart attack.[60] I couldn't catch my breath. But because we had so many memorial services going on, I chalked it up to the bad sleep patterns we were having, the way we were eating, the fact that I was out of shape, off my regular fitness routine.

But it never got better. In fact, it got to the point where every call we went on, I didn't know if I was gonna make it or not, the way my heart was beating. I was gasping for breath.

I really started to realize I had a problem around four weeks after the eleventh. We were told we could go down to the medical office and get checked out, but I didn't want to be out of work. If they put me on the sick list, they wouldn't let me help out at the Trade Center.

⫸⫷

Losing nine members in a firehouse is very hard. We had nine families we had to look after. In all, the department lost a lot of guys with over twenty years in. They could've retired. There was one guy I know of—September 11 was his last day working. He had forty years on. I think he was in Rescue Company 1. His son was in the fire department, too. They both were lost. That man's wife lost her husband and her son in one day.

I can't tell you how many memorials we've been to. On our days off, you get a printout that lists all the services going on. You go to as many as you can; sometimes you try to make two in a day. You want to show the families that you support them and that they're being thought of, that their loved one is remembered.

Before this happened, a line-of-duty funeral would have anywhere

---

60 Climbing stairs in buildings while on call.

from five to ten thousand guys showing up for a funeral. Now? You're lucky if you get a hundred, because there's so many services going on. We're spread too thin. You've got guys being laid out upstate, in Queens, Brooklyn, the Bronx. I think Staten Island's lost close to a hundred guys out of the three hundred or so total firemen lost.

⫸⫷

So yeah, a lot of us were starting to feel sick. But we wanted to wait until most of the services were done before getting ourselves checked out.

Finally, a little over two months after September 11, it was like four o'clock in the morning and we were walking up the FDR Drive, responding to a car fire. We went on foot because we couldn't get through traffic, there were too many cars blocking the roadway. After walking about ten blocks with all my gear and equipment, I thought I was gonna pass out.

I went to my officer and told him, "Boss, there's something wrong. I don't know if I'm having a heart attack or asthma." I never had asthma before. My heart was strong as an ox. They got some paramedics to check me out, and everything showed okay on my EKG. Nothing wrong with my heart. My lungs were clear. But they said, "Definitely follow up with a pulmonary doctor."

My regular doctor's a pulmonary specialist, so I went to him. He gave me a breathing test. I'd just taken one back in August, but this one came back dramatically lower.

See, there's a certain volume you push out when you breathe, which can be measured in liters. A person my size and weight should be pushing out 4.5 to 5 liters of air in an exhalation. Suddenly, I was pushing out a little over three, and I'm in shape. I decided to go for more tests.

I went to the fire department surgeon and they gave me a breathing test. The department usually gives you a full medical every six months to a year to make sure your heart's okay, your lungs are clear. You get a blood workup, the works. This time, they found out I'd dropped around 40 to 45 percent of my breathing capacity since the last time I was tested. They said, "Let's put you on some inhalers and see if that helps. Maybe you developed work-induced asthma from all the stuff down there."

I was on the inhaler for a week but it wasn't helping, so I went to see another specialist. He ticked off all the airborne particles that got into my body down at Ground Zero—wood, glass, metal, cement, and who knows what other chemicals combined in the dust. He said I hadn't just inhaled it, it wasn't just in my lungs and bronchial tubes. I'd ingested it. That crap was in my stomach, my bloodstream, and the nasal passages in my head. Plus, the combined effect of everything is keeping my tissues constantly inflamed and infected.

For the past four weeks, I've been on three types of inhalers and three different kinds of steroids. But nothing seems to be helping.

>>><<<

Some days are worse than others. I'm the type of person who enjoys getting four hours of sleep. Before the eleventh, four hours used to give me plenty of rest. Now? I can't get enough sleep; I always feel tired. The doctors told me, "Since you're not breathing enough air, you're breathing in more frequently and it's making you tired." They also say it's a form of depression, and I'm sure that's part of it, but the physical fatigue is crippling sometimes.

Normally, I just buzz along. I like to food shop. I cook, I clean, I do things around the house. My wife labeled me "Mr. Mom," but I do these things because I like doing them. They used to call me the Energizer Bunny. "When are you going to sleep, Sal? When are you going to stop?"

Now I get winded just pushing a shopping cart along.

>>><<<

From what I know, there's 400 to 500 guys with breathing problems. I heard that number from the medical officers down at the Bureau of Health Services, and from other members of the fire department with similar problems. And there's about four guys with lung damage

Researchers from Columbia University's Lamont-Doherty Earth Observatory recorded seismic signals consistent with those produced by small earthquakes when the planes hit the Trade Towers. They note, however, that these vibrations were not sufficient to collapse or significantly damage the buildings adjacent to the WTC. These structures more than likely sustained damage when they were struck by debris falling from the Towers or the massive blast of air pressure generated by the collapse.

so severe that it actually shows up on a chest X-ray—without even going for an MRI or a CAT scan, it's showing up on a regular chest X-ray. That's a very bad sign.

There's guys who went in for the blood workup and got it back with three or four different viruses showing up. Guys that had a scope stuck down their throat—the doctors saying there's a bunch of crap down there that you can actually see with the camera, but they don't know how to get it out yet. That's why they're treating us with the inhalers. Hopefully the bruising and inflammation on the bronchial tubes will soothe and the body will heal itself.

Yeah, I'm a little angry. But what am I gonna do? I'm happy I'm alive. The one guy who took my spot working that day, George Cain, is gone. I'd only known him a year, but I felt close to him. He was a really great guy. We were always around each other.

We lost a lot of guys, but I was close to George. Whenever I think of him, it hurts.

⟫⟪

When I finally got to close my eyes that first night, I had my one and only dream about George. I was hanging out in the firehouse. George and I were on a fire truck, in the engine, just driving around and around.

Then, suddenly, we were at a car accident which another fire company was at. The car was on fire, and we went in to rescue a kid who was trapped inside. We got him out, too. That felt real good. We did all the EMS stuff on him, and then we put the fire out.

When I woke up, I started looking for George and everyone else—all the other guys—looked at me funny: "He's not here," they said. It was so painful. At that point, we knew he was missing. It was so unreal for the first two weeks to know that he's not coming back.

George was a marathon runner, a rock climber, and an avid skier. He traveled all around the country. He was a health-food nut. I'm saying this guy was in phenomenal shape, and he lived for being a fireman. He loved the work so much, he'd put in for a transfer to a busier company up in Harlem because he loved going on calls, no matter how dangerous it was.

Most firefighters are like that. People ask us, "Aren't you scared to go out on a call?" No. That's what we're waiting for. We love the job, and a call means we finally get to do something, whether it's a car accident, someone's stuck, or someone's sick. It makes us feel useful. It's a good feeling to help someone.

Why do we do what we do? That's hard to say, unless you're a fireman. People say, "Why do you run into a burning building?" It's about helping the people in need, simple as that.

When I heard about the plane crashes, I knew that guys in my company would be on their way down there. These guys love what they do and they always do a great job. Always.

NICOLE BLACKMAN

Nicole Blackman, thirty-three, is a tiny, raven-haired woman with a striking voice. It can climb through multiple octave ranges of expression with startling ease and grace.

Like many hardcore Manhattanites, Nicole dropped everything when the Towers fell—her work, friends, home, and habit—to pull the city loose from the grip of tragedy. Her story is a love letter to volunteerism, the ethic that impressed the world with the tenacity of the Big Apple and its citizens in the days following 9/11.

I THINK IT was the day after. I was on the phone with a friend of mine, Sue, who lives down in TriBeCa. I called to check up on her because she's one of the only people I know who lives in that area.

She said she was spending time at a volunteer center whose mission was to provide an information clearinghouse for downtown residents: what to do if your power was out, what to do if you couldn't get back into your building, that sort of thing. Everything was changing so quickly that the community opted to organize on its own. It was the only way to guarantee self-preservation.

Sue said that several relief services had infiltrated the area and were setting up way stations to help the rescue workers coming down the West Side Highway. Volunteers were staffing up to hand out sandwiches, breath masks, and bottles of water.

I said, "Well, do they need anything?"

She said, "Last time I was there, they needed sandwiches. They have nothing to give these rescue workers, and they're hungry."

"Great."

I immediately started emailing and calling friends. We got together at someone's apartment and put together a big production line. There were five or six of us; someone had the bread, someone else had cheese, another person had turkey, and we started making

"... several relief services had infiltrated the area and were setting up way stations to help the rescue workers coming down the West Side Highway. Volunteers were staffing up to hand out sandwiches, breath masks, and bottles of water."

sandwiches. We wrapped them all up and printed out labels so everyone knew what they were. And we didn't use mayonnaise; we didn't want them to go bad.

We didn't really know where to bring our cache, though. We tried bringing it down to St. Vincent's hospital, but when we got there, they told us they weren't accepting food donations. After all the effort we'd gone to, that was disheartening.

Finally, we started walking around downtown, hoping to give the sandwiches to anybody who seemed like they could use them. We found this restaurant called Fiddlesticks that had a sign out front talking about rescue efforts. We went inside and the employees said, "We're storing food here for the hospitals because they don't have room."

Remember, it was the twelfth of September. Everyone still thought there'd be tons of survivors from the Towers, and we thought they would need supplies.

➤➤➤◄◄◄

People throughout the city were trying to donate food, but nobody knew where to bring stuff. The people at Fiddlesticks saw this development and said, "Bring the food here and we'll store it as long as we can." They had this giant cold storage in their basement.

I began to wonder—who's organizing all this? Who's in charge? But there really wasn't anyone. The rule at that point was: make it all up as you go along.

So we dropped our food at Fiddlesticks and I thought, fine. At least our sandwiches will go to someplace useful."

⟫⟪

After that, I started walking across town, heading toward the West Side Highway. I ran into a friend of mine who was sitting in an outdoor café, smiling and having a cigarette with his dog curled up at his feet.

He asked me what I was up to and I explained to him what I'd done with the sandwiches. He gave me this withering look and said, "Listen, girl. I've spent a lot of time in Paris. This kind of stuff happens all the time in the rest of the world. You can't get yourself all crazy about it."

I wanted to strangle him. He hadn't seen any of the missing posters outside of St. Vincent's, the news vans covered with flyers, the people holding up signs that said "thank you" to any cop or fire truck that drove past.

I was like, "You really don't get this, do you?"

I knew that I couldn't convince him, so I thought, this is someone who's just trying to distract me. I said, "Thanks. Good to see you. I'm gonna go." And I kept moving.

⟫⟪

When I got to the West Side Highway, I saw that tents had been set up all along the strip and people were bustling about, moving from the tent to the road and back again, handing out supplies to cars and trucks full of rescue workers driving past.

I asked, "Hey, who's in charge?" And someone said, "That girl over there in the baseball cap."

It was very organic, a real grassroots operation. The girl in charge wasn't wearing some official hat or badge of office or anything. No sign that said, "Me In Charge."

So I approached her and said, "Who needs a hand? What can I help you with?"

The tents basically had a large stock of bottled water, respirator masks, and sandwiches. There were people lined up at folding tables who were making more sandwiches. I said, "Hold on a second. Do you guys know about Fiddlesticks?"

"What's a Fiddlesticks?"

I said, "Who's got a truck?"

Someone said, "Get a truck, someone go with this girl. She's got a source."

They flagged down some guy in a van who was driving along the West Side Highway. The driver, who'd come to town from Connecticut or Massachusetts or something, had gone to a Home Depot and bought all the boots and respirators he could find, a couple thousand dollars worth of stuff. He'd thrown it all in his van and driven right down to Ground Zero thinking, this is what they're gonna need, this is what they're gonna get. After dropping off his load, he'd spent the rest of the day driving around town making himself available to anyone. "Who needs help moving stuff?"

Somebody flagged him down and said, "This girl needs to go someplace to pick up food. Can you take her?" He said no problem.

So there I was, sitting in the van with a perfect stranger who turned out to be the loveliest guy. We drove over to Fiddlesticks. I walked in and said, "I've got a van here to take some food over to the West Side Highway."

All I heard was, "Great. What do you need?"

The bartenders hopped over the bars to help. The waitresses dropped their checks on their customers' tables and said, "Dude, you're gonna have to wait for your order, I've got something else to do." Everyone took off their aprons and we formed a daisy chain, twenty people long. The dishwashers came out from the back and they helped, too, guys who didn't speak even English.

There was a door from the downstairs storage up to the sidewalk, and crates kept coming up. Water and juice, PowerBars, sandwiches, cans of soda, bags of ice. If it was portable, it went into the chain. Thankfully, people hadn't donated things like deli platters, only individually packaged items like candy bars and potato chips.

We filled up the van. I thanked the guys at Fiddlesticks, and they were like, "Hey. Great. Glad it's all going someplace you can use it."

But as we were driving back to the West Side Highway, I started thinking, wait a minute. What would have happened if I hadn't been there at Fiddlesticks and known all this stuff was there?

Do you see what I'm saying? That chance circumstance set the tone for everything else that happened next.

⫸⫷

The rescue supply game became about being a pinball that made a connection between two points. "You guys need ice? I know somebody who has some." That's how the network developed, little by little. It wasn't like someone handed out a roster and said, "If you need coffee, call here. If you need bandages, call the Red Cross." It was more like, "Okay, I need 500 pounds of coffee in an hour. Who can I call? Let's make this happen." And all by itself, this fragile little network began to weave itself alive.

We unloaded the Fiddlesticks hoard at the West Side Highway, and the people in charge said, "Oh my God! This is amazing! And the sandwiches are labeled!"

Trucks were coming down the West Side Highway, and a lot of the guys on board were reporting to the Ground Zero site for the first time.[61] They didn't know what kind of ad hoc services were available to them, so we had to make hospitality part of our repertoire.

---

61 For months after September 11, the West Side Highway became the main conduit to shuttle rescue and recovery workers in and out of Ground Zero.

We'd rush up to a truck and say, "How many guys do you have and what do you need?"

You didn't want to make them roll down their windows if they didn't have to; the air was pretty bad, and we wanted to protect them. A lot of volunteers were wearing masks. So you learned to speak a quick, bastardized form of sign language. *Water. Eat. Mask.*

Someone might sign back to us: *Four masks. Three waters. Two sandwiches.* We would collect everything in an armload and tap on the window. They'd roll down the window, we'd throw the supplies in, and they'd roll it right back up.

>>><<<

After a couple more hours, someone approached the supply camp and said, "Hey, there's another pick-up at this location. We've got lots of stuff over here that you can use." But we still had food we weren't going to be able to use that night, and we were upset our store would go bad because we weren't going to be able to refrigerate it.

The guy in the van was still driving around, so I corralled him and said, "Let's bring some of our food over to the Armory," which was where they were starting to bring relatives of the missing to get them processed and collect DNA samples.[62] Off we went.

It was a nightmare over there. Security was thick as thieves, and the cops weren't letting anyone in.

They asked, "Do you have identification?"

I said, "Yeah."

"Who are you with?"

And I had to say, "I'm a New Yorker. Look in the back of the van. Sandwiches. Here's what we have."

Basically, they had to take it all on good faith, and they did. I couldn't get angry at anyone; I knew they were just trying to do their job in a situation that changed every ten minutes. "Let volunteers in.

---

62 Located on 26th and Lexington Avenue. The Armory became the site where thousands of desperate family members filled out detailed, nine-page missing persons reports to assist in the search for survivors. Lexington Avenue became wallpapered with homemade posters showing the faces of missing persons with heartbreaking descriptions.

No! Don't let volunteers in. Check them. Okay, only let them in if they're Red Cross or Salvation Army." I understood. It was a very difficult situation.

So I just said, "Okay. Why don't you tell me what you need and then I'll give it to you." I was trying to be patient, but it was really frustrating. The traffic, for instance. To go two city blocks, it sometimes took half an hour.

>>>>><<<<<

At the Armory, the authorities rattled off a list of what they wanted and we said, "Really? Great. We've got all that. Food, toiletries, socks, and bottled water."

It took them aback, but they said, "Well . . . okay! Great!"

Some of the workers came outside and started grabbing things, but I said, "It actually works faster if we make a daisy chain and hand things off. You guys know where the supplies should go and I don't. Plus, we don't want to get in your way. Can we try it my way?"

They did, because my way was easier on security. No unauthorized people went into the building.

So we set up the daisy chain. I remember there were three or four Japanese tourists standing outside. They'd obviously been in town during the attack and at one point, they started taking pictures. I stopped for a second and looked at them. Then I said, "You can take pictures or you can put your cameras down and help."

Someone had to translate for them, but when they understood what I said, they put their cameras down and moved in to lend a hand.

That was the attitude I started developing. You could gawk at all this and you could say, "Wow, shit's fucked up, man! Look at what's happened to our city. It's crazy, man! Isn't it weird?" People were walking around on the streets with cell phones talking like this, trying to give their friends eyewitness accounts. Or you could be a part of it instead of watching it happen to other people. You could say, "Here's how I got to know someone who I'd never spoken to before. Here's how I pitched in and became part of the solution." Wouldn't that be a more extraordinary story to tell?

It was shocking to me how some people couldn't understand that attitude or outright elected to take the other stance. I thought, my God. Look at how this one event has brought out the best, the worst, and the strangest in people.

⁂

After the Armory, we were driving past one of the blockades on 14th Street, which, at that point, was still the official DMZ. We were trying to make our way back to the West Side Highway, but we got detoured. Looking back, I know all this happened on Wednesday the twelfth or maybe Thursday the thirteenth. Around this point, I honestly began to lose track of time.

On 14th Street, there were great crowds of people standing by stockpiles of donations. They didn't have any idea where to bring their donations, so they'd brought them as far south as they could before running into security. I saw piles of fruit, batteries, bottled water, and junk food that stood twelve feet high. There were all sorts of nonperishable goods stacked in blocks, too: blankets, flashlights, pick-axes, helmets, goggles, saline solution, band-aids, medical supplies. Most of the goods looked like stuff that people had donated from their jobs, but there also seemed to be a lot that people must have literally gone out and collected. "Does anyone have any socks? I'm putting together a basket of socks." The quality of goods ranged from factory-fresh items to second-hand.

We drove past this and I remember sayin', "Oh. My. God." It was . . . it was unbelievable.

Then a state trooper stopped us and asked if we needed to go below. I tried to explain that we'd just brought stuff over to the Armory, we didn't have any sort of official ID, we were just trying to get back to the West Side Highway so we could pick up more food and make some more shipments.

I nodded toward the giant stacks of donated goods and said, "What's going to happen to all of this stuff?"

The trooper said, "I don't know. We need someone to bring it down to Ground Zero, but no one has clearance."

"Well, what do you need to get it down there?" There's nothing I hate more than waste. I was looking at all this stuff piled up and thinking, we have a van but we don't have clearance. What do we need to make this equation work?

The trooper's name was Tim and he came from upstate New York. He was this big, heavyset guy, and he said, "I'll drive down with you. I can get anywhere. I'll just show my badge."

"You'd do that?"

He looked around. "They don't really need me here. They've got enough guys guarding this place."

So I said, "All right. Let's load her up."

We opened up the back doors and I stood in the back of the van, because it was the only way I'd be tall enough to talk and have people see me. I called out, "Can I have everybody's attention? We can get all of this stuff down to the site."

People cheered. "Yeah! Great! Excellent!"

I said, "What we're gonna do is try to put all the items in together in a way that's clear and easy to dispense when we get down there." I didn't know what kind of mess it was going to be at the site. "We're gonna do shoes and boots first. Find all your shoes and boots and we'll put those in the far corners of the van. After that, I want clothing items—all clothing items go in the back, then medical items next. Bottled water and emergency medical supplies toward the end so we can unload it in order."

This way, if someone else had to help us unpack, at least there'd be a layout to the van. Boots are here, helmets are there, pick-axes here, gloves and *da da da da da*. And if anyone needed med supplies right away, I wanted it in easy reach.

So we started calling out types of material, and the load commenced. I'd yell out, "Now we're doing batteries. Now we're doing flashlights." And there were twenty people or so who looked through everything and started calling out in response, "I've got batteries. Do you have batteries? Okay. All the batteries are done. Now we're doing helmets."

We loaded it all up and headed toward Ground Zero. I was sitting up on top of the equipment in the back. Tim and the driver were up front.

⇛⇚

It took us a long time to make it downtown, because we were stopped at every checkpoint. Tim had to show his badge each time and say, "I'm bringing them down. We've got all this stuff for the rescue effort." And we'd have to open the doors so security personnel could take a look. Apart from that, though, no problems.

As we got further and further down Manhattan Island, there were less people but more checkpoints, and a lot more smoke. It got blacker as we went down. The effect was as if, little by little, everyone in this part of the city had said, "Okay, on this block, ten people: turn out your lights. On this block: twenty people. On the next block: fifty people turn out your lights." We were literally sucked into a black hole.

We weren't stopping for red lights because there *were* no red

Liberty Park Plaza, directly across from the WTC, became a staging area for rescue operations. For a while, the Brooks Brothers menswear store was impressed into service as a morgue.

lights. In fact, there was no traffic at all. Occasionally, we'd run into a fire engine parked across the street and we might have to wait for it to move. Or we'd wait for rescue services to go through. Whenever that happened, I'd ask the van driver, "Do we have thirty seconds?" If I heard him say, "Yeah," I'd hop out with my respirator on, a big, plastic full-face mask, and I'd run along the line of fire trucks and ambulances.

These people—they'd obviously been down there since the beginning. They were exhausted. They had holes for eyes. They were smoking inside the cars and trucks, and a couple guys would always be asleep in the back, holding on to each other as they slept.

I'd run up to each one and tap on the window. I'd mime: *Water? Face masks? Food?* They'd nod and I'd do the sign for *how many?* The numbers came back: *one, two, three.* I'd run back to the van to pull their order.

At this point, you could feel the dust that permeated everything, making the air thicker. I had to stop often and wipe stuff out of my eyes. I was only wearing a tank top and jeans; I never thought I'd get that far south. I was completely unprepared.

When I'd collected their order, I'd go back to the rescue workers' vehicles and throw it in through their windows. Same routine as before: roll down the window, throw it all in, roll it back up. I worked the line. I would do about a dozen cars and trucks at every stop, and then go back to the van. We'd start moving and I'd use the downtime to load myself up again. Then, the moment we stopped, I'd repeat the process, approaching cop cars and fire trucks. Same thing: *Food? Water? Masks? Eye drops?*

We developed hand signals for everything. At one point, someone said, "Do you have any aspirin?"

I mimed like this: *Headache?*

It got to be so I was like a flight attendant. Whatever they needed, I got them.

⫸⫷

The thing that struck me most is how I would hand somebody something and they'd always say thank you. And I would say thank you back. No one in three weeks ever said you're welcome, I guess because none of us felt worthy of what everyone else was doing.

The firefighters were like, "Listen, we have to be here. But you don't. You're giving up your lives and your families to be here. Thank you for that."

But I was like, "I'm handing out medical supplies and sandwiches. I'm not doing anything. You're down on your hands and knees picking up bodies. You're picking up pieces. I hand you a cup of coffee and you say thank you to *me*? Please stop."

That was when I realized how we'd entered a different culture. Nothing was normal. The usual manners didn't apply. The situation could bring out things in you that you never knew were there, both good things and bad. A lack of patience, for instance, or an extreme reserve of patience. Or ingenuity. Or organizational ability.

I was astonished to see what came out of me and what came out of other people. Especially when we got to the Pit.

»»»«««

How can I describe it? Huge bales of smoke. Shit everywhere. It was so dark you couldn't see, despite the emergency lights they'd hung up everywhere. All of Lower Manhattan was painted black. No light permeated the gloom except for the beams of wandering flashlights or the headlights of your car. No televisions were heard along the streets. No salsa music blaring from somebody's car stereo. There was nothing. It was as if someone had literally burned up New York and painted everything—the buildings, the sidewalks, the gutters, the sky—black, and people were walking around with candles.

Down there, it was all pretty much rescue and relief workers with badges and walkie-talkies. Everyone had big boots on. I remember thinking, I'm gonna get thrown out of here really quickly, I'm obviously not supposed to be here so I'd better do my job fast.

We pulled the van up. I honestly can't tell you where we were because I wasn't really looking. Geography had ceased to mean much down there—everything had changed so much. Already, we found supply piles lined up on the sidewalk: boots in size order, helmets, and axes. Someone had set it up so that, if you needed anything, you didn't have to go inside a building; you just dropped your old gear, picked up what you needed, and went back down to the Pit.

We started unloading our haul. A couple of people came over and asked Tim, since he was a state trooper, "Who's in charge here?"

He pointed at me and said, "This little girl right here."

I was like, I am? My mask was covering my face and I felt really funny. I think I said something like, "Hi." The looks everyone gave me weren't supportive. But then I thought, hey! What have I been doing for the past day and a half? I have to show them I can do this. So I took a deep breath and said, "Okay. Here's what we have." And I ticked through the list of supplies in the van. "How do you want us to unload it?"

"We'll get you some help." And they brought over a bunch of guys.

Guys. That was the moment I realized that it was really all men down at the site. So few women, except for a handful—rescue workers, mostly, and ambulance drivers and some police officers. At least from what I saw, it was the Planet of No Women. Some sort of sci-fi movie where everyone female had been bombed out of Manhattan and only the men had stayed behind.

⟫⟫⟪⟪

We unloaded everything, then Tim said he had to get back up to 14th Street. The van driver said he had to get back home, too, but he'd bring me back to the West Side Highway or wherever I wanted. I said I'd like to have a moment to quietly pay my respects before we left.

Of course, by now, everyone's seen the site on television, but very few people have actually been that close. I stood at the base of Ground Zero, ten feet away from where the rubble began. The remains of the building, the façade, jutted up like big pick-up sticks. There was so much activity going on around it, like a noisy beehive. And yet there was also a sense of quiet, sort of like a drone. A background noise that drowned out everything else.

I stood there for a good, long moment because I knew that, in a little while, it wouldn't look like that anymore. And I kept trying to understand the weight of it, what it all meant. It was the kind of thing you can't really write down or explain to someone else. I wanted to take a mental picture, which is what I do in situations when I know a photograph will never capture a moment. I literally look at something for a couple of seconds and then close my eyes. I did this.

Before I left, I also asked Tim if I could have my photograph taken with him. Not a celebratory picture: "This is us at Ground Zero." He'd been showing me pictures of his wife and his kids, and I wanted him to have something to show his family when he returned. So I took a picture of the two of us standing by a fire truck. There was already a sense that "you don't take pictures down here" permeating the air. I got that unspoken vibe very quickly. For some people on 9/11, snapping pictures was like going after big game, but not at the Pit. I explained to Tim that I didn't want a picture of the site. "I want a picture of you. Because I want to remember your face and what you did."

I took our photo, very low-key, and then I put my camera away.

⟫⟫⟪⟪⟪

We drove back to the West Side Highway and I checked in with everyone at the volunteer stations. I told them their deliveries had gotten where they needed to go and everyone was greatly relieved. By now, they had shifts of people working for a couple of hours all through the evening. Essentially, they had a round-the-clock operation going and I said to myself, okay. Time to take a break. I need to go home and absorb this.

I walked from 8th Avenue all the way over to 1st and caught the L train back to Brooklyn.

When I got home, I called Sue and told her what I'd been doing. She said, "Well, if you're really into this, I hear the relief services further over on

"The remains of the building, the façade, jutted up like big pick-up
sticks. There was so much activity going on around it, like a noisy
beehive. And yet there was also a sense of quiet, sort of like a drone.
A background noise that drowned out everything else."

Chambers Street could use some help. Let's go down together
tomorrow."

"Fine."

The next day, I was more prepared. I understood, for instance,
that my clothes were going to get destroyed, so I wore a crappy
watch—an old one I wouldn't care so much about if it got scuffed up.
I brought a cell phone, too. Instead of a bag, I wore a pair of camouflage pants that had pockets where I could put identification, cash, an
ATM card, my house keys, eye drops. And I think that's what really

did the trick, those camouflage pants. When Sue and I approached the barricades on Chambers Street, the military men positioned there saw me and waved me right in. I must have been a novelty for them.

Sue's a model, by the way. She's tall and blonde and has no trouble getting in anywhere she wants to go.

⇛⇚

From Chambers, we walked over to Stuyvesant High School, where most of the relief services were stationed. A school crossing guard was pulling security at the front door, stopping everyone and asking for ID. She wasn't doing a very good job, though; Sue and I walked right on in and she started chasing us. "Hey! Hey!" We went down some hallways and hid until she gave up trying to find us.

Stuyvesant High had essentially become base command for non-medical relief services at Ground Zero. By the time we arrived that morning, organizers had already determined that medical supplies would be on the first floor; chiropractors, short-term sleep beds, and massage tables would sprawl out on the balcony. The second floor had a clothing and cantina area for food in a triangular-shaped locker area, and more cots for short-term sleep. The next floor up had classrooms where you could go in, close a door and get long-term sleep. The locker rooms and showers were all stocked up with grooming supplies—towels, soap, shampoo—ready for use.

Basically, it worked like this: any rescue worker who'd been out on the Pile could come in, swap out all his gear, get a chiropractic adjustment, talk to a therapist, eat, grab a cup of coffee, and take a nap. We set the place up to facilitate an assembly line process. "We'll put the counseling center over here so they can get coffee and eat, then go talk to someone and take a nap. Put all that on one floor." We wanted to make things easy for the workers because we found that it took tremendous inspiration for them to climb a simple flight of stairs. They were too exhausted. If only we could've relocated the showers! As it turns out, they were up on one of the higher floors, and we really had to plug them heavily to get workers to use them. Everything else was situated as low as possible to promote accessibility.

⫸⫷

When Sue and I walked in that first day, Stuyvesant High was very disorganized, a really haphazard system. There were no official directions to anything—more like paper plates taped to walls on which someone had written "FOOD ON 2" with a magic marker.

I went up to the second floor and found piles of boxes, garbage bags, shopping bags, and crates jumbled all over the place. I had no idea where they'd come from. There were a couple of card tables in the middle of the room and a couple of round picnic tables off in one corner. It looked like a ramshackle AA meeting-slash-tornado relief camp.

A woman was taking a break at one of the picnic tables. She looked as if she'd been through the wringer. So I introduced myself and said, "I'm here in case you need help."

She said, "Okay. Well. Workers basically come in and get what they need to eat, and then they go back down."

I saw some aluminum-and-steel shelving racks that had probably been rolled up from the cafeteria standing against one wall, and said, "Um, how 'bout if I organize this for you?" I figured we could use the racks to store things so that, at a glance, we could see what we were almost out of. "I could make this work nicely."

She said, "Hey, if you want to do that? Yeah. Great."

Basically, I'd given myself a job.

⫸⫷

It took two hours for the place to look like D'Agostino's.[63] I used my own system and organized things according to categories in case we needed to put together shipments for Ground Zero: this many of this thing, this many of that thing, and so forth.

When the supervisor's shift ended, she said, "Okay, I'm going home. How long are you staying?"

---

63 A popular upscale, full-service supermarket in Manhattan.

I said, "I don't know, I thought I'd work for about six hours. I'm not really tired yet, I'll just keep going."

"All right," she said, and started out.

I said, "Oh. Ah. Wait. Who's the next, you know, supervisor in charge?"

She said, "I don't know. But they should be here shortly."

"Oh. All right. I'll just . . . try to keep everything rolling."

It was kind of quiet now, around eleven o'clock. And no one ever came. Seventy-two hours later, I was running the place, the person in charge of all food services. I thought, how difficult could this be?

〉〉〉〈〈〈

Very soon, I had volunteers showing up asking me, "Do you need help?"

"Yeah," I'd say. "You can start over there."

The Guardian Angels came in and we put them on duty in the pantry.[64] We stored all the stuff we'd need during the next four hours on the ground floor; long-term storage was upstairs in the cafeteria's walk-in coolers. We'd lost power on the lower floors, so in order to keep drinks cold, we had to get big garbage cans, line them with plastic, and fill them with ice.

I put one of the Angels in charge of making coffee, which sounds like a menial task but it was actually a huge undertaking. Water had to be heated in huge vats that took from one to four hours to boil. We worked up a system where we'd heat four vats simultaneously in staggered stages so that one vat would be ready each hour.

Sue worked with me for a few hours that first evening at Stuyvesant, then she went home. She came back the next day to put in a few hours more and said, "You're still here?"

I said, "Yeah. Listen. I need . . ." And I rattled off my wish list.

By that point, we'd pretty much figured out what the main problem was. There was no real shortage of supplies; people from around the country were making massive donations. Food was largely being

---

64 The Guardian Angels are a volunteer urban watch patrol.

stockpiled at the Chelsea Market. Medicine, clothing, sundries, construction equipment, and so forth were being collected at other sites
like the Javits Center, Pier 40, and a few others. Each site was run
by volunteer crews who were doing a great job, but who all faced the
same essential problem: how to get all the goods they were stockpil-
ing past the security blockades and into Ground Zero.

So we solved that problem. In the first couple days after the attack, we developed a sort of hourglass pattern by encouraging all the
stockpile sites to ship their goods to Stuyvesant High. From there,
thanks to our proximity, we could warehouse it for incoming relief
workers or redistribute it as needed to satellite areas around the perimeter of Ground Zero. The redistribution system was especially
necessary, because a lot of workers couldn't make the journey a few
blocks uptown to Stuyvesant. They were that tired.

»»×«««

Shuttles started coming in from the perimeter sites. A lot of people drove up to the high school in Gators—those little military golf
carts? They'd dismount and approach us, saying, "Hey, I'm EMS services from blah blah blah and I need socks," or "I'm from this site and
I need thirty sandwiches, thirty bottles of Gatorade, eye drops, and
gloves."

"Okay." I'd assign them a volunteer and say, "Take them shopping."

Whatever you needed, you came to Stuyvesant. Like I said, I was
in charge of food and this girl, Karen, who's a very well-known fashion stylist, took charge of clothing. All the bags and bales of clothing
that came to Stuyvesant got handled by Karen and her teams. They
took over individual classrooms and laid them out like wholesale outlets. T-shirts here, sweatshirts there, sweatpants and underwear in
the next room, and so forth. Everything got organized on racks by
order of size. Shoes were set out in rows with size numbers taped
on the bottom and laces tied together. Essentially, we'd created the
Walmart of tragedy.

⟫⟫⟫⧏⧏⧏

I remember walking one firefighter through the whole system. I was outside getting some air and he approached Stuyvesant, totally covered in debris, totally shell-shocked. I could see in his eyes that he couldn't make sense of anything, so I took his hand and said, "Hi. I'm Nicole. You've never been to Stuyvesant, have you?"

"No."

"Okay. Well. We have these services available to you." I ticked them off slowly so he could follow me. Then I said, "Why don't we get you a change of clothes, take you upstairs to the showers, and get you clean so you can get some rest. How much time do you have on your break?"

I had to help him make decisions, because he was long past that.

We got him up to Clothing, where incoming workers undressed and threw their old clothes into trash bags. We made no effort to clean them; clothes from the Pit were considered hazmat. We got this fireman into sweatpants so he could lounge around a bit and got him a stack of brand-new gear. By that point, Karen and her volunteer assistants had the routine down so pat. They could just ask you, "Size? Extra-large? Long-sleeve? You want jeans? How are your socks doing? Do you want something to sleep in? High boots, low boots, how do you like your boots? Underwear: briefs, boxers, boxer-briefs?"

The girls would run off and fill the order while the relief workers just stood there, dumbfounded.

The showers were laid out the same way. Single-serve portions of shampoos, soaps, washcloths, towels, eye drops, and deodorant were laid out in baskets, with a garbage can set up at the end of the line for when you were finished—you could just dump your trash and move on. The supplies were lined up to be immaculate, and every hour, I sent a volunteer to the bathrooms to straighten things up.

I said, "I don't want anyone to look at this place and frown. I want this to look like the Happy Delicatessen of Plenty. There is never to be one of any item left. If we only have one of something, take it off the table and hand it to someone because, if this is the last soup spoon, no one will take it."

They wouldn't take it because every relief worker thought that someone else deserved it more than they did. I saw this happen more than once. So there was never one toothbrush. Never one sandwich. Never one PowerBar. As soon as we saw our stock get lower than six of anything, we replenished.

⫸⫷

I often found myself asking workers, "Do you have time for a nap? Can you sleep for a couple of hours?" I would write Post-it notes reminding me of the time I was supposed to wake up volunteers dozing in the short-term sleep bay and stick the notes over their heads. Then I would set the timer on my cell phone for twenty minutes, twenty-five minutes, an hour and a half, and so forth. The timer would go off and I'd start down the line. "Barry, you said you wanted me to wake you up. Rhonda, how about it? You wanted me to wake you. Do you want to sleep a little more?"

Usually, they'd say, "No, no. I have to—I have to get up."

But sometimes I convinced them. "Look. Sleep for half an hour more. I'll come wake you up. Trust me."

In half an hour, these guys were so deep in dreams, it was hard to pull them out again. I didn't want to wake them, but I knew they'd be upset and wouldn't trust me anymore if I didn't. So I'd try to wake them like my mom used to wake me, really gently.

A lot of times, they wouldn't know where they were when they came to, and it was strange to have them look at me like they did. It broke my heart every time they'd open their eyes and realize it wasn't a dream. Sleep had been their escape. My job was to bring them back. It was so hard to do that.

⫸⫷

At one point, the Board of Education came in and said, "Do you want our lunch ladies to help you out?"

I said, "Why, yes. We would love to have your lunch ladies help us out."

It was getting to be absurd, all these people asking me what to do. But of course, the only people I ever mentioned that to were people like Sue. To everyone else it was, "We need 600 pounds of ice a day, three times a day, because I have no refrigeration. How can we make this work? To everyone else, I guess they saw that my food services team was putting out 3,000 to 6,000 meals every day, and they just said, "Okay. Guess she's got it under control. No questions asked."

I realized I'd really taken ownership of my system when, at one point, a police captain approached me about two weeks after the attacks and said, "'Scuse me, who's in charge here?"

I thought, oh jeez. That's it. I'm screwed.

But I raised my hand and said, "Me. Over here. I'm in charge."

He said, "Ma'am, my name is Captain So-and-So. I want to bring some of my officers in for breakfast. They're relieving a number of officers who've been here a few weeks, but we've never been down to the site before. I wanted to find out about your outfit. How many of my people can you handle all at once, for instance? We've got 600 on our team. How would you like us to stagger their meal shifts?"

I was stunned. But instead of going, holy shit! He's asking me! I thought, bluff! Bluff!

I said, "Six hundred's too many all at once, but we can comfortably handle 100 to 120. If we stagger them in twenty-minute eating shifts, I think that might work."

He said, "All right. We'll do it by hundreds. We'd like to take six of your shifts."

Just like that, we had a reservation. Breakfast for 600.

⫸⫷

We didn't have vitamins at Ground Zero early on, so I started buying them on my own. I would go into GNC and say, "What do you have?" and I'd buy the biggest Centrum maxi-container I could find, the $180 one. I'd get six of them.

Every time I talked to the people running the distribution sites, I always asked if they had vitamins and they'd say, "Hang on, let me see if we have that." They never did.

I made sure to go around the cafeteria tables to give workers their vitamins. A lot of guys didn't want to take their pill, so I'd make a game of it. "Okay. Who hasn't taken their vitamin today?"

"Well, I don't need one."

"I don't take those."

"Well," I'd say, "Centrum is complete, from A to Z. Complete with Vitamin V: Viagra!"

"Oh, I don't need that!"

"Oh, buddy," I'd hoot. "That's not what your wife said."

And everybody would go, "Ooooooooh!" But they would take their vitamins. After three days of this, they'd see me coming and go, "C'mon, Nicole. Gimme my vitamin, gimme my vitamin." And no one got sick on any of my shifts. I made sure they got antioxidants and milk thistle, which is very helpful for clearing out lungs and for

"At least from what I saw, [Ground Zero] was the Planet of No Women. Some sort of sci-fi movie where everyone female had been bombed out of Manhattan and only the men had stayed behind."

treating liver toxicity. There was so much crap in the air, it became a matter of doing anything we could to try and help the workers clear their lungs.

Eventually, I talked to a friend of mine who said, "What do you mean you're buying your own vitamins?"

I said, "I don't have time to spend running all over the city lobbying for multivitamins at supply distribution centers. I have to get back down to the site."

So my friend looked on some websites and found Whitehall-Robins, which manufactures Centrum. He called them and forwarded them some of the emails I'd been sending out, which described what I was doing and what we needed down at Stuyvesant. Then a representative from Whitehall-Robins called me and said, "I understand you need some vitamins. We've been trying to figure out how to make donations and we didn't now who to go through. What do you need?"

I said, "A truckload of Centrum. Right now."

She said, "What have you been doing?"

"Buying the big jugs. I don't know if you have the individual packets, but those would be a lot cheaper to hand out."

She said, "No problem. How many do you need?"

"Well, we're doing between three and six thousand meals a day. Probably two and a half thousand people for breakfast. I don't know how long we'll be at Stuyvesant, but if you send me ten thousand tablets, I'll tell you how long it lasts."

"Fine," she said. "No problem. What else do you need?"

"I don't know. What other products do you represent?"

"Oh. Well, we do Chapstick. We do this and we do that . . ."

God bless Whitehall-Robins. The next day, a truck came and I had a pallet of vitamins. From there, the word went out to Dr. Scholl's that we had all these boots but no insoles, and they sent over a truckload of those. I soon found out that corporate America would send us anything we needed; they just didn't know where we were and they didn't know who to contact. It wasn't like we had a site posted on the web that said, "Call Ground Zero, Incorporated at this number to contribute."

That's when I started calling ABC News and putting things on the little zipper tape that runs across the bottom of the TV screen. So very soon, everyone who watched television would see that we need Imodium. We no longer need bottled water, and we no longer need dog food.

People thought the search and rescue dogs were starving. Let me tell you—those dogs ate better than a lot of people do. And they don't eat normal dog food anyway, they eat specialized vitamin stuff—not Alpo off the shelves. We had, like, 5,000 pounds of dog food at Stuyvesant. That's a lot of dog food.

≫≫≪≪

The canteen upstairs at Stuyvesant started looking like a Costco. We had cans of fruit and vegetables, bottled water, cans of coffee, bales of rice—boxes and boxes and boxes of stuff.

I thought, what are we gonna do with all this? We had it stacked up in boxes so you could walk through with a hand truck and off-load whatever you needed.

We'd get a food donation from Pier 40 and the driver would say, "Where do you want it?"

"Fourth floor, please." The Guardian Angels were stationed upstairs and they knew where we needed everything. They'd take care of it.

It got to the point where we were self-sufficient. But it was still frustrating that we couldn't always get what we needed when we needed it. We never knew where things were coming from. Also, the distribution centers started to get shut down as time went on. Chelsea Piers Market was shut down first, and then I think Chelsea Piers, and then Javits. Pier 40 was last, I think.

Chelsea Food Markets needed to get back to business as usual; Chelsea Piers, too. As these sites shut down, we had less and less opportunities to get resources. Suddenly, I wouldn't have a source for coffee anymore. Or medical supplies.

We had phone lists ten pages long that read: "Bob: Coffee Guy" or "Mark: Soda Guy." "Rick: Ice Guy." If we figured out a person's specialty, we didn't need their last name. We had a phone number, and that was sufficient.

I'd call them: "Hey, it's Nicole at Stuyvesant."

"Right. What do you need?"

The whole network was done in shorthand, like CB handles. You didn't know any normal things about people on the list. Like: "Oh, Bob? Sure. He works in advertising. Five-nine. Dark hair. Tennis player." Nothing like that. He was Coffee Bob. There was Leo the Driver.

But as sites kept getting shut down, we had to find new ways to get supplies in from the outside. My friends were beginning to report things to me like, "We brought donations to this site, but there was no one there to receive it. Javits got rid of their receiving area to house the National Guard, who are sleeping on the floor."

Right around then, the DMZ contracted and moved from 14th Street to Canal. A little while after that, it pushed even further south to Chambers, and closer to us. Even still, a lot of donors found they couldn't get through the gates to resupply us.

⟫⟪

People across the city took up collections at their offices. They donated medical supplies, boots, clothing, and backpacks.

A friend of a friend passed along my emails to everyone he knew, adding commentary. "They have enough of this, they need more boots and in smaller sizes."

More women workers were starting to work at the site, but we had no sizes for women. Everything was in double-XL: old sweatshirts, T-shirts, sweatpants, anything like that. Anything that no one would be too upset about throwing away at the end of the day. Clean underwear and clean socks.

People were sending us old used stuff, and it's not that the thought wasn't appreciated. But if the underwear had skid marks, we had to say no.

≫≫✄≪≪

People started bringing supplies to the Church of Scientology in Midtown, and suddenly there were Scientology members all over the place at Stuyvesant. They all wore bright-yellow T-shirts. We called them "The Chickadees." Their shirts said, "Church of Scientology" and listed the organization's address and phone number on the back.

Someone explained to me that one of the tenets of Scientology is that you help in a disaster—everyone pitches in. They're apparently very well known for lending a hand at disaster sites. I didn't know this.

If a toilet was backed up, I could find a yellow T-shirt, hand them a plunger, and say, "Listen, I'm really sorry. The toilet's backed up."

They'd say, "I'd be happy to."

No job was too dirty or weird. It was just, "I'd be honored." And not in a rote, robotic, zoned-out religious way—"*I-would-love-to-clean-up-the-toilet-for-you-thank-you.*" They honestly seemed to feel it was a privilege to pitch in. I found that 98 percent of the Scientologists were a real pleasure to work with. They were so even-tempered and gracious, so calm and soothing to be around. Even at the height of craziness, of, "Oh my God! We don't have these items in supply!" They'd say, "Okay. Relax. I'll find out about it."

I owe them a lot. They had some pamphlets and some books with them, but they weren't pushing anything. They did a lot of nerve assists, which is where someone lies on a bed and a Scientologist traces the nerve endings across your back, arms, and legs. Just tracing through the nervous system to help soothe, calm, and relax someone. They would do this for five to ten minutes with folks who were jittery. They'd sit down and talk to you if you needed someone to talk to. Anything that needed to be done.

The Scientologists also solved our drop site problem by saying, "Why don't you have donations dropped at the Church? It's a secure location. When stuff comes in with your name on it, we'll call you. No, better yet, we'll send a driver to pick it up."

So that's what we started doing.

When everyone down at the site started asking for cigarettes, we started calling cigarette manufacturers. I had started buying them myself and asking friends to donate them. Finally, I called Phillip Morris. But ever since the lawsuit settlement, they're not allowed to give away cigarettes anymore, even for disaster sites.

I was adamant. "Guys. I understand you're not allowed to give away cigarettes in bars or high schools, but this is a disaster site. Come in and back up a fucking unmarked truck full of cigarettes. Who's gonna know?"

"Oh, no. We can't really. We really can't."

"I won't tell anyone where they came from, I promise. I'll just hand them out and say they were donated. I'll even say I paid for them myself. Just bring them down here. What's it gonna cost you?"

Well, they couldn't or they wouldn't do it, and neither would any of the other cigarette companies.

But a friend of mine orders his cigarettes from Tobacco By Mail, a website catalog where you can order your smokes in bulk—exotic brands, too, things you can't get at your local metropolitan chain stores. This friend put in a phone call and the next thing I knew, I was talking to a TBM representative who called me and said, "I understand you need cigarettes."

I said, "Yes, our workers request these three or four brands the most."

She asked, "How much do you need?"

"We're going through ten to fifteen cartons a day. I can't tell you what to do. But if you want to donate a certain amount, I'll let you know how long it lasts. Then I can call you in a few days and, if you want to donate again, it's entirely up to you."

She sent me a crate packed with all different brands, something like 100 to 150 cartons. Tobacco By Mail could donate because they're a catalog company—a reseller, not a manufacturer.

Friends of mine were saying, "I want to pitch in. I want to donate something but I can't take time off from work. I have nothing that could be of use. What can I do?"

I said, "Can you pitch in five bucks for a pack of cigarettes?" Everybody could do that. I emailed everyone: "Ask all your friends who smoke if they can buy a carton of cigarettes. Put the cartons in a duffle bag or a milk crate and give me a call when it's full, and we'll send someone over to pick it up."

⧽⧽⧼⧼

A few gals who worked in the art department at *Martha Stewart Living* put together backpacks, because they knew we needed packs to transport stuff. We had to have thick bags to keep things inside clean. Open bags gathered too much contamination.

These gals asked every staffer to bring their old duffle bags to the office. Then they packed the bags with clothes and toiletries—Martha has raised these girls well. They put little American ribbons on every bag with notes next to them that said, "Good luck. We're with you—*Martha Stewart Living*."

I wept. I don't even think Martha knew that her art department did that.

Cleopatra Records send down a big duffle bag full of CDs. They said, "We don't know what else we can donate, but if some of those guys might need something to listen to, give them these." They sent major labels. So I was handing out John Cougar Mellencamp, P.O.D., and an awful lot of Bon Jovi. Anyone from Jersey got a Jon Bon Jovi CD.

⧽⧽⧼⧼

During my first seventy-two-hour shift, I hardly stepped foot outside Stuyvesant. After that, I tried to make sure I got fresh air at least twice a day, but I was afraid to leave the site because I didn't know if I'd be able to get back in. Security protocols changed so quickly that, even if you knew the cops at a checkpoint or the Army or whoever it was—even if you recognized them by sight, six hours later someone else would be in charge. The Air Force in charge. Police. Marines. It was crazy.

I'm pretty sure the head of FEMA told me at one point that there were seventeen different government agencies involved at Ground Zero, including all branches of the military, the police, OEM, FEMA, the works. Communication within these organizations is difficult enough. But imagine having basically every American security relief volunteer and military outfit on active duty at once. It was amazing anything happened at all.

It was particularly frustrating for us because we repeatedly heard people say, "No, you don't have clearance. I don't know who you are. No." I would send runners down to the site where the food deliveries were coming in, who would never come back. We were hemorrhaging volunteers, which is one reason we all ended up sleeping at the site. We didn't have passes, and if we left the building, we'd be unable to return. After three weeks, we were down to a skeleton crew.

Right outside the building, we had this little smoking area where everyone would hang out on their breaks, chatting and drinking bottles of water. I remember I was there at one point and starting to hallucinate from fatigue. I looked at my watch, which said three o'clock, and thought, wow, the lunch rush was kind of quiet today. Huh.

It took me a while to realize it was pitch-black outside. It wasn't three o'clock in the afternoon; it was three o'clock in the morning.

Working at Stuyvesant was like working in a casino. No windows, bad lighting, and all the clocks had stopped.

➤➤➤◀◀◀

Without realizing it was happening, I began to feel the stress take hold of me. At one point, I said to a young volunteer, "I need a break, can you keep things going?" I walked outside to Chambers Street, where at first I started shaking. Then I broke down crying. A couple of the guys I'd become close to—I was feeding them three times a day—came up to me and asked, "What's going on?"

I was way past my limit. I knew what had to be done and my brain wanted to do it, my heart wanted to do it, but the body couldn't.

So the triangle broke down, totally exhausted. At the same time, I was stuck. There was nobody to hand everything off to.

A Sergeant Gaita from the Marine Corps was in charge of passes at that point. They'd set up their security headquarters in a little war room tent across the street from the school. The place was a tangle of maps laid out on tables, secure phone lines snaking all over the place, computer terminals, the works. These friends of mine who saw me break down escorted me into this tent, which petrified me. I knew I'd totally dissolved, and I knew this couldn't look good. But all I could do was weep and think, I've lost my shit and they're not gonna let me back in. Get a grip! It was like when you come home drunk to your parents and you try to sober up really quick.

Sergeant Gaita gave me a hard look and said, "What do you need?"

I said, "I need to get my people back on the site. I need to put together viable shifts so that we can have humane, sensible conditions for the volunteers. I've been here so long because I can't find anyone to hand this off to. You're locking out all my good people."

He said, "Our first concern is you. We don't want you messed up. We want you to go home and rest up."

He was talking to me a little patronizingly, like you'd talk to a crazy person. And I guess I can understand. From their point of view, I was just this crazy civilian who was working too hard. But the NYPD and the fire department guys told the soldier, "You don't understand. If she's not here, we don't eat. Give her whatever she needs. If it wasn't for these people . . . please."

So they handed me forty all-access colored, numbered passes, and I had to give them the names, phone numbers, and social security numbers of every volunteer who received one. The volunteers would have to show their passes as they came into the site. If their name didn't match the list, they'd be taken away, and it was my ass. I only gave them out to the most trusted workers we had, and whoever was in charge of a department at Stuyvesant got a couple of passes to do likewise.

I said, "If you smuggle someone in, we all lose our passes. Do you understand this?" Everyone did, and that was that. The situation was going to work out.

Sergeant Gaita handed me the forty passes and said, "Okay. You have twenty minutes to hand these out and then we're escorting you home. You can't come back for eight hours. Get some rest."

"What are you talking about?" They were treating me like a crazy person again.

He said, "Look. We need you here. If you break down, there's no one else to keep the machine going. You have to sleep."

That's when I realized that they understood what I was doing. I'd become a very important idiot savant.

I walked back across the street to Stuyvesant with the passes, and some friends of mine there were like, "Hey, Nicole. How's it going?"

The police officers on either side of me said, "She can't talk to you right now, she's got to get some paperwork done and after that, we're escorting her home." They wouldn't let me carry my own backpack. "No, ma'am," they said. "We've got it." They escorted me to the ladies' room and stood outside the door. They put me into a squad car and drove me back to Brooklyn. One of the cops knew my neighborhood and said, "We'll drop you off on the corner. We don't want your parents to get worried."

I said, "How old do you think I am?" I didn't have any makeup on or anything. They thought I was nineteen.

I took a shower and really slept. And then I went back down to the site. I spent many more overnight shifts there, twenty-four and forty-eight-hour shifts. It's what needed to be done.

⟫⟪

One of the things I learned working at Stuyvesant? What's essential and what wasn't. Laundry and getting your hair cut aren't important. Neither is cleaning your house or cooking. Shopping, reading, watching television. Keeping up on your email. Going out to museums, going out to shows. Seeing your friends, putting on makeup. Not important.

Every morning before going back down to the site, I'd re-assess things while getting dressed. Should I wear rings? No. Unimportant. A watch? Important. Nail polish? Not important. Nail file? Important—I don't have particularly long nails, but if they got in the way, you'd cut them off. Hair barrette or a rubber band, get the hair out of the way, pull the bangs back. Is this jacket important? Yes, it warms me and protects me. A notebook? Not really. A cell phone? Yes. Everything had to earn a place in my pockets or my bag. It became an exercise in "what can I lose?"

Must call my mother every other day. Must put quarters in my pocket in case I need change for a pay phone. Must have eye drops. Must carry Vaseline for my cut-up hands. I'd think, yesterday, we were running out of pens—let me grab some of those, and ziplock baggies for people who went through the food lines and didn't know when they'd be back. "Take some more," I could say, and hand them a bag. "Take some for one of your pals who doesn't have the energy to walk up to Stuyvesant, and give it to them."

I started opening up the different pockets on their uniforms and shoving in PowerBars, eye drops, vitamins, Imodium, sunblock, candy bars, anything I could get in there so they'd have it down at the site. The rescue workers would protest and say, "No, no. I don't need it. Really." But they'd come back later on, saying, "I handed everything out, do you have any more?"

I also found myself getting very frustrated with people who weren't at the site. People who were doing things that now seemed trivial to me. "I'm gonna do brunch. I'm gonna go to the library. I'm gonna go walk the dog."

Walk the dog? You're kidding, right? Hold the dog out the window and squeeze it's ass. Figure out a better system for walking the dog, and that's half an hour you can use to feed someone.

Most of all, I had to learn to recognize that not everyone functioned the way I did. Not everyone thought it was important to help. At one point, I saw a young family going out to a restaurant on a Sunday morning in Lower Manhattan, and I thought, my God. That's what a person *should* be doing. But I honestly didn't know how they did it.

Friends from all over the country would call me, the only person in Manhattan they knew; they were trolling me for experience. They wanted to pick out the pearls and live vicariously. That way, they could call their own friends and say, "Did you hear about Nicole working at Ground Zero? Did you hear about the guy who came into her place to eat after picking up human hands?" Like it was the biggest party of the year, and since they couldn't get in, they wanted to say they knew someone who was there. It infuriated me, so I stopped talking to them.

I feel the same way when people go down to Ground Zero now, as if it's a tourist attraction. I can understand how people want to go down to see it, to understand it, to pay their respects. But then I heard from a friend of mine in California who was coming to town. I said, "What are you gonna do while you're here?"

"Oh, it's gonna be great. I'm gonna get my hair cut, I'm gonna go do yoga, I'm gonna go to Ground Zero, I'm going to the MOMA, and I'm having dinner with so-and-so . . ."

Great. You've just dismissed one of the most profound experiences this country has ever had. I hope they go down there, glib and giddy, and get the shit scared out of them by the words still etched in the dust of the buildings all around the site.

"God help us."

"Pray for us."

"This way to the Morgue."

There's a shadow history on this city that might never go away.

❧

We were finally running efficiently and we still hadn't seen anyone from FEMA or OEM. No one ever popped in and said, "How can we help?"

I'd taken to staying over at the site again. Why not? We had our own little city with clothes, beds, showers, food, a radio with batteries—everything you needed. If you brought a cell phone charger down with you, you could basically run the country from there. It was easier, psychologically, to stay there rather than to get distracted by the outside world. You got more done.

We never knew how long it would go on. A campaign of Chinese whispers began: "I heard we're gonna get ousted today." "No, I heard tomorrow." "Should we order more coffee?" "Should we order more water?" "They're changing the color of the passes again. Yellow, then red. Then I hear they're moving into blue."

Finally, the powers that be ordered a shutdown at Stuyvesant. Rumor had it that one of our senators had a daughter who was a student there and didn't like being bussed to another location. They wanted to turn the school back into a school and move all the relief services to a big cruise ship over on the waterfront. But we had millions of dollars' worth of supplies in there, and I wanted to know what was going to be done with it.

I was told, "Sanitation's coming tomorrow and will throw it all out."

"No, no, no!" I said. "Give me three days. We'll find people to take it."

They gave us the days. We called every homeless shelter and church, every volunteer organization, soup kitchen, and volunteer ambulance corps we could think of and told them, "Make an appointment, come on down, bring your vans, and shop. Take whatever you want." We gave the food supplies to the school as thanks for hosting us, and found homes for about 95 percent of the stuff we had.

While we were packing everything up, the head of FEMA finally came in, a huge man with huge hands. He seemed very sweet. The heads of the police and fire departments were with him.

He said this to me: "Wow, you guys really filled a gap. You've done an amazing job." It turned out that no one had ever stopped in on us because they thought we were an official organization, like the Red Cross.

"Well," I said, "I'd like to take you on a tour so we can show you what we've been doing."

I started doing a walk-and-talk. "And here we have the Beverage Center. You can get a trolley here and take what you like. Just sign here because we need to know your name and phone number so we know which deliveries went where. Now, if you'll follow me downstairs . . ."

I wasn't looking, but Karen, who'd run the clothing department, said, "I wish you could have seen the look on the FEMA director's face. He couldn't believe it." Apparently, he'd run the Oklahoma City operation, and he couldn't believe how we'd organized the Clothing Center, the kitchen, the sleeping bays, the Massage Floor.

When we were finished, he turned to us and said, "This is the most impressive volunteer operation I've ever seen. I have to thank you, and the mayor will be congratulating you, trust me."

I never heard from him again. But in all honesty? That doesn't matter one bit.

UPDATE

Within a week of September 11, 2001, the EPA issued an "all clear" to the citizens of Lower Manhattan. Essentially, EPA said that no toxic chemicals existed in the air or water as a result of the Towers falling. This report was directly contradicted by several leading independent firms whose instrumentation showed levels of mercury, lead, benzene, silicon, sulfates, and other hazardous materials that literally went off the charts.

The students of Stuyvesant High School, where Nicole Blackman worked, were asked to resume classes at the facility on October 9, 2001, despite the fact that fires still smoldered nearby and workers in hazmat suits were busy carting debris away from the school premises. Similar situations occurred in nearby schools PS/IS 89 and PS 234.

Life went on.

In the fall of 2006, however, a group of Stuyvesant High School students and alumni held a press conference with Manhattan Borough President Scott Stringer. The group demanded that the federal government admit it had misled minors regarding potential health concerns present in Lower Manhattan in the immediate wake of the 9/11 attacks. A petition was presented that had been signed by more than 170 Stuyvesant alums requesting a federally sponsored health program of screenings, treatment, and insurance for former Stuyvesant students.

Stringer took the stand and testified that the Stuyvesant Parents' Association had heard from 400 Stuyvesant alums who reported suffering from unusual first-time illnesses. These illnesses included, but were not limited to, sinus infections, worsened allergies, bronchitis, asthma, and the so-called "WTC cough." One student had even been diagnosed with Hodgkin's lymphoma and believed that his disease was caused by exposure to toxic dust at Stuyvesant High.

To date, the federal government has not responded.

TONY RASEMUS

Tony Rasemus, fifty-four, served two years as a marine in Vietnam. A lifelong resident of New York City, Tony has learned many skills over the years: he trained in ironworking and construction and volunteered his skills at Ground Zero the day after the attack on September 11.[65]

Tony is a wiry man with a bristling reddish mustache and unstoppable energy. He frequently leaps to his feet in order to re-enact the scenes he describes. He pantomimes how he lifted rubble with his hands, and illustrates the proper posture for crawling into a debris cavity.

THAT FIRST DAY, I went to volunteer down at the Javits Center and nothing was organized.[66] There must have been 10,000 people from all walks of life. People wearing shorts and sandals . . . I don't know what they were thinking. That's totally inappropriate clothes for rescue work. They had various tables set up for construction workers, ironworkers, riggers. I said, "Where do you want me to go?"

"Go over there. They're taking names."

I saw a couple of guys hanging around with tool belts; I had my Carhartts with me.[67] So I went toward them. My wife had gone down with me. She was trying to find a place to give blood. She said, "Do you want me to hang out with you for a while?"

I said, "Nah, I don't know. This might take a while." So we said goodbye.

She wasn't gone five minutes before we got loaded onto a bus—a variety of guys—and it was *zip!* Right into Ground Zero.

---

65 Iron and construction workers were in high demand because of all the metal debris that had to be cut away in order to check for survivors.

66 Referring to the Jacob K. Javits Convention Center, called the "Marketplace for the World," located at 34th Street and the West Side Highway. A positively mammoth center that can be adapted to fit any sort of gathering imaginable.

67 Carhartts is a well-known brand of heavy-duty work pants.

>>><<<

There was all kinds of people on that bus, but mostly construction workers and ironworkers. They let us off a few blocks away from Ground Zero. Don't ask me exactly where we were. I didn't know the geography of that area when it was functional. I'd been in Windows on the World, and I think at one time I knew somebody who had an office in one of the Towers. My knowledge of the geography basically consists of the subway tunnels and the PATH trains.

We couldn't go directly into the rubble. We had to move west and swing around, I know that much. They took us down the West Side Highway, people cheering with signs up on the sides of the road.

I can tell you one thing that you should probably note in your thing there: as my wife and I went down to the Javits Center, I was looking at the various construction sites around the city. I noticed that all the cranes were at a rest position. Right? There was no iron-work being done. You want to find heroes from the rescue workers; those ironworkers are the guys to talk to. I'm telling you right now—outside the EMS people and the firemen, there was nobody in this city stood taller than the ironworkers. They shut down every con-struction site in New York City. I heard some of them talking to each other, and they said, "This is the only job we got now." And I'm telling you, you could tell. You saw nobody climbing the iron all over the city. Nobody up there riveting. Nobody doing bolt-ups. I think they did an across-the-board union call. They shut down and headed in.

The second group I saw the most of down there was the electrical workers. Lots and lots of IBEW.[68] They had apparently lost some people.

>>><<<

Firemen were still suppressing fires in the rubble. We had a couple of cutters, a couple of burners, some small pieces of heavy equipment. I don't know which Tower I was working in. You couldn't tell anything

---

68 International Brotherhood of Electrical Workers.

from what you were stand-
ing on, I can tell you that.

We were all on the
bucket brigade that first
day. A whole bunch of guys
would go up, pick up a piece
of debris, stick it in a bucket, and pass it back down
the line. Empty it out and
pass the empty bucket forward. Buckets. Whatever
you could pick up with
your hands went into the
buckets.

The constant outpouring of citizens' grief
immediately following the 9/11 attacks often
expressed itself publicly.

You'd create a cavity
in the debris. Then you'd hear somebody say, "Stop! Bring the dogs,
bring the dogs!" The rescue dogs would come up; mostly German
shepherds, but I saw one golden retriever. They'd get in there and
sniff around. Next word you'd hear: "Bring the body bag up." The rescue workers would go in and drag out whatever they could by hand.
We didn't find anybody alive.

Twice I heard rumors that they'd brought people out alive. I
think the last group was on the thirteenth, which was Thursday. A
fire truck had been buried, and I heard at first that they'd found five
guys, but later I heard it was two.

All I really know is this: I personally saw no one taken out alive.
And I never saw a whole body, either. Just parts, everywhere. Everywhere. Pieces strewn in with the rubble, not readily apparent until
you got right up to them. And construction workers didn't touch anything. The protocol was to call for the EMS people, and they'd come
up to handle it. Then you'd go right back to the Pile. You'd leap back
in and get to work again.

꙳꙳꙳ꙿꙿꙿ

There was one section that had been a bridge between two buildings, and the dogs were going crazy over there, right? Me and the ironworkers went over to it and some battalion chief, some fire guy, said, "No, you can't get in here, this is unstable."

And we were like, "Yeah, we know, but the dogs. There's something in there. Let us go in."

The guy kept telling us it's dangerous, but the ironworkers were like, "We walk around thirty stories in the air on bare beams, okay? Trust us. We can do this."

So about two hours pass by and they finally let us in. We brought out twelve bodies. Later on, I talked to a fireman and I learned that this location had been one of their command posts.

See, when the firemen showed up at the Towers, because of the immensity of the disaster, they set up command posts so they could say, "This company goes here, this company goes there."

We brought out nothing but firemen from under that bridge. Damn thing must've dropped right on top of them.

⫸⫷

The second day, Thursday, I went down to the Javits Center, same as before. It was now a lot more organized, but it was also taking a lot longer to get people dispatched. They were trying to segregate people by skills, and this time they said, "We need acetylene burners."

There was a bunch of us who stuck up our hands. "Yeah, that's us."

They said, "C'mon," and they moved us to the front of this long line. There was, like, eighteen or twenty of us, and everybody had to sign up: what your skills were, your phone number, your address, all this and that. But after we did the paper, we stood around and waited. And we waited. And we waited. And we waited . . . for whatever vehicle was supposed to take us down.

This stake-bed truck pulled up and a crew of guys, ironworkers, got off. They were wearing dark-blue T-shirts that said, "Ironworker Local, Mackinaw City, Michigan."

I went up to one guy and I said, "Are you really from Michigan?"
He says, "Yeah. A bunch of us came down. Five of us."

I said, "Not for nothing, but how'd you get here?"

He looks at me, he grins real big, and he says, "Drove all night."

Right then, we're standing there and the guys in charge, the fore-
men, called out that they wanted a burn crew. Like I said, there were,
like, twenty of us, and these guys are ready to go. I mean ready to
freakin' God-damned go, man. These guys were like marines. But
they sent another crew instead.

After about two hours, we got sick and tired of waiting. Some
of the local guys from New York City and Jersey? They just started
walking down the West Side Highway. I mean, you could see where
the smoke column was above Ground Zero, right? So we started out.
A group of twenty guys straggling down the road with equipment.

⋙⋘

At one point, a truck goin' north on the West Side Highway stopped

"My wife's manicurist is from Russia; she's lived here about eight years. She says to me
just the other day, 'I've never seen Americans be like this. I never knew this is how
Americans could be. Especially in New York.' I think that's what a lot of people think.
And that's a shame."

and we talked to the people inside. It was this pickup truck with a young couple in it.

"Yeah," they're saying to my guys. "We love you. Thank you. Way to go."

Next thing I heard was one of my burners say, "Can you drive us down there?"

I have no idea who this couple was. They were in a brand-new pickup truck, and they thought about it and said, "Yeah. We can get you down there." So fourteen or sixteen of us jump up on the flatbed—*boom boom boom*—of this regular old-fashioned American pickup truck. I'm sitting squashed in next to the tailgate. There's an ironworker to my right who's French Canadian, must weigh at least 250 pounds. I got him around the neck and if he falls off the truck, he's gonna take my arm with him. His neck was the size of my thigh.

Another guy was holding on to me, right? Everybody's just grabbing on. All we needed was a little olive oil on us. We were in that truck like sardines.

And these guys were going into Ground Zero for the first time, so everybody's like, "We gotta come up with a story to get through the blockade." See, we weren't officially cleared 'cause we just walked away from the Javits Center. We didn't want to wait.

But I told the guys, "Look. We don't have to come up with a story. I was there yesterday. The firemen and the policemen ain't gonna stop you. They got too many brothers buried underneath. The only problem we're gonna have is the military."

My crew had all sorts of battle gear. Tools and pry bars and the like. And this couple with the pickup, all we heard out of them was, "Watch the paint! Watch the paint! Watch the paint!"

»»«««

So we got down there, and I'm trying to lead the guys back to where I was the day before. But by this time they had the whole thing barricaded off; we couldn't go in. Then all of a sudden this group of guys—there was about a dozen of them wearing those orange reflective road

crew vests that say "CONTRACTOR" on the back? They had some
kind of pass. I think they were being brought in to adjust for safety.
They looked like engineering types. But the orange vests were being
let through, so this crew I was with, we immediately piled in behind
them to get through the barricades.

This national guardsman stops us and says, "Wait a minute,
what's going on here?" We said, "We're the burn crew, we're with the
contractors! We're supposed to go through with the contractors!"

The guard's standing there, about to give us a hard time, when the
contractor turns around and realizes all of a sudden that he's got a lot
more guys than he came with. He grins and says, "Oh yeah. They're
with us. Let them through."

The guard's like, "Yeah. Uh—okay. Sure. Bring them through."

And that's how we got in the second day.

⫸⫷

I took over an acetylene torch from a fireman crew. These firemen
were not leaving, right? Their battalion chief would tell them, "Go
home. Get some sleep." They would stand up and shuffle off to somewhere until the battalion chief left. Then they would go back in. They
were bringing in trucks from welding suppliers because nobody had
proper acetylene gear.

And there was this one fireman who I found slumped up against
a wall, wearing his burn clothes. I went up to him and said, "Listen,
I'm here with a burn crew but I don't got the appropriate stuff. Can
I . . . ?"

The guy started to get up. He said, "I'll go. I'll go back in."

I said, "Look. I'm an ironworker. Let me take care of this for you.
Get some sleep."

So the guy gave me his stuff, and I wore his gear and went back
out into the Pile. A leather jacket so the sparks don't bother you. The
goggles. Heavy-duty gloves that don't burn. And my Carhartts.

See, you couldn't burn a hole through a twenty-foot I-beam,
whatever the dimension is, and jerk it out with a crane. There might

be somebody trapped underneath. So you cut it off here, cut it off there, have three or four guys lift it out and put it on something, haul it away. Build another cavity, start all over again. I put in twelve hours on Thursday, September 13.

※※※

I didn't go back down on Friday because I knew it was gonna be ridiculous getting back through security. We got lucky those two days. But late Saturday night the Javits Center called me, saying they needed more burn people. Because I'd filled in that form on Thursday, they said, "We gotcha down as a torch guy. Can you come in?"

"Yeah," I said. "Sure."

I was back down at Javits by six on Sunday morning. And it was the same thing all over again.

※※※

I was so proud of my city. This is my home. The way everybody stood up. There wasn't any crying, there wasn't any weeping, there wasn't any pulling of hair. It was just, "We're gonna deal with this." And nothing was gonna stop anybody. If anybody wanted to see what this city is truly all about, it was down there.

My wife's manicurist is from Russia; she's lived here about eight years. She says to me just the other day, "I've never seen Americans be like this. I never knew this is how Americans could be. Especially in New York."

I think that's what a lot of people think. And that's a shame.

UPDATE

Tony Rasemus still resides on the Upper West Side of Manhattan after thirty-one years in the neighborhood. I bumped into him in mid-September of 2006, and we headed for a local bar. Over draft beers, I brought up the results of recent polls, which indicated that approximately half the U.S. population surveyed believe that the federal government participated in or allowed 9/11 to transpire. What, I wondered, were Tony's feelings on that?

"Totally ludicrous," he said. "Anybody who believes that needs massive doses of serious therapy."

Then he sprung a bomber on me. In 2005, Tony was diagnosed with a particularly virulent form of prostate cancer. "Guys my age are prone to it," he said. "But I got myself screened over at the VA, just to make sure. Turns out I tested positive for Agent Orange."

Agent Orange was a corrosive defoliant used to melt the jungles of Vietnam so that American troops could better flush out the enemy. It took over twenty-five years for the Pentagon to acknowledge that the high incidence of joint aches, night sweats, bloody feces, migraine headaches, rashes, violent behaviors, and cancers found in many Vietnam veterans were linked to this substance.

I pointed out to Tony the eerie parallel between Agent Orange and the recent outbreak of Ground Zero workers who suffered from untreatable respiratory diseases. In recent months, the EPA and other government agencies had come under fire. Surely, people said, they must have known how toxic Ground Zero was? Reports from several independent experts conducted in late 2001 contradicted the "all clear" given by the EPA. I wondered aloud if Tony felt angry. The evidence indicates that his own government exposed him to health-damaging chemicals.

"Not angry in the least," he said. "[The government] doesn't owe me anything. I got a free education from them, and benefits. If I'd wanted a house years ago, they'd have helped me pay for it. That's a part of my service.

"By the way, we should clarify something here. There's no scientific proof that a link exists between Agent Orange and vets dying, vets getting cancer, and children being born with birth defects. No proof at all. Just an extraordinarily high statistical probability."

I asked Tony, "When does an 'extraordinarily high statistical probability' cross the line and become bona fide proof?"

"I'm not qualified to say that," he said. "I can only tell you what

I know. You got exposed to Orange? You got problems. That's the practical point of view."

He returned to the subject of 9/11. "In the case of volunteers down at Ground Zero? The fact that all these formerly-healthy fire-fighters, thirty years old, all of a sudden have lungs like they're ninety? There's no scientific proof there, either, far as I've read in the news. But again: what's the practical point of view. We all know what's going [on]. You don't need a test to figure it out.

"I remember all those college students down there, crawling over the I-beams in their Doc Martens right after the Towers came down. They were digging up rubble, handing out water, handing out sandwiches. They were bright enough to know that wasn't a good idea. We all were. So what? Thank God we had them. Thank God someone was there.

"Something definitely has to be done about these people. I don't know what we can really do now except shovel money at the problem, put them in programs, try and find cures. But we have to do something. The way we're treating these people? It makes me wonder. Who do we think's going to risk their neck the next time something like this happens?"

CASSANDRA MEDLEY

Cassandra Medley has been a staff writer for an ABC soap opera, a Walt Disney screenwriting fellow, and an award-winning playwright. Her work has garnered her an Outer Critics Drama Circle Desk Award, a New York Foundation for the Arts Fellowship, and a playwriting grant from the National Endowment for the Arts.

Like many other New Yorkers, Cassandra refused to be denied a chance to help at Ground Zero.

LET ME SET the tone of what I'm about to tell you. Last week, I was in Union Square—this was a week after the attack. And I overheard two men talking. One of them said, "My office is down on 20th, and there's this hot dog vendor who I always buy lunch from. He looks like one of them."

The other guy said, "I knew it, they're everywhere."

The first guy said, "Yeah, and just two days before the attack this vendor says to me, 'You know what? Saddam Hussein does not like America.'"

The other guy said, "You're kidding me."

And the first guy said, "Nope. That's what he said, that's just what he said. So you think I should call the FBI and report him?"

That's the vibe in this city right now. Blind, unreasonable, paranoid fear.

Or is it?

⋙⋘

On September 12, I went down to visit a very close friend who lives on Laight Street in TriBeCa. She'd been evacuated the day before and had just got back into her apartment. I went so we could comfort each other.

I made it down to 8th Street by train, but from there I had to walk further down since the subways were all shut down further south. I walked as far as Houston Street, where I ran into a total blockade. The police had set up blue sawhorses and wouldn't let you go any further south unless you lived in the neighborhood or you were an aid worker. They determined if you matched either of these criteria from your ID. Now I was stuck. I didn't fit the qualifications. But ironically, I ran into somebody I hadn't seen in years: Pat, a painter who lived on the next block.

We hugged and I said, "Would you say that I'm visiting you so I can get through the barriers?"

We got in line and this one policeman—a big, big guy—had seen that I'd been on line before, and he knew that I'd been refused. When we reached him, I pointed to Pat and said, "I'm visiting her."

The policeman kinda looked at me. Then at Pat. Then at me. Then he shrugged and he let us through.

>>>><<<<

After you crossed Houston and Canal, you got hit by the smell; it was like tire rubber combined with bitter tobacco. A sickening sweetness. Pat had an extra painter's mask with her, and she gave it to me to wear because the reek was so overpowering.

I walked up to Canal Street and over to Laight, where I hung out at my friend's place. Across the street from her, a gourmet caterer had opened up his shop and was cooking all the food he had—these huge meals—for rescue workers. We joined the owner's two teenage daughters and a couple of neighbors in this troop of people volunteering to deliver food.

There was a police station and a triage center a short block away, and we figured the workers there would be hungry. But to reach these places, we'd have to cross the blockade again. Same burly guys, same strict faces. We figured we'd risk it. It was interesting: the moment the security people saw we had food, we had no problems, no problems at all.

We stopped at another deli to pick up more provisions, and here were these tall teenage boys on the corner, I'd say they were seventeen or eighteen years old, watching us.

One of them approached and said, "Hey. How're you doing? You all delivering food? And they let you through, is that right?"

I said yes, that was the case.

"Well, we want to get through, too," he said. "We want to go down to Ground Zero and help pick up the bodies."

I said, "Why on earth would you want to do that?"

And this boy said, "We want to get some training. You know how graveyard workers get paid really well? We want to get some training in the field, something we can put on our resumes . . . that we helped pick up bodies."

We recommended that they go further down Canal Street. And after we'd passed them by, my friend said to me, "You know? There's some things you just can't make up."

⋙⋘

As we got closer to Chambers Street, the landscape began to re-semble a war zone more and more. You could see smoke and rub-ble everywhere—in the streets, on the sidewalks. We were suddenly surrounded by Army jeeps and soldiers and national guardsmen. Sniffing dogs. Doctors and medics standing around. Waiting. Vol-unteering. Personnel in blue hospital scrubs had set up all these spaces with IV stands. There were hundreds of empty beds with clean, white sheets, waiting for people. But nobody was in them. They'd set up this ultimate reception and treatment center for survi-vors they couldn't find.

I heard somebody on the phone saying, "No, I didn't get their name, I just told them to keep breathing. I think they're at Roosevelt or Beth Israel Hospital, but I didn't get their name. I told them to relax." It sounded like someone had been rescued and they'd had trou-ble identifying that person.

The vibe was spooky at this triage center. You had total efficien-cy and total silence at the same time. And now a crowd of rescue

"It was so important for me to experience that human contact and to feel that change in my experience. For me, it was mutual empathy and sympathy of that kind that let everyone know we were all in this together."

workers started coming in off the Pit, firemen and policemen. They were dusty and sweaty. Beleaguered. Men and women both. They were asking for sandwiches and lots of ice, because it was a hot day. We scurried out to get as much ice as we could find from area restaurants with their doors open. We put the ice in large plastic bags and brought it back to the triage centers.

For us, it was all catch-as-catch-can that day. We wandered the streets, creating jobs for ourselves and helping out whomever and wherever we could.

><><

When we got back to the gourmet place, they were already making sandwiches—some vegetarian, some with cold cuts. We took up the duty of wrapping them in plastic. It felt so good to be doing something. Through all the checkpoints we passed, we began to learn what the true currency for passage was: if you had food to offer, you were waved through. All you had to do was appear with a cake or something.

Later that day, we were making our rounds again and everyone started yelling, "Get down!" We hit the ground. It turns out, the commotion was caused by additional parts of 7 World Trade Center falling down.

I'm telling you, Lower Manhattan was like a war zone. A battlefield after the battle.

⟫⟫⟪⟪

I think what moved me the most . . . see, I've always had an ambivalent attitude toward the police. As a black woman, I have relatives and friends who've been the victims of racial incidents. You've heard about profiling on the news? Well, I've lived through situations like that. It changes your attitude toward law enforcement. It changes your attitude about a lot of things. But what I saw that day was a complete change.

We'd be in the process of delivering food, and neighborhood people would approach us saying, "You know what? The policemen and firemen around the corner don't have anything to eat." So off we'd go to find them something and bring it to them.

There was a phalanx of uniforms all along North Moore Street, policemen—women and men, white and black—running in and out in shifts, standing guard. We gathered up some food and brought it to them. Their faces! Such glowing appreciation. "Oh, thank you! Thank you!" Real, personal, eye-to-eye contact.

At the mere mention of food, more police and firemen would emerge from the backs of station houses. They'd start to gush. "Oh, this is so great! Wonderful! Thank you!"

It was so important for me to experience that human contact and to feel that change in my experience. For me, it was mutual empathy and sympathy of that kind that let everyone know we were all in this together. I experienced the most profound and unexpected shifts in my perception whenever a person said, "Oh my God! A salad! Thank you!"

See, everyone was broken. And everyone was tired. Overwhelmed.

It was the day after, we were all still in shock, and the folks in uniform had been down there since it happened, working round the clock. They needed us as much as we needed them.

>>><<<

I feel that times like these call for us to look at our collective humanity, and that's the reason why some of the current flag-waving disturbs me. The way that public figures are speaking about the attack on America, the attack on this country. They're going on and on without any empathic acknowledgement that we're all in this. The whole world. Every nation has been wounded by September 11.

For myself? I would prefer . . . well. If there were an international flag? If there were a flag for the Planet Earth? That's what I'd be waving right now.

UPDATE

Cassandra Medley's latest play, *Relativity*, opened at the legendary Ensemble Studio Theatre in Manhattan in the spring of 2006. The *New York Times* Theater section reviewed the piece as "guaranteed to send audiences out with plenty to think about . . . the production offers . . . two dazzling performances and two especially dazzling scenes."

Relativity focuses on the story of Kalima, a brilliant young African American geneticist who must choose between her love for pure science and her love for her mother, Claire. Claire has founded an institute supporting melanin theory, the notion that black people are genetically superior to other races because of the melanin content in their skin pigmentation. Kalima, proud of her mother's work and her African American heritage, can nonetheless find no scientific proof that melanin science is valid.

In the ensuing two-act drama, all that Kalima cares about is placed on the scales of judgment. Which will win out? Her ethnic pride or her training as a geneticist? Her love for her mother or her belief in the scientific method?

Medley's writing draws Claire's viewpoints liberally from the works of Frances Cress Welsing, Carol Barnes, and Leonard Jeffries, and crackles with the authentic pain Kalima experiences as she makes one choice after another, hoping to arrive at a position she can believe in with both her large, willing heart and her incredibly bright mind.

Relativity has also been produced at many regional theaters across the United States.

ANTONIO "NINO" VENDOME

In the wake of the attack on the Trade Towers, Canal Street turned into a highly organized, bustling refugee camp. The change happened practically overnight. Restaurant owners like Antonio "Nino" Vendome opened their kitchens, and their employees scrambled to feed thousands of hungry rescue workers, police, and firemen. Many establishments covered their initial expenses, estimated in the millions of dollars altogether, from their own pockets.

Nino Vendome owns Nino's Restaurant, a neighborhood favorite at 431 Canal Street. Mr. Vendome is a square-shouldered, barrel-chested man who appears to be in his fifties, with spiky, steel-gray hair.

WHY DID I open my restaurant to these people? The way I figure it, it's not some kind of birthright to have people risk their lives and their families on your behalf and not be appreciated. Let me tell you something. My family came here from Italy in 1955 with four suitcases and $40 to get started. I put down roots in real estate and ended up doing pretty well. I'd established myself in business by the time I was twenty-one.

This city was different back then. A lot different. I put a key in the door of my very own office one morning at 4:00 A.M., and I turned it. I knew there were risks being out on these streets, but I also knew there were men in blue around to protect me. I could never have established anything if these men in uniform weren't out there, putting their lives on the line. So yeah, I feel like I owe them.

➵➤✦◄➵

The attack happened on Tuesday morning, and I organized the restaurant on Wednesday so that we were up and running as a relief shelter on Thursday. We've been going 24/7 ever since, and it's already been a month.

When we started, it was obviously an emergency situation; none of us knew whether we'd be operating for one day, two days, three. But as long as I'm around, we'll stay open until somebody tells us we aren't needed anymore.

Our location is ideal—we're about fifteen blocks from Ground Zero, a distance where the air quality is acceptable. Workers can actually enjoy their food while they're here. And I'd say we're feeding between five to seven thousand people a day, which includes everyone involved in the rescue efforts—policemen, national guardsmen, Con Edison power company workers, sanitation workers, utility company workers—everyone working in the rubble right now. We don't ask questions. Our doors are open, whether you want to come in and cook for yourself or you want a meal prepared. Or maybe you just need a place to sit and take a nap. That happens a lot.

The outpouring of support by New York City eateries—and the number of free meals served to rescue workers in the months following 9/11—was nothing short of staggering. General manager Nick Pasculli said that keeping Nino's open twenty-four hours to serve nearly 5,000 meals a day cost the restaurant at least $80,000 a week.

I'd estimate we've served about 100,000 meals so far to thousands of different people who come in here bone-tired. Exhausted. They come in from all different types of situations. But you know what? I have yet to hear one of them complain. Make sure you write that down.

＊⫸＊⫷＊

I set my own staff of about ten to fifteen people to work. Then I hired fifty more and took in at least a hundred volunteers to round out the ranks. We're handling an incredible volume right now. On a daily basis, we'll prepare 2,700 eggs, 400 pounds of potatoes, 350 pounds of meat, 180 pounds of bacon, 150 pounds of sausage, and 125 loaves of bread.

We're going to need more bodies as we become more organized. Volunteers have been coming in from around the country and that's great, but we have no idea where they're staying. All I know is they're coming here selflessly to do what they can.

For instance, across the street there's a barbecue truck run by a church that drove up from Texas. That's right, you heard me: Texas. They're cooking ribs and chicken in this submarine-like oven mounted on the flatbed outside. This thing must be thirty feet long and it's cooking twenty-four hours a day, seven days a week. There's a tractor-trailer behind it full of chopped wood to keep the grill fires going. And this is what Americans are doing. We're very resourceful people.

⟫⟪

We were originally producing all the food we serve here, but the volume of workers grew so rapidly. My place can only handle 150 people at a time. So the question became: How do you serve 7,000 people? It's a game of logistics.

I've recruited other restaurants in the community to help prepare food. Immediately, we were looking for products with nutritional value. Carbohydrates and proteins; lots of pastas and chicken. The mainstay theme is Italian, but we have some French menu items plus all different types of vegetarian cuisine. We've asked suppliers for donations of stews, chickens, frozen pizzas; romaine and mesclun lettuce; sports drinks and sodas. Kitchen stuff, too: garbage cans, paper napkins, folding chairs, and toilet paper. There's a list outside that specifies who's contributed everything. And people have astounded us with their generosity.

Right after this whole thing happened, we had survivors from Windows on the World working with us. One of their managers was working here one night. His name was Steve—I forgot his last name. After all he'd been through, losing all his people, here he was, laughing and joking to keep people's spirits up, serving chicken and salad.[69] A great guy to be around.

He was working with us night and day. Then they had a memorial for some of his co-workers, and he just fell apart. He hasn't been back since. We're just letting him be for now. What else can you do? He's been through a lot, but he gave us a lot. We'll reach out to him in time. For some of these people . . . what else can I say? It's going to take a lot of time.

⟫⟫⟪⟪

I started my first business right around the corner from here about thirty years ago. I've been involved in restaurants for well over twelve years. In all that time, I've seen the selflessness of people, and I've seen the selfishness. I don't want to cast aspersions but, on an honest assessment, this situation has brought out the worst in some people.

For instance, at one point early on, I needed more refrigeration. So I went to a local distributor and he dropped off a refrigerator unit. The thing was worth $500 and he wanted to charge me $1,000 a month to rent it. I agreed, because I needed it right away to do the job. But I knew I was getting robbed.

So I explained to this guy that he's a thief and a crook and that this is not the time to be doing that sort of thing. Then I cut the check for $1,000. He came around to the restaurant and said, "What about another thousand for the deposit?"

I said, "You know what? Do I look like a fucking idiot to you? Get out of here before I decide to do something stupid."

So I've experienced that kind of idiocy. It doesn't matter. I've experienced some unbelievable unity as well.

⟫⟫⟪⟪

There's a big sign out front that reads, "Feel free to share your thoughts with our nation during this tragic time." People have taken us up on

---

69 Windows on the World, the famous 30,000-square-foot restaurant located high atop the North Tower, lost seventy-three employees.

the offer. The walls and windows of buildings up and down Canal Street are covered with stickers as far as the eye can see. And each sticker bears a unique message from a rescue worker:

"Love like your life depends on it."

"From the ashes, we will rise and become even stronger."

"It's time for America to bless God."

"Dennis is gone, a wonderful spirit."

"Life is good even when it's bad."

"How much foreign oil are you using? It's now our war."

"New York: May we never forget how close we've become. Let's stay this way."

There are drawings made by children, too. Crayon-on-oak tag images of Captain America and Superman. I saw the cartoon hero Wolverine slashing through Osama bin Laden with his razor-sharp claws. And inscriptions are posted from representatives of many religions and countries: the B'nai B'rith, the Jews for Jesus, the Virgin Islands, Argentina, and the Dominican Republic.

I read these notes, and I was blown away. They started out as a way to help the rescue workers with their mental fatigue and stress. Then we issued everyone coming through our doors some paper and pencils so they could express themselves, whatever their thoughts might be. The terror, their families, the war, whatever. It started small. People would write a note and stick it to the wall. Now the entire block's covered. We've encapsulated them under plastic to protect them from the elements.

I've been talking to the New York Historical Society and the Museum of Modern Art about making sure these notes get curated. This is something I feel needs to be documented for the world to reflect on in perpetuity. A thousand years from now, people will want to know what went on here. People will want to read what our reactions were and wonder what it was like to be alive during all this.

>>><<<

All these fellas, these uniformed officers—we serve them a meal and they're so grateful. "Thank you, thank you, thank you." That's all I keep hearing. These are the guys who were running into the buildings as they were collapsing, and everybody else was running out. They've lost their dear friends, but they still stop to say thank you when someone hands them a bottle of water.

We want to make a statement here that identifies unsung heroes. I am so grateful for this privilege.

>>><<<

I'm no one special—write that in your story. I'm like everyone else. We're all constantly working to keep a roof over our heads, working to nurture our children. These people we're feeding? None of them live in three- and four-garage homes. None of them is secure with their children's educations. They're just men and women whose families live with the idea that every day they go to work, they might not be coming back.

In the '60s we used to call them pigs, and God knows what. But it's time we stopped cursing at them and spitting at them and taking them for granted. It's time to take a step back and appreciate what these uniformed people do.

So you plant the seed of knowledge. You plant a vision. Maybe now some coffee shop in Utah will look at that uniformed individual a little differently. And maybe they can't afford to give him a free meal, but they can afford to treat him with the respect that he deserves.

That's our goal. To protect these people who are the mainstay of this country.

BOBBIE-JO RANDOLPH

Bobbie-Jo Randolph, twenty-seven, is a volunteer firefighter and on-call EMT from Hermiston, Oregon. Bobbie-Jo is a member of the Disaster Medical Assistance Team (DMAT), a branch of FEMA. She was one of several rescue workers from all corners of the nation who responded to the call for assistance at Ground Zero.

A FEW YEARS AGO, I met a pediatric emergency physician in Portland named Dr. Helen Miller who worked for Oregon Health Science University. She had moved to Oregon from Seattle, where she'd been on the DMAT team. She'd really enjoyed working DMAT, but there was no team in Oregon, so she decided to put one together. When she started recruiting people, I went to an emergency medical conference in Sun River, outside of Bend, to meet her and throw my hat into the ring.

Initially, we had less than twenty members. In order to qualify for a team, we had to get more people interested. So we went out into our communities and said, "This is what we do. If you're interested, come talk to us and we'll try to push your applications through." That was in 1999.

At first, we made ourselves known by doing some local events with the Seattle county team. In Oregon, they have what's called the Gorge Games, a large athletic event where participants do everything from windsurfing to running to biking. It's a televised event, one week long, and we provided medical care. But we kept training and training over the past two years, drilling ourselves to handle any disasters that may or may not occur.

When New York happened, we thought we were ready. Ground Zero was the first time the federal government deployed us.

>>><<<

When a national disaster is declared, DMAT teams from around the country send their rosters to the head honcho at FEMA. We were one of the first teams to get our roster in. We said, "Look, we have an entire team ready to go."

Normally there are different team levels: One, Two, and Three. Level One is the highest priority, with teams that have more people and more equipment. Oregon is currently at Level Two, so we're not normally the first people to get called. But having our rosters together helped. There were several other teams that were closer to New York, like Ohio and North Carolina; those teams were deployed first. Each team went to Ground Zero for a two-week period before getting rotated out and replaced by another team.

Oregon team members were asked to go in mid-October. We sent a first team out, then the government asked for more. I was on the second team. As I recall, I left the fifth of November, 2001.

≫≪

I was in bed when I heard about the attack. Someone called my phone and said, "Turn on your TV right now," so I did. It was just before the second plane had hit, maybe 5:00 or 5:30 in the morning on the West Coast.

I was watching when the second plane hit. At first I thought it was a replay of the first plane's impact. Then I realized, no, that's a different building—there are two buildings on fire now. I'd never been to New York City. I'd never seen the Trade Towers except on TV or in photos.

Honestly, the first thing that came to my mind was that I wanted to jump on a plane, get over there and help. That, and my concern for the safety of the people in those buildings. Before the buildings collapsed, I wondered what the chance for that was. These are things that go through your mind when you're a firefighter.

I remember thinking: not to worry, those buildings are huge. A few floors might collapse, but nothing else. It was never in my mind that the entire building could fall. But when they did, I also remember thinking, there hasn't been enough time for the firefighters to get out. I wondered whether there were people still alive in there . . . or did they all evacuate? The news wasn't coming as fast as my mind was moving.

I remember sitting there, watching everything and wondering if this was real. It seemed more like a movie. I guess everybody says that, huh?

>>><<<

After the buildings fell and we knew that it was definitely going to be a disaster site, I called up my team leader. Dr. Miller had been inundated with phone calls, but she told me what she'd told everyone else: she'd already called FEMA and told them we were available if anyone needed us. At that point, nothing was set up yet. It was too soon to tell. This was the day of the attack.

She asked us all to keep a watch on our email rather than to keep calling her. She wanted the phone lines open in case. And every day she'd send us an update: "We're still on the list. Keep your bags packed, we don't know when we'll go."

DMAT wants to know that you can be on a plane immediately after they call. Usually you have between twelve and twenty-four hours from getting the call to leaving for a disaster location. That makes it difficult in Oregon, which is a huge state. I live three hours from the nearest major airport. Plus I had my kids to think about. If I have to leave town, I'll do different things with them on different occasions. When I left for New York, my mom, my ex-mother-in-law, and the boys' father took turns watching them.

>>><<<

I remember getting the call. Helen didn't make it because she was already here in New York with the first team Oregon sent out. With Helen in New York, Steve Myron was the acting team leader in Oregon. He happens to live twenty minutes from me—we were the only two people from our team living in Eastern Oregon—and we're good friends of six years. Steve's a police officer, an EMT, a firefighter, and he does hazmat. He's the king of all trades, an awesome guy.

Steve and I'd been involved in something called the Hometown Heroes Ball, which was sponsored by our local country radio station. It was a huge dance with a few famous singers—New Yorkers probably wouldn't know them because these folks are country singers. But we had the dance to thank all the local heroes, our firefighters, policemen, EMTs, servicemen, anyone with a badge. They all got in for free and their guests paid a nominal fee, and all of that money plus money from a silent auction went to the charity funds in New York.

I'd been listening to the radio and planning on going to the ball. Steve had put together a PowerPoint program about September 11, a very moving presentation with music under it, about three songs long. He'd shown it to a few people and everyone cried when they watched it, but he hadn't done anything else with it. I thought, "Wouldn't it be great if we could do the PowerPoint show at the fundraiser?"

So I called up the radio station. I told them we had a team that was working in New York right then, and that we'd love to show the presentation and talk about what we do. They said, "Awesome. We'd like to see it."

⋙⋘

We went to the dance and showed the PowerPoint program. About halfway through the slide show, there are pictures of the firefighters, paramedics, and police who died, fifteen or twenty slides with fifteen or twenty people on each slide. People started clapping as the pictures came up. They offered a standing ovation and continued clapping until the images of the people were done and the show went back to slides of the site. I looked around the room and there wasn't a table where people weren't openly crying.

We were sitting at our table when Helen called us on Steve's cell phone.

"Put a second team together," she said. "You're coming out here on Monday." Just like that, we were being deployed.

We got right up from the table, left the dance, and went home to pack.

⫸⫷

We have such a large team now that I wasn't positive they'd have a spot for me. Steve left the dance and drove the two and a half hours to Boardman, where he lives. He found out he needed two doctors, two nurses, two paramedics, a team leader, a logistics officer, and an administrative officer to round out his team.

Then Steve called me up and said, "I can't use you as an EMT, but I need an administrative officer. You're it." Our regular AO was in Maryland, and I could fill in during a pinch.

The ball was Saturday night, and Steve called me at about two o'clock in the morning on Sunday. We left that Monday morning, the fifth of November, on Delta Air Lines. We landed in LaGuardia Airport.

⫸⫷

Getting on the plane was difficult for some of the team members. Some of them were pretty nervous about the previous hijackings. I only found myself anxious during the take-off and landing; I was fine once we were in the air.

Normally we wear uniforms on the plane, but this time we were told by our team leader that DMAT didn't want people in uniforms on the aircraft.

I'd been fairly quiet, into myself during most of the flight. I was sitting next to three women. I heard them talking as we flew in over New York City.

The Ground Zero cross, which stands more than twenty feet high, is shown here atop its previous pedestal at the site of the World Trade Center.

They asked me what I did, and I told them I was coming to help with recovery and to provide medical care for the workers. They were very excited about that.

I asked them, "What do you do?"

They said, "We work for Martha Stewart. We're her aides."

"That's great," I said. "I love Martha Stewart." I was looking out the plane's window and, since I figured these ladies lived in New York, I asked them to start pointing out the buildings.

They pointed out the Empire State Building. Then we saw lights and smoke—you could see it real clear from the plane, and one of the girls said, "That's it. That's Ground Zero."

One of the girls suddenly had a hard time talking. She turned her face away from me.

⟫⟪

We landed and entered the airport. Most of us were carrying enor-

The Ground Zero cross was relocated off the World Trade Center site to make way for new construction. It now stands on the side of St. Peter's Church facing the WTC on Church Street, where it looms over passersby.

mous hiking backpacks, since we'd often been deployed to places where there was no running water, no bathrooms, no anything. We'd found out at the last minute that we'd be staying at a hotel, but we still brought the bags. Normally, I carry cooking utensils. Salt and pepper. Dehydrated meals that you can buy in camping stores—the kind you can make by tearing open the packet and adding water or clicking to heat. But I took all that out.

We waited in line for a van that picked us up and took us to the Sheraton New Yorker.

That van ride? I thought I

was going to die. It was the worst driving I'd ever seen, my first taste of New York traffic. Our driver was from Maryland—some kind of volunteer. He'd been here since day two, picking people up and dropping them off at the airport, shuttling them back and forth between the hotel and Ground Zero. I guess he'd learned a lot about driving in Manhattan, and fast. He drove as badly as I thought New York cabbies were supposed to.

We went over two or three of those concrete lane dividers, and the wrong way down one-way streets. I had a middle seat in the front of the van with nothing to hold on to. I was literally grabbing the bottom of the seat. My knuckles turned white.

>>><<<

I wasn't expecting to stay at one of the nicer hotels in New York, either. The first night we were there, Mayor Giuliani was holding some sort of event. I remember having my pack on as we walked up the stairs ... glancing up and seeing all these video cameras and photographers lined up behind red velvet ropes, their flashbulbs going off.

I guess they were there to take pictures of celebrities, but when they saw us, I guess they felt it was some kind of photo opportunity. Flash, flash, flash!

I was overwhelmed. I couldn't understand how anyone would have any interest whatsoever in taking our pictures. The way I saw it, I was there to do relief work. I felt that the moment wasn't about pictures of me, it was about the policemen, the firemen, the rescue workers who had been there since day one. They were doing the work, not me.

>>><<<

FEMA had commandeered the whole top floor of the Sheraton. That evening, they sat us down in a room and debriefed us for fifteen minutes. We were told to turn out in uniform in the hotel lobby the next morning at seven o'clock. Our first shift would start at eight. They didn't tell us what we'd be doing or what we'd see, but we had a rough idea. We figured we'd be running a medical tent down at the site. And we'd already talked to Helen, who'd been here for some time; she'd told us a little about her experiences.

We knew we'd be caring for construction workers and firefighters. We knew that the medical teams were mostly handling foreign bodies in the eyes, respiratory problems, lacerations, things like that. As administrative officer, I would keep track of the team members' hours, get everyone's social security number correct, handle paycheck administration, that sort of thing.

Essentially, we weren't told much at the briefing. Just when and where to meet, plus hospitality things like where we could do our laundry, where to get food, and so on.

We also had our ID pictures taken. We were told we'd need to have two cards with us at all times in order to get through the Ground Zero security checkpoints. We wore them on lanyards around our necks. The first card was from the Mayor's Office of Emergency Management. The second was our National Disaster Medical Systems ID issued by FEMA; it had a logo of the Trade Towers in the background, and an American flag. At the bottom it said, "September 11," and listed our team designation as Oregon 2 DMAT.

≫≻≪≺

After the debriefing, we got a fifteen-minute break. Then they took us down for a quick tour of Ground Zero.

We rode over to the site in the van. Again, I pulled that middle front seat. I was looking forward through the windshield. The first things I saw as we sped down the West Side Highway were the cranes and smoke.

We went through a few security checkpoints. Then, to my left, I saw a building with computers hanging out the windows by their cords. I don't know why that was, although it's not an odd thing to have happen during a fire. Maybe the firefighters had gone in spraying water and blown the equipment right out the window. Or the wind kicked up by the blast had done it. I didn't know. This was nearly two months after the disaster, so who can say? But the building was charred on the outside. All the windows and most of the wall structures were gone; you could look right inside and see the offices. Everything was so burned, it was hard to tell what was what.

Then I saw the Cross.[70] It was sticking out of the ground down in the Pit, perched on a mound of debris about three stories high. You've seen this on the news, these two beams, brown, rust-colored, one horizontal and one vertical. They were riveted together in the perfect shape of a cross. I would guess it was probably twelve feet high from the ground to the crosspiece, with maybe another six feet above that to the top. There was a firefighter's jacket hanging off one of the spars.

Personally? I took the Cross as a sign that God was there. In fact, I got a little teary-eyed when I saw it. But then I came to the realization that I didn't have a right to cry. Ground Zero wasn't my turf. It hadn't been my family and friends who'd perished. The tragedy hadn't happened in my town, my state. I had no right to grieve as the other people did.

Right next to the Cross was a small makeshift building where all the firefighters were stationed. You could see them walking across the dirt road to and from the site, sitting along the road in their heavy uniforms, sometimes wearing their helmets, sometimes holding them in their hands. They looked like soldiers, come in off a battlefield. Dirty. Exhausted. Changed. Some of them would nod their heads and wave as we went by.

I realized they couldn't see me in the van, but still, it didn't seem right to let those people see me cry. This was their site, not mine.

➤➤➤◄◄◄

---

70 The Cross Bobbie-Jo is referring to, one of several found at the disaster site, is a crucifix-shaped hunk of I-beam more than likely recovered from the wreckage of the U.S. Custom house at 6 World Trade Center. It drew the attention of the international media when clergy blessed it in a solemn ceremony held outside the building on October 4, 2001. In October 2006, in accordance with the effort to finally rebuild the World Trade Center site, the now-famous Ground Zero Cross was removed from the pedestal on which it had stood, watching over the site, for approximately five years. It was remounted a few hundred yards away outside St. Peter's Church, and looms over passersby walking south toward the World Trade Center on the east side of Church Street.

After passing the Cross, we continued on down the West Side Highway until we came to our tent. Our assignment had us relieving two teams: Seattle, King County DMAT 1, and another from Oklahoma, I think. Our medical tent was positioned under the walkway that used to connect 1 World Financial Center to the Marriott Hotel. But the bridge had collapsed. All that was left was the stubble of the walkway jutting out from the building. We entrusted ourselves to the firemen, who told us that this was the safest place from falling debris.

When I say "our tent," I should clarify: we actually had three. The first tent was our treatment center. The one behind that held our medical supplies, and the tent closest to 1 World Financial served as our command tent. There was one doctor, one nurse, and one paramedic assigned to each tent.

We got out of the van and got hit by the smell. Later on, I'd find that the intensity of the odor depended on the wind; sometimes you'd smell nothing, and sometimes it was very bad. Contrary to popular belief, it wasn't so much the smell of death and decay. By the time we got there, it was more like the odor of ground cement and sulfur and burning rubble. But it definitely stunk. A couple days after we arrived, we were issued heavy industrial respirators to assist our breathing.

Inside the command tent I found two team leaders, two logistics officers, and two administrative officers—one from each of the two teams we were replacing. They were downgrading the site; our one team would replace two. When we arrived, there were twenty people working the site in two teams, ten and ten. After the downgrade, the ten from my team would provide the care that twenty people had offered before us.

I assumed the downgrade happened because the site wasn't as busy, medically speaking, as it had been in previous weeks. And we knew that sometime in the near future, DMAT would pull their tents out completely. But for the moment, we were needed.

⇒⟫⟪⇐

We didn't bring our own medical equipment. Everything was

provided for us, from gauze to defibrillators. We had a full mini-ER, like a MASH unit, running in each tent. We had a huge Ryder truck stocked with pharmaceuticals. Our team pharmacist kept track of everything we dispensed, from narcotics to ibuprofen.

I had to learn the administrative system each day as I went along. The paperwork, the computer system, tracking information . . . we had laptops in our tents connected to the city, the mayor's office, and our own command center at the Sheraton. Everyone needed to know how many people we treated, who we treated, what we had treated them for, whether or not they were transported to a hospital, whether or not they were transported by paramedics or had walked in on their own, what medications they had been given—everything needed to be tracked. That was also part of my job.

⇶⫸⫷⇶

I did take a moment here and there to meander over to the treatment tents so I could get an idea of what was going on. Normally I work as an EMT, so, of course, I had curiosities.

For me, if there was anything difficult about being at Ground Zero, it's that I wasn't able to really treat anyone. Instead, I helped the team leader arrange to clean the outhouses that hadn't been emptied by the Sanitation Department when the site was closed on Veteran's Day. I guess you could say I was needed for different purposes.

So, after our orientation of Ground Zero, most of us were pretty tired. We went back to the hotel and spent $30 on one meal at TGI Fridays. Welcome to New York.

At seven the next morning, we reported to the lobby. By eight o'clock, the teams we were relieving had left, and we were on our own to take care of everything.

⇶⫸⫷⇶

I was in the command tent when I first saw them pull a fireman's body out of the Pit.

The paramedics used to park their ambulances next to our tent;

they'd come in all the time and chit-chat with us. While I was talking with one of them, another guy came in and said, "They just found another one."

The paramedic I was with said, "All right, let's go."

He walked out. I wanted to go, too, so I talked to my team leader and told him where I was at with my job. He gave me permission to go on outside. One of our paramedics, Christie Wells, wanted to go, too. She and I walked down the ramp that led to the site, down into the Pit with its thirty-story cranes.

An ambulance had already backed in, with its rear doors open toward the Trade Center. The ambulance had its lights on. People lined up along either side of the ramp. There were stairs going down into the Pit—someone had shored them into the ground—and there were people at the top of the stairwell, plus paramedics, firefighters, construction workers, and a fireman with "Chaplain" written across his helmet. There were several Red Cross volunteers. Everyone was waiting for the remains.

We all waited—no more than ten or fifteen minutes, but it seemed like a long time. They knew this body belonged to a firefighter because they had found a jacket.

When the procession finally passed by me, I saw firefighters carrying a Stokes basket, which is a metal mesh basket used to extricate bodies from wherever they're found, beneath a cliff or under some rubble. The basket was draped with a white sheet. The firefighters stopped at the top of the stairs and draped an American flag over the body. The priest said a few words I couldn't hear, a prayer of some sort, I guess. All activity had stopped in the Pit.

When the priest finished, I saw people make the sign of the cross. Then everyone stood at attention. Someone told us to salute. They got the basket into position and put the body in the ambulance. Then they gave the basket to the paramedics. A couple of firefighters got in the ambulance and closed the doors. The sirens were turned on, and they drove from the site heading north along the West Side Highway.

There was a point where someone said it was okay for us to take our hands down from the salute.

When the ambulance was gone and people started to disperse, Christie and I walked back toward our tent. I didn't run, but I walked really fast because it was all I could do to keep my tears from flowing.

I got into the tent, I took a deep breath, and immediately started crying. I'd wanted to wait until I was hiding because I still didn't feel I had the right to cry.

»»«««

The two-month anniversary of September 11 was also President's Day and my son's birthday. He had a dinosaur birthday cake at the same time Hillary Clinton, Mayor Giuliani, and Governor Pataki signed my helmet.

I met the President of the United States; he talked to me while walking by. He was shaking everyone's hand, and he reached out and shook mine. We were wearing different uniforms than everyone else, and he noticed that.

He said, "Who do you work for and where are you from?"

I said, "I'm from Oregon DMAT."

He said, "That's a long way to come. Thank you for coming. We appreciate you."

I'll bet he had no idea that, by saying that, he would make me so happy. I live in a town of 13,000 people. I'm just a small-town girl who never thought I'd meet the President of the United States, let alone hear I was appreciated by him. I shook his hand, and in two seconds he made me feel like I'd made a difference.

»»«««

The next day, an aircraft crashed out in the Rockaways.[71] It was a

---

71 American Airlines Flight 587 crashed shortly after 9:00 A.M. on November 12, 2001, while taking off from John F. Kennedy International Airport bound for Santo Domingo. All 260 people aboard were killed. While the crash was inevitably attributed to an accident rather than sabotage, the emotional impact on New Yorkers was especially harsh. The city was still reeling from a similarly horrifying wake-up call on a beautiful workday morning not two months before. The public was still justifiably anxious about additional terrorist attacks.

tough time—to stand at Ground Zero and hear the calls for the airplane downed. To see everything stop. They evacuated the Pit. I could hear what sounded like every siren in New York wailing out toward Queens. I remember what an eerie feeling it was, and I thought, this must be just a tiny taste of what it must have been like for some of those other firefighters and paramedics on the eleventh.

We went back to the hotel, back to the Living Room Area, as I called it. They had put out about fifty recliners in an old ballroom with a couple of big screen TVs, and we sat down in them. Everyone was silent, glued to the television, watching it all happen, trying to figure out why it had happened again.

I remember looking in the eyes of some of the rescue workers and seeing them relive what had happened before. Some seemed fearful, while others seemed full of utter disbelief. It was one of the only times in my life that I was truly scared.

⋙⋘

I bought four T-shirts, one for each of my children. All the guys and women that I worked with signed them. Their signatures say everything from, "Thank you for letting your Mom come," to "Always remember that she is a hero." To this day, I can't pick up those T-shirts without crying.

It helps me to remember that other people actually thought I helped. Other people thought of me as a hero. But I never did anything heroic. I don't *feel* like a hero; I'm *not* a hero. I don't even feel like I should be in this book. But that's what these inscriptions say. Hero.

I wasn't home two months when my son's teacher asked me to come visit his class. I went. I took the helmet and the T-shirt that I'd made for Brandon. There must have been twenty to twenty-five children in this classroom, and they glued themselves to me. They wanted autographs, they wanted to touch my helmet, they looked at all the pictures, over and over and over again. What a great feeling to go to your child's classroom and have all his friends think that you're a hero.

I've been enjoying the kids a lot more lately. Mostly because, between my divorce and my trip to New York . . . well, it was an enlightening experience in a lot of ways. It made me realize something I'd heard a lot before but never paid much attention to: life is short, and only a few things are important enough to focus on. Unfortunately, we don't always do this. We focus on things that aren't really important at all.

I don't want to be thirty years down the road now, saying, "Why didn't I do this? Why didn't I do that?"

I want to say, "I did all the things I wanted to do. My life was great. I lived it the best way I could, and I'm happy with all I did."

⫸⫷

Now I feel I have the right to grieve. After being there—the firefighters, the policemen, and the paramedics all made it clear to me that they not only appreciated me coming, but that I had just as much right to be there as anyone.

RICK ZOTTOLA

The firm of Leslie E. Robertson Associates (LERA) has designed some of the pre-eminent buildings of our time, including the Bank of China Tower in Hong Kong; the Continental Airlines Arena in East Rutherford, New Jersey; the International Trade Center in Barcelona, Spain; the Crystal Cathedral in Garden Grove, California; and the World Trade Center. LERA also serves as a consultant for many of the world's current architectural marvels.[72]

Rick Zottola has been the LERA partner in charge of the World Trade Center for several years. He rushed to the Towers in 1993 to spearhead damage assessments after a terrorist bomb exploded in the basement. He knows the World Trade Center complex as well as any person alive.

In his calm, soft-spoken manner, Rick describes the unique role LERA has taken in the Ground Zero clean-up. He also details his firm's love for an architectural miracle that will never again command the New York skyline.

AFTER THE DISASTER, we all had great hopes that there would be significant rescues. But it quickly became apparent that wasn't going to be the case. The collapse, the devastation, was so horrible that very few people survived. So the rescue effort is now over.[73] Now we've switched over to two different efforts: clean-up and recovery.

The DDC is responsible for clean-up, but we've been retained by them because we know every nuance of the facility.[74] It was a

---

72 LERA founder Leslie Robertson is credited with designing the Twin Towers' innovative tubular steel frame. A week before the hijacked planes struck the Towers, Robertson addressed his colleagues at a conference in Germany. He noted that the Towers were strong enough to take a direct hit from an aircraft [*Philadelphia Inquirer*, September 12, 2001]. No one can fault him for underestimating terrorism's resources. The destruction brought to bear upon the Towers on September 11 was beyond the scope of anyone's imagination.

73 This interview took place in November of 2001.

74 The DDC stands for the Department of Design and Construction, a New York City agency.

magnificent structure and we loved it. So we consult with the DDC and with demolition crews on the structural integrity of the rubble that's left in the Pit. It's a very big job, as you can probably imagine.

The recovery effort, on the other hand, is all about retrieving remains. The fire department and the police department—plus other emergency workers—are responsible for that, and we're assisting them however we can.

⫸⫷

Some last details were still being implemented, but the Towers were pretty much completed before 1976. LERA designed the Towers' structures. We had an ongoing contract with the Port Authority to provide maintenance and services over the last thirty years since the original design was implemented, and we were contracted as consultants to the Port Authority and to the architect Minora Yamasaki and Associates. It was a big project.

A lot of people don't understand this, but buildings are living organisms; they're not static things. They age, they wear out, parts need to be replaced. As office tenants change and technologies advance, the buildings' internals underwent maintenance and a steady stream of capital improvements. For example, a tenant might move into many contiguous floors and want to put in their own interconnecting staircases. This would require a structural cut in the slabs, so we'd have been involved in that sort of work.

I have to say, the Port Authority really takes care of their property well—much better than private organizations. So our work centered around a continuous structural integrity inspection program. We inspected columns, slabs, and structural things throughout the complex. External and internal—wherever you can physically access and visually see. Some places we used to inspect . . . well, the layperson can't see them. For instance, to see some of the columns inside each Towers' central core, we'd climb on top of an elevator and ride inside the shaft. We could inspect the structure much better from that vantage point.

We had the same view inside the Towers' guts as a doctor might have during his patients' surgery.

≫≪

The footprint of each Tower was an acre square, so the two Towers made up just two of the sixteen total acres of the World Trade Center. The sixteen acres comprised six buildings: World Trade 1 and 2, the Towers. There was Marriott Hotel, which is 3 World Trade Center, though no one ever called it that. Then there are WTC 4 and 5, which are low-rise buildings. And 6 World Trade Center, which was the old Customs House.

Seven World Trade Center was actually across the street. We didn't do the original design for it; I think we may have worked on some of the early foundations. The Port Authority owned the property, but it was developed, built, and operated by a private developer.

Six months ago, Silverstein took over a ninety-nine-year lease on World Trade 7 and the entire sixteen-acre World Trade Center complex.[75]

Essentially, I'm trying to convey to you how huge the site is. Yes, the Towers came down, but every single square foot of the overall structure wasn't destroyed.

Over that sixteen acres are two distinct sections of basement. You may have read in the papers about something called the Bathtub, which is surrounded by something called the slurry wall that's stabilized by tie-dash anchors that keep the river out. A parcel of property on the eastern edge of the complex incorporates remnant levels of an old railroad station; the Hudson Manhattan Railroad Station was an underground rail forty to fifty feet below street level that was

---

75 On April 26, 2001, Silverstein Properties, in partnership with Westfield America, gained control over the World Trade Center by signing a ninety-nine-year lease worth $3.2 billion. This deal put control of the largest U.S. office complex in private hands for the first time. Previously, the Trade Center had been managed by the Port Authority of New York and New Jersey. The destruction of the Towers did not release Silverstein from having to make approximately $100 million a year in payment to the Port Authority. Silverstein filed an insurance claim for $7.2 billion, which became a hotly debated topic. September 11 dealt a devastating blow to the American and international insurance trade, which were strained by unprecedented payments.

demolished to build the World Trade complex.

At its lowest part, the basement runs seven levels deep to include parking, mechanical space, storage space, FBI and CIA parking. The vault, which you've heard so much about, was in that old H&M basement facility. Built around the turn of the century, it held gold and silver for the Bank of Nova Scotia.

Immediately following the attack, the vault became a huge security issue. The bank needed our assistance because they didn't know how to get their trucks in there. The New York City and Port Authority police were able to extract a lot of precious metals under . . . well, we're not talking about the most favorable circumstances. But considering the security risk those metals posed, everyone was happy to get that stuff out, and the sooner, the better.

The World Trade Center came about through the shared vision of New York governor Nelson Rockefeller and his brother David. Initial plans, which were made public in 1961, place the WTC site along the East River. The Port Authority later switched the site to the west side of Manhattan by demolishing the old Hudson Terminal for the bankrupt Hudson and Manhattan Railroad.

»»»«««

Even though so much of the basement structure was damaged, as I say—parts of it weren't. Just luck, really. These were big buildings, but they fell as they were designed to, more or less straight down. When we were poking around the rubble, we found three different levels of damage, crudely speaking.

First, you had the parts that weren't really damaged. Second, you had parts that were damaged, but accessible; slabs, for instance,

In total, the Twin Towers cost the Port Authority $900 million. Tenants first moved into 1 World Trade in December 1970; 2 World Trade opened for business in January 1972.

that broke away from their columns but which you could still move over and around by crawling on your hands [and] knees. The third condition was total collapse—that is, just a big pile of debris. These are crude increments, of course. We find many gradations in-between.

Right now, we're still doing condition assessments for the DDC underground. This means we suit up in hard hats, respirators, flashlights, knee pads, elbow pads, and a good pair of waterproof boots, since there's a lot of water down there. You've got to get down on your hands and knees and crawl around.

Unfortunately, we have significant experience with all this thanks to the 1993 bombing. I've got a team working with me to gauge the strength of remaining beams, the slabs. It's all visual work. There's no other way to get a sense of how they're holding together than to eyeball them.

How do you know if you're safe? Ah . . . you don't, really. Things are a mess down there, horribly wrecked and precarious. The weight of all that damaged stuff is tremendous. A square-foot concrete slab certainly weighs much more than I do, but the good news is that a person walking through the rubble is not adding any significant load. That's why rescue workers, right after the Towers came down and there was the frantic urge to get survivors out . . . they were literally able to jump right on top of the Pile.

But machinery is a different story. Machinery can weigh tons. That's important to keep in mind because, if you have heavy equipment treading around, you need to know where there are voids below. Areas for potential collapse.

We know for a fact that early rescue workers who went down to look for survivors were able to get everywhere that you could imagine. As they went in, they would spray-paint the walls fluorescent orange and yellow with their call signs. They would identify their emergency unit, like "ESU Indiana" or "ESU New Jersey," and they'd log the date. While doing our condition assessments, we couldn't find a single place that the searchers hadn't marked. It's remarkable.

Going down into the wreckage is very much like walking down into a coal mine. It's not a straight path; you have to meander down stairs, negotiate over piles of rubble, squeeze through holes that have torn open in walls, maybe go down another set of stairs. And it's dangerous; it's not humanly possible to remember how you got in there. The rescuers would paint arrows on the wall showing the way out. There's an element of spelunking to it. But like I say, those guys are trained. We found their markings going down all six levels, all the way to the bottom. They left no stone unturned. They did a wonderful job.

Wall Street firms did not occupy the Towers throughout their early years. It wasn't until the 1980s that the city's financial state began to boom and an increasing number of private businesses became tenants.

>>><<<

Our role is different compared to other engineering firms that are down at the Pit right now. No one can get around underground like we can—we know that place so well. It's a good thing we're there, too. See, the disaster not only destroyed the buildings, it destroyed the management systems. Those systems, and the people from the Port Authority with the knowledge of how those systems work, just disappeared. Blown to the four winds within seconds. The FDNY contacted us because, essentially, they had no one else to turn to.

They don't know where the fire stairs are, for instance. Three hundred and fifty lost firemen were in fire stairs and places of egress, so they want to know where those stairways are. We're trying to show them the access points. And they'll say, "Over there? Under that pile of debris? Okay, let's dig there."

Keep in mind that the World Trade Center was one of the most complicated complexes in the world before the disaster. What with the main basement, the shallow basement, the old basement . . . when the Towers stood, you could imagine the Center as a complete subterranean city with buildings on top that were as big as cities themselves.

The firemen began their struggle with no information whatsoever, no drawings. That's when we stepped in. One of the services we provide [is] we appraise dangerous areas and hanging debris. We advise whether it's safe or not to go in, how far to go in, how much digging they should do, what tools they should use, whether it's safe for machinery. We'll say things like, "There should be a stairwell over here. There's a corridor down there, straight down about ten feet."

There's a lot of camaraderie that makes it all work. It wasn't a mandated activity. We just saw the need and began to assist the Port Authority employees on an ad hoc basis. For us, it's been important, therapeutic work.

>>><<<

On the morning of September 11, I was sitting with another engineer, hunched over some drawings and talking in our offices eight blocks from the Trade Center. All of a sudden this blizzard of paper—snow-flake-sized particles—flew by our window. We're only eight blocks away from the Towers, like I said, but we didn't hear anything—I don't know why. The first thing I thought of was a ticker-tape parade, but it was coming from too high up.

I got up and looked out the window. We have this wonderful view from immediately southeast of the complex. We saw smoke coming out of the North Tower, but we didn't know what it was. We thought someone's floor had caught fire.

Within five minutes, I got a call from Frank DeMartini, one of our colleagues at the Port Authority who helped us with reconstruction after the 1993 bombing. A very good friend. He said, "Rick! There's been a massive explosion in Tower 1. Grab a few engineers and some drawings. Come right over."

He didn't know what had happened. His office was on the 88th floor, the plane hit his building on 92. His wife, an employee of ours, was with him. Normally, she was stationed at a small LERA office in Tower 2, but that morning she was over having coffee with Frank. She'd been getting up to leave when the plane hit.

We were all thinking of the 1993—a terrorist bomb. We thought, here we go again.

We got our gear and left.

⇉⇇

People were running down the street in the opposite direction as we hustled over there. We heard them say that a plane had hit; we figured it was a commuter plane. We had no idea how big that hole was.

We were just two minutes away from [the] South Tower and about to go up to our office when we heard this roar overhead; we looked up and there it was, flying low over the city.

The second plane impacted the South Tower while we watched, and the explosion spat fire out into the air. We watched the whole thing, completely dumbfounded.

I don't know how to explain it, that feeling you get just before you go into shock. Everything drains out of your consciousness; everything unique about you is drained out. I'm convinced that everyone standing in the street looking up at the Towers at that moment was the same. It didn't matter who you were or what your life experience was. At that moment, all of that stuff that was you drained right out, and you were just another human being looking up into the sky, afraid.

⇛⇚

Our first inclination was to keep going, but then our senses came back to us. We realized that the North and South Towers had just been attacked. Therefore, we needed to turn around. There's nothing a structural engineer can do in an attack situation, and who knew what else was going to happen? We returned to our office eight blocks away, where our goal became about attending to the safety of our employees.

We stayed here the whole time and encouraged people not to leave. We didn't know if more planes were going to come. Fortunately or unfortunately, the people here had to witness the South Tower falling. After that, we couldn't see anything. The wind was blowing in

". . . when the Towers stood, you could imagine the Center as a complete subterranean city with buildings on top that were as big as cities themselves."

our direction, and Lower Manhattan was engulfed in a cloud of dust like nuclear winter.

⫸⫷

Everyone who normally reported to our office in the South Tower survived. Nicole DeMartini, Frank's wife, got out safely. By happenstance, the other engineers from that office reported to our central office that day. One of them had been scheduled for outside scans of the building that day; he was supposed to ride the window-washing maintenance platforms from top to bottom. Obviously, he was very, very fortunate to have not been out there when everything happened.

Frank DeMartini didn't make it out. He stayed with a few colleagues from the Port Authority, assisting and ushering people out. We can piece this together from calls made by fire marshals.

It was a very bad situation up there. People were trapped in elevators. Firemen came rushing up, trying to find those elevator cars. No one had any clue as to what was about to happen.[76]

I miss Frank very much. He loved the facility, and he knew it like no one else. From all reports, he had his walkie-talkie glued to his ear and was talking to people trapped in elevators. The last anyone heard from him, he was in one of the elevator rooms saying that the equipment was ready to collapse.

"Send some engineers up right away. We've got to get these people out of here." That's the last thing he was reported to have said.

⫸⫷

Before the World Trade Center was built, that side of Lower Manhattan was a bunch of low-rise, three-to-twenty-story brick buildings. Even though it was private development, the Trade Center was an urban renewal project. It cleared out a lot of those old buildings, including the old H&M train station. And when it was built, quite frankly,

---

76 Tom Haddad (see his story in the "At the Towers" section) later saw a picture of Frank DeMartini in a television special, and recalled that Frank had been one of the men who'd come to rescue him after the first plane impacted.

it looked stupid. These huge Towers with nothing else around them.

As you move toward central downtown and the Wall Street basin, you can still find pre-war buildings, but the West Side of Lower Manhattan essentially grew up around the Towers. In fact, it's probably safe to say that this entire city grew up around the Trade Center. And now they're gone. You'll never see that panoramic view again.

But maybe a part of it will live on. When southern Manhattan grew out into the bay over the century, the area we now call the Trade Center was muck. The H&M station was built around 1920 and, essentially, its basement had to be sea wall, constructed with eight-foot-thick concrete. That wonderful old piece of construction was incorporated into the World Trade Center. It's intact, even after all that happened—a surviving piece of history. We're hoping that it will be used just the way it is in the next piece of development that takes place on the site.

⫸⫷

Yes, we're already involved with the rebuilding process on a consulting level. It's very early, though. The city says they'll be cleaning up until the late spring of 2002. Essentially, they're stabilizing the site so they can turn it over to whoever develops it. And that gets complicated.

The Port Authority owns the land, but Silverstein owns the ninety-nine-year lease. The government has pledged billions of dollars to reconstruction; with insurance companies involved, that was an economic as well as a political decision. The way I see it, all anyone can realistically hope for is that the right things happen and something important gets built on the skyline.

LERA is unique in our sensitivities to the project. We have little actual influence over what new structures are built, but I don't mind saying that our dream is to have portions of the structure built in the '60s remain. This way, you'll have three tiers of history: the 1920s, the 1960s, and the new construction.

We also think that the salvaged structure has certain undeniable technical uses. For instance, it protects a portion of the PATH train

By February 2007, the WTC site had been cleared and lay in wait for reconstruction to begin.

station in the lowest basement. If retained, it should help speed up the return of PATH train service.

⇉⟫⟪⟫⇇

An organization called the American Society of Civil Engineers is undertaking a structural study to understand the collapse mechanism [of the Towers]. Keeping in mind that people above the impact zones had no way out, ASCE hopes to improve the design of buildings in the future to include better safety features.

Frankly, I'm not sure how much good that'll do. What you learn about the World Trade Center applies to the World Trade Center; it was that unique. How what happened here will translate to other buildings is a little unclear to me, but I suppose they have to try. I'll tell you something, though: what saddens me most is that no one's going to remember all the wonderful intricacies of the complex because of the thorough destruction.

See, our structural assessments went way beyond just looking at the columns. We crawled through tiny spaces in the old H&M basement and saw the building's mechanical systems firsthand, which were tremendous, like no other because of their size and magnitude. There were six stations, each the size of a small house, that controlled air conditioning, heating, electricity, and emergency generators. River water was pumped in through two pairs of pipes five feet in diameter to cool the air conditioning systems. Our inspections took us to all these places and more.

We rode the tops of elevators looking at the guts of this building. And outside the buildings, we rode through midair all the way up to the top on window-washing platforms two feet wide. How many people can say that?

The North Tower was close to 1,400 feet tall; the TV antenna added another 360. We inspected that antenna, too, you know. You had to climb up a ladder inside it until you reached the tippy-top where the flashing light was. At that point, you weren't inside the antenna, either. You were climbing outside, alone, and 1,750 feet in the air.

There aren't many chances in the world to get that high.

MIKE POTASSO

Mike Potasso, thirty-three. Paramedic. A strong back, and a crushing handshake. He has jet-black hair cut close on top and shaved to a buzz on the sides. Small round spectacles accentuate an intelligent, sincere face.

On the ride to Ground Zero, Mike steeled himself for what he thought would be the hardest day of his professional life. Instead, he found himself confronted with the frustration that many emergency workers felt that day, waiting on the front lines for survivors who never arrived.

YOU SEE A lot of strange things on this job. Some real characters. I've picked up Elvis a few times, picked up Jesus. I had one hysterical woman who thought she'd dislocated her fallopian tubes. You can't make this stuff up.

For instance, three weeks ago, I responded to a call. "Pedestrian struck. Someone's been hit by a car, resulting in cardiac arrest."

When we got to the scene, we saw a long street stretching off in either direction with a car pulled up on the sidewalk like it had spun out and crashed. So we hollered to one of the cops and said, "Where's the cardiac arrest?"

The cop said, "Arrest? No, no, this guy isn't under arrest. We're just giving him a ticket."

"There's no one here in cardiac arrest?"

The cop shrugged. "Not that I know of."

Whatever, right? "Okay," we said, "we'll see you later."

Then we noticed another ambulance at the end of the block and we went to check it out, just to see if they needed help. As we approached, another cop came up to us and said, "Hey! Where you goin'? We got a cardiac arrest in the back of the bus!"

Aha. "Where'd he come from?" we asked.

It was the pedestrian we'd been called about. Apparently, this is what happened: the car we'd seen up on the sidewalk had spun out and hit a street sign, which fell over and struck the victim, killing him instantly. He was just some guy walking by, an innocent pedestrian walking down the street. But here's the irony. He was killed by a "No Standing" sign. Get it? No standing.

Well, we laughed. You have to, right? I know, it may seem callous to look at a situation like that. But when you're constantly exposed to this stuff, you tend to separate yourself from the situation through humor to protect your own well-being.

≫≫≪≪

Medic school was rough. I'd work my regular forty hours, plus one to two tours of overtime a week. Then I'd have to go to class three days a week for four hours, eight hours on alternating Saturdays. Plus, I had rotations to do: 150 hours in the ambulance; 150 in the ER; forty hours in the ICU; forty hours OB/GYN; forty hours geriatric care; twenty-four hours pediatric; twenty-four hours OR; twenty-four hours Psych; forty hours of internship.

This went on for eleven months. But the good news is, when you get out of all that, you're ready for anything.

As a medic, you learn basic pharmacology and cardiology so you can handle respiratory and metabolic emergencies. Along with anatomy and physiology, we're also responsible for twenty-six different medications and the performance of certain skills, such as synchronized cardio-verting, cardio-pacing, and EKG interpretation. We can start and maintain IVs, do endotrachial intubation, needle decompression, and drug therapy.

None of it helped one bit on September 11. Not one bit.

≫≫≪≪

I work for FDNY*EMS, Battalion 31, out of Cumberland Station in downtown Brooklyn. We're on the Brooklyn side of the Manhattan and Brooklyn Bridges, a stone's throw away from downtown Manhattan.

I worked the evening shift, 3:00 P.M. to 11:00 P.M., the night before September 11. When my partner and I got off work, our lieutenant told us there was overtime available the next morning and my partner was trying to talk me into working it. I refused. I was already scheduled to work a double the following day. So he took the overtime and I went home.

A friend called me at about 9:30 the next morning, and she said, "You're never gonna guess what happened." Then she told me someone had just bombed the World Trade Center and the Pentagon.

"Okay," I said. "You're full of shit. Look, I'm tired. I had a really busy tour last night, so stop playing games."

She said, "Shut up and turn on the TV."

So I put it on. And then I sat there, just watching. I couldn't believe it. Both Towers. And I thought, I gotta go.

Just then, my mom called me. She said, "Where are you going?"

I said, "I'm going into work."

"What do you mean? Don't go. Please."

But you see something like that happen? You don't even think. You just start going through the process: How am I going to get to work? If I take my car, I'm never gonna get in there—it's bedlam down there. I lived in Rosedale, which doesn't have a subway—it's the most southeasterly part of Queens, the last town in Queens on the south shore. We have the Long Island Railroad, but I wasn't about to wait on that.

It's only about eighteen miles from home to my station house. So I grabbed my bike.

»»»«««

I strapped on my tech bag. I didn't have any uniforms in my locker at the station, but I always keep one spare uniform at home, so I packed that, too, along with my boots. My helmet and my utility belt was in the station locker, thank God. The utility belt's got my shears, my catheters, a clip for my radio, my narcotics, et cetera.

This sort of trip wasn't unprecedented. I'd biked to the station before during nice weather. Normally it took me an hour, but I didn't think about the time or the distance. I was just pedaling. It was harder than usual this time, because I was laden down with equipment: the fifteen-pound tech bag, which I'd strapped to the bike, plus another ten pounds or so on my back.

I took the Conduit to Atlantic Avenue, then Atlantic all the way down to Carlton Avenue, which I cut across to get up to my station. Nobody was on the road. Normally, you could see the Towers clearly from the Belt Parkway, but all I saw was smoke. It was just after 10:30 in the morning, and I think [both structures] had already collapsed.

>>>«««

As soon as I got to Bedford Avenue, I noticed more congestion, more people. So many things were going on at once. Crowds of people were coming out of Manhattan while more people were trying to fight their way in. The end result? Everybody got stuck. Nobody was moving anywhere. Everything locked down.

A mosque in that area was chanting over their PA system and their daily prayers seemed to resonate, echoing over the gridlock on

Emotions ran high among American citizens immediately following the September 11 attacks on the World Trade Center and the Pentagon. Many people clamored for some sort of retaliatory action—but against whom? It would take several months for the FBI to name Mohammad Atta as the head suicide pilot of a terrorist ring comprised of nineteen hijackers.

Bedford.

Good thing I'd taken my bike. My car would've been stopped dead. I was able to pick my way through and got to my station around 11:30.

There was a lot of confusion. Nobody knew exactly what was going on, so everybody was running around getting extra equipment ready. It felt like we were going into a battle. It was that kind of tension.

I got to work running through my checklist and packing supplies. Trauma dressings, blood pressure cuffs, narcotics, goggles. Bandages, shears, stethoscopes. The bigger stuff was already down at the site: longboards, collars, oxygen, IV bags, and intubation equipment.

We heard that a city bus was coming to take us into Manhattan. NYC EMS handles an average of 3,000 to 3,500 calls every day, so some of us had to stay behind. The overnight crew was mandated to cover the day tour while the rest of us went to Ground Zero.

We were just getting ready to go when one of our ambulances came back covered in rubble. So we paused to treat a couple of our own guys who were—quite frankly?—overwhelmed. They'd been down there just before the Towers collapsed and described what they'd seen. People jumping out of buildings. The debris, the explosions. The Towers coming down.

We gave them oxygen and started IVs. While we worked on them, another guy came in covered in debris with a separated shoulder—don't ask me how that happened. So we took a spare ambulance and ran them over to Brooklyn Hospital, two blocks away. To a man, they were in shock. And they kept muttering, over and over again: "We did our best, we did our best."

⤜⤜⤛⤛

That's when I learned that my partner, Gary, was missing. Those men who came in from Ground Zero told me.

Our unit was one of the first to respond to the emergency, and initially we had six guys missing from my station. But all I heard was:

"They can't find Gary. They can't find Danny. Where's Gary?"

The worst possibilities resonated in my head. Gary was missing? He took the overtime from me so I could get some sleep. We'd talked about it, and I'd made all sorts of excuses. "No, no. I can't do it. I'm working the night shift instead . . ."

He'd looked at me and said, "Listen. Why don't you just tell me you don't want to work the overtime, champ?"

For all I know, things could have happened differently. I could have been right where he was.

»»«««

They herded us onto the buses, and that's when the emergency mentality really set in, that feeling of, okay, shit's going down. Here we go. And you separate everything at that point, you block it out. Go numb. You just focus on the job. You're running on automatic pilot, reviewing all your protocols.

What do you do when you first see a patient? We use the START System: Simple Triage And Rapid Treatment. You quickly assess life-threatening injuries and stabilize them as best you can.

Is the patient breathing? No? Then try to establish an airway. Still not breathing? Try again. Still not breathing? Black tag him, there's nothing you can do for him. Move on to the next patient.

Is the patient bleeding heavily? Yes? Then stop it as best you can. Red tag him and move on to other people who need the attention.

The walking wounded get green tags. Everyone in between gets a yellow.

Once your triage is done, you sort your patients. Do they need immediate transport to the hospital, or can they be treated and released at the scene? Or do they go to the morgue?

It's an archaic way of looking at things, but when you're overwhelmed by a staggering number of patients, you have to follow protocol, do the greatest good for the most amount of people. I've been in situations where you have ten to fifteen patients drop down on you at the same time. Like car accidents. One time I worked in the Bronx and a livery cab blasted up the sidewalk, plowing down six people. I'd only been on the job for a week.

We were the third or fourth unit on the scene. The first woman I dealt with had her leg completely amputated. Another woman had bilateral, mid-shaft femur fractures. There was a kid pinned under a car and the driver had a broken arm. The whole area'd been cordoned off. The fire department was on the scene, extricating people from vehicles. There were helicopters overhead and spectators.

And that's what I expected to find at Ground Zero.

⋙⋘

We got down to the site and found that the command structure had already collapsed. For a while, we just stood there, taking it all in. The smoke, the fire, the confusion. Then they finally deployed us over to Stuyvesant High School on West Street, where we set up a triage center in the hallway. And there, we waited some more.

For a while, we were just standing there in this dark room, waiting, and I felt weird. EMS teams were rotating in and out on the site perimeter. I wanted to be of use, to help people, but there was nothing to do except stand there, holding our position, ready to work, ready for that first patient to come in.

⋙⋘

One of my best friends, a guy I've known for fifteen years, is a firefighter for 16 Truck from the Upper East Side. I knew he was working that day, and I wondered where he was. Wouldn't you know it? I happened to run into him in the midst of everything.

I said, "Are you all right?"

And he said, "Fine. I'm okay."

He didn't have his cell phone with him, so I called his wife for him to let her know he was alive. "Freida. I'm here with Joe. He's okay."

Then I called his brother and let everyone know that we were together. I saw that happen a lot out there, this makeshift method of communication.

※》※《《

So. Standing in a dark room. Waiting and waiting to go in. It got so frustrating, but I kept reminding myself, this is what I came here to do. To get my hands dirty, treat whoever I gotta treat. But I felt like a spectator, which was horrible. And this went on for hours.

I had two people on my team who'd just got their EMT cards two weeks before. This was their first big job, and I tried to help them stay focused. They were so eager, like: "We have to go in, we have to go in." I understood. Of course I did. It's what happens on a job. You get pumped up, but you have to restrain yourself. We couldn't all go in because we'd end up getting in the way of each other. EMS isn't designed to work in a pit like that. You're there to treat people. If you get injured yourself, you're just adding to the problem, not the solution.

And there were more people helping out at Ground Zero than anyone knew what to do with. Throughout the day, they came pouring in from all over. A fire department from Nova Scotia, Canada arrived—where the hell had they come from? Teams from Boston and Pennsylvania. They just came—you'd be surprised how fast. The Red Cross was already organized, handing out bottles of water. Hatzolah, the volunteer Jewish ambulance company, was making kugel.[77] It was unbelievable.

An auditorium at the school we were in became the main staging area for the rescue efforts. We set up our makeshift command post there along with NYPD, K-9, and ESU. ESU is the police department's Emergency Services Unit—Special Ops, tactical. They respond to things like barricaded patients, hostage situations, rescues, subway jobs. They're trained as EMTs, but they're paramilitary, like a SWAT team. All that training to save lives and, as it turned out, it was total overkill for this situation.

We just sat there, watching people shuttle back and forth. I felt so useless, like I didn't even belong there. And I kept wondering what

---

77 An Eastern European baked pudding, often made with noodles or grains and usually featuring a sweet element, such as raisins or apples.

had happened to Gary.

Block it out, block it out, block it out.

>>><<<

I didn't feel like I was contributing at all.

I mean, people can relate to a fire emergency. They see flames coming toward them and think, hey! Get some firemen over here on the double! Same thing with a police emergency: you can see what's going on, the effect that policemen have.

But with EMS, you're not plunging into a fire, you're not in danger of getting shot. Our enemy is far more subtle, often airborne or blood-borne. You may not see it until it's too late. When you work EMS, you worry about contracting HIV, TB, or hepatitis. You hope you don't bring it home to your family. It's a more cerebral job. You're directly involved, one-on-one, with people in need. You deal with people when they're vulnerable, really hurt. And since you can't fix everything—that's outside the scope of first aid—you try to make patients as comfortable as you can, often as they're dying in your arms. It's an astoundingly intimate job.

And there are incredible upsides to EMS. Sometimes you get to know your patients. You might visit their house four or five times, get to know their families. The bottom line is that we sometimes save lives. When you save someone's life, you very often become a member of their family.

I remember when I delivered my first baby. So far I've done six. Intimate? Fulfilling? I walked home on air that night. And the only thing that kept echoing through my head was, this is what I did today. This is what I did.

>>><<<

The OEM's office was in 7 World Trade Center, but they had to evacuate it before the building collapsed. Once OEM was lost, the command structure had to be completely rebuilt from the bottom up.[78]

It was an amazing effort. You saw people dragging equipment to a forward center, which had dug in at the American Express building, 3 World Financial Center. A forward is important because it becomes your initial casualty center. In an MCI—multiple casualty incident—the forward becomes the first safe zone out of harm's way. Incoming patients stop there first. From there, they get stabilized and shipped out to one of the triage centers for further examination. Then, we decide whether they're going home or to the hospital.

Standard procedure says that EMS will set up a staging sector where ambulances come in; it's like a transportation hub where dispatchers tell you, "You have to take this patient to that hospital." The staging sector is especially important because, if all the patients went to the same hospital, that hospital would be overwhelmed and wouldn't be able to treat anybody.

And New York City has a very particular hospital system. Certain facilities do specialty referrals. Montefiore is a replantation center; you take your amputees there because they have surgeons specially trained to reattach limbs. Jacobi is an antidote hospital; snakebites go to Jacobi because the Bronx Zoo is right next to it. You have special trauma teams at Bellevue, St. Vincent's, and Jacobi again.

Depending on what your patient needs and depending on their stability, you take them to the specialty hospital best prepared to treat them. That's how it's supposed to go, at any rate. But when no bodies were found, we just waited. And waited.

I found myself remembering an earthquake that happened a few years back in India. Thirty days after the earthquake struck, they were still pulling survivors out of the rubble.

I hoped that's what we were facing.

⋙⋘

And I remember it had just gotten dark. Eerie silence, maybe eight o'clock at night. A few rescue workers who'd been out on the Pile

---

78 The mayor of New York's Office of Emergency Management. When 7 World Trade showed signs of collapsing early on the afternoon of September 11, the OEM was forced to abandon its crisis headquarters (for additional information, see: Ken Longert and Fred Horne in the section "The Aftermath").

stumbled into our area. We washed out their eyes and treated them for minor lacerations. Nothing serious, though. People were still going up to the site, coming back, going up, and coming back. I took a walk with one my lieutenants to keep from going crazy.

The neighborhood was all shut down. There was no electricity or plumbing in all of Lower Manhattan. The only lights were from generator-powered halogen lamps, the kind you see hauled out in paramilitary operations, movie shoots, or major disasters. The reflections from the light bounced off the burnt cars and crushed fire trucks. The only sound was the generators in the background chugging away, like sitting down on your porch and hearing a lawnmower in the distance on a quiet Sunday afternoon.

Two blocks from Ground Zero, we started walking through a snowfall of memos and papers from people's offices in the Towers. I picked up some of the sheets and read them. Reports for that day. Spreadsheets. Someone's shopping list. There were also pieces of coffee mugs mixed in with the papers, and personal effects of people who'd been sitting at their desks one moment on a bright late summer day. Then, *bam!* It's over.

This was quite a ways from the actual site of the Towers, too. The debris had scattered far and wide.

At one point, we came to a clearing in the buildings. You could see where Towers 1 and 2 used to be. In the background, a building was still burning inside, like a scene from a movie. *The Terminator*. Firefighters were scurrying around all over the place, trying to put the fire out. They'd been at it for hours, and they were dead tired.

>>>><<<<

We walked back down along the lip of the site and over to the high school, which is when I realized: I can't stand here and watch this anymore. There's nobody coming out. There are people in there who haven't had relief all day. Somebody's got to help them.

At that very moment, there was a stretcher full of equipment going down to the Pit, masks and boots mostly. So I grabbed my team and said, "Come on. We're going."

At that point, I didn't care anymore if I was going to get in trouble. I couldn't take standing there doing nothing anymore.

We went into the forward center and I said, "We're here. Where do you need us?"

The looks on the faces of the people manning that post. I knew right away they weren't going to turn down helpers. And then I kicked myself for having waited so long.

≫≫≪≪

Down in the Pit, we pulled out body parts. Parts of bodies, not bodies themselves. In all, I think we only retrieved one whole corpse.

I remember looking at the faces of the new guys on my team. They were like, "What do we do?"

Not having an answer for them, I just looked away and kept digging.

The forward center had turned into a morgue. There was a woman's severed hand lying on a table; you could still see the engagement ring on her finger. Over there was a torso. The constant smell of burnt flesh was everywhere, hanging in the air. It *was* the air.

At one point, we saw a rope sticking up from the ash and everyone started running toward it, hoping it was a firefighter. Ten of us jumped onto that pile and started moving shit out of the way, hoping it was something. Well, it wasn't. It was a piece of rope, all right. But there was nobody connected to it. If anyone had been at the other end, they were lost now.

It was a long night, and I tried to keep my emotions in check. But it was tough.

≫≫≪≪

At one point, we got word that they were shutting down the forward triage. NYPD had taken over and officially made it a morgue. So we retreated to our triage area at Stuyvesant and continued helping rescue workers and construction workers with minor injuries.

We slept a few hours upstairs on the third floor of the high school. And like I said, there was no power. One of the firemen brought his bolt-cutters and ran upstairs to the cafeteria. He clipped all the locks on the freezers. He did this because we were all hungry. We ate cold chicken patties. They were much better than nothing.

After I'd been there for twenty-four hours, they ordered us home to get some rest. I went home, got six hours of sleep, and went back to work at midnight on the twelfth. I expected to right back down into Ground Zero. But no. The command structure had reformed, and the orders were firm: "Just go down to your regular line unit."

I felt horrible. But I knew what they were doing. A person that has a chest pain in some other part of the city needed us as much as anybody else working the Pile.

Luckily, everyone from my group had made it out okay. I learned that Gary was alive. He'd been hospitalized for injuries sustained try- ing to rescue people, but he went back to the site and started treating people the moment he was released. He'd been right there in the thick of things all along.

≫≫≪≪

I remember coming home that night after being at Ground Zero and walking down my block. Everyone was honking and yelling this pro- USA stuff. People were shaking my hand, saying thank you. And I felt guilty. Someone called me a hero. I didn't feel like one. What did I do? What had I accomplished? I didn't help anybody out, I didn't make one bit of difference. This, more than anything else, was the thought that stayed with me.

So, as days went by, I kept going back there. I worked my regular shifts, and on my days off I worked overtime at Ground Zero or I at- tended a memorial service. I did that right up until November, when my father passed away and my family obligations didn't leave me any time to spend down there anymore.

Still . . . you know? Part of me wonders if there was something else I should have done. Maybe I should have worked the overtime that morning. Maybe I should have just gone down earlier on my own, not waited for someone to tell me what to do. So many people went down there on their own, you know? Of course, a lot of them died, too.

I'm thankful I'm alive. And I try not to feel guilty about it. But the truth is, I do.

UPDATE

Mike Potasso grinned as he slid into the booth and extended his hand. "I've got so much to tell you. Man, I've been keeping busy."

We were in a pub down on Liberty Street, a hundred yards from Ground Zero. It was a cold night in late January 2007, and the site, as we walked past it, was lit up with cold halogen light. Mike didn't pay much attention. He was more interested in the girl on his arm, his fiancée, Adrian Colon. The two of them had just gotten engaged.

Mike had asked Adrian to marry him at midnight that past New Year's Eve. They'd been dating for two and a half years, and Mike popped the question by hooking an engagement ring over the end of the noisemaker Adrian was blowing to summon the New Year.

"That's exciting enough," Mike said. "And then there's work. I'm on the list to make lieutenant."

Mike was still with FDNY*EMS, only he worked out of Station 57 over by the border between Brooklyn and Bed-Stuy. Since 9/11, the city had gone for broke in terms of how it trained its EMS responders. Mike and everyone he worked with had been Haz-Tac trained, which meant they were the only EMT/Paramedic personnel qualified to enter the "hot" zones of a chemical, biological, radiological, or nuclear (hazmat) disaster.

Haz-Tac units are usually the third specialized unit to arrive at a hazmat scene after firefighter and firefighter Special Operations units. "We're trained to assist in decontaminating the populace," Mike explained, "while still dispensing life-saving medical care. And if there's any situation involving nerve agents—organo-phosphate poisonings, sarin gas, for instance—we're the only ones qualified to administer antidotes on the scene."

Mike's unit was also one of only five throughout New York City whose members had been trained as Rescue Medics. These units specialized in first aid and extraction rescues in situations of extreme confinement, such as a collapsed building. "We're trained to rappel several stories, to tie knots and package patients for removal from very tight places," Mike grinned. "It was an optional program, but not for me. Not really. When they offered it to me, I was like, 'Who wouldn't want to do this?'"

On top of all this, Mike served on New York's Task Force 1, the statewide, FEMA-deployed search and rescue team. He served as a volunteer firefighter in his hometown, and he was also on the dignitary protection unit that deployed whenever notable figures came to town. "I was in President Bush's motorcade once," Mike said. "And Cheney's, too, although that was easy. He's got a whole team of doctors with him because of his pacemaker. And one time I rode with the president of Afghanistan."

"He's always busy," Adrian said, shaking her head with a smile. "Always."

After a drink, we headed back outside and Mike looked toward Ground Zero. "Politics," he said, apropos of nothing. "I kind of expected it."

I didn't know what he was talking about, and I said so. He explained, "I've got a lot of friends in Oklahoma City. After that incident happened, it took them something like three years of bickering to get the wording right on the memorial. It's been nearly six years since 9/11, and what've we done with this site? Nothing. Politics. Everyone's playing the blame game. Nobody can agree on anything, so the whole situation's an embarrassment. All this time I've been thinking, everybody shut up and just build something. Please!"

Mike kept talking, and he confided something that he hadn't mentioned before. A lot of people he worked with—EMS personnel who were first responders on 9/11—were getting sick. They were dying.

A few more people every year, Mike said. "One guy I know of was twenty-six years old and died of lung problems. Explain that. And my current partner has sarcoidosis. The other day, his lung collapsed for no good reason at all. He's still working, though; most of them are. They don't go on technical disability, but the department gives them something called a reasonable accommodation, which means they pull less physically strenuous duty. Me? I've still got this nagging cough that I never had before 9/11. But it's small stuff. What can you do?"

He switched subjects fast and told me that he participates in the National EMS Memorial Bike Ride, a 500-mile event from Boston down to Roanoke, Virginia, to honor any paramedic or rescue worker who had died in the previous year. "Because life goes on," Mike said. "You take what you can from it. You participate in something. You learn. You adapt. You don't look back and get sad. Who's got the time?"

He looked toward the empty socket in the ground where the Trade Center used to stand and said, "I'd like nothing better than to see two towers here again. But I know that's never going to happen. Take what you can and keep going. That's what we do in life."

THE AFTERMATH

JESSICA MURROW

The heart of Morris dancing is unadulterated joy. It is art too blissful for soldiers. Still, Morris dancers die in war. Take the case of Steven Adams. Steven danced the Morris his whole life. He died in the World Trade Center on September 11.

Jessica Murrow, fifty-one, tells the story of the marriage she shared with this rare and wonderful man.

STEVE WAS A very different kind of man. He was quiet, reserved, an incredibly gentle person. When I first met him, I thought, wow. What a relief from the other men I've known! Steven wasn't New York City fast-lane. He was country. He was simple. He was also a single, good-looking guy. He was fun, and he was available! I mean, come on. In this world, how many men in their forties in this world are available?

Morris dancing is a huge community, and I've played the Morris for years.[79] I'm a musician. The Marlboro team started coming to New York to dance on Easter. That's how Steve and I met twenty years ago—we'd bump into each other. See, Morris dancing is all about tradition, and it became a tradition that Steve and his friends would come down from Vermont and stay with me each spring.[80]

Then, one summer, we all rented a house together near Amherst

---

79 The ancient art form of Morris dancing arose from the primeval mists of England as a form of harvest celebration and agrarian ritual. Over the centuries, participation in the dance dwindled until it found a home on academic campuses in England, Canada, and America. Morris dancers are a colorful sight, with their bells and waving hankies; they move to simple tunes played on fiddles, melodeons, or pipes and tabors.

80 Steven joined the Vermont-based Marlboro Morris team in 1980. His friend, Christoffer Carstanjen, danced with the team for ten years. These two friends were strangely reunited by the tragedy of 9/11. Shortly before 9:00 a.m., United Airlines Flight 175, flying from Boston to Los Angeles, struck the South Tower with Christoffer on board. Within half an hour, the North Tower was struck by a second hijacked plane. Sadly, Steven was working on the 107th floor. Neither man was seen alive again.

and that was it for Steve and I—our relationship just started working. I had my eyes set on him, I don't mind telling you. I was 44 and
I'd had a lot of relationships, none of them really successful. I'd never
been married in all that time, and I was at a point where I really wanted to make something work.

⟫⟫⟪⟪

He'd had problems making a success of his life. He'd applied to law
school, but he didn't get in. He was in debt up to his ears; in fact, he
had to return his car because he couldn't make the payments, and then
he owed money on it just the same. He had huge tuition payments
due to Marlboro College, where he'd put himself through school and
graduated at age thirty-four. Frankly? He was kind of a mess.

Steve had a real blue-collar background. His father and mother
were cooks. They never earned a lot, so Steve never learned how to
deal with money. He'd struggled all his life to make ends meet. He
would always tell me that it wasn't that he didn't know how to handle
money, it was just that he'd never made enough to have any to handle.
Day in and day out, he was always robbing Peter to pay Paul. It's a
whole way of being when you're broke all the time, and it's not fun.
It's not easy.

I remember I thought, well, this isn't so bad. I've always been successful, I can help him out. I can fix him right up in a heartbeat.

See, I come from an upper middle-class background. I never had
money trouble; I've always made enough. It's all about habits you
learn from a young age. I've never spent a dime if I'm not making
money. So . . . you know, I just knew how to do it. Steve didn't.

As years went by, I realized this was a major problem. We were
really starting to get our relationship together, but I found myself
getting pissed off more and more. Steve was living in Massachusetts
and I was in New York. One winter, he was riding his bike to work,
fifteen miles each way, to earn six bucks an hour as a meat cutter. It
was the worst kind of job at the worst kind of pay. Here he was, badly
in debt and sinking further fast, and what was he doing? Threatening

his life every day to keep the whole ridiculous cycle going. I'd go up to visit him and he'd come home from work with icicles hanging off his mustache. It was pathetic.

I cared so much about him, so I said, "You can't do this anymore. You're going to get yourself killed." And with that, he let me take over.

He came to New York, moved in with me, and ended up staying six months without ever getting a job. But I couldn't get angry with him because he was the most humane person I'd ever met.

Like our first Christmas, which was great. I'd never done Christmas before because I'm Jewish. I was so excited. Steve: my first Catholic boyfriend. We had a wreath and a tree. He got me lots of presents, things I really needed though I'd never said a word. It was hard to not be happy with Steve.

Finally, he got a paralegal job and started making real money. Things got better. We both said, "We're gonna try living together for two years. After that, we're either gonna get married or bag it." See, I'd lived with people for upwards of five and seven years. I know that if you don't make the commitment, you never will. And by this time we were older. Myself? I wanted a kid, although I was having serious doubts about having a kid with Steve.

When two years rolled around, I have to say, I still had my doubts. But I said, "I'm not gonna be the one to end it, so yeah. Let's get married." No, it wasn't the best way to get married, but there are worse ways, I suppose.

᠉᠊᠊᠊᠊᠊᠊᠊

I was in such a state of terror the night before the wedding, I almost bagged it. That morning, Steve and

Steve Adams, shown here in the midst of a Morris dance.

I had a long talk. Typical Steve. He said, "Look, I know you're afraid. You think I'm not gonna get myself together. Well, don't worry about it. If it doesn't work out, we'll just say forget it." That sounded pretty good to me.

We went to France on our honeymoon, and for the first three days I was gonna leave him. I thought, this is the most horrible thing I've ever done in my life. I'm fast-lane. I speak French. Steve was lost in France, a country bumpkin. I found myself apologizing to everyone I knew for my husband.

At that point, I thought we were doomed.

≫≫≪≪

The next couple of years were interesting. Steve kept working at the law office and I lucked out—I got a job mixing sound for an off-Broadway show. That sent me off on a career path I had no idea was coming. I wound up mixing *Smokey Joe's Café* on Broadway, and suddenly everything started feeling pretty good. I began to feel like I didn't need this guy I was married to anymore.

Plus I met someone at the show who knocked me out. A fast-lane jazz guy. Real smooth. Real gorgeous. And I didn't resist. Physical things in my marriage had deteriorated. So, to make a long story short, I ended up with this other guy, and Steve was heartbroken. He went back to Massachusetts two years into our marriage.

Sure, we had our problems. But through it all, Steve had been such a sweet man. I remember him standing in our living room saying, "You're making a huge mistake. We're meant to be. This is a good thing for both of us."

I told him he was wrong. I was a fucking flake. I hadn't grown up. So Steve took off. I filed papers and just like that, Steve and I were separated.

I hung out with this other guy, but it fell apart after two years. Mark dumped me in a pretty hard way; I freaked. And Steve? He was right there. He came back, stood by me, and saved my life. And we rode that out. It was crazy, but we did it.

⫸⫷

I have this cousin who's very practical. And one time, I was pining away over Steve, not knowing what to do. I kept saying, "I want a good marriage. Why can't I have a good marriage?"

She looked at me like I was a complete idiot and said, "Open your eyes. You've got one."

I mean, what is marriage? You make the commitment. You say, "Okay, we get along, we like each other, let's do it."

I don't know any couple that doesn't struggle in one way or the other. But just like Steve wasn't very good with the whole money thing, I guess I had my weak spots, too.

⫸⫷

Steve loved to cook. Back when we were still married, I'd come home to these great meals, really incredible spreads. And I'd go off to work the next day with my little lunch bag of leftovers. He'd have made me tapenade and people would stare at me while I was eating. I'd smile and say, "Oh, this? It's nothing. My husband made a little something for me."

My parents could see what Steve was interested in—it was written all over him. They said they'd pay for him to go to French culinary school. So he went, and he was in heaven. He was on a roll.

We thought, he'll get a job as a chef and he'll rise quickly. But it didn't happen like that. Steve was a great cook at home, no question. But in a fast kitchen with a million people running in and out and a chef screaming and ten guys chopping celery? Steve was not a fast person. He hates people who multitask. He thinks multitasking is rude.

So he quit the chef's job and got a job as a steward. He did all the ordering for the restaurant. The head chef really liked him, so he put Steve in charge of hiring. Everything looked fine on the surface, but I could see that Steve was starting to fail. Every night, I'd come back home to find him sitting on the couch drinking beer. He couldn't take the grind.

One day he said, "That's it. I'm through. I'm going back to

Massachusetts and I'm gonna write about food and wine."

I had never seen him write anything, not so much as a letter. I said, "Steve, what are you talking about?"

He said, "This isn't working, this is not my thing."

I was exasperated, after all we'd been through. So I said, "Fine. Go up there. Get a job. Make money. Buy a house. Make payments. When you do that—call me."

So he went.

⸎

He took a couple of jobs where they treated him like a dog. Again, he was making practically nothing, eight bucks an hour. He worked in a huge wine store that featured thousands of labels. And working there, reading, studying hard, he taught himself about wine.

Not that his employers knew that. His employers thought he was lazy. Their approach to wine was very different than Steve's. They'd put two Burgundies together in a rack just because they looked the same, and Steve would say, "Look, you can't do that. This is a $25 bottle and this is a bottle for $8.99. See? They don't go together."

His boss just said, "You know what the trouble is with you? You don't put enough bottles on the shelves every day." They wouldn't give him a raise.

Steve and I started seeing each other again. I loved driving up to visit. But we weren't making enough money to do both—to live in New York and have a place up there. That's when he started to apply for jobs in the city again.

⸎

On a whim, Steve wrote to the French Culinary Institute and they immediately hooked him up with Windows on the World. Windows was looking for a wine cellar master, and they hired him the day after he interviewed.

The guys at Windows went, "We love you! You're exactly what we're looking for!" Steven was ecstatic. After all the shit he'd been through with people treating him like shit and me treating him like shit . . . life suddenly made sense for him. Within two months, he was sommelier once a week at Wild Blue, Windows' smaller restaurant. Then he was made the beverage manager.

Things were going well for us all around. I went off to a summer music camp so I could fall back in love with the oboe, and I remember Steve calling me with such joy in his voice. "Can you believe it? After only two months!"

I said, "Does this mean we're gonna open one of those special bottles of champagne when I get home?"

He said, "You bet!"

We were so happy. When I came home, he cooked something great. He seemed like a different person, the way he walked, the way he talked.

And that was September 4. We had seven days like that.

⟫⟪

September 10 was our anniversary. I was going to cook a great meal for Steve and sort of turn the tables on him, but I got really sick. I could tell he was disappointed. But he said, "Oh, don't worry about it." He never let the small stuff get to him.

Outside, it started pouring sheets of rain. He was wearing these nice, new shoes that I'd bought him, and I said in this little girl voice I do, "Steve, you can't go out. You'll ruin your shoooos."

And he wheeled around and said, "I'm not going to ruin my shoes! I mean, 'shooooos'!"

We both cracked up. So stupid and silly. He went out to buy a steak, but I knew he'd be disappointed because he was always going on about how there's no good cuts of meat available at 8:00 p.m. Sure enough, he comes back moaning, explaining to me, "This one's not so bad. The fat is in the meat, so you can cook it slowly and it'll melt in. Bad cuts of meat, you have to sear really fast. The fat's on the outside and it won't permeate the texture, you won't get the flavor."

I remember sitting there thinking, this guy really knows his stuff.

It was the first time I'd really understood that.

See, all those years I'd been admiring other people who I thought were fancy and bright and talented. People who were really good at what they did. All along, I felt that that's what I wanted all along, a man like that. And the night before it all happened, that's when it hit me: he'd been right here in my own backyard all the time.

We weren't wearing our wedding rings that night. I remember wanting to say, "Let's put our rings on." But I felt so sick. I told myself, I'll put it on tomorrow, and I went to bed.

He was gone the next morning when I woke up to the ringing phone.

⟫⟪

It was Steve's mother. She'd seen everything happen on the news while I was still asleep, and she asked, "Did Steve go to work today?"

I said, "Yeah. Why?"

"Oh no."

I turned on the TV and saw what was happening. Then I said, "I'll call you back."

⟫⟪

I called my brother, who lives four blocks away. He already knew, and he said, "I'll be there in two minutes."

He came over, and we sat here watching as Steve's Tower fell.

I'm not sure how it happened for him. If he was knocked out right away. If he survived the impact of the plane. Sometimes I imagine it was the smoke that got him before the building collapsed. But I still don't know. I guess I'll never know.

Later on I was told that one of the general managers at Windows got a call on his answering machine at home. A woman on the recording said, "There's been a huge explosion. All the windows have blown out and there's tons of smoke. The fire marshal told us to wait. We don't know what to do." That's the only clue I have to what they all went through up there.

I replay it a hundred million thousand times in my head. Did he try to call me? Did he try to make it to the roof? Did he suffer? I've never seen Steve afraid. He was a rock.

I'm the crazy one. I'm the one who weird things happen to. Not him. Not my husband.

⟫⟪

I used to say, "Promise me I'll die first."

He always just shrugged. "Okay."

When we first broke up, I'll never forget how angry he was, how hurt. He screamed at me, "Do you still have to die first?"

⟫⟪

It turns out that the FBI or FEMA or whoever it was comes to your door and officially tells you when they find them. "He's been identified," they said. So I went down to Pier 94, where the morgue is set up, to get Steve's remains.

I wanted to take him home with me but the people there said, "You're not allowed to take them." I was angry at that, but they explained, "You have to call a funeral director, who will get the remains. This is a homicide. There's no other process you can follow."

I told them, "I'm not religious. I don't want a ceremony. I just want this little piece of my husband back so I can dispose of it the way he would have wanted." But they were adamant. So I got out the yellow pages and picked a funeral home that seemed innocuous enough, and went down there with a friend the next day.

The funeral director wrote out a bill, which I didn't have money enough to pay for. Some agency stepped in and took care of it, I'm not sure which one. I know that the maximum allowance for funeral arrangements was $6,000, and I was presented with a check to cover Steve's expenses. These words were written on the check: "For the Victims of the World Trade Center."

Since then, I've gotten two other checks, one to help pay the rent and one for cash to get by. The funny thing is, I'm still working. I was always the money-maker. I know the money's there if I want to claim it. But in the end, what difference does money make?

UPDATE

Jessica Murrow became very frustrated by the fact that no one in the news media—her own field—would allow her to go on record stating her true feelings about the Bush Administration's response to 9/11.

From the World Socialist Web Site:

"In the first weeks after the tragedy, [Jessica's] network did a report on Windows on the World, where seventy-three employees, including Steve, were killed. . . . Looking into the camera, she said that her husband would have been 'mortified' if he knew that the U.S. government was preparing to take military action on the pretext of avenging his death. 'Are you going to kill someone else because my husband is dead?' she said. . . . Her next sentence, however, was edited out of the broadcast. 'What evil have we created that would bring people from another nation to do this to us?' she asked. 'Don't we need to look at our own actions?'"[81]

In subsequent interviews for television, Jessica's pieces were cut down to showcase her relationship with Steve without touching on her political viewpoints in the slightest. During one of these broadcasts, Jessica noted, the first portion of the show was dedicated to trumpeting how George W. Bush's Q rating had soared after 9/11.

Over the ensuing months, Jessica became very outspoken about the incredible inequities she perceived were afoot in the survivor benefit program, the gross mismanagement perpetrated by the American intelligence community, and the Bush Administration's invocation of 9/11 as a pretext for war. This last development was, as Jessica put it, "the most hateful thing that could ever happen to [Americans]."

---

81 Bill Vann, "September 11 Widow Condemns US War Plans," the World Socialist Web Site, December 2, 2002.

VINCENT FALIVENE

Vincent Falivene, twenty-eight. On the evening of September 14, feeling disconsolate and under-utilized, Vincent walked seventy blocks from his job at the Metropolitan Museum of Art to Union Square Park. That night, a candlelight vigil had been scheduled, and all of New York was invited.

As he walked down Fifth Avenue, Vincent took in the lampposts papered with color computer printouts of missing persons. "You'd often see copies of the same image," he says. "There was a guy I went to college with, and I remember another picture that showed twins—apparently both had been lost. It was overwhelming."

When he arrived at Union Square, the entire plaza was covered with mourners.

IT WAS STARTING to get dark. As I got further and further downtown, closer to the square, I started noticing the smell of—well, it smelled like burning hair to me.[82]

There was a line of Buddhists with orange robes and shaved heads walking through the park with candles. Some people in the line were dressed regularly . . . jeans, T-shirts, that kind of thing. The people in the line were predominantly Asian, and everyone was chanting. The words they were saying weren't English, so I have no idea what they were saying. But you got the idea from their mood. I didn't join the line, but I did follow them through the crowd and into the park.

I'd kind of expected to see a lot of disjointed people milling about the square, but this wasn't the case. I knew the Buddhists had organized the vigil. They'd had only a day to organize their whole congregation, and this huge gathering was the result, in such a short amount of time. I thought it was pretty amazing. See, I'm not talking about a short line of people; there were tons. It was like being at a party.

---

82 The smell of the burning Towers laced the air of downtown Manhattan for months after the eleventh.

Kinda like a conga line.

I saw all these placards and posters, you know, people leaving messages of peace. More images of missing people. Several quotes. There was one long quote from Gandhi . . . I mean, it was *long*. They had to write it on a white bed sheet with black acrylic paint. I started feeling heady. It was difficult to stop and read them all.

I'm telling you, it was like being in a crowded party, being shoulder to shoulder.

At the center of the square, three Buddhist monks were handing out candles, lighting them for people going by. Just

Directly following the attacks of September 11, some citizens saw war as the ultimate and only solution.

simple, long white candles. The monks stayed completely silent as they went about their work. They wore orange and yellow or red sashes, and they had their eyes down, somber. It was like the whole park was a funeral, and the monks were trying to be deferential to the people who were hurting. There were no smiles. There was no laughing and there was no conversation.

»»»«««

Things were different on the south side of the square. A number of people sat in drum circles, where three or four guys played bongos while everybody else sang, "Give Peace a Chance." Guys in the center were dancing. If you've ever gone to a Grateful Dead concert, you know what I'm talking about. They were dancing like that. Spastic. Reaching up toward the sky, looking up, looking tripped out, singing very loudly, like they were in church.

This one girl in particular I remember was singing between the pauses. While everyone else was singing "Give Peace a Chance," she was singing "One Love" by Bob Marley. Her voice was quite bad, but you know. The words. It was a point well taken.

The next circle I got to had a couple people sitting with guitars and another bongo drum. Here they were singing "Kumbaya" over and over and over again. It was nice and it was soothing, but that's kinda when I got a little distracted by the sound of people arguing.

One person shouting, "You're fucking crazy! We should bomb these people! There's no other response!"

Other people shouting back: "There's gotta be a peaceful response to this. There's gotta be another way to go about it. We can't let them goad us into a violent response!"

I could feel the tension building.

One argument broke out between this African American guy, who was very tall and had full dreadlocks, and this Young Girl, probably an NYU college student who wore a red, white, and blue bandana and an American flag shirt. He called her a bimbo, and she lost it. She called him "a fuckin' asshole."

People chimed in from all sides. People shouted flack. A couple more guys got involved, I guess to defend the Young Girl's honor. "You shouldn't talk to her like that, man," they said. "You definitely shouldn't talk to her like that."

The Dreadlock Dude retorted, "Hey! She called me stupid."

I started to get nervous. This gathering had started out peacefully, and now it was turning into a mob.

But the Dreadlock Dude stood up and apologized to the Young Girl. "Look," he said. "I'm sorry. I shouldn't have called you a bimbo. But you shouldn't have called me stupid. Obviously we have different views on this."

A guy from the crowd thanked the Dreadlock Dude: "That was very big of you to say, man."

The Young Girl was silent for a moment. Then she called Dreadlock Dude "a fuckin' asshole" again and walked away. But it wasn't over.

≫≫≫≪≪≪

A Latino man standing nearby said, "How could you say that America has done things that pushed these people to the point where they're willing to lay down their lives to kill us? How could you say that?"

Right then, it all broke open. People started talking over each other; the crowd surged and gathered strength. But Dreadlock Dude held up his hands and cried out, "Okay! Hold it! There has to be some kind of forum here!"

He had a piece of poster board that he'd rolled into a kind of baton and he held it up. "Whoever wants to speak should come up here and hold up this roll of poster board to signify you are the speaker."

Now he had the attention of all the people in area. People behind me started yelling, "Speak up! Speak up!"

The first person stepped forward and grabbed the baton. He started talking, but the crowd yelled over him. So Dreadlock Dude said, "Whoever's speaking should be able to speak. I don't know about all of you, but I don't have anywhere to go tonight. Everyone will get their chance."

Then another Latino guy came up and started talking. He said, "We should all love one another," which didn't get the best reception.

Then this other guy came up and asked for the baton. He was

"Other people shouting back: 'There's gotta be a peaceful response to this. There's gotta be another way to go about it. We can't let them goad us into a violent response!'"

In counterpoint to those citizens urging politicians to move America toward war, peace vigils were held across the country during the weeks following the 9/11 attacks.

a Big Dude, well over six feet tall. His head was shaved bald like a neo-Nazi. He wore a skin-tight T-shirt, tight jeans, and suspenders. His arms were real thick, and covered with tattoos. When the baton was handed to him, he said, "Listen. In 1983, I lost eighteen of my friends to the terrorist bombing in Beirut. Really close friends of mine. After that, America did bad things. But my philosophy in life is peace through superior firepower. And that's all I'm gonna say." He gave back the baton.

A woman in African garb wasn't about to let that pass. She started yelling at the Big Dude. She said she'd lived in Jamaica and used to tour as a backup singer for Bob Marley. She kept calling Bob Marley "the Prophet." As in, "the Prophet Bob Marley said we should all live as one! We need to change our view of the world! It has to be done by loving each other!" Then she broke into "One Love" while holding the baton, and everyone started singing along with her.

It's kinda funny describing it now, but it was very powerful at the time. At the time, I thought this was all wonderful, the kind of discourse people should be engaged in all the time. Obviously, this won't occur on a daily basis. But to really sit back and challenge your own belief system, or to try to bring about change? To engage in dialogue—honest dialogue—about what's working and what isn't, about

where we've been and where we need to go? That's one of the beauties
of living in this country. It's one of our rights as American citizens.
For some people who started talking to one another that evening,
however, that was as far as they'd ever gone with it.

⤞⤝

It was getting dark quickly and the air quality was deteriorating. The
wind had shifted north, and the smoke from the Towers was blowing
into the park. You could hear it in people's voices; they started to get
raspy. At that point, a lot of folks put on those surgical masks. Then,
the people who'd been singing "Kumbaya" started singing "New York,
New York" over and over again.

It all happened so quickly. Suddenly, a Rockette's line of people
from all walks of life linked themselves arm-in-arm and started doing
this absurd version of a kick line. It was insane, but it made me smile.
It takes strength to do something so odd. There was truth in the mu-
sical number.

One more thing I want to recall. As I left the square, two sculp-
tors were at work, sitting on the ground, a man and a woman. They
were working on a gold and silver plating in the shape of an American
flag, four feet wide and a few feet high. It was two-dimensional but
made to look fluid, like it was blowing in the breeze. Each plate alter-
nated gold and silver.

As they fashioned this piece, they inscribed names from the posters of missing people right into the metal plating. It was a very intricate task. And as these artists worked, people stood around and
watched them in complete silence. The artists never looked up. They
were utterly absorbed in their work. Two days later, I know they auc-
tioned the piece off. I have no idea what they did with the proceeds.

⤞⤝

It was something I was glad to have seen, but something I hope I'll
never see again. A funeral for the entire city.

PATRICK CHARLES WELSH

Patrick Charles Welsh, forty-four, is a man of tall carriage with salt-and-pepper hair and ruddy cheeks. He exudes the natural charm of a gifted raconteur.

Patrick's story begins as an American fable. How it ends is open to interpretation.

I'M AMAZED that I actually survived the '80s in New York.

I struggled when I came here in 1981. Got caught up in the bartending scene. Back then, everybody was riding the wave of Republican funny money. Father Reagan was protecting us all from the Evil Empire, and everything was, "Ain't life great? Gimme another line of cocaine! America's Number One!"

New York has always been a great place to live, but it's a love/hate relationship. If you're not financially independent, it can be extremely difficult. The guy who takes a town car back and forth and rides an elevator up to his penthouse isn't seeing the homeless person who vomits on his steps. But that's the daily reality I knew back then—the street-level view, I guess you might say.

It can be a bit abrupt. A bit shocking. But you get a little numb to it after a while. And that's when you find your niche.

>>><<<

I was going through a series of different bartending jobs and found a new one at a place called Boxer's down in the Village. It was St. Patrick's Day in '87 or '88, and the following day, I met this new waitress named Debbie.

You couldn't miss her. She lit up the room like a psychedelic Auntie Mame. When she walked in, everyone knew she was there. We hit it off right away, driving each other insane across the service bar like Diane and Sam Malone from *Cheers.*

For our first date, we went out and saw *The Adventures of Baron Munchausen.* Then we polished off a fifth of tequila at a bar I used to work at called the You're It. It was a hell of a first date.

Debbie was wild. She had this incredible zest for life. She embraced it fully. We hit it off and never looked back.

Four or five years later, I proposed on New Year's Eve.

⫸⫷

We lived in a studio on Bleecker Street, between Charles and Perry Streets. We got a Dalmatian named Dylan that was like our kid, and Debbie found this coat in a thrift store window—a black-and-white spotted coat that was awful, just awful. I used to imagine how every other customer in the thrift store had walked past that coat, saw it hanging on the rack, and said, "I won't go near that thing with a ten-foot pole."

But Debbie said, "Oh my God! That's perfect!" Of course she did, she was ecstatic about this treasure. She brought it home and showed it off for me, and what else could I say? "Baby, it's you."

A black-and-white spotted coat for when she walked our black-and-white spotted dog. Deb had a great appreciation for the ridiculous and the absurd.

She was unafraid to talk to anybody. That was another thing about her. Back then I called her The Mayor because she knew everyone in our neighborhood. Everyone.

⫸⫷

As we spent our lives together, I learned so much more about her. She couldn't read music, so she'd taught herself to play the piano by ear. She could play *Rhapsody in Blue* like a professional—it was amazing.

I would say, "How on earth did you learn that?"

And she'd say, "Oh, I just banged it out on my own."

She played the keys by memory and picked up the guitar this way, too.

She was older than me, born in Darby, Pennsylvania, right outside of Philadelphia. She went to Notre Dame High School. For a brief time, she was a Flyerette for the Philadelphia Flyers—not really a cheerleader, but a staff member for promotional things, in the press box at the games, that kind of thing. Debbie was very *rah rah rah*, so it was a perfect job for her. Shortly after that, she got a job as a flight attendant with Eastern Airlines and did that for a very long time.

Prior to my meeting Debbie, Eastern went on strike, which is when she got the job waiting tables at Boxer's. If it weren't for that strike, she would have still been flying and I would never have met her. I think about that sometimes.

Well, the airline industry eventually became a big part of my life because it was such a big part of hers. Debbie was very pro-union. She was a people person. She had no tolerance whatsoever for financial or political tyrants. In fact, she had tremendous vehemence toward Frank Lorenzo, the guy who tried to dismantle Eastern Airlines, cut it up, and sell it off to Continental. That guy was a real bastard. According to Deb, he ruined the lives of people who'd worked for that company for years.[83]

She was based in New York but traveled the world on her time off. She went to Peru and learned the customs and the language; she hiked the Inca Trail all the way up to Machu Picchu. Then she went to Bali, where she survived a near-fatal bout of pneumonia. After that, it was Hong Kong, Malaysia, Germany, and Greece using only a Fodor's book.

She always traveled by herself. She was fearless like that, a person who embraced different cultures. And in terms of her demise, this was the most ironic thing, to me. She wasn't isolationist, she was a worldly person, always down to earth. Lots of humor, no stuffiness. She was a beautiful and accepting American, quite the opposite of what many people in the world think of our people today.

⋙⋘

---

83 The movie *Wall Street* was loosely based on what Lorenzo tried to do to Eastern.

By the time we met at Boxer's, Debbie'd worked her way through a series of different restaurants. She didn't know if she was ready to go back to the airlines. They'd broken her heart. At first she took work at the Amazon Club over by Chelsea Piers, where part of their proceeds went to save the rain forests—it was a famous place in the late '80s. Then she was at Boxer's for a while. But for the sake of better benefits, she finally decided to go back to work as a flight attendant.

Some former Eastern Airlines people had put together Kiwi International Airline, a small company based out of New York which flew routes up and down the East Coast and as far west as Chicago. It was a fledgling airline, so they named the company after a flightless bird. The people who started it felt that their wings had been clipped by Eastern. It was a tight-knit group, and Debbie loved the notion of it.

She explained to me how, when a flight attendant leaves a company, she loses all seniority. Even though you may have years and years of experience, if you change companies you have to start back at zero as a buck private and go through the whole process all over again. And seniority is what you leveraged to arrange your work schedule. What it all meant was that she'd be the low gal on the totem pole for a long time to come, but despite all this, Debbie was thrilled to get back to work.

I remember going to her graduation from Kiwi's training program. I was so proud. Each graduating class put a skit together. Her class took the music from Kriss Kross's "Jump" and changed the words. I helped her write the lyrics. Debbie coordinated this whole hip-hop dance routine, and it was hysterical to see these flight attendants breakdancing in their uniforms.

⇒⟫⟪⇐

Well, Kiwi hit bad times when the airline industry struggled, and faltered through the early '90s. The company was going into a burnout phase, and Debbie began to get overscheduled because the airline was losing people. Doing a job like that every night is like being a baseball pitcher and having to throw several nights in a row; you just can't do it. You'll hurt yourself.

Debbie found out United was hiring and said, "I think I'm gonna make a move. Even though I'll have to start all over—again—my benefits and schedule will be a lot better." And that's what she did. She started training with United and was truly happy.

In fact, both of our lives started to take off. I started to have great success as a commercial actor. Finally, I didn't have to take bartending jobs anymore; I was living off my craft. In fact, I vowed that I'd never set foot behind a bar again unless it was for a friend.

Debbie and I had more time together now, and we got to travel a little. After all our years of struggling in New York, we were starting to get some payoff.

❧❧❧❧

Debbie's mother confided something in me once. She said, "You know, I have tremendous admiration for your marriage. You two just laugh from your heels."

She had us pegged. The night prior to the eleventh, we'd gone to a comedy club where a client of my manager was performing. I thank God for that because our last moments together, we were laughing uproariously, just like we did through most of our marriage.

The eleventh wasn't a normally scheduled workday for Deb. She'd gotten an email from another flight attendant who asked, "Would you cover this shift for me? I have a special event I'd like to attend."

Debbie said, "Fine. I'll take yours if you can take this shift for me." It was a normal swap.

The woman actually emailed her back later, saying, "My plans fell through, if you want to switch back."

But Debbie said, "No, that's fine. Take the day off. I'll cover it."

In a lot of ways—to her friends, her family, and me . . . we figure it was destiny. The way Deb was, I know she would have been doing her best to comfort the people on board that plane. She would have been inspirational to a great many people. I know this for a fact.

⫸⫷

Normally when she flew, we'd exchange information about where she was going. But I didn't know she was going to San Francisco on the eleventh. She just said, "I'll be back in two days, I'll cook a great dinner for us, and we'll go see a movie."

I said, "Perfect. Give me a call when you get in." This was normal enough.

Ever since I got a computer, my routine is to get up early in the morning, like 5:00, to work. Deb had to be out of the house at about 5:30 to get to Newark Airport. I made some coffee and took it to her. She was like Dagwood Bumstead getting out the door that day, with papers flying all around her—a real mess. I helped her carry her bag downstairs, kissed her goodbye, and off she went.

⫸⫷

I had a couple auditions scheduled for that morning. The first one was for an industrial film, and I was getting ready to go out the door when I turned the TV on to New York 1. The sound was off. The first plane had already hit and I remember thinking, my God, what the hell is that?

But I was already running late, so I ignored it and kept getting ready. The news wasn't even sure what had happened. And then the second plane hit. That got my attention.

My first thought was, I have to think of something to say because Debbie will be so upset when she calls. Any type of airline disaster affected her deeply.

So I went to the first audition. On the streets, people were gathering in front of TVs, in front of shops and diners. I gleaned information little by little on the way to my destination. By the time I got to the casting office, I knew it was a terrorist attack and I was filled with rage.

It was absolutely unfathomable to me, this deliberate mayhem of biblical proportions. It was like Genghis Khan coming through and decapitating children in a village. It was unthinkable that anybody could be so maligned, so full of fear and hatred. Everybody I met at the audition was the same way, inflamed that anybody could do this to fellow human beings. To call it troglodyte or Neanderthal behavior is insulting to the Neanderthals and troglodytes. Here were people who were so miserable in their lives, so full of fear, which I believe is the basis of hatred. Fear of freedom, or the fear of women being intelligent and non-submissive. People so lost in their byzantine, perverse mindset . . . so enraged that the world won't conform to their oppressive way of life that they would lash out in this fashion.

But at no time did I think my wife was involved. I was still thinking of things to say when she called. I knew that she'd not only be upset, but furious.

⟫⟪

My auditions were canceled, so I went straight home knowing that such a huge event would stop the whole world. I got to our apartment and immediately turned on CNN. The report came in that another plane had hit the Pentagon. I felt fear for all of us because those actions looked like the prelude to nuclear Armageddon. I remember thinking, oh my God, this is it, this is the day. The horns are blowing, the Seventh Seal has broken, and any moment now the Four Horsemen of the Apocalypse will be let loose. That was the first real glimmer of fear that passed through my mind for Debbie's sake, but I ignored it. Looking back, I can see I was in denial the whole day.

I'd already heard that United planes were involved. In fact, I'd heard that one originating from Newark bound for San Francisco had suddenly switched directions and gone down outside Shanksville, Pennsylvania. My mind was racing, unable to compute all the information.

Then the phone calls started coming in from friends and family asking about Deb, and this cemented my denial as the day wore on. "She's fine," I said. "She's fine. She hasn't called me yet because they probably told her to keep the airwaves clear. They probably redirected her plane to someplace, I bet they're already in the process of landing."

Remember? I didn't know she was going to San Francisco.

≫≫⋘

Then a dear friend called whom we'd run into the night before outside the comedy club. A bunch of us had stopped and chatted on
the street. This woman called and said, "Patrick, have you heard from
Deb?"

I said, "No, but it's all right, I'm sure she's gonna call me soon."

She said, "Patrick. I'm really worried. Last night she said she was
going to San Francisco, and that plane that crashed in Shanksville
was bound from Newark to San Francisco."[84]

I swear to God, at that moment, I felt like somebody'd hit me
across the bridge of my nose with an eighty-pound bat.

I snapped at this woman. "There are many flights from Newark
to San Francisco," I said. "She's fine. She'll call me as soon as she gets
an opportunity. Debbie's a professional. She's got people to take care
of, she's fine . . ."

To me? The odds were unfathomable. It was like I was really
saying to this poor woman, "I'm sorry. You've got me confused with
someone else. Things like this don't happen to me. It's just something
somebody like me would only ever read about."

≫≫⋘

But, of course, the day went on, and I was becoming more and more
unraveled, fighting my own mind. I was bug-eyed, glued to the television, pacing. A wreck of a man spiraling downward. By late afternoon,
all planes were ordered to the ground, and I had yet to hear from her.

People were calling left and right. Debbie's sister called; her

---

84 Four planes were hijacked and crashed on September 11, 2001: American Airlines Flight 11,
bound from Boston to Los Angeles, which crashed into the North Tower of the Trade Center
at 8:45 A.M.; United Airlines Flight 175, bound from Boston to Los Angeles, which crashed into
the South Tower of the Trade Center at 9:06 A.M.; American Airlines Flight 77, bound from
Washington, D.C., to Los Angeles, which crashed into the Pentagon at 9:45 A.M.; and United
Flight 93, bound from Newark to San Francisco, which crashed inexplicably in Shanksville,
Pennsylvania, at 10:10 A.M. Cell phone calls from the Shanksville plane confirm that the passengers staged some sort of revolt against the hijackers shortly before the plane spun out of control
and crashed. Experts theorize that Flight 93 may have been heading toward Washington, D.C.,
to attack either the Capitol Building or the White House.

mother called. "No," I kept repeating, "I haven't heard." Realizing I was in denial. Realizing I was in this incredible ghost of gloom that drifted around me, like a nightmare that I couldn't wake up from.

My mom was trying to comfort me. "Maybe she's all right. The cell phones are still out of whack. She'll call as soon as she can."

It was right then that the call waiting beeped. I told my mom to hang on and I clicked over to the other line. "Yeah?"

It was a United Airlines representative. "Hello? Mr. Welsh?" I can't remember the woman's name on the other end. My mind was reeling. I didn't want her to say another word. I was like, please, not one more word. But she said, "I'm so, so sorry to inform you that your wife, Deborah, was on the manifest for Flight 93 that went down in Shanksville."

That poor woman. I can't imagine what she had to go through to tell me that. That job? I wouldn't give it to my worst enemy.

»»«««

Right at that moment, time stopped. I can't tell you what it felt like. I was so devastated by this unheard cry of souls, all the people who'd been killed that morning. This moan of humanity going straight up to heaven. I was already shaken, but when this woman told me Deb was gone, I fell to my knees and dropped the phone.

It was no accident that my mother was holding on the other line. There I was, down on my knees, weeping uncontrollably. I don't know how long the woman from United stayed on the phone. Finally, I said, "I'm so sorry. I can't talk right now. My mother's on the phone . . ." I don't know what else I said.

"I understand," the woman said. "I'm so sorry."

I clicked back to the other line and said, "Mom, they just told me that Deb was on that flight in Pennsylvania."

I know I said more, but I honestly don't know what. At that moment, I didn't know who I was anymore. Everything about my life had lost meaning. I felt like the shell of a person, like somebody had scraped out my insides. I couldn't stop weeping. I couldn't talk.

The phone started ringing mercilessly, and I took a few calls. Then the pastor from our church called, Father Brett Hoover from St. Paul the Apostle. And I told him. And he said, "Patrick, I'm coming right over."

I said, "I'll meet you downstairs."

I dragged him to a bar and threw down one drink after another. I didn't know what else to do.

He understood perfectly. He said, "Don't worry, I'm right here with you."

⟫⟪

People from our old neighborhood still remembered her. After September 11, people put memorials in their windows. There were flowers everywhere on Bleecker Street. The Mayor was gone.

Dear friends of ours, Pam Moss and her husband, Tim, took this beautiful picture of Debbie when she and I first got together. They framed it in black with an American flag that said, "In Loving Memorial."

She would have been fifty this July 20. And we would have been married for eleven years.

⟫⟪

Two weeks later, I delivered my wife's eulogy at a memorial in her honor. I didn't think I would be capable of it, but I think she was there to help me. I knew I had a responsibility to my wife, that she needed a wonderful, lasting tribute, and I made sure she had it.

"The world has been transformed," I said. "The transformation isn't in the malevolence of these madmen. It isn't found in the scarred skyline of our great city. It isn't in the broken walls of our proud Pentagon. It's not in the charred crater of courage in the gentle fields of Pennsylvania. The true transformation is how all these people—our countrymen and the world—came together. That's what we must take away from this. That transformation is the divine rescue of God among man."

I remember it was near sunset and so many friends had come. We had a lovely Irish wake up on the roof of our building. We'd had lots of parties there over the years, gatherings of very creative people. Now we grabbed hands and said the Lord's Prayer, and each person had a moment to impart something about how Debbie had touched their lives. It was incredible.

People were weeping incessantly. I was just barely holding myself together. I thought it was my duty to do that.

I looked around and saw how Debbie had touched the lives of all these people. And once again, she had touched my life from beyond her own. She's forever a part of me, forever a part of my life.

For two months after that, I was . . . I was not good.

>>>><<<<

I'm a different person now than I was then. I'm not just Patrick anymore. I feel like I'm Patrick and Debbie and a lot of these other people. I'm the person who's going to mold his new life in whatever direction God has chosen for it to go. I struggled for a long period with this. But you have choices to make in life, and life is very hard.

M. Scott Peck started off his book *The Road Less Traveled* with "Life is difficult." He said that when we finally understand that life is hard, and that anything easy is the gravy, then it's actually not so hard anymore. But if you think that the world owes you a living, for instance, and everything should be a silver spoon in your mouth, well, you're gonna have a hard time.

Editor's note: Patrick wanted to be sure to thank Greg Wolfe, Madeline Klinkova and her sister Vanessa, Barbara Sinaris, and many other dear friends for their remarkable friendship and support during his grief. "They came to my rescue," he said. "Please make sure to mention them."

UPDATE

In his book, *Among the Heroes: United Flight 93 and the Passengers and Crew Who Fought Back*, Jere Longman evaluates the voice recordings that were eventually analyzed by the U.S. intelligence community: "A few minutes after 9:31 A.M., a hijacker on board Flight 93 can be heard on the cockpit voice recorder ordering a woman to sit down. The woman, presumably a flight attendant, implores, 'Don't, don't.' She pleads, 'Please, I don't want to die.' Patrick Welsh, the husband of flight attendant Debbie Welsh, is later told that a flight attendant was stabbed early in the takeover, and it is strongly implied it was his wife. She was a first-class attendant, and he says, 'knowing Debbie,' she would have resisted."

A *New York Times* reporter, Longman is perhaps best known as a sports writer, though he did extensive coverage for the *Times* concerning the developments surrounding United Flight 93.

While the exact events that took place on United Flight 93 will probably never be known, some events have been ascertained by careful evaluation of phone calls made by passengers as the hostage crisis ensued. The 9/11 Commission Report cites that Deborah Welsh, the flight's purser, was held in the plane's cockpit and killed there early in the crisis.

LAUREN ALBERT and KAROL KEASLER

Lauren Albert, thirty-five, describes a situation that thousands of families throughout the New York metropolitan area were forced to participate in following the attack: the search for a missing family member or friend.

Lauren went down to the Red Cross the day after the attack to register her friend Karol Keasler as missing.

I WAS HERE in my Murray Hill apartment on Tuesday morning, the eleventh. I'd made some coffee and was drinking it when I watched the first plane hit on TV. The first thing I did was call my mother who lives up in Maine and say, "Oh my God, you're not gonna believe what just fucking happened."

Then the second plane hit. I thought I was seeing things. My hand went to my mouth and I kept saying, "Oh my God, oh my God, oh my God." I was in shock. Who wasn't?

Right after that, my phone went dead, so I got online immediately—I have a cable modem, and there was this flurry of emails. A tight-knit group of my friends rent a house together every summer out on Fire Island, and everyone was asking each other to check in. "Please! Please! Hit 'Reply to All.'"

It took a little while, but everything seemed fine, everyone seemed accounted for. Until we remembered Karol and Mike, two friends who worked for the same company. No one had heard from either of them.

Karol worked on the 89th floor, Mike on the 88th of Tower 2. Which I guess is what eventually made all the difference, that one floor of space that separated them.

>>><<<

To say that everyone was frenzied wouldn't do it any justice. When the phones came back on, I called the Chicago offices of Karol's company—Keefe, Bruyette, and Woods—to find out if they had any information. I told the woman in Chicago Mike and Karol's names, and she was really helpful. She said, "Oh, I know Karol. Look, we know some specific departments escaped entirely, they've already checked in. But we don't have any information about Karol or Mike right at this moment."

I remember thinking, well, okay. There's confirmation that some people as high as the 88th and 89th floors got out, so there's a good chance for both of them.

Just to be sure, I called Keefe, Bruyette, and Woods' Boston office and got a guy who also said he knew Karol. In fact, he said he used to sit right across from her when he'd worked in New York. This man said, "We haven't heard anything. All I can tell you is to keep calling. And pray." He was definitely not as optimistic as the woman in Chicago had been.

But now I thought, well, he's just being emotional. People did get out. It's probably okay. It's just really hard to get in touch with people right now, since the phones aren't working.

Well, around three or four o'clock that day, I got word from my friends that Mike had checked in. He'd fled Tower 2 and called Rho', who got in touch with all of us through the network we'd set up.

Mike had worked in the Towers for years and was there when the first bombing happened in '93. He's an ex-marine who worked in a small department. He said that everyone heard it when the first plane hit. They felt it, too. Folks in his department looked at each other and said, "Let's get the fuck out of here." So they left.

He made his way over to the World Financial Center and found his girlfriend, who worked in an office there; she was suffering from pretty bad smoke inhalation. They took the ferry to Staten Island, where she lived, and that's where he finally called everyone from.

But [by] four or five that afternoon, no one had heard from Karol.

The Chicago office was nice enough to call me back to say they hadn't heard from Karol, either; they had heard from Mike.

I said, "Yeah. Okay. I got that. I know."

That's when I started to feel numb. It was starting to sink in.

⟫⟪

I'd known Karol for four years. She was vice president of events and communications for KBW, which is a securities broker and investment bank. She coordinated events and road shows for her company, and you could tell she was good at what she did. Karol was a one-woman party. She could light up a room just by walking in the door.

Early on Wednesday morning, the twelfth, I talked to my friend Elizabeth. She said, "I have some upsetting news."

"What is it?"

She said, "Karol's fiancé, Michael, has been living in Moscow . . ."

"Right," I said. "I know." Karol was gonna move there. Michael had been calling frantically from Moscow. He'd obviously heard, but he couldn't get in touch with anyone. Our network of friends was still in operation—if anything it had gotten larger. Karol's mom had been in touch with somebody, and it ultimately got back to Elizabeth. This is the way it happened for a lot of people, I later learned, this round robin of diluted information that went on for days afterward.

Elizabeth said, "After the first plane hit the first Tower, Karol called her mom. She told her, 'Mom, I'm okay. We know what happened and I'm all right.' But then the phone went dead."

When Elizabeth told me the phone had cut off, I knew. I just knew she was gone.

Desperate for their loved ones' return, the families of those missing in the Towers created homemade flyers like these and plastered them all over the city. Buildings and street posts in the Financial District were wallpapered with them.

⟫⟪

That afternoon, my friend Jason called and said that the Red Cross had opened up a Missing Persons Center at Bellevue Hospital on 1st Avenue. I was the closest to Karol out of our group of friends, and maybe I was the most equipped to handle what had to be done. I don't know. Everybody was pretty much in a state of shock.

At any rate, I had a bunch of pictures of Karol from this luau party we'd thrown out on the island the summer before. She was gorgeous. Really short, platinum blonde hair. Her huge, megawatt smile. In the picture, she was wearing a sarong and a coconut shell bra and hugging another friend.

That was the best picture any of us had of her face.

I took it to Kinko's, made a bunch of color photocopies, and went down to the Red Cross to wait on line.

⊁⟫⟫⟪⟪⊰

When I got to Bellevue, the line was three blocks long. All these people and everyone was clutching photos. It was very organized. The line was very quiet. Some volunteers were giving out boxes of sandwiches and coffee and cookies and bottled water.

There was a white guy, about thirty years old, walking up and down the line with a list on a clipboard. He was tall and thin and looked like a Midwestern farm boy with strawberry-blond hair. The list recorded the most recently updated casualties, and he was going person-to-person to see if anyone's missing person had been found in the hospital.

He didn't find anyone.

As he came closer, I asked if he could check to see if Karol was on his list. Now that we were standing next to one another, I could tell that he was exhausted. By now it was four o'clock in the afternoon on Wednesday, September 12. He looked completely overwhelmed. I had to give him Karol's name five times. His hands were shaking.

I saw an older man with white hair and a chaplain's collar call out to a little ten-year-old girl who was standing on line with her mother. The chaplain said, "Come here, honey. Come here. What was your daddy's name again?" The mother burst into tears.

I was standing next to a group of four or five girls my own age, and I figured out by overhearing their conversation that they were there on behalf of their friend. They were saying things like, "How's she gonna get through this? She hasn't even written the thank-you notes or gone through the wedding pictures yet."

I thought, Karol was going to get married, too. She'd just gone to Quebec City with her mom a few weeks before to buy her wedding dress.

≫≫≪≪

When I finally got to the end of the line, they handed me a question-naire to fill out on Karol's behalf, but I found I couldn't answer a lot of the questions. I could do the basic descriptions they asked for, like hair color, skin color, weight, appearance. But the rest? I wanted to make sure, you know? I wanted to make absolutely sure she had, like, blue eyes and not green.

MISSING
Winston Grant
Hgt 6'2", Wt. 180lbs, Age 60yrs,
Hair Black/Grey at temples

Worked at Blue Cross/Blue Shield
30th Floor of 1 World Trade Center
Please call (866)761-8265 with any info.

It's tough to describe, but suddenly there I was, standing in that line, and I didn't know anything for sure anymore. Like, I couldn't remember if Karol had pierced ears or not. I couldn't remember exactly what her engagement ring looked like. The little things eluded me and made me wonder . . . had I ever really known her at all?

I guess that's when I realized I was in shock. I also realized the importance of the little things you've seen a million times but never really register. Questions like: How long were her fingernails? How long were her toenails? Does she have any scars, birthmarks, or tattoos?

I'd seen Karol practically naked; we spent summers together out at the beach in little bathing suits. I was almost certain she didn't have any tattoos . . . or did she? Then there was stuff like: Broken Bones? And what was she wearing that day? I had no idea. I hadn't seen her that day. Was she right-handed or left-handed?

I just wanted my friend back.

I had my cell phone with me, and I had to call a lot of friends to get that form filled out. I asked, "Do you know this about Karol? Would so-and-so know that about Karol? Can you call her mother for me? I need her dentist's name, does anyone have that information?"

⋙⋘

Then they brought us into an auditorium to get a case number for the person we were going to declare missing. I was sitting in a row next to a woman about my age, and at one point she just broke down and started crying. So I started crying, too. I wasn't doing it for her, specifically. After all that had happened, I just had to.

This young woman kept repeating things like, "Well, we checked his answering machine. Employees are calling in to see if he's okay, but we don't know. We checked his answering machine . . ." It was awful.

But then, something really curious came over me. I don't want to call it a calm or anything like that, but it's like something inside me clicked on or clicked off, I can't decide which. I started looking around, because I felt like I wanted to just . . . bear witness. I looked directly into people's faces and saw a lot of people staring into space, shocked, expressionless. People with tears in their eyes who were quietly crying on their own. I made it a point to look at their faces because I wanted to remember that. I didn't ever want to forget what this was or what any of it meant, although I'm still not sure what that is.

I got a case number for Karol: 759. I assume that meant that, by that point, they'd registered that many people as missing. It must have been early in the process.[85]

---

85 It soon became apparent that approximately 3,000 people were missing from all four 9/11 attacks. Later, 2,973 would be accounted for, with 24 still missing. This number does not include the 19 hijackers of the four jetliners.

>>>><<<<

DOUG JASON IRGANG
(last name commonly misspelled... ERgang, URgang)
AGE: 32 years old
weight : 140 lbs
height : 5'8"
eyes: hazel
identifying scar on right side of his stomach. (large scar)
LAST SEEN @ 2 WORLD TRADE CENTER
WORKS @ Sandler O'Neill Fl. 104
IF YOU HAVE ANY INFORMATION
please contact us ....
(212) 388-9382
Steve & Sari : (631) 721-4815

Sandler O'Neill and Partners, L.P., is a New York-based investment banking firm that suffered especially horrendous losses on 9/11. Headquartered on the 104th floor of 2 World Trade Center, Sandler O'Neill lost sixty-seven of its eighty-four Manhattan-based employees when the planes struck the Towers. (See the story of Brendan Ryan and Kristin Irvine Ryan on page 432.)

A friend who lives in Stuyvesant Town, on Avenue A below 14th Street, mentioned to me that she'd been walking home on Tuesday evening and seen something amazing. Somebody had painted a huge mural on the side of a building. They must have done it fast, in the space of time between the planes hitting the buildings and that same evening.

The mural showed the New York City skyline with the Towers on fire. And the artist had written: IN LOVING MEMORY OF OUR FAMILIES AND FRIENDS. Then the date, and an inscription: REST IN PEACE. People had already begun to embrace the place. Candles and flowers and offerings had been left at the foot of the mural, as if it were some kind of shrine.

I decided to pass by there on my way back from Bellevue. I brought some flowers for Karol, pink star lilies because those were her favorite. When we used to go out to the beach for the weekend, she always brought star lilies, and before she even put her bags in her room, she'd have them cut and arranged in a vase on the kitchen table.

The mural was overwhelming. Whoever painted it had made the sky orange. The buildings—the Towers—were gray. I put the star lilies down along with all the others' offerings, a vast sea of bright-colored flowers, and just stood there. I thought of Karol. And I guess I stood there a really long time.

⤜⤜⤜⤜

It's early October now, and we've already had a memorial service for Karol. Michael, her fiancé, flew in from Moscow. At first her family was fixated on things like going to the morgue. But then they just made a decision that she was gone based on the information they heard, which seemed pretty clear.

For instance, a guy who worked on the same floor as Karol apparently called his wife after the second plane hit Karol's Tower. Nobody knows how his call got through, but it did. And that wife eventually got in touch with Karol's mom and relayed her husband's last words.

Apparently, the man had said, "There's smoke. The heat is really bad. I'm not going to make it out. People are dying all around me of smoke inhalation. It's bad."

And another person who was running to evacuate after the first plane hit said she'd seen Karol. She'd asked Karol, "Aren't you coming? Why don't you come? We've got to get out of here." But Karol told her, "No. I'm staying right where I am."

That's about all we know. Just those two things. But I guess it's enough.

There's dust all over the city now. In the past two weeks, I've breathed it in. I catch myself thinking that Karol was incinerated and therefore I'm breathing her in when I breathe in the dust. It seems a little weird, but it's also oddly comforting. Karol loved New York, and right now she's a part of it—not just in one place, but everywhere.

I've been numb, pretty much . . . that feeling you get when you've slept on your arm all night. But when you wake up, all the blood comes rushing back in. It's a sudden rush of sensation, so sudden that it's painful. The feeling's coming back to me now, and I wish it wouldn't.

I've accepted that she's gone. Now I just want to believe that she didn't die in vain. I can't feel hate for anybody, I just want her death to have meant something.

I'm still waiting to see what this meant.

KEVIN KILLIAN

Kevin Killian, forty-three, is the chief information officer for Verizon. He's in charge of support and direction for all the systems, needs, and strategies for the Enterprise Solutions Group, which supports large business customers: commercial, city, and federal.

Kevin recounts how he and Verizon labored to resurrect one of America's greatest institutions—the New York Stock Exchange—as quickly as possible in the wake of the attack.

ON THE MORNING of the eleventh, I had a meeting at our headquarters at 1095 Avenue of the Americas. I arrived at around nine o'clock, and they had a large-screen TV mounted on the wall as you came off the elevator. The picture showed smoke pouring from one of the Towers of the World Trade Center. Beneath the picture, a caption said that officials believed a plane had hit the building. At that point, the media was still thinking that the aircraft had been a small twin-engine plane or something of that nature.

But then, as I watched, the second plane flew in. It was definitely not small. From the TV camera's view, you couldn't see the 767 hit the building, but you could sure see the fire coming out the other side.

We were on the 23rd floor of our building, so we moved quickly to the windows to see if we could catch a glimpse of what was happening downtown. Then we started to hold our meeting, but news that the Pentagon was also under attack arrived and we realized the situation was getting bigger and worse. A bunch of us went to the windows again and witnessed the Towers' collapse.

I used to work in the brokerage industry for nine years. In that time I was downtown every day, so the situation hit close to home. That night, I couldn't get out of the city. Part of me wanted to leave, sure, so I could see to my family. But another part wanted to stay and see what I could do to help. It turns out I was about to have my hands full.

⟫⟪

People who tried using their phones in New York on September 11 may have gotten what's called a "fast busy" signal. This may have continued for the next few days. The lack of service was due to the sheer volume of calls we experienced all at once. We had to reroute so many of them. And people whose service would normally ride over cables that were severed by the Towers' collapse didn't have service at all until we installed the temporary—what we call "bypass"—cables. High-speed internet was affected, too. It runs on those central office cables, same as the phone lines.

But like a lot of telecommunications networks, Verizon's web is built with a lot of automatic, diverse routing points. Essentially, the network is designed to provide alternate ways to go. If, for instance, a cable gets cut—if a backhoe digs up a cable during some street construction—the network will automatically reroute traffic to different facilities.

So, the upshot was that a lot of the call service throughout Manhattan was instantly rerouted. For example, we never lost 911 emergency services in New York. It automatically rerouted to alternate facilities and networks, despite all the damage our web had sustained.

⟫⟪

The next morning, Wednesday the twelfth, I reported back to 1095 headquarters to get together with my group and see what we could do. I met with some of the senior executives in the crisis center and listened to all the things they told me needed to be done. Basically, we had to reconstruct 2 million circuits and reroute 1.5 million lines. Even more circuits—a tremendous amount, in fact—would have to be rerouted through some of our different switching offices in order to bypass the ones that were down. We had to rebuild eighteen sonic networks. And then there was the big problem of the network management platform that supports the New York Stock Exchange and all the member brokerage firms.

It was at that meeting that I learned we had to totally rebuild the network within five days in preparation for the Stock Exchange's proposed opening on Monday, September 17.

⇻⇺

A brief item on how the Stock Exchange is set up, from our perspective:

Each of the brokerage firms in the Exchange has dedicated facilities on the network and gives Verizon the ability to manage the system. Let's suppose that a brokerage firm wants a private line, or a voice ring-down line to call their representatives on the Stock Exchange floor. Or maybe they want a line between one member firm and another—we already have the facilities set up for that. Through our network management platform, we just connect a circuit in one location to a circuit in another. Normally, we can set it all up in a matter of hours.

But a lot of damage was sustained by the Towers' collapse. A whole lot of damage. The main systems supporting the Stock Exchange platform were located on the 23rd floor of 140 West Street. That facility was one of our center-most circuit hubs in all of New York City. But after the eleventh, we weren't able to get inside.

⇻⇺

140 West Street stood directly adjacent to the Trade Center. By Wednesday morning, our next-door neighbor, 7 World Trade, had collapsed. The steel structure of 7 World Trade was about forty-nine floors high; when it collapsed, it literally slid into our building, peeling it open like a can opener. The bottom six or eight floors of 140 West were completely exposed to the elements. Plus, a steel beam had

shot out from one of the Towers and pierced the left side of 140 West Street around the 15th floor, completely destroying two floors.

Personnel had been evacuated and the power had been shut down. Despite the trauma it had sustained, the building was still standing; that in itself was promising. But we had no idea what condition our equipment was in after being exposed to the dust and the smoke. Obviously, the building had internal damage. The question was: how much?

And there were other considerations. The fires that raged around 7 World Trade were in the process of being suppressed by the fire department, so there was a tremendous amount of water pouring into all the buildings in that area. Water had flooded out the cable vaults of 140 West Street—these are the basement vaults where all the cables that run underground in all the manholes of New York City connect. And now it was underwater.

As I said, 140 West constituted one of the largest central offices for switching equipment we had in the city. All the cables from the surrounding buildings connected there, as well as all the facilities connected to other central offices in downtown. Basically, 140 West was a hub for the whole Manhattan area. We had reports that the first ten floors were saturated, totally compromised from the water. Every circuit had shorted out. Our cables offered no conductivity.

This was going to be a very big job.

⋙⋘

On Wednesday, we started scrambling to rebuild the network management platform from scratch. We got vendors like Cisco Systems involved and contacted different groups within Verizon, like corporate IT, to whom we gave a very long grocery list. We needed routers, we needed servers, we needed all sorts of equipment, and we needed it fast.

We started plans to locate all this equipment on Wednesday. We sent people down to the D.C. area to locate servers we could use. Alcatel was helping us out—they're a vendor with parts that support the network management platform. Basically, by late afternoon on the twelfth, we had parts coming in from everywhere, down from the New England area and Canada, up from D.C. By midnight on the twelfth, we had people all over the country shutting down equipment that wasn't classified as vital to their operation and putting it on trucks that drove through the night. We wanted to receive everything by Thursday so we could check where we stood. Our deliveries were complicated by all the restricted access in and around Ground Zero, so we had to work very closely with the police and the Office of Emergency Management people. We had to make sure those trucks carrying equipment got through to us.

Through it all, we kept lines of communication open to four or five different command centers who were each working round the clock on a different piece of the network: the facilities, the systems, the connectivity within the cables. One center was verifying each of the two million circuits, one by one. Try to imagine the blizzard of conference calls we had with all these command centers: "Okay. Where are you on this? Where are you on that?"

On Thursday, we started rebuilding the platform at our Pearl Street location, where many people who supported the network are based. But as we started reassembling the network, we realized we'd forgotten something vital. We needed the hardware to rebuild, yes, but we also needed the databases, which had resided on the old platform. And those databases resided at 140 West Street.

The databases were invaluable. To manually rebuild all that data—populating the field tables, entering the information, plotting connections to all these circuits—well, we could do it. It would have to be done manually; it would be a tremendous exertion of effort, and the entire process would take about ten days, minimum. But we didn't have that long. The stock market had to be back up and running for Monday morning, September 17.

>>><<<

From Verizon's point of view, we sustained more damage from 7 World Trade collapsing than from the Towers' demise. When 7

World Trade came down, it crushed a lot of underground cables. A quick survey of the damages told us it would take months and months, if not years, to rebuild—this was obviously not an acceptable time frame in an emergency situation. So we went for the quickest fix. We connected cables to the switches housed on the upper floors of 140 West Street and literally threw the cables out the windows, running them like spiderwebs over and around other buildings, stringing them along to various other points downtown and splicing them in wherever we found cables that hadn't been destroyed.

Over the next couple of days, Verizon employees ran cables outside the building from the 6th and 7th floors, draping them across the streets to provide local service for the disaster recovery efforts. The city, the police, and all sorts of people had lost communication—and communication, as you can probably imagine, was paramount in the aftermath of the attack.

So we ran the cables wherever we could. They strung over the streets, ran from building to building through windows, from rooftop to rooftop. In some cases, they snaked right out the front door of our headquarters and meandered off into the city along the sidewalks.

❯❯❯❮❮❮

On Thursday afternoon, I visited the crisis center along with the senior management team, and indicated that we'd done all we could at that point. Now we needed to get into the 23rd floor of 140 West Street and grab the necessary equipment to rebuild the Stock Exchange platform.

People had already gone into the lower floors to assess damages to the structural stability of the building, but there was still a lot going on down in that area. Smoke. Fire. Chaos. The military, the firemen, the police, and just about every government agency you can think of had set up shop, and who knew who was really in charge? We feared there were all sorts of toxins in the air. Management wanted us trained in the use of respirators and "moon suits" before we entered the building. So that's what we did.

I left on Friday morning with five other people. We were up in Midtown and had to take a subway as far downtown as we could, which turned out to be 14th Street. From there, we walked down to Canal. Along the way, we stopped to pick up some flashlights and tools from one of our central offices. And we decided that, if we were really going to bring these servers down from the top floors, we'd need something to protect them from the dust and dirt that was blowing through the air outside. So we picked up a bunch of garbage bags, too.

We'd walked about a mile from the 14th Street subway stop when I was able to stop a police van and ask for a ride. The van drove us the rest of the way down to West Street and dropped us off a block from 140.

⋙⋘

I'd prearranged to have some of our facilities people know we were coming. When we got to 140 West Street, we found a lot of folks doing cleaning and abatement on the building. We asked eight of the cleaners to help us carry the equipment down; this way, we wouldn't have to make multiple trips. This was early on Friday afternoon, the fourteenth.

We donned our environmental equipment and went up to the 23rd floor with flashlights, tools, and the garbage bags. At this point, no one had been above the 10th floor; the cleaning crew had focused on the physical equipment in the central office. We were told point-blank by facilities that we weren't allowed to go on one side of the building because, structurally, they weren't sure it was sound. So we started up the stairs.

We stayed in the stairwells running along the center of the building, and we didn't stop to scrutinize any of the damage on the lower floors. Frankly, we didn't have to; the damage was fairly obvious. There was a lot of dust on those lower floors, a lot of exposed steel beams and concrete. The ceilings were falling down, the floors were cracked wide open. Desks, cubicles, and switching equipment were strewn all over the place, as if the place had been hit with a tremendous shockwave. Simply put, there was a tremendous amount of devastation.

We went up as slowly and carefully as possible. We didn't have many flashlights, so we tried to stay together. On the upper floors, things didn't look too bad, actually. It was dark and dusty, but other than that, there wasn't much devastation. The data center was in a more controlled environment and there were several doors in place there. We had to break a window to get into one of the rooms because we didn't have a key.

We cut the cables that connected the servers to make them easier to get out, unscrewed them from their racks, put them into the garbage bags, and secured the bags to keep them dust-free. In all, we were carrying ten Sun servers that were the main databases; size-wise, they were each the size of a PC tower. Not a massive burden, but heavy enough. We trucked them all the way back downstairs to the lobby.

>>><<<

We had a truck on standby to pick us up, but President Bush was in the city that day. As you may recall, he spoke to the crowd at Ground Zero, and he was standing right outside our building at the corner of 140 West Street when we finally walked outside.

You know how it is when the president comes to town. They shut everything down. There's no traffic, no movement at all. We couldn't get our truck in for a pickup, so I made phone calls to our folks, who dealt with the police to see if we could get a police van to come pick us up. They couldn't get through, either, so we ended up sitting there for a few hours until the president finished.

I stood outside, waiting, listening to the president's speech. It was an emotional moment. When he finished, he went through the crowd, shaking hands, and I happened to be standing next to the truck he was coming back to. I got to shake the president's hand, and then Governor Pataki's.

>>><<<

We took the servers to the Pearl Street location and started the rebuild. We worked that whole weekend, coordinating with different
groups all through the night, every night. To pull the data out from
the servers, we had to rebuild the entire system and bring the platform up gradually. By Saturday we had it up, but to bring the network
fully back online from there, one of our corporate planes had to go to
Texas and retrieve some additional equipment. All this was going on
while equipment from other places around the country kept arriving
in the middle of the night, after which it was shuttled to different
central offices who'd develop different aspects of the new network.

I remember walking downtown to one of the NYSE offices on
Sunday night, the sixteenth. I was trying to check conductivity so
that NYSE could access the network management platform and
could make any necessary changes before the market opened. I was
there until the middle of the night trying to get that aspect up, then I
went back to working with different people until dawn.

Frankly? At 5:00 A.M. on the seventeenth, I was still wondering
if we'd be able to pull it all together. Certain things were working, but
we still didn't have full conductivity.

But in that last hour—between five and six o'clock in the morning—everything started to click. I don't know how else to explain it;
the last pieces fell into place. At six o'clock, we finally had the ability to
access the network and make immediate changes. We asked the folks
at NYSE to come over and sit in our Pearl Street office, so we could
tackle everything on a priority basis according to what the Stock Exchange needed. And we worked right up until the point the Stock
Exchange opened at 9:00 A.M. that morning.

❯❯❯❮❮❮

At 8:59 A.M., I'd been holding my breath all night. I think one of
our executives described the situation as "a diving catch in the bottom
of the ninth." The opening bell sounded at the Exchange and everything . . . everything went pretty flawlessly. Obviously, certain firms
weren't fully operational and scrambling to have their people work at

different facilities, since their regular offices weren't up and running. But the network worked. It held under what turned out to be a record day for trading volume.

Chairman Grasso from the Stock Exchange was very happy. We got a tremendous amount of recognition from the government and the Stock Exchange, and from all the member firms who were elated we'd been able to pull off the job.

>>>>‹‹‹‹

I can only describe the teamwork within Verizon as incredible—everyone, all the different groups, focused on getting things done. People started working hard the moment we got over the initial shock of the attacks on Tuesday the eleventh. I can't tell you how many hundreds—maybe thousands—of people within Verizon never went home from the eleventh till a week later. They lived in their offices. They slept on floors and sofas. They got an hour's sleep here, an hour's sleep there. They just kept doing what they had to do. Some went out and got new underwear and shirts when they had to, but they didn't go home.

You know, one of the first things you think about when something traumatic happens is the desire to be with your family. We all wanted to be there, with our loved ones. But these people stuck it out. They're very emotional about their jobs. And there was never any feeling that we wouldn't get it done. Everyone knew we would. Frankly, everyone knew that we had to.

The prevailing attitude was this: "The president of the United States wants this to happen. The governor, the mayor, and the president of the Stock Exchange want this to happen. Getting the markets up and running is critical to our country. We have to show the terrorists that they can't stop us, they can't keep us down."

I get choked up thinking about it. The dedication, the commitment, the teamwork within Verizon and all the other businesses that assisted us. It was an incredible, incredible effort. I've never seen anything like it. And yes, without question, I am very, very proud of the contribution we made.

CHRISTOPHER CASS

Christopher Cass, forty-three, grew up in Cold Spring Harbor on Long Island and says he was a Yankees fan from the day he was born. He lived in Manhattan for many years before moving to Los Angeles.

I'D PURCHASED a ticket weeks before it all happened, to fly from L.A. to New York on September 13 on the red-eye flight. Well, the eleventh happened. My sister, Nancy, was in the World Trade Center, on the 44th floor of Tower 1. Air travel across America shut down for three or four days, and my flight was canceled.

I called the airlines and was unable to get through, but I live close to a hotel in Beverly Hills that had a satellite office for United Airlines. So I walked in, took a number, and waited in line. It was a big crowd and everybody was asking the same question. "I was supposed to be on a flight—what's happening? When can I get outta here?"

Finally, I met with the travel agent and she switched my flight to Monday night, the seventeenth.

⇒⇒⇒⇐⇐⇐

LAX is a messy airport—it's self-contained, with all the terminals in this large horseshoe. Because of 9/11, authorities were saying, "Get here early for your flight. Two hours minimum for domestic, three hours for international." For the first time, they actually meant it. I had a 10:00 P.M. flight, so I made sure to get there well before 8:00.

Unfortunately, security wasn't allowing anyone to drive into LAX, not even to drop off or pick up passengers. Authorities were telling everyone to park in, like, Parking Lot Z, which was nowhere near LAX; it was, like, somewhere out in Long Beach. So my wife drove me out there, and I joined this amazingly long line of people with luggage queuing up to get on shuttle buses that would take us to the terminals. I could tell then that I was in for a strange evening.

On the shuttle bus, I threw all my luggage onto the racks. Passengers were packed in like sardines. The driver got on the microphone with that insanely pleasant voice saying, "Terminal One," and a few people got off.

"Terminal Two." A few more people got off.

"Terminal Three." One or two people got off.

Then: "Terminal Four," which is the international flight terminal. Everybody got off the shuttle! It was mass exodus, except for me and one other guy. Everybody who got off at Terminal Four looked foreign to me, and I got the distinct impression that they were eager as hell to get out of America.

⇻⇺

Fast-forward a bit. At the United terminal, I checked in, went up to the counter, handed over my ticket and my passport. I asked the woman if there was any way I could get a window seat. She tapped her keyboard, glanced at her screen, and said, "Everything's all booked up, but ask the attendant at the gate. There'll probably be cancelations. We might be able to fit you in."

That day, I was concerned with security—obviously. So while I was at the counter, I asked the woman specifically, "Look, I've got this laptop I'm gonna carry on. Is that okay? Should I put it in my bags?"

She said, "No, don't worry about it." And I thought, fine, fine. I left the United counter and headed toward the security checkpoint.

The queue for the metal detector was long and slow. Everyone was going through one security checkpoint—there was only one conveyor belt for luggage, one metal detector, one set of guards. I started to fidget; I could sense that everyone was getting antsy. There was an Arab-looking man in line, and it was impossible not to notice him under the circumstances. And this woman with a baby stroller turned to me and decided at that moment to say, for whatever reason, in a voice loud enough to carry four or five people forward, "I'm going to Baltimore and I hope that guy's not on my flight!"

She made no bones about it. She didn't even try to clean up her tone. Didn't whisper it under her breath. It was like, "To hell with being PC, this is how I feel, so this is what I'm saying."

I ignored her and pretended I was distracted with my own thoughts, doing the half-polite, gee-I'd-rather-not-talk-to-you-right-now sort of airport body language. I didn't know how to deal with her and I didn't want to. What she said made me sad. Ugh! The Ugly American!

⇥⟫⟪⇤

At the security checkpoint, I threw my laptop, backpack, and fanny pack up on the belt. I usually carry a little Swiss army knife on my key chain, but I'd already taken that off because I'd heard that nothing even vaguely sharp would be allowed on board. Not wanting to get hassled over a two-inch pocket knife, I'd packed the knife in my luggage.

I noticed that every item going through the X-ray machine got stopped. The guys working the belt would back it up, examine whatever they saw through their X-ray screen, then run it through again. This happened with everybody's stuff: forwards, backwards, forwards again. I'd never seen so many security people at an airport checkpoint, by the way. There were U.S. marshals in blue windbreakers with yellow, bold lettering on the back. LAPD officers. L.A. airport transit cops. National guardsmen. The works. We'd entered a police state.

My laptop went through, and I was prepared to deal with some questions. The sir-could-you-step-over-here, turn-your-computer-on-please deal. My case held the computer, lots of phone cord for the modem, an extra battery for my cell phone, and a tiny travel alarm clock, plus a couple of camera lenses and film canisters—what I supposed would look like the makings of a small bomb through an X-ray machine.

But the security guys slipped my computer case through the machine once. Twice. The attendant nodded to me, I grabbed the case, and was on my way. I took about three steps past all these men wearing uniforms and guns, and I thought, are we really any safer than we were a week ago?

I was struck with this insane urge to just call one of these armed guards and say, "Look! I just breezed on through here and nobody checked anything. What the hell is going on?"

>>><<<

By that point it was nine o'clock, and I walked up to the gate counter because I wanted to get that window seat. This woman, whom I'll call United Employee Number One, took my boarding pass and typed my name into her computer. I told her how I'd prefer the window, and she said, "We're gonna start boarding in about twenty-five minutes. Why don't you come back and I'll see what I can do for you then? I'll hold on to your boarding pass in the meantime."

Twenty-five minutes later, I went back to the gate and United Employee Number One was nowhere to be seen. In her place stood United Employee Number Two, so I approached her and explained how Number One had my boarding pass, how I wanted a window seat, and blah blah blah blah. Number Two said, "We're not boarding just yet. She'll be back. I'll keep an eye out for you."

Off I went to find a chair and sit down amidst this crowd of people who were all . . . watching everyone else. Everyone in the waiting area was sizing each other up. Who are you? Why are you flying on this flight? *My* flight? This sense of vigilance permeated everything. We'd been in shock all week, and I think we all felt a little paranoid.

I did notice at that point that there were two or three Arab-looking guys. And I *noticed* that I noticed them, you know? I thought, God, now I'm like that woman with the stroller. But I just couldn't help it. I noticed them and I felt bad for it. But I noticed just the same.

Then this announcement came over the speakers. "Sorry, we're experiencing a slight delay. The pilot is having a staff meeting with the crew. There are five flight attendants on this flight. Three have checked in, and two are still going through the security checkpoint. They're on the way up, and we apologize for any inconvenience."

I thought, that's the most information I've ever heard an airline disclose about a flight delay ever.

When the two flight attendants came rushing down the concourse, it certainly felt like a validation. Aha! They were telling the truth. It's a nice feeling when an airline tells the truth.

⟫⟪

Now the passengers began lining up at the gate, and I went back up to the counter. As it turned out, United Employees Number One and Two were gone, and I was faced with Number Three, an older woman with a nicer uniform and a bright-red scarf; she appeared to be some sort of senior United official. And I struck up a conversation with her about, "I gave my boarding pass to a woman who used to be here, she told me not to worry. I was trying to get a window seat."

Number Three found my boarding pass and said, "Yes, we have a window seat available. I'll change it for you." By now, we are over forty minutes late. It was ten o'clock and we hadn't even gotten on the plane.

More PA announcements came in: "We're sorry, we're sorry."

Finally, they called my chunk of rows and I got on the plane with my laptop and my backpack.

Now, prior to going to the airport, I had—for whatever reason—pulled a note card out of my drawer at home and scribbled a few lines to the crew of the flight I was going to be on: "Dear Crew, I know we've all had this horrendous week and I just wanted to share my sympathies with you, your company, and your fellow workers. This is a tragedy of epic proportions, blah blah blah . . ." You know what I mean? It was just a sympathy note to let them know that some passengers care about them and what they do for a living.

I'd never written a note like that before in my life. Why did I do it? I just wanted the employees to know that they were appreciated. We still don't know what happened to that one plane that crashed in Pennsylvania, but it could very well have been that the crew and passengers worked together to stop any further disaster from happening.

I walked down the gangway to get on board, and as soon as I hit the threshold of the airplane, there were two flight attendants who were all smiles. "Welcome! Welcome! Hello!" And the first one I saw, I just reached in my pocket and shoved the envelope into her hands. I barely even made eye contact with her. I just mumbled, "This is for you." Then I hiked my bag up onto my shoulder and walked off down the aisle. Didn't want to make a big production out of it.

I went toward my seat, looked down the fuselage of the plane, and there, sitting in the seat next to mine was—well, for lack of a better word—"Abdul."

⬫⬫⬫◀◀◀

I don't know what the proper phrase is. A Middle Eastern man? An Arab-looking guy? He had olive skin, brown eyes, black hair, and a mustache—a fairly nondescript man, but most definitely of Mediterranean or Middle Eastern origin.

So I did the airplane nod, that piece of body language that says, "Hi, I'm going to be living in that seat right there, and you need to get out so I can get in." He understood. He stood up right away and I threw my laptop in the overhead, scrooched into the row, and put my bag under the seat. I pulled my newspaper out and thanked him and he sat back down, started futzing with the seat belt. There were elbows flying and I folded my paper, but before I began to even read the paper ... and I never do this, I mean I don't talk to anyone on airplanes. But I thought about it for a long moment, and then I turned to this man and said, "So. How was your week?"

⬫⬫⬫◀◀◀

It was a heightened moment. We were all on edge. By taking that plane, I was engaging in something that people were frightened to do at that point. Fly to New York. Go to Ground Zero. I admit I'd been making calculations in my head all evening, saying things to myself like, okay, if I'm taking a red-eye flight in a plane loaded with 60,000 pounds of jet fuel and we're leaving Los Angeles, the terrorists are not going to crash us in New York because there's not going to be any fuel on board by the time we get there. No fuel means no explosion, so they're going to crash here in L.A. Obviously, they'd want a flight where they knew they had less passengers, so there won't be any more Shanksville incidents. But hang on a minute. My flight is full . . .

This was the kind of shit floating through my head.

⟫⟫⟪⟪

"So. How was your week?"

He looked at me and said, "Fine." Just one word. A cold delivery. And it felt like, after the word "fine" left his mouth, a big white sheet of cardboard came up that read, "That's it. That's done."

Then I thought, cut the guy some slack, huh? If it wasn't this particular week, if anyone had asked me the same question two weeks earlier, I would have said, "fine" too. So I put my newspaper up in front of me and went about my business.

But then I had a thought right after that. How can you just say "fine"? How can anyone just say "fine" after the week we'd just had? September 11 was . . . it was a Kennedy moment. Like, where were you when JFK was shot? Everyone knows where they were when John Lennon was killed. Everyone knows where they were when the space shuttle blew. It's a Kennedy moment, a Pearl Harbor moment.

I just didn't expect to get "fine" as a response, and then have him drop it so suddenly. So I sat there and pretended to read my paper, but now I couldn't help but preoccupy myself with questions. Why did he say "fine"? What does he really want to say? And I started looking out the corner of my eye, thinking, wow, he really does look like an Arab.

That's when I noticed there weren't any airline magazines in the front pocket of my seat. I found out later there'd been a picture inside the magazine showing the World Trade Center, so United had decided to pull them.

⟫⟫⟪⟪

Now it was twenty minutes after ten. We were still at the gate. The flight attendants had run down the aisles, taken their head count, and whacked down the doors to the overhead compartments. We were all ready to go, but now my thoughts were going positively crazy: If this guy *is* a terrorist, what do I do? I've just put my rinky-dink, little Swiss army knife in my bag; it's packed up and stowed below. I've got this copy of the *L.A. Times*, though. Maybe I could roll it up and hit him with the Sports section. Hey! I've got a blanket and an airline pillow. I could throw the blanket over his head, try to smother him with the pillow . . .

Then I thought, why am I having these thoughts? He's just a passenger on a plane, no different from me.

For those ten or fifteen minutes we were waiting, I got a little wigged out. Abdul crossed his legs—his right leg crossed over his left, just barely sticking out in the aisle. He had the right-foot-leg-tap thing going. This was all registering to me. Sharp. Surreal.

⸙⸙⸙

Another ten minutes went by. Then I saw a flight attendant coming down my aisle. She stopped right in front of where Abdul and I are sitting, hunkered down, and looked at us. She said, "I'm sorry to do this, gentlemen, but you fit a profile and the captain would like to see you both."

My mouth fell open. "Me?" I said, almost choking on the idea.

The attendant smiled. She kept smiling the whole time. "Yes. If you could just follow me, please?"

For a dramatic beat, neither of us did anything. Then I unbuckled my seat belt and Abdul unbuckled his. He stood up. He wasn't in any hurry to go. I, on the other hand, couldn't wait to find out what was going on. I fit a profile?[86] I had my American passport out and I was thinking, what is it? My goatee? But then I thought: Aha! The card! Someone gave the flight attendant my card and they must have thought, he's out of his head! He's the good cop, Abdul's the bad cop!

---

86 At this point, it's probably important to describe Christopher Cass as a Caucasian male with brown hair and blue eyes who was, at the time, wearing a goatee. On the day of the flight, he was dressed casually in a jacket, denim shirt, tie, and khaki pants. He is not the first person I'd pick to be a terrorist of any sort.

He's too nice. Why did you give us this card, sir? Let's question him!

Well, I got up. Abdul got up. He was walking in front of me down the aisle, right up ahead of me, and every head on the plane turned to look at us. Figuring my passport wasn't going to be enough, I started fumbling for my California driver's, digging it out of the little fanny pack I was wearing. My thoughts were starting to turn manic: Okay, I know I'm not in any kind of trouble. If nothing else, I'll have a good story to tell when I get off the plane.

But I was insanely curious. And it wasn't even an option to protest.

I thought we were going up to the cockpit. We didn't. We de-boarded the plane on the gangway. I remember thinking, oh, wow. I didn't expect to leave the actual airplane. Aren't there merchant marine laws that go into effect when you get on and off a plane? I had this little moment of "what are my rights?"

I stepped out and saw a small crowd of United employees standing around: the captain and a U.S. marshal, plus other United security guys with their blue blazers, and the two flight attendants whom I'd given my note to hovering by the door, but still inside the plane. And two other Arab guys were there, too. A total of three Arab-looking gentlemen, and me: the suspects.

>>><<<

The captain was engaged with the other two Arab men. His posture was rigid and he was shaking his head back and forth, back and forth, staring at the passports he was holding in his hand. The look on his face wasn't pleasant, more like he had a bad case of gas. He took a couple of deep breaths, and I saw him hand the documents back to the two Arab guys. Then he turned to Abdul and said, "You've probably been getting this all week and I apologize, but I need to see some identification."

Abdul pulled out a piece of ID that looked like a driver's license. At that point, I started getting tunnel vision; I couldn't focus on anything but my pounding heart. I started getting sweaty, thinking, what am I nervous about? Why is my adrenaline running?

I remember hearing one of the blue coats say, "Do you have any-thing else? Where are you from? Where are you going?" The captain was rolling his eyes now and shaking his head. I kept repeating this inner monologue of, I don't want to be here, I don't want to have any-thing to do with this at all. Meantime, everyone else was just watching.

The pilot finished with Abdul and looked toward me. I looked at him—then past him, over his shoulder. And that's when I saw an-other person who'd been standing there the whole time, about five feet away, the Senior United Woman with the red scarf. We made eye contact and her face went all bug-eyed. She mouthed, "What are you doing here?"

I shrugged my shoulders and mouthed back, "I don't know."

The captain started toward me but the Senior United Woman intercepted him, grabbing him by the bicep. Then she dragged him toward me, grabbed me by the bicep, and herded the three of us off to one side. Our heads were really close together and she said to the cap-tain, "Steve, this is Mr. Cass. He's fine. We talked a little while back. His sister was in the World Trade Center, and he's going to New York to see her. I put him in that seat twenty minutes ago, a last minute switch—he wanted a window."

The captain looked at my passport, then at me, and said, "Well, aren't you traveling with this guy?"

I guffawed. "Nooooooo!"

He looked back at Abdul and asked, "Are you traveling with him?" Abdul looked at me, then back at the captain, and shook his head no.

The captain turned back to me. "I'm really very sorry, Mr. Cass. I assumed you were traveling with him. These other two gentlemen are traveling together. I'm very, very sorry. Please accept my apologies. You can go back to your seat."

My pulse rate was peaking by now. The lovely United employee was holding on to me with both arms saying, "I'm sorry. So sorry. Please. Enjoy your flight."

I felt like I was being genuinely sincere when I looked at both of them and said, "It's fine. Really." And I walked back into the plane.

>>>«««

The first person I saw was the flight attendant whom I'd handed the card to. I looked at her and said, "Is this because I gave you the card?"

She gasped. "Oh, you're Mr. Cass! I'm so sorry. No, we loved your card! I've passed it around to the entire crew—we've all read it. So-and-so cried when she read it. They took you off the plane? Oh my God, please!"

She grabbed her co-flight attendant and said, "This is the guy that wrote us the card." Suddenly everyone wanted to kiss me.

Well, I walked back down the aisle again. Every head turned to watch me, and everyone was asking each other, "What happened?" I wasn't back in my seat for a beat when two heads popped over the chair in front of me, and the guy sitting behind me stuck his head up over my seat like we were in that old E. F. Hutton commercial. People all the way on the other side of the plane were straining to get an earful of what I was about to say. But I didn't know what to say.

I abbreviated my experience by saying, "I'm not sure what's going on, but it's pretty serious."

About ten or fifteen more minutes went by. Then the two flight attendants came down the aisle. One of them sat in Abdul's vacant seat and put her hand on my arm. "We're sorry," said the other. "Please accept our apologies, we're all under a lot of pressure right now."

Two other flight attendants suddenly appeared and walked quickly toward us, one down each aisle in the plane's fuselage. The attendant in my aisle stopped at my seat, while the other stopped where the other two Arab guys were sitting toward the back of the plane. I saw the overhead bin over my head open up—the same thing happened to the compartment over the other two guys' seats. The attendants rummaged quickly through all the luggage, then whoosh, they took the bags of the Middle Eastern men right off the plane.

Now it was past eleven o'clock. We were over an hour late. The pilot got on the PA and said, "We'll be taking off in a few minutes.

Right now we're just removing some luggage from down below."

And then? Applause. Not a standing ovation, but there was quite a reaction.

※»※«

My emotions were mixed. That's the best way I can describe it. I'm as angry as the next person about what happened on the eleventh, but I don't want to run around killing all Arabs, all Muslims, because that's not what it's about. What I'd just seen happen was a "let's intern the Japanese" move. It was suddenly very clear to me that we, as a culture, were going to pigeonhole these people—or at least we were going to that week. The political and moral machinery inside my head was grinding, and not grinding easily. The situation was confusing and it was awkward.

※»※«

We finally took off. By the time we'd been in the air an hour, every single flight attendant on that plane had come by my seat to apologize.

Now, there was a young black woman sitting one row behind me in the center section. She was clearly in view of what had happened, but not within earshot. At some point in the flight she got up out of her seat and sat down next to me. She asked me, "Hey, what happened?"

An older black couple was sitting nearby—they looked to be in their seventies, at least. Very nicely dressed, middle-class, knowledgeable. No one had to say what we were all thinking; it was clear that everyone felt it. Immediately after the eleventh, there was this sort of unspoken communal pain among people. We were all in tune with some sort of human wavelength that allowed us all to communicate, practically telepathically. Everyone's senses were heightened.

The young black woman said, "Boy, I'm so relieved they took those guys off." And she got up and walked away.

A split-second later I wondered, would she have been saying that forty years ago if a black person had been escorted off the plane? This woman, who was barely in her thirties, had missed the hardcore civil rights movement, but here she was, certainly benefiting from it.

I kept trying to look at the older black couple, trying to read in their faces what they thought about all this. But they kept to themselves and never looked over. I just wanted to get a feeling, some sort of expression. But they didn't share it with me. All I know is this: a black man in his seventies has faced discrimination in this country.

I was hoping to find some wisdom in that man's face that I could learn from. But nothing came.

SCOTT SLATER

Scott Slater, thirty, a New Yorker . . .

AFTER THE ATTACK, I holed up in my apartment, compulsively
watching the news for two days. But then I felt the need to get out
and do something. I grabbed my camera and started walking, visiting every site in New York I could possibly think of. Lincoln Center.
Union Square. Canal Street. The Empire State Building. The Armory. I walked all around the city.

"It was a pronounced statement of sorrow. Despite all that
had happened, our flag was still there."

"The single flag had been replaced with more American flags than you can imagine . . . all flying full staff, a tremendous show of strength. On that second visit, I looked at the flags and thought, we've risen."

At Rockefeller Center, I was struck by an image. Normally, the flag posts fly banners from all different nations. On September 13, there was a single American flag flying at half-staff. The other poles were bare. It was a pronounced statement of sorrow. Despite all that had happened, our flag was still there.

A few days later, I happened by that area again with my camera. The single flag had been replaced with more American flags than you can imagine. One for every single pole, all flying full staff, a tremendous show of strength.

On that second visit, I looked at the flags and thought: we've risen.

BRENDAN RYAN and KRISTIN IRVINE RYAN

If you follow the music scene in Manhattan, you've surely heard of the Bogmen. In the mid-1990s, the band became the toast of the town, playing rock music they smirkingly described as "Hi-Fi/Lowbrow Super-Charged Lounge Fodder."

Brendan Ryan, thirty, founded the band with his brother, Bill, and their friend, Bill Campion. Brendan's wife, Kristin Irvine Ryan, co-founded a charity called Secret Smiles, which, in the wake of September 11, took on a mission its founders could not have possibly imagined.

Brendan tells us his story—about music that plays again, charity that finds new purpose, and a love that refuses to die.

WHEN THE FIRST plane hit, Kristy called me and said, "Put the news on."

I saw what was going on and said, "Are you guys going to evacuate?"

At first, she thought the explosion was in her building, but I was watching it all on TV. I said, "No, no. You're the Tower without the antennae, right?" Just to be clear. "No, it's in the other building. Are you evacuating?"

"No." Still very poised. Kristy had nerves of steel.

"Why aren't you evacuating?"

She didn't know. But then she told me that an announcement came on saying that everybody should relax. The fire was in the other building and it was being contained, the announcement said.

I thought, contained?

She said she wanted to wait for more instructions, and she wanted to call her dad to let him know she was okay. "I'll call you back," she said, and hung up the phone.

※※

I'd known Kristy since I was twelve. We grew up together. When we met, she went to a Catholic school and I went to public school in Huntington, Long Island. We became very good friends. Like best friends.

We talked about getting married and having kids when we were in ninth grade. We went to proms and dances together but we weren't "boyfriend and girlfriend." Kristy always thought that if we got together too young, we'd never last. She always said, "After college." As if she had a crystal ball. "After college, we'll get serious."

We went to college and wrote letters to each other. We called each other all the time; she was in Dayton and I was in Providence. It was a . . . you know, it was a healthy relationship.

After college, we were together a long time. Eight years. Engaged for a year. Then married last June, 2001.

Ninety-four days. That was the duration of our marriage.

※※

Kristy had worked at the equities desk of Sandler O'Neill and Partners since '93, ever since she graduated college. She loved that job. She loved the people there. One of the drawbacks to a job in investment banking is that you spend a lot of time with your colleagues; the people at Sandler were together all the time. There was very little privacy. If Kristy had a doctor's appointment, she couldn't hide it. Everyone was right there, everyone knew about it.

But they were like a family. They were all so close, such a special group. They really enjoyed each other's company and got along well. When you work that closely with people, tensions are bound to get high and relationships get strained. But Kristy's equities group remained close friends throughout. How often do you see people stay at the same job on Wall Street?

Kristy was there for eight years, and she never wanted to leave.

When we were preparing for our wedding last June, we reviewed the guest list and I said, "Wow, there's a lot of Sandler O'Neill people here. We've got to cut it down."

We ended up inviting ten, and every person we had to cut from the list was a major sacrifice.

>>><<<

When she called back, I said, "Look, I'm watching this on the news. When you go downstairs, don't go outside. I can see debris falling off the first Tower."

I didn't imagine another plane coming in. Who could have possibly imagined that? The first plane hitting defied everything.

I was hoping Kristy and her group would leave soon. I looked at the fire in the North Tower and got concerned. I'd just watched a TV special two weeks before where a fire in a Californian suburb spread too rapidly to be stopped.

"When you get downstairs, stay low," I said. "Go into the subway and call me. Call me when you get down there. What does it look like where you are?"

She said, "All we can see is black smoke."

I was on the phone with her, watching the TV, when I saw the second plane hit the South Tower. Kristy was working on the 104th floor.

The phone went *sssssshhhhhhhh*. Then it came back in.

She said, "We're going down now."

I said, "I love you. Call me when you get downstairs."

But the phone went dead. And that was it.

>>><<<

We went for a walk the night before, on the tenth of September. We talked about . . . everything. I guess it's kind of strange to have that kind of talk the night before she passed away.

The subject of her job came up, and she mentioned how a lot of our friends who worked on Wall Street were struggling and looking for new opportunities. But Kristy said she felt fortunate. Sandler O'Neill was a great place to work. "It's secure," she said. "I love everybody I work with."

She told me this on that Monday night.

Also that night, the subject of Sandler O'Neill's lease came up. Kristy told me the firm might move out of the Trade Center in January or February. I hadn't heard Kristy say anything about it until that night, so I said, "You never told me this."

"Oh, yeah," she said. "No big deal." Which was a typical response from Kristy because she took everything in stride.

"Well, what do you think about it?"

She said, "Well, to tell you the truth, I'm sick of the whole Trade Towers thing. The elevator systems are inadequate. Like once you're up in the office, you're up there. You can't go down."

I said, "What other 110-story buildings do you have to compare the elevator systems to?"

She said, "Well, anyway, I wouldn't mind moving."

So there was talk of them moving to Midtown. But not fast enough, I guess.

⁂

I'm a musician and I've always traveled a lot. But Kristy was very patient. She held on to our relationship, saying, "I have no choice. You're the one I want to marry."

Music was something I did in junior high, high school, and college. Early on, the Bogmen had interest from the manager who handled Miles Davis and Cyndi Lauper. He said, "Look, I'll pay your rent, I'll get you guys a studio. We'll get a record deal with Warner Brothers." So we signed a full-time contract with him, but it didn't work out.

After that, we toured around the East Coast without representation. We played here in New York a lot. Within that year, we became the biggest unsigned band the city had to offer. Then we signed a deal with Arista Records in 1994, and ended up having a long four- or five-year relationship with them. We put out two albums plus a live album, did a little bit of MTV, toured some, had some success. Then the group broke up about two and a half years ago.

Why did we do it? It just got old. It wasn't fun anymore for us. It's so hard to keep a band together.

But here I had this relationship with Kristy that was so easy. She encouraged me to keep going, to work through it. She wanted me to do whatever made me happy.

The last year I was with the Bogmen was not a good year for me. I was pretty miserable. But she supported me emotionally through it all.

≫≪

It didn't hit me right away, what had happened. I thought that the fuel tank had exploded from the first plane and spread to Tower 2—that's how it looked at first from the angle of the news camera, and that's what the commentator said had happened. So, thinking that the explosion had only hit the edge of Tower 2, I tried to convince myself that she was okay. I kept thinking, she can get below that. From 104? She can get below.

But then they replayed the second plane's attack from different angles and it began to sink in. I kept dialing her number, but the line was dead.

That's when I realized there was no chance. Nobody who was up that high could have gotten out.

I knew early that day that it was over. I just hope and pray, like all the family members of people who were in there, that it was painless and quick.

Whichever version of an afterlife you believe in, you have to believe those people are in a special place. I believe Kristy is because she, as much as anyone, deserves to be.

≫≪

Let me tell you a little about Secret Smiles. It began with Kristy's best friend, Meredith O'Neill Hassett, who's a schoolteacher in Harlem. Her father is Tom O'Neill—that's how Kristy got her interview at Sandler right out of college.[87]

---

87 Brendan notes that, thankfully, Tom O'Neill had business on the West Coast on the eleventh of September.

In '98, Meredith felt really bad for one of her outstanding students. The boy's mother was a single parent on welfare who didn't have a refrigerator, a stove, and lot of other necessities. This woman was a very caring mother who worked very hard for her child. She'd try to get a part-time job somewhere, at the Gap, for instance. But the way the system works, her salary would get deducted from her welfare, and she'd make less money than if she stayed at home. It's a paralyzing system.

Meredith saw the poverty this woman was in and the commitment she had to her son, so she raised some money. I think Meredith may have contributed some of her own; Kristy did, too, and so did Tom O'Neill. They ended up buying necessities for this mother right before Christmas. Secretly. Meredith wouldn't stand to have the mother know that she was behind the gift. Instead, she sent Kristy, Kristy's sister Kerry, and me uptown to the woman's apartment two or three days prior [to] Christmas.

Since we were strangers, we could pose as representatives from a bank without being found out. And we told her what was being delivered. We said, "Congratulations, you won a raffle." We met Meredith's student, who was so happy to receive the gifts.

Well, the mother stood there in disbelief. All this went on as Meredith waited in the car outside the apartment, anxious to hear about their reaction.

The following year, Meredith and Kristy thought, why not start this as a charity? And we've been doing it ever since, always donating anonymously. It was, and is, such a beautiful thing.

⋙✕⋘

Kristy has four sisters, three of whom live far away. They all drove to New York as soon as possible—they had to, because the airlines were grounded after the eleventh. They wanted to support one another and their father, Stu; Kristy's mom had passed away eight years before.

The days that followed September the eleventh were long and filled with rumors. Out of concern for each other—and since we all hoped for survivors—family members from the firm called each other, asking questions. "Did Frank get out? Did Bruce get out? Where's Craig? Where's Stacey?"

All these people. Confused. Ridiculous. It was, and still is, a true nightmare.

Survivor lists circulated through different hospitals and somebody put Kristy's name on one of them, as well as two other people from her desk. This created a painful sense of false hope.

I remember someone calling me more than a week after the attacks saying that they're all still alive, in a hospital somewhere in New Jersey. I had to hang up the phone.

Including Kristy, nine people who were at our wedding passed away in the Towers. Everybody at her desk. Gone. Including Stacey McGowan, who was one of Kristy's bridesmaids.

And it really made me angry, prolonging everything.

There's no blueprint for this kind of tragedy. People were and are simply devastated.

⋙⋘

It's funny. Kristy went to Meredith's school one time and read children's stories to Meredith's students. Unexpectedly, that mother arrived—the one we'd helped out by posing as bankers—and she noticed Kristy, who was hard to miss because she was so beautiful. Looking at Kristy, the mother said to Meredith, "I know that woman. She looks familiar."

Meredith played dumb. "Oh? Really?"

Meredith and that mother eventually became friends. The woman attended Meredith's wedding in October of 2001. Even after Kristy's death, she still had no idea that it was Meredith and Kristy's charity who had delivered those items.

I played piano at parts of the wedding, and the woman kept saying to Meredith, "I'm telling you, I know that guy from somewhere."

Good Morning America produced a segment on Kristy and Secret Smiles, which aired on Christmas Eve of 2001. It was set up so that the mother could finally meet Kerry and I. So now the secret's over. The mother looked at me and said, "I knew you! I recognized you!" I just wished Kristy had been there. She would have loved it.

⋙⋘

The Bogmen reunited to play a benefit concert for Secret Smiles in memory of Kristy. We performed two nights at Irving Plaza. Gordon Gano, the singer/songwriter for the Violent Femmes, did the shows with us. We're all friends who go to the same bars.

Gordon and I wrote a couple songs together with my brother, and I put a CD together with some musician friends in memory of Kristy. I wrote the lyrics to one song, "You Make Me Happy," for Kristy.

The band hadn't played together for two and a half years, so we were originally going to perform one night. In doing so, we set a high ticket price. But the first night sold out so fast that we added another. The Bogmen raised $100,000 from those two nights, and all proceeds went to Secret Smiles.

We've parlayed Secret Smiles towards what happened downtown. We're getting the word out and have done some press. We have a website now, at www.SecretSmiles.org, and we're still very un-bureaucratic. We're public, but small. We act quickly to get relief right out.

We're not just helping in Harlem, either. We're in Long Island and the tri-state area as well—wherever we feel we can help. We're working hand-in-hand with Safe Horizon and some other charities to find out who's really the neediest of the needy, and we're focusing on that: the window washers, restaurant workers, and the receptionists from the Towers, and their families. The lower-income households who may have lost earners.

⋙⋘

I think about Kristy all the time. Of course I do. She was filled with happiness and virtue. Life is hard without her. But the mourning process isn't focused. When a group like hers gets taken out . . . it doesn't make grieving any easier. I think it actually makes it harder. I know the saying is that "misery loves company," but it doesn't pertain to this situation. It just doesn't.

I talk to family members of people who worked at Kristy's desk, and it's very difficult because the losses are inconceivable. How could so many innocent, young, and talented people be gone? It's different for everybody. I've talked to some widows—many of whom have kids. They have to step it up for their kids, and they're doing it. This takes a tremendous amount of strength.

I don't have any children. I often wish Kristy could have left more of herself behind, an extension of her.

>>><<<

I ran around for the last three and a half months, not sure how to approach each day. I didn't sit at home all day crying. I went out a lot and kept moving, doing what I had to do. I planned the shows, worked on the CD, the charity. I started a new job.

But dealing with paperwork and certificates is hard because the process is so cold. I've been down to Pier 94 probably eight times now, to surrogate court three times, to Worth Street four or five to visit FEMA, HRA, the Salvation Army, the Red Cross.[88] I get all these letters from Kristy's company saying, "Make sure you register for this, and make sure you call these people." Meanwhile, there's a lot of people out there trying to milk the system who weren't even involved in September 11. It has a dehumanizing effect, which I really don't like.

I kept busy, but I hated coming home. I dreaded it. I moved to another apartment three weeks ago in early December 2001, and it's helped. I dreaded the other apartment. I slept on the couch for three months with the news on, waiting for the next catastrophe.

>>><<<

Terrorists piloting a plane to hit American targets is like a midget hitting Mike Tyson in the face and knocking him out. I'm still wondering

---

88 HRA stands for the Human Resources Administration, a city agency.

where our intelligence was, where our defenses were. For two planes to hit the Towers? And another to hit the Pentagon? It's as if our nation's biggest targets sat defenseless.

If we sat around a think tank and wondered, "What would someone do if you were an enemy of the United States?" we'd probably come up with this scenario.

People believe what happened that day was inconceivable. I don't. I believe that our government failed Kristy and all of those people. It's the government's job, first and foremost, to protect its citizens. And on the eleventh of September, it simply did not do that.

※※※

Things are a little better now, although nights can be rough. It's hard to fall asleep, and my dreams are often difficult. I'm not a pill person, I'm not into medication. Still, the loss of Kristy causes a pain that comes in waves, and it's difficult to control the tempo of those waves.

Sometimes when I wake up, I still smell the fumes from Ground Zero through the bedroom window and I think, this isn't really happening. Or, I'll see Kristy again, she'll come back. Or, this is just a dirty joke someone's playing on me.

But then I always realize it can't be changed. Like so many others from this catastrophe, my life has changed, and this, unfortunately, is the new world.

I guess I have to do something to make a difference. Kristy did. I can't just stay in bed and do nothing. Some days are really bad, but I get up every morning and try to get something done.

Kristy was loved by so many people. She's sorely missed, and she always will be. Her friends and family miss her beyond belief. But what I truly find amazing about Kristy is that, even after her death—because of her work with Secret Smiles—people who never even met her feel her presence. And those people miss her, too.

※※※

The following lyrics have been excerpted from the CD produced by

the Bogmen, Gordon Gano, and the Knockout Drops for the Irving
Plaza benefit, Kristy's Smile.

"You Make Me Happy"

Walked through the sunbeams from your eyes
Cracked up and laughed all alone
It's not just me on this island
You're with me now to the stone.

You make me happy
You make me happy
You make me happy
It's just a brief separation
Close your eyes, grab onto faith
Rock away all of your demons
Faith is much harder to face
It was too early for sundown
No more predictions of fate

Swam through blue water with dolphins
Kissed a stingray on the lips
Sailed a boat straight through the ocean
Tried to just get one more kiss

You make me happy
You make me happy
You make me happy . . .

UPDATE

The Bogmen came together as recently as late December of 2006 to
play performances at Webster Hall and the Bowery Ballroom in New
York City to benefit Kristy's Smile, a non-profit association dedicated
to charitable giving. In 2010, the group released its fifth album, the

studio EP *Looking for Heaven in the Barrio*. Adding to their slate of well-received holiday shows, the Bogmen played a benefit show at the Paramount in their hometown of Huntington, Long Island, in December 2015.

Brendan Ryan and his brother, Bill, have kept busy composing and producing music for films and television commercials. They have reunited in the band Mad Larry, which, according to their website, "takes influences from a wide range of artists such as Tom Waits, Talking Heads, the Platters, and Neil Young." The website also mentions that, "In a Samuel Beckett kind of way, Mad Larry often sings about finding hope and serenity in the midst of the absurdities and tribulations of the wayward world. Confessing flaws, compulsions, indulgences, and failed relationships, Mad Larry writes and plays about the frailties of artists and all of us."

MARK LESCOEZEC

Mark Lescoezec, thirty-two. A placid guy you'd probably miss in a crowd, but someone who can keep a company afloat in the middle of a catastrophe by letting his deft fingers work a keyboard.

YOU KNOW, it's funny. People who work in technology? Nobody really knows about us until something goes wrong. Then we're the most important people in the world.

When the Towers went down, the destruction wasn't limited to the physical devastation of the Trade Center buildings. Massive stores of information were annihilated. To me, that's an interesting [historical] footnote: that in this age of technology, people and equipment are often replaceable. Information, however, is priceless.

Everybody lost people. Cantor Fitzgerald, you've heard about them? They were huge into bonds. Seven hundred people out of a thousand were lost. I can't fathom that. There were actually concerns over the liquidity of the entire bond market because of one company's sudden destruction. Imagine that.

⤗⤗⤗⫷⫷⫷

You may have heard that Sandler O'Neill was a company pretty seriously affected by the attack. They were up on the 104th floor of Tower 2. Their offices were . . . well . . . pretty heavily hit.

My boss is Stan Druckamiller, who founded the company I work for, Duchesne Capital. And Stan just asked the folks at Sandler outright, "How can we help you?" See, he knew the guys in upper management at Sandler. I assume they were good friends because our industry is like any other—people get to know one another. One big happy banking family.

Sandler wasn't in a position to refuse. And this is the solution we came up with:

Just before September 11, Duchesne Capital was all set to open a branch office in San Francisco. I'd already staged and prepped all the necessary equipment at our New York office. It was all set to ship out to San Fran, so the guys out there could take the stuff out of the boxes, plug it in, and boom. Ready to go.

When we heard about the attack, we just . . . well. We basically gave all that equipment to Sandler O'Neill.

※》《※

My company only has, like, twenty-five people in New York, so we only have two technology people here. We do the networking, the servers, the T-1s, all that. We work with market data. It sounds dry, but imagine a bank without client information. Imagine a broker who loses all his transaction information. The banking industry rides on the back of electronics. State-of-the-art electronics—the faster, the better. Understanding this, our attitude quickly became: "Whatever you need."

For instance, I go over to Sandler after work every day and put in a few hours to get them moving. My time's been donated by my firm. Temporarily, Sandler O'Neill's working out of the Bank of America on 57th Street. Bank of America loaned them space until they get back on their feet and find something long-term. It may take two or three months, it might take longer, no one knows. Believe me when I say it's the least of everyone's worries.[89]

So my company gave Sandler all the equipment we'd intended for our San Francisco project, and I set up a sequel server for their accounting system. They have a portfolio management system, of course, and I spent a few years in source fund management, so I've worked with those systems in my previous job life. It's all foreign for them, but it's simple for me to come in and do it.

The guys in Sandler's accounting office know how to use sequel servers—packages like Solomon database and Nextiva and all that. They just don't know shit about setting them up. Funny, really, what

---

89 This interview was conducted less than three weeks after the attack.

becomes life or death for a company. You follow a question tree of very simple, but very important questions. Were their backup systems good? Were they tested? Did they keep the backups on-site or off-site? Fortunately, Sandler was very compliant with all of this.

I'm sure a lot of companies from the Trade Center didn't follow the procedures that Sandler did. And now their business is gone. Completely wiped out.

⟫⟪

That first week after the tragedy, the first week I was helping out, these people—the survivors—they were walking around the office with these . . . eyes. They were lost in a daze.

It was an epidemic of white-collar shock. I found one of their portfolio managers working with the computers, actually making things worse. She had no idea what she was doing. It boiled down to advising her and the other people who were there: "Please don't think. Let us do the thinking. There's only one goal now—just get your networks up and running."

I work with these people every day, and it's really wild to see them like that. Burnt out. Stumbling around. Broken. I go outside to have a cigarette and see the rest of the city scrambling as well, scrambling to get things moving again.

Business has to exist. It has to move on. You have to go back to work, keep things running. Client accounts are still open, deals are still up in the air for trading firms. And underlying this all is the void of so many lost friends. Faces, once familiar, that no one will ever see again. The disorientation is incalculable.

I go back inside the building and people glance up at me, so thankful. They're so happy we're there to do whatever we can for them.

⟫⟪

This past week I went into Sandler, and you could feel the relief. Their network was finally up and the primary server was running smoothly. Given the circumstances, it all happened pretty fast.

Like I said, Sandler had their tapes. Every company backs up
their servers; it's something most people don't even think about. Very
critical data gets backed up on those tapes. A lot of companies store
them off-site, and Sandler was no different. They kept theirs in a
vault at HSBC downtown. One little hitch: HSBC was close enough
to the disaster so that no one could get into the vaults—the power
was cut off.

But somehow, Sandler retrieved those tapes. For one second,
would you just imagine if they hadn't?

Here's what the scene would look like. You've got all the hardware. You've got rows of talented people sitting in front of dark
screens, waiting. But all the data you've been collecting for the past
thirteen years—spreadsheets, documents, emails, portfolios, memos,
protocols, payrolls, Christmas card lists—it's gone. All gone.

We recovered the data from the tapes last Saturday night at 2:00
A.M. You can't imagine the huge sigh of relief.

»»«««

Yeah, Duchesne Capital still plans on opening our San Francisco
branch. But for right now, we're just helping out at Sandler O'Neill.
That's the focus.

I was thinking of volunteering downtown at Ground Zero, but it
sounds like they have a lot of people there already. And data is what
I do; this is what I *can* do. So I do it. I could dig for bodies, I guess.
I could prepare food. But I honestly feel that I'm making a contribution here. Everyone helps in their own way.

Sandler's not out of the woods yet, not by a long shot. I want to
get them up to where they can make their own decisions, function
independently. They're gonna have to staff up, bring in new people,
good people. It's like they're starting all over again.

At least they get the chance.

»»«««

Let me end with this little story. Because, for me? This is how September 11 affected me in both a small and a large way at once.

There's a company Duchesne Capital uses for marketing services. I called them the other day, looking for one of their technicians I like. We're converting to a T-1 line from the system we're using right now, and this guy of theirs is very cool. He knows his stuff, he's easy to work with, and he solves a lot of problems. I've known him for years. His name is Wade.

The other day I was having difficulties, so I called up the marketing service and talked to the woman who answered the phone. I said, "Look, can you send Wade over? I've got a glitch over here I can't figure out, and I need to finish this conversion."

There was this pause on the other end of the line, and she said, "Wade was in the World Trade Center."

See, we weren't best friends. I just knew the guy. He was very cool and he knew his stuff. He was easy to work with.

But now he's gone and I mean . . . I mean . . . you know?

OMAR METWALLY

Omar Metwally, twenty-eight, lives in Brooklyn. He's of Egyptian descent. His dark features and olive complexion could very well be mistaken for many ethnicities.

His words come easily when he tells his tale, but once or twice they catch in his throat and he takes a deep breath before continuing.

SEPTEMBER 11, I was working in Midtown at a temp job. They let us all out when we heard the news, but nobody really knew what to do.

I walked around Central Park for a while. Normally I take the F train home to Brooklyn, but I couldn't go home; they'd shut down the trains. So I walked around the park, looking at people's faces. Lots of blank faces.

It was . . . I don't know how to describe it. I was alone. I felt lost. I had nowhere to go. I couldn't get any friends on the phone to set up a place to stay in Manhattan. I didn't know where anyone was. It was awful.

So I went down to the East Side and was walking down First Avenue. I stopped at a pub, just to get off the street for a bit. By that point, I'd walked around for a couple hours.

There was a crowd of grief-stricken people watching the TV. You couldn't really hear what was being said on the broadcast, what with everybody talking and all, but you could see the images. And also pictures and video of Osama bin Laden. It was the first I'd seen of Osama bin Laden.

I leaned over to this guy next to me and I said, "What's the deal? Did they pin this on the al-Qaeda? Do they know?"

He just watched the TV and nodded. Said, "Yeah, yeah. I think it was them. I think it was bin Laden. We should bomb those fucking Arabs."

He was talking over his shoulder. He wasn't looking at me.

I didn't know what to say. But eventually, I turned to him and I said, "You know, I'm Arab."

He didn't say anything for a second. He just sort of stared at me. Frozen. Then he started stammering to apologize. "Sorry," he said. "Sorry. You know, I'm . . . Turkish."

⋙⋘

I've dealt with that kind of racism growing up all my life, the way the media and films portray people of Arab descent as gun-toting madmen.

You know, there was Reagan's war on Gaddafi. Then the Gulf War in the early '90s. That sentiment's been around, and you learn to deal with it. But once I'd left school, I thought I could avoid it. I guess not. It's in there, and it's insidious.

How does it make me feel? Hopeless. I hold the media responsible to a large degree. For years and years, there's been a barrage of certain images. If you recall, after the Oklahoma City bombing of the Federal building, there was so much speculation. Pictures were shown over and over again, pictures that have a very powerful effect. They have a powerful effect on me, and I'm part of the ethnic group that's being poorly portrayed.

When Oklahoma City happened, they showed countless images of Arab terrorists. Then, after they found out that Timothy McVeigh was responsible—a white American—no apology was extended to the Arab community. But the damage was already done.

I saw the same thing happen in this situation. The media flooded the nation with images that weren't put into proper context. You know, already the number of hate crimes on record has skyrocketed. There were only 250 hate crimes reported against Arab Americans last year. Well . . . [laughs] *only* 250. It's up to four or five hundred now, less than two months after the attacks. It's doubled and it's growing—and it's early.

What do I see happening now? I'm afraid we're going to war.

I'm worried about our basic freedoms. I'm worried about our society. The Bill of Rights. The ideas that we, as a nation, were founded on. They're good ideas. But people have been put into camps in this country, remember that?[90] It's a part of our history that lots of people tend to forget. I don't.

I think there are people who are going to take advantage of this situation, political advantage. And my fear is that those problems, which are really the root of what happened at the Towers, will be ignored so that the government can push the American people into a really frightening right-wing agenda.

Fear can be used to such great effect. The problems that need to be addressed in the world are problems that need to be addressed in this country. Problems of social justice, problems of poverty, problems of racial equality, problems of class. But we push it aside, we push it aside, we push it aside.

We only reconsider our actions when it's already too late.

UPDATE

Omar Metwally's career as a professional actor took off not long after the attacks of September 11. Among many other credits and awards, he received the 2008 Chopard Trophy, presented at the Cannes Film Festival, for playing the role of Anwar El-Ibrahimi in Gavin Hood's *Rendition*, which also starred Meryl Streep, Jake Gyllenhaal, Alan Arkin, and Reese Witherspoon. He played Dr. Vik Ullah between 2015 and 2019 on Showtime's series *The Affair*. And he won an Obie Award for his performance in the Atlantic Theater's production of Rajiv Joseph's *Guards at the Taj*.

---

90 Following the attack on Pearl Harbor, Congress passed certain laws and the executive branch issued certain exclusion orders meant to protect the West Coast military areas from sabotage. As a result, over 120,000 Japanese Americans were required to report to internment camps, regardless of evidence of their loyalty or disloyalty to the U.S. At the time, there was little protest from Americans. The U.S. Supreme Court ruled that the internment camps did not violate the constitutional rights of Japanese Americans (in *Korematsu v. United States*, 323 U.S. 214, 1942).

KEN LONGERT and FRED HORNE

Ken Longert is the owner and operator of Ken Longert Lighting, a New York City theatrical lighting business. He's been lighting films, television programs, commercials, Broadway and off-Broadway theater productions, tradeshows, and special events since the 1970s.

But all of his skills were put to the test when September 11 unexpectedly turned the Chelsea Piers into the mayor's emergency management nerve center.

Ken and his partner, Fred Horne, review their experiences.

Ken: TALK ABOUT weird luck. The OEM was training cadets at Pier 92 on September 11.[91] Two or three hundred cadets were there, learning the proper procedures in case some kind of disaster hit New York. Total coincidence. We were booked four or five days before the attack happened, since we're the normal special events lighting subcontractors for the Pier. So we got there about seven o'clock in the morning to set up.

We were doing our job and everything was routine until we looked off the south side of Pier 92 and saw smoke coming from the first Tower. Everyone assumed a plane had hit the Trade Center, that it must've been an accident. Nobody thought much of it until a few minutes later, when we witnessed the second plane's impact. I should qualify that. The plane came from the south and we were standing at a northerly position. So we didn't actually see the impact, but we sure as hell saw the flames gushing out the building's exit wound.

Within seconds, all the people from OEM disappeared. That's when we knew something big was going on. This was at 8:45 in the morning.

We took a coffee break about 9:15 and made a decision not to

---

91 OEM is the New York City mayor's Office of Emergency Management.

continue setting up because we didn't think the OEM guys would be back. I had fifteen or twenty guys floating around the Pier—electricians, carpenters, and soundmen. I went up to the roof of Pier 92 to see what was going on, and witnessed the buildings come down. Couldn't believe my eyes.

So the job was halfway finished. We were in limbo. Around noon, we called it quits and dispersed.

I'm a bike rider. I train every morning in Central Park. I rode my bike from the Pier back up to my home on the Upper West Side. Let me tell you what I saw: there was this peculiar feeling in the air. People were in a daze. Thousands of people walking uptown, like some sort of catharsis had happened and people were in a trance.

⫸⫷

Ken: OEM had opened its new Emergency Operations Center in February of '99, this state-of-the-art facility designed to operate as a stand-alone center from which New York City government would operate in a time of crisis. The EOC was in 7 World Trade, within walking distance of City Hall and most city agencies. It was an engineering marvel. The EOC facility is powered by three 500-KVA generators that act as emergency power sources totally independent of the building's backup generators. In addition to a 6,000-gallon fuel tank, there's an 11,000-gallon potable water supply for sanitary and domestic water needs, plus a backup system for heating, ventilation, and air conditioning. Computers, phone systems, and radios are all individually set, with uninterrupted power supplies. The EOC can withstand winds up to, like, 200 mph, and in the event of a hurricane, the exterior walls are constructed with steel framing, plus numerous layers of drywall and Kevlar.

Within the EOC is seating for sixty-eight agencies to operate during an emergency, with each agency assigned its own workstation. In the event of a major incident, they can rig up another forty workstations. These workstations are set up in groups to facilitate interaction with other agencies in the EOC. The groups are broken down into Health & Medical, Utilities, Public Safety, Infrastructure, Human Services, Transportation, Government, and Administration.

You have to appreciate the planning this all took. But it all proved useless. Later in the day on September 11, 7 World Trade Center collapsed, and OEM suddenly found itself homeless.

>>>><<<<

Ken: The next day, we heard they were going to use Pier 94 as a morgue. This is where our in-house office was, so we scrambled to get the place ready. We hung a lot of curtains to serve as temporary mortuary chambers. Policemen and firemen started coming in, but we never saw anyone bringing in bodies. As it turns out, there weren't any to be found right then.

Then Mayor Giuliani showed up. He came in with Judith Nathan and a whole entourage of people whom I assumed were connected to OEM.[92] A whole parade of suits came through, debating what to use the Piers for.

The Chelsea Piers are owned by the City of New York. They're very well-located. Basically, the authorities were able to close down the West Side Highway and have one lane open for emergency traffic on its way down to Ground Zero.[93] Pier 94 is easily accessible from that.

Giuliani had never really seen the Piers set up for a trade show: carpeting laid down, booths set up, the works. I think he was impressed. The upshot is that OEM completely took over Pier 92 for operations. Everything that should have been down at 7 World Trade Center moved in here.

I heard later on that they scrambled to find a location as soon as 7 World Trade crumbled on the eleventh. I also heard that they moved into two or three places, trying them on, before they settled into the Pier. What's not to like about this place? There's parking, windows all around. And it's a ship terminal. If worse came to worse, you could

---

92 Judith Nathan was Mayor Giuliani's girlfriend at the time, and now his ex-wife.
93 The West Side Highway is the thruway that runs along the westernmost side of Manhattan, alongside the Hudson River.

pull an aircraft carrier right up the Hudson and dock it outside.

Keep in mind . . . at that point? No one knew if we were going to war. Or with whom.

※»≫»×≪≪≪

Ken: So the Family Assistance Center moved in from the 23rd Street Armory to Pier 94, and OEM moved into Pier 92. We got the word they were coming in to set up on the night of the fifteenth. By that point, we were basically ready to go. Our production schedules tend to run like everything is a last-minute emergency anyway; we're used to dealing with rush jobs.

Fred: We get calls for big jobs all the time at the last minute. Go into a hotel ballroom; go into a park, into the street; go anywhere. Create an environment, create a production. Work on the fly. That's what we specialize in.

Ken: So we went ahead and started laying in electrical lines as groups of people started showing up.

Fred: Verizon showed up and set up hundreds and hundreds of phone and T-1 lines for the OEM.

Ken: Trucks pulled in. One of the major telephone companies pulled up and started letting people make free long-distance calls. They needed all sorts of power.

Fred: Fiber optics came in, Time Warner came in to lay cable so every OEM office had their own TV set to watch the breaking news.[94] There was no cable at the Pier before this.

Ken: We had to take care of the news teams, the television stations, camera crews, ABC, CBS, everybody making requests all at once. The cafeteria needed power lines for refrigeration. Verizon wanted power. People needed lighting. They wanted sound. On the fly, we designed a sound system that would break the place into three zones, so whoever was at a podium could switch on Zone 1, Zone 2, or Zone 3. We

---

94 Time Warner City Cable of NYC, a cable TV and high-speed online service provider.

hung fifty speakers, set up hundreds of track lighting instruments. We already had some items at the Pier, and I have a warehouse in the Bronx where I store the rest of my lighting, staging, sound, audiovisual, and video equipment. For this job, we cracked into everything, pulled out all the stops. This was serious business, and it was all about saying, "Yes, we can."

>>><<<

Ken: We became the de facto power distribution specialists at the Pier, but really, we had no idea what we were doing. There was no blueprint on file for anything like this. So we laid in a very intricate system. I have a supply of multi-cables that drop circuits into quadrants all along the Pier, so we just started dropping circuits all over the place, treating the whole place like a giant theatrical lighting grid.

Power is universal. How it's distributed is not. There's a million different connectors—two-wire, three-wire, four-wire. Twist locks with the pin in, twist locks with the . . . sheesh. Don't get me started. And every connector is rated by voltage and amperage.

Naturally, every agency had different requirements, but we accommodated everybody.

Fred: We had this huge toy box of everything you could possibly imagine, and from that we pulled equipment to outfit everyone, no matter how weird their request was. Some agencies had color Xerox machines four or five feet wide that worked on "two-away" plugs, a very weird type of plug. We got that problem solved within three hours using a very simple system: locate the part, send someone to get it, install it, done. If they didn't have it in town, call someone who had it, tell them to ship it immediately, and I'd pay for it. I'm still holding the bills.

Ken: Keep in mind that Pier 94 is huge. It's a T-shape, about 600 feet wide with a finger that juts out from the top about 900 feet. ConEd ran 16,000 volts into the basement. Then they did substations, which eventually transformed the power down to 480 volts. On Pier 94, I installed 480 to 208-volt transformers; the higher the voltage you

transport, the smaller the wire you need. And right at specific locations, I broke it down from 208 to the 110 that was needed.

I set the system up on a temporary basis, so it could move and
accommodate different situations. A certain amount of it was perma-
nent, but there's a whole secondary distribution phase which moved
around as needed per show. We had that same situation on Pier 88,
90, and 92.

Fred: To make sure the light distribution was right, I marked out a
row of klieg lights on the ceiling. At any one time, six were being used.
But if any went out, I had it rigged so that six more were ready to go. I
had a backup system, and a *backup* backup system. If Number 3 went
down? No problem. Boom! I'd cut to Number 4. It was absolutely
seamless.

>>>><<<<

Ken: They set up the war room on the mezzanine of Pier 92. That
was Giuliani's private conference room. We went in and set up a
sound system, cable mikes, the works. Video monitors outside the
room.

The top tier of the mayor's office sat in the war room, bigwigs
from every possible area you could imagine—traffic control, sanitation, fire, police, Amtrak, Metro North, bridge and tunnel.

Fred: The heads of all the departments would receive their updates,
figure out who's problem it was, then work together to solve it.

Ken: And that jives with the way we operate. We don't take no for
an answer. Nothing is impossible for us. When somebody came to us
saying they needed some obscure, cockamamie electrical connector?
It wasn't like you could call your super and allow it to go undone for
three months. We got it done, man. Period.

It was inspiring to see the city government functioning that way.
No politics. No dickering. Just *boom!* Get it done. In fact, I was struck
by how amazingly fast the OEM could put a plan in motion. If there
was a hole between the walls? They got on the phone and the hole's

filled in an hour. In front of Pier 94, if there was a fire hydrant that wasn't working? They got the fire hydrant fixed in two hours. This is unheard of for the way the city normally operates. Amazing.

Fred: And then the *Comfort* arrived.[95] It shipped out from North Carolina or Delaware, I think it was.

Ken: We're saying that overnight, the facility we'd worked at for eighteen years, staging events and trade shows, was turned into a military facility. Overnight! The whole complex, the whole environment changed. For instance, the *Comfort* has its own hospital, operating rooms, emergency rooms, and water desalinizing plant. When she pulled up, this place became like a fortified city, everything all ready to go.

Fred: You could opt to stay on the ship. They had rooms prepared for you. They had mess halls you could eat in and people on duty to do whatever you wanted. You could get your laundry done if that's what you wanted. That ship was of great service to the people working at the Pier.

>>>><<<<

Fred: The thing I'll take away from all this? You couldn't do anything without somebody asking if they could help. I'm talking about people from different departments. Whether they were walking by with a press folder, in a group, solving some problem . . . a guy from the phone company grabbing a cup of coffee or a janitor passing by with a mop. If you looked like you had a problem putting a ladder up, there were two other guys there helping in the blink of an eye. "Can I hold that ladder for you?" They'd do it, and then off they went. You had time to say thank you, and that was about it. The camaraderie was absolute.

---

95 USNS *Comfort III*, hull number T-AH-20, commissioned in 1987. The crew that arrived in New York included some 300 navy medical personnel and 61 civilian mariners. The *Comfort* actually departed Naval Weapons Station Earle, New Jersey, at 3:00 p.m. on September 14, under orders from the commander in chief, U.S. Atlantic Fleet. She sailed under Captain Ed Nanartowich.

The Pier became a very intense environment to work in. Suddenly, the Red Cross was coming by every hour with fresh coffee and stuff to eat, saying, "Is there anything special you guys want?"

Ken: Everyone wanted to take part; everyone wanted to do something. From our point of view, we felt, hey, this is what we do best. We're our own emergency management for theatrical and trade shows, and here we were, a perfect fit. We were able to move into action for the cause. We had our hands full.

If there was a downside at all, it might be that we kind of felt isolated. The whole world was down at Ground Zero, but we were up at the Pier. And when you work day and night, day and night, day and night . . . eventually, you're working in a fog. It begins to take on its own sense of reality.

It really hit home when we lit that Memorial Wall outside the Pier. I think that was a focal point. That became our connection.

Fred: They never had one technical problem here. I've done a lot of trade shows in my time and I used to be an equipment rep. I traveled up and down my area, Florida to Maine, hitting every freakin' trade show east of the Mississippi. In a trade show, you set up your electrical, and sometimes it works. The thing that really blew me away about what we got done at the Pier—there was never a problem with the electrical.

The true test? The OEM, FEMA, the Red Cross run the Piers now 24/7, and they haven't had one problem. The stuff that we built is still working 100 percent.

Ken: Nothing's done half-assed. Not in my business, not in any business. There's no learning curve anymore when you've been on a job eighteen years. Not even for something like 9/11. You just put your nose down and get that job done. The rest works itself out. We were truly proud and happy to make a contribution.

JEAN KNEE and MICHAEL CARROLL

Jean Knee has been a social worker for a private school in New Jersey for nine years. She categorizes her school as a "challenging, nurturing, caring atmosphere."

Jean's cousin, Michael Carroll, was thirty-nine years old and a New York City fireman for sixteen years. He was killed in action on September 11.

Jean tells how her family was affected by the passing of their kinsman.

MY DAUGHTER Elizabeth's wedding was planned for September 15, 2001. On September 11, we heard that Michael was one of the first firemen on the scene at the Towers. Soon after that—in the midst of this very confusing day—we understood that he was missing.

My son works in the city. He was on 18th Street and had to evacuate his building. He knew his cousins lived up on 86th Street, so he took off for Michael's mother's apartment. When he got there, the family was trying to get news about Michael, who came from a family of firemen. This situation was their worst nightmare come true.

For the longest time, incoming reports kept repeating the same thing: "He's missing." I don't know if you remember but they kept listing people as "missing" instead of declaring them dead outright, so everyone was tremendously hopeful that they'd find survivors. Gradually and gradually, though, that hope slipped away.

In my own mind, I kept saying, "Michael is safe." I told my daughter that over and over again: "I know Michael's safe. He's somewhere right now and we just don't know where he is."

※※※

They closed my school on September 12, but I met with people from the upper campus to decide what we were going to do. We brought the faculty in early and talked to them about what types of behavior they could expect from children who'd experienced trauma. "Let the children talk about whatever they want," we told them. "Don't censor anyone. Let them have their experience." Many of the children had parents who'd worked either in the city or at the World Trade Center.

When a child is in pain, there's a tendency among adults to say, "It's going to be all right. Don't worry." But the adults just want children to be quiet. In this case, it was more important to let the children talk about how they felt.

⫸⫷

You know the video clips of the planes hitting the Towers, the ones they played over and over and over again? We found that the young kids, kindergarteners and first-graders, couldn't distinguish that it was one event played over and over again on television. They thought it was happening anew each time. So some of them thought that all of Manhattan had been destroyed.

Their perceptions of the experience came out in their outside play; they reproduced what they'd seen, smashing into blocks, knocking down towers. Some of the children finished their milk and made planes out of the cartons.

This is all normal. Children express how they're feeling in play. They don't necessarily talk about it. Parents kept asking us, "What are they saying? Are they talking about it?" No. They weren't. They hadn't formulated it in their heads, and there was nothing about it they could relate it to, nothing at all.

But my real concern is for the people who survived. They went through horrendous things to get out of those buildings. They walked over dead bodies. They thought they were going to die. It must have been a terrible experience, and many of them aren't getting help. They aren't talking because they don't feel they have any right to, since they're still alive. And if this sort of emotional trauma is allowed to go untreated, there's a very real danger there, not just to the individual but to society as a whole.

>>><<<

On September 14, we heard from Michael's family. They'd canceled their hotel reservations and wouldn't be able to come to Elizabeth's wedding. They were waiting to hear about Michael's condition. Perfectly understandable.

My daughter asked, "Am I really going through with this wedding? Is that right? What should I do?" After a lot of deliberation, we decided to go ahead.

The wedding was on the beach in Provincetown, Cape Cod. Since it was a destination wedding, many people couldn't fly there; the airlines weren't operating yet. Flights were still grounded. A lot of people from the Washington, D.C., area drove up instead. It was actually incredible how some people got there.

I almost didn't go myself. I felt that, in my ten years at the school, this was the time I was needed most. The principal finally had to tell me, "Go to the wedding. Nothing's going to fall apart while you're gone for the weekend." So I drove from New Jersey to Massachusetts on Friday night, the fourteenth.

All the way up to Massachusetts, every overpass had flags and signs up that said, "God Bless America." It was a six-hour ride, and I cried the whole way up.

When we got to Provincetown, candles were lit as a memorial in the center of town. People knew people who had died on the planes. This tragedy reached everywhere, you know?

>>><<<

On October 20, the family decided to hold a memorial Mass for Michael. The wake was held the day before at Campbell Funeral Home on Madison and 81st. The entire fourth floor was reserved for Michael's wake. The rooms and hallways were filled with firemen, family, and friends.

When the firemen entered the building, they took the stairs—that's what firemen do. They don't take elevators. Stairways are the safest part of the building, and I always imagined that Michael was in a stairway at the World Trade Center when he perished.

Mayor Giuliani came to the wake. I think he attended all the services for the uniformed men that died at the World Trade Center, though how he was able to schedule that, I don't know.

Elizabeth was at the wake, and her family kept asking about her wedding. She was touched. They'd all sent flowers to her wedding with a note saying, "Thinking of you on this day. From your family in New York." She was so overwhelmed that, in the midst of this difficult time in their lives, they had been thinking of her.

>>><<<

The day of Michael's memorial, I decided to take the ferry with my children from Hoboken to Ground Zero. As we were going over, I talked to a ferry worker who told me about all the boats that came to help people get away from the area on September 11.

He said, "It was an incredible scene. People with private boats and anything that could float were pulling up and taking survivors to New Jersey."

We landed and walked over to Broadway.

Members of the FDNY mass outside of Trinity Church in preparation to enter Ground Zero and dig for survivors—and their brother firemen—shortly after the Towers fell.

I had made the decision that morning not to take my camera. The devastation at the site was overwhelming. At that time, thousands of bodies were still missing, but many individuals hadn't been declared dead yet. And I thought, they're here at Ground Zero. Buried in the gray dust.

That dust was everywhere—it was on the leaves of the plants, on the trees, in the flowerbeds that lined the streets, on the buildings. We walked past window washers who were busy trying to clean the façade of a building scheduled to open that week. I stood in silence, wanting to touch the dust but at the same time feeling it was somehow sacred.

⇶⇜

We went to Ladder 3 on 13th Street, which was Michael's company. Thirteen men died from that firehouse. Twelve of them worked there, and one man had been there waiting for an assignment. I felt compelled to talk to Michael's firemen friends. I know how close these men are; they're like a family unto themselves. I wanted them to know that it was good they were alive.

From there, we took a cab to the Church of St. Ignatius Loyola.[96] The cab driver asked which side of the street the church was on. I said I didn't know. But as we went over a small rise in the road, we saw hundreds of uniformed firefighters standing in rows on Park Avenue. I said to my children, "This is going to be big."

We got out of the cab, crossed the street, and a fireman asked if we were family. He told us to stand to the right side of the church entrance and assured us that seats were being reserved for family. The bagpipers were there. A man with an American bald eagle perched on his arm was standing on the street.

The church was huge, and every seat was filled. I didn't know who many of these people were—family, firemen, others. Carroll is an Irish name, so we have a large extended family. The women in the family tend to live till their nineties; Michael's grandmother died in

---

96 Located on Park Avenue at 84th Street.

her nineties. This was the first death I could remember in a long time. The first, and certainly the most unexpected.

There were several eulogies. Keith Gessner, a long-time friend of Michael's, spoke along with Robert Burmeister, a friend from Ladder Company 3. There were representatives from the mayor's and governor's offices. Michael's brother, Billy, spoke; Billy is also a New York City firefighter. He spoke eloquently about Michael and his love for his wife, Nancy, and their two children: Brendan, six, and Olivia, two.

There wasn't a dry eye throughout the entire ceremony. After a while, I stopped blotting the tears and just let them fall. All around, these big burly firemen had tears running down their faces.

The processional hymn was "Be Not Afraid," and we sang "Amazing Grace" and prayed. The recessional hymn was "On Eagle's Wings."

⪼⪻

As we left the church, a fire truck pulled up. The family lined up behind it and firemen lined the street, standing at attention, saluting us as we walked behind the fire truck down Park Avenue.

There was so much confusion in my mind, between the public events and the personal fact that I was at "little Michael's" funeral. Michael, the little boy in pajamas who used to watch Saturday morning cartoons when I slept over on the couch at this parents' house.

⪼⪻

Last week, Michael's body was recovered from the scene. This is a good thing. Without a body, we all clung to the hope that somehow he would be found safe—many people clung to that hope.

Some families are still hoping that their loved ones might be found someplace, that they're unconscious in some hospital somewhere—that they'll wake up, realize they've been missed, and come home.

It's so very sad.

Early on, I told Michael's brother, Billy, "Bill, even now, I keep thinking that they'll find him alive."

He said, "Jean. That's not going to happen."

At least now they can bury him. There'll be a grave and a place his family can go, a place his children can visit. That's very important in the grieving process.

UPDATE

In the final assessment of the attack on the World Trade Center, 343 New York City firemen, 23 New York City policemen, and 37 Port Authority police officers were killed.

JOHN McGRATH

John McGrath, thirty, started his law practice at 160 Broadway, less than a full block east of the World Trade Center. He is no stranger to the Trade Center or the particular culture that surrounded it—John worked for the firm of Ohrenstein & Brown on the 85th floor of 1 World Trade before founding his own company.

He talks of the massive damages sustained by the area and the local businesses, as well as the loss of many dear friends.

O'HARA'S. What a place. It had two bars on the bottom floor. It was located one block from the Trade Center. There was a door on the north side of the room that faced out onto the Towers—that's how close you were. They had all Irish bartenders at O'Hara's, except this one Japanese guy named Kato. He always bartended upstairs with my friend Brian McCabe, whom we referred to as "The Other Middle-Aged Guy with Gout."

The rules at O'Hara's were simple. You had to be a lawyer or you had to work in the Towers to drink there. I met up with another lawyer friend of mine on the evening of the tenth to watch the Broncos on *Monday Night Football*. Then we got a car to go home.

I remember driving past the Towers and talking about them. I don't remember what we said exactly—I made some kind of joke as we drove by. That was the last time I ever saw them.

O'Hara's is gone now. The building's still there and it's sound; I've seen it on the news videos. But the windows are all blown out and the place is filled with shit.

A lot of people from Cantor Fitzgerald hung out there, and Cantor lost 700 people, I think. *Seven hundred.* This woman I knew was seven months pregnant. She's gone, too.

See, I still had a lot of friends who worked up in the Towers. But I'll get to that in a minute.

＊＊＊＊＊

I never thought it was a jetliner. When I first heard a plane hit a Tower, I thought it was a Cessna. When you worked in the Trade Center, you always saw Cessnas and other little planes flying below you. I figured some idiot had lost control and flown into the building.

In retrospect, that was a little naïve. A Cessna would just bounce off those buildings like a bug.

When I watched the attack on TV, the impact of the first plane looked like it might have gone through my old office at Ohrenstein & Brown. It didn't, though. Even when I worked in the Towers, it was always difficult to tell which floor was which when looking at them from the outside. They were just too damned big.

＊＊＊＊＊

My current office is on the ninth floor of our building at 160 Broadway. It used to be that 70 percent of the view from our window was 1 Liberty Plaza. The rest was dominated by 1 World Trade. Where we once had a relatively nice view out the windows, we now have a view of carnage. And through that: New Jersey. You can see right through where the Towers and 7 World Trade Center were. They're just . . . gone.

Sure, I was concerned that my business was gone. The Wednesday or Thursday after the attack, I was watching the TV coverage and they said that 1 Liberty Plaza was about to collapse. That's right across the street from my place but what could I do? We weren't allowed back in the area until Monday, the seventeenth, but even then, we had limited access. You had to get past several security checkpoints.

I'd actually tried to go to my office that first Saturday, the fifteenth. My ID as a local business owner let me in through the first few checkpoints, but I couldn't get all the way down to my office because security was still afraid that stuff was falling off 1 Liberty Plaza. My whole section of Broadway was shut down. No luck there.

As it turned out, my building had survived, by which I mean it was structurally sound. But the heating, ventilation, and air-conditioning system is probably destroyed. Before evacuating on the eleventh, the building owner didn't turn these systems off. The first Tower hadn't fallen yet, and I guess he just hadn't considered what might happen if the intake fans were running and two massive skyscrapers collapsed next door. All the pulverized debris from the Towers got sucked into the air ducts and distributed throughout the building.

>>>«<<

When I finally got into my office on the seventeenth, I found that everything was covered with dust. Curiously, however, the windows were intact. Which tells you the force of the debris that was flying: it was strong enough to get through cracks in the ceiling, the window seals. It covered my desk, my chairs, my papers, everything.

This is a sample of the debris taken out of my office.[97] My girl-friend's father is a PhD in chemistry. Technically, he's retired, but he still has a lot of friends at the University of Connecticut and volunteered to have this stuff analyzed. The tests came back showing that this dust has a little bit of everything in it. Little pieces of paper. Silicates. Concrete and glass fibers.

I don't know why I keep it. I guess I just don't want to throw it away. It's been sitting on my desk in my apartment; I've been working out of there since 9/11. Looking at it, it's kinda hard to believe that the Towers were reduced to that in a heartbeat. All those big things were turned into little things in an instant.

Little things matter a lot to me now, you know? Like, I was going through some old things the other day, and I found my men's room key from when I worked on the 85th floor of 1 World Trade. For a split second, I had this insane thought that, gee, I'd better give this back.

I'm keeping it. I don't think they'll miss it.

>>>«<<

Right after the attack, things got worse before they got better. I started hearing from people I used to work with and friends from high

---

97 John held up a small vial of gray dust.

school. That's how I found out that four people from my high school class were killed. One was a guy I'd gone to high school with. We'd lost track of each other for a couple of years. Then, over the last three years, I started seeing him all the time. Mike Duffy. He became a regular at another place I hang out at. After all this happened, I half-expected to see him. In fact, I found myself looking for him every time I went to the bar. I never ran into him, and I didn't think much of it until I got a newsletter from my high school.

Another guy I graduated with—John Schroeder. I played lacrosse with him. In my junior year, he was captain of the team. He'd gone off to school at Princeton, but we started bumping into each other occasionally when I was working at the Trade Center. He was on the 87th or 89th floor of 1 World Trade, right where the plane went in. He'd married a girl from our high school class, and I think they'd been husband and wife for just about three months before this happened.

Then there was this friend of mine's father. And the guy who was at my brother's wedding. And my good friend's brother. And this other guy's cousin. Just more and more names. They keep rolling out in the papers every day. It sucks.

But I think the most disorienting part of all this is the number of people I sort of knew who are gone. All those people from Ohrenstein & Brown and all the other firms who used to hang out at O'Hara's—the ones I only knew by their first names. And now I have no idea whether they're with us or not. I may never know.

⤜⤛

At first, I was upset with the tourists going downtown, especially when they first opened Broadway on September 20 or 21. There were people climbing on light poles, hefting cameras in the air, taking photographs, and crowding the streets—you couldn't walk on the sidewalk, it was so crazy. A three-minute walk to my office ended up taking twenty.

I thought it was disrespectful to come as a tourist and gawk. There were people having their photos taken, smiling and posing with what was left of the World Trade Center in the background. At that point, we still thought there were 6,000 people buried. So these people were taking snapshots of a graveyard. That's how I see it. Disrespectful.

I made comments. One guy was fighting with police to get a picture. I walked up to him and asked, "Where's your family buried?" He was caught off-guard, and I said, "Really, tell me where your family members are buried. Because I'd like to dig them up and take their photograph."

He wasn't from New York. But he kinda got the idea.

In fact, one of the restaurants down there printed some signs outside their restaurant: "This is hallowed ground. Show some respect."

That was appreciated.

⋙⋘

I was out of my office for about a month before the building management finally got everything cleaned up. When I re-opened and started seeing clients again, you could tell it was a dramatic experience for them. It was the first time a lot of people had been downtown, which must have been sobering. And someone involved in litigation isn't usually happy to begin with. I've had a couple clients come in, look out the window, and start crying. I let them have their moment and then try to get them back on track.

I understand what that's about. It's very tough for me to sit here in the office and perform work when I recognize I'm just a couple hundred yards away from a mass grave for thousands of people.

And I know that approximately 20 to 40 percent of the lawyers in New York City either couldn't get into their offices or had them destroyed. The damage to business in this city has been unbelievable. For instance, the phones didn't work for six weeks, but that didn't really matter. In all that time, I had nothing to do.

That first week we were anticipating about $20,000 in revenue. We got maybe $500. It's only been this last ten days or so that business has picked up again to the levels prior to 9/11. I've already had

one case pulled from me—a criminal defense client hired a new lawyer because he couldn't get in touch with us for a week. And I couldn't
call him, since I had no access to my case files, no phone numbers.

RETROSPECTIVES

ALICE GREENWALD

What is the point to a headstone on a grave? Why have human beings captured the ashes of loved ones in urns since time immemorial? How do the living cope with the memory of the departed, especially when those who have left us did so under tragic and confounding circumstances?

These and other questions were very much on my mind when I interviewed Alice Greenwald, who currently serves as president and CEO of the 9/11 Memorial and Museum.

Built directly upon and within the World Trade Center campus, the memorial and museum shoulders the awesome responsibility of welcoming visitors from around the globe as they seek to connect—and, in many cases, reconnect—with all that happened there twenty years ago.

"I see the 9/11 Memorial and Museum as the container for the nation's grief," Alice says. "It's a very important function."

If this sounds like an understatement, it is. But Alice has earned the right to be pithy. Her extensive career in remembrance affords her a viewpoint into the process few people can match.

She began her journey in remembrance at the Spertus Museum of Judaica in Chicago, the Hebrew Union College Skirball Museum in Los Angeles, and the National Museum of American Jewish History in Philadelphia where she served as executive director for five years. Between 1986 and 2001, she provided expertise to clients including the Baltimore Museum of Industry, the Pew Charitable Trusts, the Historical Society of Princeton, and the United States Holocaust Memorial Museum (USHMM). Her work with USHMM evolved into a nineteen-year affiliation where, among other assignments, she served as associate museum director for museum programs.

The author of several articles and books, Alice was executive vice president for exhibitions, collections, and education at the 9/11 Memorial and Museum from 2006 to 2016, and assumed the chief executive role in 2017.

Perhaps unsurprisingly, the list of Alice's accomplishments goes on.
For all these reasons and so many more, I was grateful to speak with
her by video conference in the closing days of 2020.

I'VE BEEN IN the memory business a long time. People ask me,
"Why do we remember?"

Well, there's a great quote from Elie Wiesel in one of his books:
"If we stop remembering, we stop being."

I believe that memory is essential for moral conscience. If we can't
remember what happened to other people, we can't possibly determine what's right and wrong. Remembering becomes an existential
imperative so we can learn to be better human beings.

As I see it, this imperative has two parts. First, we could say that
remembering is simply one of life's obligations. That we have a fundamental obligation to remember those who have died. And when
I say "died," what I really mean is that we remember how they lived.
This isn't just a human response. As far as we know, elephants do
the same thing. But it becomes especially important when we try to
breach this interesting chasm between the profundity of loss and the
outrage over a loss that's unjust, as in cases of criminal inhumanity.

That's just one part. I said there are two. The second reason we
remember is to ask ourselves what we're capable of as human beings,
both at our worst and at our best.

Human beings make choices. The nineteen hijackers, Osama bin
Laden, and everyone affiliated with al-Qaeda . . . they made a choice
to perpetrate that horrific attack on 9/11. But on that day—and in
the weeks, the months, even years that followed—people made other
choices: to respond with empathy and compassion, from a deep sense
of public service. Service to one another, not to oneself.

I've seen this over and over again, both at the United States Holocaust Memorial Museum, and now with the commemoration of
9/11. We learn that, in our worst moments, in the most egregious

examples of inhumanity, we also see people acting their best. Yes, it's true that, sometimes, heroism comes to us via instinctual courage. But many other times, it's simply a choice.

That's a big part of what you experience at the 9/11 Memorial Museum. We put these stark choices in front of people. Of course, you encounter the horrific story of that day. You may find yourself devastated by the unjust, indefensible loss of human life. But also, I think, you'll be ennobled by stories of justness, generosity, and incredible spirit. By the people who went out of their way to do whatever they could to help each other. We've seen incredible resilience come out of those kinds of responses. And they were all choices.

That's why I think we remember. We're essentially asking ourselves, "What choices are we going to make when presented with our own challenging circumstances?"

⸎⸎⸎

Grief requires that we find a place to *put* our grief, or else we can't function. That's why we have cemeteries, why we have monuments and memorials.

It's like Gettysburg. I wasn't alive during the Civil War. But Gettysburg is the container for that experience. It allows our country to acknowledge what's happened, but also to move beyond it. And we had to go on. To rebuild and renew. We had to do that in order to be resilient.

I see the 9/11 Memorial and Museum as the container for the nation's grief. It's a very important function. In normal times, we welcome three million people a year from all over the world.[98]

How do they react to their visit? Obviously, experiences are different for everyone. If you'd asked me that when the museum first opened in 2014, or even when the memorial opened in 2011, I would have given a different answer than how I respond today. Because at

---

98 This interview was conducted in December 2020, in the midst of the COVID-19 global pandemic.

that point, the majority of visitors came with their own 9/11 narrative imprinted in their memories.

If we're making gross generalizations, I think the museum experience is definitely different for people who lived through the event. They have a memory of it, and they're coming back maybe with some hesitation. They don't want to re-experience this horrible day.

We found this with New Yorkers in particular. The local audience only tends to come when relatives come in from out of town and say, "Take me there, I want to go. The museum's got such a great reputation. That's the one attraction we want to see."

For people who lived through 9/11 but were not so closely affected by it, either through loss or experience, there's a real desire to come. It's a pilgrimage of sorts. The event is ingrained in their consciousness, and they come to pay respects. For those people, I think— for the most part—the Memorial and Museum provides an elevating experience.

But the event was very personal for New Yorkers; 9/11 is still very much on their minds. It's a prism through which we still view the world.

For myself, I'll look up and, if it's a crystal-clear blue sky, I'll still say, "Oh, it's a 9/11 sky." It's just so much in my head.

I think New Yorkers still have a bit of anxiety below the surface. Maybe less so now than five years ago. Certainly, less now than ten years ago.

For instance, a couple of years ago there was a flyover of the Statue of Liberty, and people here freaked out because they heard that sound of a plane flying way too low. There hadn't been enough notification, and people thought it was another terrorist attack.

People in other cities understand this. In Boston, certainly. Areas around Washington, D.C., L.A., San Francisco, and so on. But I don't think that reaction happens to people in other places around the country. It's not as visceral.

Still, as I say, if they lived it, they remember it. And the museum affects them, too.

⟫⟩⟨⟪

One of the funny things about 9/11 is the way the event cut straight across different sectors of society.

We have all the blue-collar service workers for whom 9/11 is very much their story—law enforcement and firefighters. First responders. Construction workers. All the civic organizations. But 9/11 was also deeply personal to people in different economic positions.

Think of all the financial services organizations that were at the World Trade Center. The banks and the brokerages, the bond traders. 9/11 was just as personal for these people.

The fact that people of every denomination and persuasion were killed on 9/11 is what makes the event so universal, what allows it to transcend.

We have to remember that, while 9/11 happened to us, on our soil, it was experienced as a global tragedy and a global loss. A lot of Americans come to pay their respects, but people from over ninety nations were killed that day. Every year, we have heads of state who come during the United Nations General Assembly to pay their respects. Prior to COVID, about thirty percent of our visitors were international.

Another important point is that 9/11 was an unprecedented moment of collective global witness. An estimated one-third of the world's population witnessed the attacks in 2001. People watched it happen literally around the world, in real time or in the news broadcasts that ran endlessly throughout the day. It was a shared experience. A universal wound. And a wound that united us as human beings, beyond boundaries of nationality, region, and ethnicity.

Here in the United States, we know it as a watershed event. Certainly, the world order has shifted in interesting ways in the aftermath of 9/11. But it was also a watershed event for people around the world. What I've learned is that, even in countries like India, for example—which has some of the highest, if not *the* highest rates of terrorist incidents in the world—they were as shocked and unprepared for what happened on 9/11 as we Americans were.

People have told me that, "Here in our country, we never know when the next event is going to happen. We feel vulnerable all the time. But America was safe. For us, it was the last best place."

That was taken away from everybody on 9/11.

That's one of the things we thought about a lot when creating the museum experience: this sense that all these people would be coming with their own 9/11 story. We knew we couldn't be a conventional museum, an expert voice telling people what they already knew. Instead, we designed the museum as it is. It takes in all those voices.

For instance, when you walk into our memorial exhibit, you see that all four walls, floor to ceiling, are covered with nearly 3,000 faces. Right away, you see that every ethnicity is there. Every faith tradition. People two and a half years old to eighty-five are represented. And you can tell by the names, they're not all from one place. It's an immediate experience of the scale of the tragedy.

We worked very hard not to politicize the event. It's a fine line. We talk about the rationale of al-Qaeda; we give you that background. But our goal is to communicate the human experience of a historical event. It's always about what happened to people. Because if you get at what happened to people, you transcend the politics, you transcend the differences, and you start seeing yourself in the story.

When you look at those 3,000 faces, right away you understand: "This happened to all of these people? This could have happened to me."

It's about seeing yourself in the history and building up a fundamental intolerance for the use of terrorism as a tool of grievance.

⤛⤜

So the people who were alive during 9/11 and remember it—that's one group of people with one set of reactions we tried to consider. But it's now twenty years after the event. We have a large number of visitors who didn't live through 9/11. They have no personal memory of these events.

I call them "young people," but some of them aren't that young now. Some are in their twenties. They may have been three or four years old when 9/11 happened, so they don't have a memory of it. And of course, this group includes anyone younger than that.

We find that many students who come to the museum know very little about 9/11. When I speak to young people, they begin to tell me their parents' story! I've talked to our educators about this. It's fascinating!

The young people didn't live it. But because 9/11 was such a moment of rupture for so many people, their parents will say, "Well, this is what happened to me on 9/11. This is my story. This is where I was, this is what I was doing." So these young people tell you their parents' story as if it's their story. I just think that's a fascinating transmission of family history through a historical event.

And young people certainly have no context for the changes that came after 9/11.

"Of course, you always take your shoes off when you go to the airport! Isn't that what always happened?"

No. That didn't always happen.

"Well, of course when I go to a museum or a library or a public space, I open my pocketbook or my book bag and they have to rifle through it!"

No! That didn't used to happen!

People in this age group have no counterpoint for what's going on now. So that's where we focus a lot of our educational resources.

We speak to a lot of people in this generation as they enter the service professions. Police officers. Firefighters. The military. Intelligence agencies. A while back, several of these agencies came to us (the FBI is a case in point) and they said, "We need these young analysts and young agents to know about what happened, so they understand the agency they work for."

We were unprepared when they first made that request. But over the years, we've developed many wonderful professional training programs that help young recruits appreciate the agencies and organizations they've chosen to join. To have a deeper understanding of the role they play in society, but also the role that members of their organization played on 9/11.

They're the ones taking responsibility for our security and safety in a world that, in so many ways, was engendered by 9/11. And yet they have very little understanding of it. And each year, the people we talk to get younger and younger!

⇢⇤

I'll never forget this. It moves me so much just thinking about it.

We were training a new group of detectives with the NYPD. And we had a former NYPD detective, a man by the name of Jimmy Luongo.

Jimmy got up and talked about how, when 9/11 happened, he was deployed immediately to the site and that afternoon was assigned to be the Incident Commander at Fresh Kills (in Dutch, that means "fresh water"), a recently closed landfill in Staten Island that was re-opened for the massive forensic operation of shifting through millions of tons of debris from the World Trade Center site.

Now remember, there were 1.8 million tons of debris at Ground Zero. Huge pieces of steel. Pulverized concrete. Molten building materials. Tangled rebar. And you had the rescue operation going on. They were searching every iota of material to recover personal property, and because human remains were in there. People, too, had been pulverized. And there was a deep dedication to try and return some part of them to their families.

Jimmy was ordered to set up the operation at Fresh Kills so that the wreckage at Ground Zero could be transported by truck and barge over to Staten Island. His supervisor said, "Oh, and we need this to start tomorrow morning."

Jimmy was flabbergasted. He didn't know where to begin! He expressed his concern to his supervisor, who ordered him to "just figure it out!"

So Jimmy was telling these young detectives his own story from a moment of duress. He was telling them, "Be prepared to go beyond what you think you can do, because it's going to happen in this line of work."

And then he said something like this: "At some time in your career, somebody is going to give you an order to do something you're going to think you can't do. But you know what? You're going to just do it. You are going to just figure it out. Because you don't have a choice. The situation demands it. The moment demands it. And in that moment, you will rise."

It was a very personal story, and it came right out of a personal 9/11 experience. But it transcends that history to become an educational guidepost for another generation of service.

⟫⟪

Here's another story that took my breath away. It taught me so much.

When I first came to the project, I met a woman who's since died, Marilynn Rosenthal. She was a professor of sociology at the University of Michigan.

Marilynn lost her son on 9/11. He was a passenger on hijacked United Airlines Flight 175, which was crashed into the South Tower. And she wanted to meet the family of a young man who was one of the hijackers, Marwan al-Shehhi.

Somehow, she was able to get in touch with Marwan's family. She flew to Abu Dhabi in the United Arab Emirates and was met at the airport by a cousin who basically said, "We're honored to have you with us. We're so sorry for your loss. But our Marwan wasn't one of the hijackers. Our Marwan could never have done such a thing."

They took Marilynn to see the family, who were very hospitable. She had a whole conversation with them, and she asked, "Is Marwan around?"

"No," they said. "We haven't seen him in years."

This was a few years after 9/11. In their minds, there was no connection between their relative, Marwan, and the Marwan al-She-hhi who was a hijacker on the airplane.

"Something terrible must have happened to him," they said. "Marwan's passport must have been stolen. Maybe he was kidnapped or killed."

The family admitted they didn't know what had happened to him. But they kept insisting, "He would never have done that. This is not the person you're looking for."

When it was time for Marilynn to leave, the same cousin took her to the airport. This time, when he looked at Marilynn, he said, "Why would he have done it?"

And so it began. That person, and that family perhaps, began to think . . . could this be possible?

Now, Marilynn Rosenthal was a sociologist. She had this innate sense of "you talk to people as people." You know? Because politics is one thing. Journalism is another. But Marilynn functioned from a standpoint of "I'm a mother who lost her son. You are people who also lost someone close to you. So I want to talk to you. I want to understand, because we are connected profoundly by the loss of our sons."[99]

It comes down to seeing each other as human beings. This is what we strive for at the Memorial and Museum when we communicate both what happened on 9/11 and the human response to it.

What allows people to commit mass murder is that they stop seeing human beings as human beings. Now they're targets, right? They're expendable, collateral damage, whatever you want to call it. They're not people anymore. That's where atrocities always begin.

Right now, there's a fundamental absence of empathy in this crazy, messed up world. But if we can get to empathy, if we can get to connection, there's a kernel of possibility that we can make change.

⤜⤛

---

99 To read more about Marilynn Rosenthal's incredible journey, see the *Washington Post* article "Sons of the Mothers: Marilynn Rosenthal Struggles to Understand Her Child's Killer, the Boy Who Grew Up to Be a 9/11 Hijacker" by Tamara Jones, September 11, 2006.

A few years ago, we had Justice Sonia Sotomayor in to speak. She's a New Yorker and a real teacher.

There were a number of young people in the audience, and she went right over to them. Drove her Secret Service crazy because she literally got off the stage to talk to these kids! She wanted them to know her 9/11 story, but the story she told wasn't about 9/11 at all. It took place about a day or so afterward.

She said she was on the street somewhere and she saw somebody, a stranger, who appeared to be in emotional distress. Maybe they'd lost somebody. Maybe they were just still in shock or whatever. So Justice Sotomayor crossed the street to give this person a hug.

That story said everything to me. Transcending differences by recognizing the common wound.

But somehow we didn't hold on to that. After 9/11 . . . you remember? We had this coming together of our society, our country, the world. Everybody said, "We are there for you!" "Nous sommes tous américains" was the headline of Le Monde on September 12. "We are all Americans."

You had this sense of people caring for each other. This acknowledgement that we're all in this together. That our wounds would bind us to each other, make us more compassionate toward one another.

It was too short-lived. Whether that was because of political decisions or whether that was just because you can't sustain that level of caring? I don't know.

For me, the question remains: Why does it take an event like 9/11 for people to show what they're capable of as compassionate, caring human beings?

It seems to take something, some event, that breaks the dream most of us find ourselves in most of the time. To remind us what actually matters.

For many people who lived through 9/11, they're shocked that it's been twenty years. The twentieth anniversary has a great deal of resonance for these people. Certainly, this is true of people like first responders who lost so many of their colleagues and family members. Sometimes they have a hard time coming in. And, as I said, New Yorkers in general have this built-in reaction of, "Well, we lived it! Why do we need to go? We already know what happened!"

I think a lot of people from these groups come to the museum bearing this worry about: What am I going to experience? Is it going to be painful? Is it going to re-traumatize me? Will I be able to handle it? But many times, I think they're . . . how should I put it? Surprised. Shocked, maybe. By their reaction to being in the museum's physical space.

I don't want to be overly ambitious about our project. But I think it's an almost therapeutic experience. You know how they say in psychology that, when you re-encounter trauma, that's the only way you can actually get beyond it?

We did not want to create a museum that was a three-dimensional version of a history textbook. The museum provides a safe space for re-encountering the events of that day and for commemorating people in the fullness of their lives, not as victims of mass murder. The historical exhibition takes you through the narrative of the day. Every moment, including its antecedents. What led up to the 9/11 and the world we found after 9/11.

This is very much a storytelling museum. Yes, we're an archive, but we're a living archive. Like a living time capsule. This makes the experience very immediate. Very present.

Our stories are told in the voices of people who lived the event. You begin with the voices of multitudes, remembering what happened that day. We use all the retrospective oral histories. We have the in-the-moment radio transmissions, the cockpit voice recorders, all the media that was capturing so much of the story. The news radio broadcasts on the day of 9/11, which is how so many people were taking in the information.

So you experience what people twenty years ago experienced when they heard the 1010 WINS broadcast, or see a first responder interviewed on the news as if you were watching it that day. And, as I mentioned before, in the world after 9/11, you begin to see these acts of coming together in generosity and empathy.

Then our guests leave the gallery and enter Foundation Hall, this cavernous space with a sixty-foot-high ceiling. Cathedral-like, if you will. And there's this sense of "I can breathe again. We can go forward. We stand at the foundation of the World Trade Center. But look. The World Trade Center has been rebuilt." There's this sense of possibility and potential.

Obviously, I can't speak for everybody's experience. But I would say that journey's a fairly typical experience for people who didn't want to visit the museum in the first place.

⪼⪻

Right now, we live in a world where the distinctions are going away. Our economies, our health, our environment. God knows . . . what we do here, or what somebody does in Russia or Australia, it can affect the entire world.

COVID has shown us this. If there's a fly that gets on an airplane or in a suitcase and comes to New York, you've got West Nile virus, right? If a virus in Wuhan, China, comes about, the entire world is affected. The same is true of the economy. What happens in the Hangseng in the morning has an impact on the New York Stock Exchange by the time I wake up. Or greenhouse gas emissions. So many examples.

So the world has gotten much smaller. And because it's smaller, we're going to have increasing points of tension. We've got to figure out a way to negotiate these tensions that doesn't involve the mass murder of innocent human beings.

That may sound overly simplistic, but it's certainly an aspiration of this project. The Memorial and Museum stands as a focal point for healing and affirms the commonality of seeking to understand the world we live in through remembrance. We remember these people who were so senselessly killed so that—and I know it sounds corny, but—so that it shouldn't happen again.

Well, it will happen again. It did happen again. And it does happen again. But if we collectively have the will to say, "No, that's not the way to negotiate," then other avenues can open up as ways to resolve our tensions.

≫≪

How have people changed when I see them leave the museum? I hate to make generalizations about other people's experience, but I can tell you that people leave deeply moved. The experience affects them. What happens after that? No one can say.

When you leave the museum, there's no moment of "Now I get it!" We don't have a call to action. There's no rallying cry of "Now you've experienced it, go out and do something good!"

Still, our hope is that what's affecting our visitors is that recognition: This is not somebody else's story, it's everybody's story. It could have been me. It could have been my child. It could have been my neighbor. It could have been my son's teacher. My daughter's friend. It could have been any of us. And is that okay?

That's really what we want people to be thinking about.

When that first group of FBI agents came to us for what's now their required training, the bureau's director, Chris Wray, gave them a speech. He quoted lyrics by Leonard Cohen: "There is a crack in everything, that's how the light gets in." It blew us away. We thought, That's it. That's absolutely right.

None of this is to say there are easy answers. The world is complicated. We acknowledge that. But when you leave the Memorial and Museum, you might have a new set of questions. And these questions will be on two levels.

First, the intellectual level. You might find you have a greater desire to understand how tragedies like 9/11 come about, and how we respond to them. You'll probably see that our responses are complicated, too. They have their own repercussions. But here we are at the World Trade Center, so let's try to figure this out together.

Then, on an emotional level, we remind people that even in these horrible moments, we have the capacity for resilience. Hope is still possible.

On the foundation level of the museum, as you're leaving the building, there's a single quote on the wall. It comes from Joe Bradley, an engineer and recovery worker. It's something he said on the day they ended the nine months of rescue and recovery at Ground Zero:

"We came in as individuals, and we're leaving together."

That's what we want people to think about when they leave the museum. Because I think, for all of us who work there, that summarizes what our project is all about.

TOM HADDAD

I re-interviewed Tom Haddad, forty-nine, in late September 2020. It was a turbulent time. The world was seven months into the COVID-19 pandemic. The economy was teetering toward a recession. Debate over how to respond to the virus had highlighted divisions in a country that was already polarized.

But COVID-19 seemed to be the least of our problems.

The murders of Breonna Taylor, Ahmaud Arbery, and George Floyd had rocked the United States all summer. Protestors marching against institutionalized racism and police brutality had been met with armed responses in cities like Philadelphia, Atlanta, and Washington, D.C. Day by day, the divide between citizens shouting that black lives matter and all lives matter seemed to be widening. Plus, all this was leading up to a stormy presidential election between the incumbent, Donald Trump, and former Vice President Joe Biden.

Due to pandemic restraints, Tom and I spoke by phone. Despite the seriousness of the times, we found ourselves laughing over days gone by— like the time we'd first met eighteen and a half years before.

It was a bright, clear day in the spring of 2002. I interviewed Tom on a bench in Madison Square Park, here in Manhattan. Back then, I was still recording my interviews on magnetic tape micro-cassette. Digital wasn't a thing yet. And in those days, two complete strangers thought nothing of sitting less than six feet away from each other, as the pandemic precautions dictated. That was part of a normal life.

Not that there's anything normal about Tom. There's a reason I've begun each edition of Tower Stories *with his account. Tom had an incredibly visceral experience on 9/11. One that, sadly, few people lived to talk about.*

If you haven't yet read his original interview, I suggest you go back and do so before reading this.

When I first met Tom, it was six months after the Towers had fallen. I found him distracted. He was very intelligent. Certainly present. But distant. Not knowing him personally then, I assumed this was how he typically presented.

But the man I spoke to in late September 2020 was happy, easygoing, generous, funny, and quick to laugh. He represented almost a complete turnaround from the sullen guy I first met nearly twenty years before.

I asked Tom how this change had occurred. His answer left me inspired.

FOR A LONG TIME, I was a salaried employee. And in 2010, I was kind of led to believe that the company I worked for—same company I'd worked for on 9/11—wouldn't be long for the world. I was a senior vice president. So I decided it would be better for them if I got off the payroll. They wouldn't have to pay my benefits, my payroll tax. It would be a huge savings for them. I'd keep working for them freelance, and maybe they could stay afloat a little longer. I thought this was the right thing to do.

We went from fifteen or twenty employees with an office in the World Trade Center to . . . well, now they're down to just the two owners and one employee, I think. Basically, I went from having, like, a 401(k) match and really terrific benefits to having to do all this stuff for myself. It was a bit of a shocker.

If I had to grade being a freelancer, I would give it a solid B. I don't like having to worry about where my next gig is coming from, you know? I don't like that. I'd always been a very traditional guy as far as employment. My dad worked for IBM for something like thirty-five years. So the idea of independence was never appealing to me. But now that it's been ten years—which is shocking, by the way—I do appreciate it.

Like, with the COVID pandemic. My youngest son is in the third grade. He needs somebody sitting there with him for his remote learning. Otherwise, he gets distracted. So I sit with him, doing my work off-camera. But I wouldn't be able to do that if I didn't have this kind of flexibility.

Originally, people were so psyched to be working from home because of COVID. Now, it's just normal for people to constantly be
working. Plus, there's the constant fear we all live in of, you know . . .
tomorrow, the place we work for might close. It makes people even
more terrified, so they work even more now than they used to.

I wonder if they'll ever get that time back. I don't think we will.
I think that, in a lot of ways, COVID-19 has changed our lives far
more than people even realize at this point.

»»«««

The first eight or ten years after 9/11 were rocky for me. Really bad.
I had a lot of anger, but also a lot of detachment. There are whole
blocks of time post-9/11 that I have no memory of at all. My wife will
say, "Hey, remember when we went on vacation to Rhode Island?"
And I'll be like, "No, I don't." I don't remember it at all.

It's funny because I was in this weird, internalized place . . . I just
shut it all out. I mean, I was still functioning. I could tell people what
happened on 9/11. How I ran through the street. It was logical for
me to say I was scared, and so I would tell people I was scared. But
I didn't really feel it. I wasn't processing anything emotionally. Like,
zero percent.

But then I took part in an experimental therapy program put
together by New York Presbyterian, the New York State Psychiatric
Institute, and Columbia University Hospital. It was one of the best
things that could have happened to me. And like most good things
that happen to me in my life, my wife found it.

Right after 9/11, she saw that I was struggling. And me being
an artist, she decided that, "Well, he's never been one for words,
but maybe he'll keep a diary of pictures as opposed to writing." She
bought me a sketchbook, and she says, "You know what you should
do? You should start making drawings and just let it all out. Don't
think about what you're drawing. Just draw." So that began this nearly twenty-year journey of drawing pictures and sort of working my
feelings out like that.[100]

She found this study when she realized I was getting to a place she could no longer help. I had, like, four interviews before I was accepted into it.

It was basically a study where they were trying to come up with ways to treat soldiers returning from the Iraq War. They were looking for candidates who'd suffered what they referred to as "cataclysmic PTSD." And the way they explained it to me was that anybody can have post-traumatic stress. You get in a car accident, for instance, you can have post-traumatic stress. But by "cataclysmic" PTSD, they meant that the world experienced it with you. It was your experience, but the world also watched. If you're there on the ground during a mass shooting that got televised, it's something you can't escape because everybody's watching it, everybody's talking about it. They're curious about it.

The way the doctors explained it to me is that, when you experience trauma of this level, your mind basically has two options. You can detach your factual experience from your emotional experience. Or you can go crazy. Those are your two options.

Fortunately, for me, I detached. Which is why, in the first ten years after 9/11, I could tell my story in such incredible detail. I described what happened to me in a factual manner. Almost emotionless. That was this detachment I'm talking about. Detachment of the factual experience from my emotional experience. The therapy was designed to combine the two again.

They made these MRI maps of my brain at the beginning and then at the end. I was in the tube for, like, five hours. They taped a computer monitor to my face, like goggles, and they would show me pictures of things so I would react to them while they were mapping my brain. Sometimes they asked me questions and I had to answer them. And sometimes it was just showing me a series of photographs. It was an intense, intense experience.

---

100 Tom talked about this in our first interview, back in the spring of 2002. He calls it the Bus Drawing project. When he started it, he literally used to draw on the bus while commuting to work in the city after 9/11. To see Tom's pictures from the Bus Drawing project, go to: www.coroflot.com/thaddad/Bus-Drawings-Project.

Then, the way it worked, I had to relive my experience of 9/11 for an hour and a half each day, every day for fourteen weeks. I liken it to . . . you know that scene at the end of *A Clockwork Orange* where he's put in front of the TV with his eyeballs held open?[101] This sort of extreme exposure. Actually, that's what they called it—extreme exposure therapy.

They were looking for people who could emotionally handle it, and I guess they thought that I could. And did, by the way. So I guess they were right.

They didn't put me in front of a TV screen. Not in the beginning, anyway. All I did was tell my story as it happened from the moment I woke up that day until the moment I got home. I had to tell it in as much detail as I could possibly remember. They recorded this on audiotape.

So one day a week, I would go up to Columbia Presbyterian all the way up on the East Side. The psychologist would record me telling my story, what I did on 9/11. Then, once a day for the next three days, I would listen to myself telling the story. At the end of the week, I went back up to Columbia Presbyterian and listened to the recording with the therapist. And we would talk about it.

Sometimes I'd tell the story and more of the details would start to come out. But you could also hear in the tape sometimes, I was annoyed. Like, I didn't want to be there. I didn't want to be doing it.

Then, on week ten . . . I don't know if you've seen it, but there's this totally amazing documentary that was made by a couple of French documentarians. They happened to be downtown filming on 9/11, and by accident they recorded everything as it was happening. So as homework on week ten, I had to sit and watch that movie.[102]

---

101 Tom's referring to the 1971 Stanley Kubrick film adaptation of the Anthony Burgess novel. At the end of the film, violent hooligan Alex DeLarge (played by Malcolm McDowell) is subjected to a form of extreme aversion therapy. His doctors pump him full of drugs and strap him to a chair. Metal clamps are used to hold his eyelids open. This forces Alex to stare at a video screen that plays images of some of the most violent abominations human beings can inflict on one another.

102 This film is called *9/11*. It was directed by Jules and Gédéon Naudet and James Hanlon, a member of FDNY, and produced by Susan Zirinsky of CBS News.

There's a part in the film where they were actually inside Tower 1. And there's a sound that would happen every now and again. This horrific loud thump and crunch sound. And that sound would haunt me. I could never quite figure out what it was.

But when I watched the film, I saw that it was the sound associated with jumpers hitting the ground. And it all flooded back into me. Emotionally, I remembered it all. In my body. All of a sudden, I collapsed to the ground and started crying uncontrollably. Fortunately, I was at home. Even thinking about it right now, it makes me upset.

And you know what's funny? By that point, I'd told the story of 9/11 so many times in front of so many people. At college symposiums. Radio tours. I told my story, and I never once remembered that I actually saw people hit the ground.

When I was able to piece it together, watching that film, it was like … I can't even explain what it felt like. Like being punched in the gut. I physically collapsed to the ground and started crying uncontrollably.

That is the exact moment, according to the therapist, that my emotional experience reattached to my factual experience. And suddenly I realized this whole thing I lived through, it really happened to me. It was like years' worth of emotion all came out at once. I was completely spent for four days afterwards.

⟫⟪

At thirteen weeks, I had to go back to Ground Zero. It was my first time back there. I went alone. And when I got there, I had just a terrible feeling. I just felt awful. I didn't want to be there. But I knew that I had to do it for the therapy.

I don't know if you recall from my story, but for me, the hardest part of my experience on 9/11 was when I got out on street. So I had to retrace my steps in the street as a part of the therapy. The idea was to help me know that this place was real, it all really happened. And so I went there. And at first, I was just like, this is stupid, I don't want to be here, I'm just going to go home. And then I decided, you know what? I'll do it. All right? I'll humor you. I'll do it.

I tried to retrace my steps, but I couldn't at first. The site was under construction back then. There were all these barricades up and fences. I couldn't get to where I'd started: Point A.

So I was standing there in the middle of the street and I thought, you know what? I'm close enough to where I started that day. And on 9/11, I ran. So I'm just gonna run and see what happens.

People must have thought I was nuts. But then again, it's New York. So I started at Point A, close to where I figured I must have started that day in the street. And I just started running. And before I even knew it, I was sitting in the Au Bon Pain where I ended. I mean, I was sitting in the exact same seat where I wound up that day all covered in dust, and this time I actually started yelling and crying. I was like, "I'm doing it again! I'm doing it again!"

It was such an exhilarating feeling, I did it a second time. I went all the way back to Point A and started running again. And then, like, as if it was a blur, I'm sitting in that seat again. And I was like, this is the coolest thing ever! It was like it was all stored there in my muscle memory, you know?

Then I felt something miraculous. I'm sitting there in the Au Bon Pain. And I'm thinking to myself, I don't have to do this anymore. This whole thing of, like . . . carrying this weight on my shoulders. It all started to fade.

It was almost as if my mind was allowed to let it go. And I let it go. I let it go. It all started to fade, and it's no longer a part of my everyday life.

My relationships started to change. Before the therapy, I was a short fuse, ready to explode at any minute. I was this lit powder keg. But I've lived a lifetime beyond it at this point.

I've got three boys. They're amazing. My oldest is seventeen, so he remembers me prior to therapy. And he'll say, "Angry Dad." Or he'll say, "Oh, Dad used to yell a lot." My two oldest, they talk about it sometimes. "You remember when Dad used to yell all the time?"

But now? It's the craziest thing. Now I'm like, the mellowest person I know. I'm the calm one. I just don't do it anymore.

The whole reason I did therapy in the first place was because I didn't want to be that person anymore. I wasn't that person before 9/11. I was goal-oriented. I wanted to move up the corporate ladder. But that slowly started to fade. Post-9/11, none of it matters, you know? I started letting my hair grow. I have a big bushy beard. I've become The Dude from *The Big Lebowski*. I don't yell anymore. And just . . . none of it matters, you know?

It's something I say a lot now. People get themselves all worked up about work. But everyone's replaceable at work. You're not replaceable at home. And that, I think, is where my head is now.

I've got these three amazing boys. My wife has been the rock of my whole existence. Best thing that ever happened to me. She has been my everything through all of it. Patient and loving and understanding. She helped me get home on 9/11, but she also helped me find peace after. So, you know, people get themselves all worked up and angry and yelling about politics. It matters to me, but I'm not going to get myself worked up about it.

The final week of that therapy was just me talking about how I got to this place of peace. I have to tell you, it comes and it goes. I have all these other issues that I can go into for hours regarding how our country is treating survivors. But I recently had to speak to the psychiatrist that was in charge of the therapy program. We spoke on the phone. We talked about my well-being, and he wanted to know—are there any lingering effects from 9/11?

I was honest. I said I still have anxiety. I still have panic attacks. They don't happen much. But they taught me how to handle them. It's not completely debilitating.

They actually gave me the final cassette of me telling my story. The very last time I told the story? I have that tape.

>>><<<

Years ago, when you first interviewed me, I said I believed that if you went back to work after 9/11, you were just as much a hero as anybody else. I still believe that. The very notion that there were some people that were "heroes" and some people that were "victims" and some people that were damsels in distress . . . that's just not the way that it was.

Right after 9/11, there was this great opportunity for us all to come together. And we did, by the way. On 9/11, or shortly thereafter, everybody was one solid unit. That's the way I remember it. Even in Washington. Everyone came together and rallied behind a president who was largely hated, by the way, and only became more so as his presidency continued. But his response to 9/11 was terrific. He did his best to unite the country.

Everybody was proud to be American. The same thing happens every couple of years at the Olympics. We're all one country together, as opposed to you're black or you're white, you're a Republican or a Democrat. Gay or straight, whatever. At that point, you're an American and it doesn't matter.

After 9/11, there was common cause. It was really inspiring. And then . . . it faded. Was it Hurricane Katrina? Or the souring on the Iraq War? Was it the realization that there were never any weapons of mass destruction? I don't know.

Since 9/11, we've grown further and further apart, whether it be economically or ideologically. And it's sad. There's a lot that should have been learned from 9/11. And maybe it was, briefly. But just like cramming for an exam, it's forgotten the next day.

⋙⋘

There's always pain and suffering. If all you do is focus every minute of every day on the horrors of the world, we will never have happiness. Right? I learned a lot of that from my experience of 9/11. If all I do is focus on the horrors of what happened that day, I will never have any time for happiness. There's only twenty-four hours in a day. So, in a lot of ways, I had to let it go.

I have found happiness in the small moments. And certainly, through the eyes of my children.

STEPHEN ADLY GUIRGIS

Meet Stephen Adly Guirgis, fifty-five. He calls himself an actor and he is, make no mistake. But he's also one of the most gifted playwrights working in America today.

Stephen is a founding member and a former artistic director of the groundbreaking LAByrinth Theater Company. But perhaps most important of all, he's a native New Yorker. You'll know this the moment you see his work.

Stephen's plays exalt in this city. His characters hail from its taverns, prisons, brothels, halfway houses, and churches. They are drug dealers, crack-smoking hookers, ex-cons, recovering addicts, and cops gone to seed. They are curbside poets, angels who strum their harps in the sewers, and serial losers with gonzo dreams.

Many Americans write such people off as the flotsam of our society. Stephen Adly Guirgis lifts them up. Again and again, he shows how the marginalized and the dispossessed know more about life than those whom our society tends to reward. Witness how deftly he handles his work in Our Lady of 121st Street, The Motherfucker with the Hat, In Arabia We'd All Be Kings, *and* Between Riverside and Crazy, *which, in 2015, won him many awards including the Pulitzer Prize for Drama.*

A consistent feature of Stephen's plays is his gift for conversations that bounce from one extreme to another. That's not just how he writes. It's how he talks.

He'll speak about something awful and, right in the middle of that, you'll find yourself laughing. And vice versa.

We talked at an outdoor café in October 2020, on Manhattan's Upper West Side.

I GREW UP here. My father came from Egypt. This was back in the early sixties, when being from another country was a big deal, you know?

My mother was Irish Catholic. From Jersey. Their first year together, my dad was going crazy. He couldn't handle Kearney, New
Jersey. It was Podunk. It was too slow. He grew up in Cairo. So he
was, like, "Can we go to New York? Let's go to New York. Let's please
just move to New York."

My mother'd always dreamed of it. But she was, like, "Honey,
you're new to this country. How are you gonna make it work?"

Well. The moment he got here, everything clicked. He found a
job. He found the shops. He knew how to get to the subway. It was
just boom, boom, boom. So that's how I ended up living here. I was
three months old when we moved.

We got this rent-controlled apartment. We were living above our
means. All my friends who lived in this neighborhood, they could
all afford going to sleepaway camp. They could get leather sneakers
before—remember when there was no leather sneakers? They would
have after-school classes in, like, clowning. Stuff like that. And I'd be
like, "I want to take clowning." Or the guitar. "I want to learn how to
play guitar!"

So in this neighborhood, I didn't fit in economically. But I kind of
fit in socially. I went to kindergarten and grammar school up on 121st
Street where I fit in much better economically, but socially there was a
bit of adjustment. Basically, I was a white kid where there weren't that
many white kids. Plus, I wasn't a good athlete. I wasn't fearless. Like,
I was smart, but back then that wasn't necessarily a positive thing.

I had to learn to get by. And I did.

A while back I realized that, if I have a talent for writing, it's because, when I was a kid, I fucking listened like my life depended on
it. I'd wear my pants one way in this neighborhood, go uptown and
I'd roll them up this way, that way. I was always trying to figure out
how to just be accepted, you know? And that's built into my writing.

Basically, I've lived here on and off my whole life. And this neighborhood back then . . . growing up, my mother would send me to
Zabar's, which only has, like, a couple items that are cheap.[103] The

---

103 Zabar's is the iconic specialty food store at 2245 Broadway and 80th Street.

only thing we could afford was the rye bread. So she sent me to get the rye bread. And right in front of Zabar's, it used to be like . . . what's that place in London where they argue about politics? In public? Trafalgar Square!

Right in front of Zabar's, they used to have every left-wing, communist organization. People screaming, "Register! Sign up! We need to get this guy on the ballot!"

That's what this neighborhood was. Traditionally, it was crazy fucking communists, intellectuals and artists, opera singers and Puerto Ricans. It was middle-class, Jewish, liberal Democrats.

I lived on Riverside in the eighties. And back when I was growing up? We'd say, "Are you going up to Broadway? You'd better walk up 84th Street. You walk up at 85th Street, you may not make it to West End." There were gangs, drug rehabs, SROs. Like, all that shit.

But it's not that now.

Now this neighborhood is, like, baby strollers and a lot of entitlement. It's not the same. For me, New York is different now.

Like, a year ago, I was on my way to my therapist. And there was a guy with a folding table, you know? Doing politics. And I look. This guy is doing this fake thing. He's saying, "Well, I'm a libertarian." Which really means he's, like, a fucking Trump supporter.

Now, look. I'm a normal person. But I lost my fucking mind. I fucking screamed. This cocksucker coming here with his . . . I lost my mind. I fucking knocked over his table.

These two old drunks, they grabbed me. And they were like, "Calm down!"

I'm like, "I'm calmed down! I'm calm!"

They were like, "Look at your hands."

They were shaking so badly.

><><

Ric Burns. He did that New York documentary series? Watching that documentary, I was very struck by this thing that, like, New York is an idea. You know? In the same way that the United States started out as an idea. New York is actually a microcosm of this idea.

For the first wave of immigrants, there was a social contract. It basically said, you're gonna come here and you're gonna work your ass off. You may live in substandard conditions. There's gonna be rats, there's gonna be roaches. But you can earn enough money to improve yourself. And here in New York, we're going to educate your children for free. Because back then, it wasn't just public grammar school and public high school. The CUNY colleges were free.[104]

So that was the deal we offered. You come here, you're leaving your home behind. You're gonna break your ass, and some of you are gonna fall off of buildings or whatever. But your children are going to have this thing that you couldn't have. You'll give them a chance.

Oh, and P.S.? Not everyone around you is gonna be French or whatever. There's going to be Polish and Italian and black people here all together, and blah blah blah. We all ride the subway system and everyone has to be together. It's a melting pot, okay?

You know Robert Moses? Like everyone thinks of Robert Moses, rightfully so, as a fucking evil demigod. But in the beginning, Robert Moses was a fucking socialist. Robert Moses built the beaches on Long Island and took the land away from the rich people. He was like, We're making public beaches so that people who work so hard during the week can take a bus and take their families to see the ocean.

Just look what this city did in a couple generations. They made something spectacular, the envy of the world.

But unfortunately? Post-World War Two? By the time Puerto Ricans started immigrating? It changed. Like, some of that shit was dried up. Manufacturing and . . . it wasn't the same. They didn't get the same deal. It was different.

Same idea, but different.

⇶⤛

---

104 CUNY stands for City University of New York. With twenty-five campuses, eleven senior colleges, seven community colleges, and seven postgrad schools, it's the largest urban public university system in the United States.

I got a 9/11 story. But I wasn't in New York. I was in L.A.

I was writing on a TV show. My whatever, my career. It got to the point where all my agents were pushing me to do television. But I didn't want to do television. I just wanted to be a playwright.

And so, to get them off of my back, I said, "I'll do television, but only if it's David Milch or Tom Fontana.[105] Otherwise, I don't want to do it. Don't call me. Don't bother me."

Two days later, I was sitting in this hotel on Park Avenue with David Milch. And he hired me on the spot for this show called *Big Apple*. It only lasted, like, eight episodes on CBS. This was in 2001.

So that was my first time working in TV, and it only lasted two months. Life lessons. I was still trying to decipher if the guy's, like, a legit genius, then it was over.

And [my agents] were like, "Well, would you just take some more meetings?"

So I took a meeting with this guy. He was younger than me, but he had his own show on NBC, Sunday nights.

We did an interview. He was a good salesman. And I decided to go to California and work on his show.

He really sold me on the idea. It was a cop show. I like cops and stuff.

I got a place in L.A. It was like a *Melrose Place* type of place. Little apartment, cheap complex. Some friends of mine from New York were there: Gary Perez and Marlene Forte. Marco Greco. They're all New Yorkers, all members of my theater company.

Now my boss's idol was . . . let's call the guy Gary DeVanne, okay? This famous director/producer/screenwriter. So my boss loved Gary DeVanne so much, he made us watch all of his movies. To get a feel for them, you know? And then he asked us what we thought. Me and the other writers.

---

105 David Milch is a multiple Emmy Award-winning writer who created or co-created several iconic NYC-based shows, such as *NYPD Blue*, *Brooklyn South*, and *Big Apple*. Tom Fontana has also won many awards. He lives in NYC, where he's had several plays produced while working on shows like *Oz* (which he co-created), *The Beat*, *Homicide: Life on the Streets*, *St. Elsewhere*, and *The Jury*.

I said, "I think Gary DeVanne is style over substance." And look. Back then, he was. He's gotten deeper now. But back then?

So my boss was like, "Who the hell are you?"

I probably would have been fired or quit. It was a really rough experience.

Like, keep in mind . . . during all this? I was eating out of the gas station on the corner. I'd been working three months and still hadn't gotten a check from the studio. So I'm drinking, like, the seventy-nine-ounce Big Gulp. I'm eating the pre-packaged hardboiled eggs, cause there's no craft service for me.[106]

But then my boss gave me an episode to write. He comes into my office. He throws down a script and says, "Rewrite."

I was like, "Okay, what do you want me to rewrite?"

"Start at page one."

So that became my thing. I was doing page one rewrites of all the scripts. And fortunately, cause I guess I wasn't arrogant and the other writers liked me, they weren't deeply resentful I was changing their scripts. Also, they were still getting their money. And their scripts were much better, you know?

Well, as soon as I turned in the writing, everything changed. All of a sudden, it's like, "You want craft service? We're getting you a refrigerator." I got an office with a couch. I got promoted.

But, see, I have this aversion to writing. Basically, I can only write at night when there's no one around. So during the day, people would be doing their work. And I'd be like, jerking off, you know? Because I can't work.

So it got, like, at the end of each day—I would say five days out of seven—I'd be pulling all-nighters. I'd come to work on a Monday, maybe leave Saturday, late afternoon. Take Sunday off and come back. I would wash up in there.

Basically, I was living at the office.

I think my boss felt I needed a little inspiration. So one night, I'm

---

106 Craft service is the department in film and TV productions that provides cast and crew with food and beverages.

working. My boss comes in and says, "Stephen, come outside to the parking lot right now."

This is, like, on a Tuesday.

So I go out with him to the parking lot. And I'm like, "Yeah, what's up?"

"You see that light? You see that office?"

I look where he's pointing. "Yeah."

"What time is it, Stephen?"

"It's two in the morning."

"You see those lights are still on? You know whose office that is?"

"No, I don't know."

"That's Gary DeVanne's office. It's 2:00 a.m. and Gary DeVanne's still working. That's why he's Gary DeVanne. He's got the whole floor of that building."

And I was like, "Great. Can I go back to fucking work now?"

➤➤➤◄◄◄

So 9/11, I was pulling another all-nighter. It's 6:00 A.M. L.A. time. It's just me and this security guard in this mini studio on Bundy. We were the only ones in the building.

The guy was from South America or something. He comes in, started talking to me. I couldn't figure out what he was saying. So he goes out and comes back, rolling a TV in. And he turns it on.

What I see . . . it's fucking 9/11, you know? I was like, "Oh my God."

And he was like, "*Dios mio! Ah-bah-bah!*"

I saw the second plane come in [on the TV]. And I thought, we're at war.

We didn't know what was going on.

Then the phone rang. It was my boss. He was like, "Oh, my God! Thank God, you're here! I need you to write an episode!"

"What? You need me to write—"

"I need you to write an episode *right now!*"

"About what?"

"About *anything*. But it needs to prep in two days."

See, the episode we were scheduled to start was about terrorism. So we couldn't do it.

I was like, "Yeah, okay." But I was like . . . fuck! 9/11 is happening!

I couldn't get through to my mother [who was in New York City]. I'm like, is my family alive? What's going on?

Then, my theater company. They're like family to me, but I knew a lot of them were at an intensive retreat in upstate New York, at Horton Foote's farm.[107] We got in touch on 9/11. I remember it was a huge weight off my mind, because at least I knew everybody at the intensive was safe.

But the next call [I got] was from my friends at the apartment complex. And they're like, "Oh, my God! We're so glad we got you! We're all here together. It's going to be all right. We're coming to get you."

I said, "Marlene, I can't."

She said, "What do you mean?"

"I have to stay here."

She wanted me back at our house in L.A. so we'd all be together while we watched our city burn. But I said, "I have to write this episode."

≫≫≪≪

The block I was on got cordoned off for the next two days. The studio was closed. Nobody could get in. It was just me, the security guard, and a cop. And for the next two days, I wrote this episode about a prison break. It was just as unsubstantive as it could possibly be. Like, of course, I'm trying my best. But I'm just so aware that I'm essentially writing bullshit while the world is ending. You know?

And I had a moment where I said to myself, the second I can get out of this job and get the fuck out of L.A., I'm going back to New York and I'm going to write about shit that means something to me.

---

107 Horton Foote (1916–2009) was an award-winning American playwright. He founded the outdoor summer theater Horton by the Stream, in Tannersville, New York.

That hopefully means something to someone else. Because this is just bullshit.

※※

So remember how—I forget how long it was after [9/11]—you couldn't fly? Remember that? It was maybe a couple weeks or something.

I wanted to go home. But my boss didn't want me to go home. He wanted me to keep writing.

I was like, "Bro, I think I gotta go home."

The day before I was supposed to leave, he was like, "Stephen come into my office." So I did.

"You know," he says. "My best friend is so-and-so from the FBI. Right? And look. I'm not allowed to say anything. But there is a *severe red warning*. Do not fly! That's what they're saying. Do. Not. Fly! Now, it's up to you. It's your choice. But please, do not fly. Can I pay you not to fly? Can I fly your parents out here?"

I'm like, "You just told me we can't fly . . ."

※※

That show got canceled three or four months later. And my managers were like, "Can you just take a couple more interviews?"

"No, no, no."

"Just take a couple. You can always say no."

So I did some interviews. Got some offers.

One was this show on CBS with this blond-haired Australian guy. It was actually a good show and they were offering me more money than I thought I'd ever make in my life. But I didn't want to do it and I was afraid to turn it down because I was, like, I'll never make this much money again.

But right around then, I flew to London because we were doing *Jesus Hopped the 'A' Train* in London. Phil Hoffman was the director.

And I said to Phil, "I don't know what the fuck to do. Because I want to be back in New York and I want to, you know, do my thing.

But there's this offer and bah bah bah *bah*! And I don't know what to do. So. What do you think?"

I remember Phil said, "I can't tell you what to do. But I'll just say this to you. If you're gonna say no? Learn how to say no now, at the beginning of your career. Because if you don't learn how to say no in the beginning, you'll never learn and you'll spend your career doing shit you don't want to do."

So I turned the show down and came back to New York.

I think I had, like, $150,000. I thought I was a millionaire. But then, after not paying taxes, it ended up being much more profitable if I'd never gone to the state of California.

At least I was back in New York.

When I got here, I wrote *Our Lady of 121st Street*. That play did well for the theater company. I did some acting.

And I never looked back.

⟫⟪

I did *not* have friends who died on 9/11. But yeah, I knew people who knew people. Which I learned subsequently.

Like, I used to have this old Romanian couple in my building. The Toledos. The husband looked like . . . you know the millionaire dude on the Monopoly board? That's what he looked like. Little big boss man.

His wife was Mrs. Sophia Toledo. She was, like, eighty-three years old. Still working. Tough European stock.

She was a translator for immigration. And so, she was down at World Trade Center on 9/11. And everything came crumbling down.

She was rescued from the rubble. Basically, some big black guy just picked her up out of the rubble and put her, like, upright on her feet. Little ancient Mrs. Toledo.

He made her count to ten and then he was gone, she said. She never got a chance to thank him. But, you know. He saved her life.

⟫⟪

My experience of 9/11 felt like being in an existential French novel.

For me, hell was being alone in that big studio in L.A., writing something meaningless when literally everybody and everything I love was in dire straits.

It felt so horrible to be in L.A. Fluorescent lighting. It wasn't creative. It wasn't real.

I'm from New York, you know? So that's what I write about.

I mean, L.A. . . . . it's nice. I enjoy L.A. I know it's the town they built over the graveyard. I don't care. I've got depression, so the weather, the moon, everything. The food. It's easy to be healthy.

But I've always felt like, if I ever left here permanently, I'd lose my edge. Like, if I left, I'd turn into one of these bitches. You know?

I remember this one time, I'm talking to this guy out there. A writer. He led his own show. Some really big Mucky Muck. And he's like, "Stephen, why don't you move out here?"

I said, "Yeah, man, I love it out here. Maybe I will someday. It's better for me in so many ways. I'm just afraid I'll lose my edge. I need to feel connected, you know?"

And he was like, "Ha ha! You know, Stephen? I was the same as you ten years ago. Ha ha! And I told my wife—honey? Remember, I told you that? I can't be out here, I said. I won't be able to write. But I came out, and it's fine. I do the same work out here and it's great!"

But I was like, "No, I've seen your work, man. See, you lost your fucking edge."

⤐⤙

There's a reason New York was the hardest hit on 9/11. When people come to the United States, they don't fly into Peoria and catch a connecting flight to fucking wherever. They come to New York City. It's the port of entry to the world.

And look, I'm disappointed in our sports teams. They fucking suck. The Jets. The Mets. But, you know . . . we're in the middle of a pandemic, right? And again, people are predicting, like, the doom of New York City. Like, they're saying New York is gonna go away.

Where's it gonna go?

It's change, that's all. It's *got* to change. And you have to allow for that.

Every time some beloved place closes here, I mourn it. And I feel like this is the end. Like, "No more H&H Bagels? Fuck New York!"

But you know what? Let's say, God forbid, there's another, horrible second wave of COVID. And there's more economic devastation, so buildings and businesses are abandoned, blah blah blah.

What's gonna happen?

Someone's gonna take over those buildings. And they're gonna do this thing where they start selling food. Someone else is going to start a theater. That's how it goes.

Like, remember the Bleecker Street Theatre? It was down around the corner from Lafayette? It was gonna close down, and everyone got so upset. They were outraged.

But like, the whole reason they were being squeezed out was because thirty-five, forty years ago, rent here was nothing. Now it's like prime real estate. So that's part of the process.

You have to be open to how the next generation is going to find the next big place. And I'm sorry. It might not be downtown New York. It might be someplace else.

That said . . . yeah, I still believe in New York.

I grew up in the building I live in. And I went through this period where, when I'd walk through the front door, my neighbors didn't hold the door for me. Maybe they thought I was a fucking robber or something. Which is funny since I've been living here longer than any of them.

Like . . . you're *what*? An investment banker from Estonia? Like I said. Now the neighborhood's all about privilege and entitlement.

So I get in the elevator. I've seen these people, like, hundreds of times.

I say, "Hi."

Nothing.

This one guy, my neighbor. He lived on my floor. It got to the point where I wasn't even going to try and talk to this guy anymore. He did this to me all the time.

But then. I'm fortunate enough to win the Pulitzer Prize. I go up in the elevator one time, and my building is suddenly like, [urbane accent] "Excuse me. Are you the fellow who won the Pulitzer Prize?"

"Yessir."

"Oh my god! This is my wife, Mary! This is Susan! You have to come back to our place!"

It was like, everything changed. Like *that*. Word spread. "You know that fat, dirty guy who brings in the blacks and Puerto Ricans? He's actually *somebody!*" Suddenly, everybody started treating me nice.

Yeah, man. I'll take it.

Still, there's a part of me that misses the old days. Like, when you interacted with people in the street, you did it through the filter of We Live in New York.

Now? If I told you how people talk to me in the fucking street? You wouldn't believe it.

Like, I'm walking the dog and some fucking pesky motherfuckers be like, [high-pitched voice] "How come you don't have your dog on a leash? You gotta have that dog on a leash!" You know how they do?

So many times, I just want to turn around and be like, "You know this is New York, right? Is there some reason for you to assume that I'm not insane? That I'm not gonna take out a knife and fucking plunge it through your neck? Huh, motherfucker? Because you want to fight with me about the dog peed too close to the rose bush? Shut the fuck up."

But you pick your battles, you know?

FATHER JAMES MARTIN

Father James Martin, sixty, is a Jesuit priest, a New York Times *bestselling author, and a consultant to the Vatican's Dicastery for Communications.*

His books include Jesus: A Pilgrimage, The Jesuit Guide to (Almost) Everything: A Spirituality for Real Life, *and* A Jesuit Off-Broadway: Center Stage with Jesus, Judas, and Life's Big Questions.

In 2002, James wrote Searching for God at Ground Zero, *a thoughtful and thought-provoking memoir of his time ministering to courageous rescue and recovery workers at the Pile. He also serves as editor-at-large for the Jesuit magazine* America.

After listing these and other honors, comedian Stephen Colbert once introduced Father Martin by saying, "More importantly, you are the chaplain of the Colbert Nation." Without missing a beat, James quipped, "Much more importantly."

Father Martin began working with LGBT communities after June 12, 2016, when an active shooter entered Pulse, a gay nightclub in Orlando, and killed forty-nine people and wounded fifty-three more.

In response to this tragedy, Martin wrote his book Building a Bridge: How the Catholic Church and the LGBT Community Can Enter into a Relationship of Respect, Compassion, and Sensitivity. *He told the* Washington Post *he was "disappointed that more Catholic leaders did not offer support to the LGBT community."*

This stance attracted controversy. While many bishops and cardinals applauded Father Martin's position, others flatly denounced it. Backlash from the Christian far right was as violent as many found it predictable.

Still, on this and other issues, Father Martin persists in pondering God's infinite love. He talks open about what he calls "the mystery of suffering" and the Christian imperative of forgiveness.

When viewed through the lens of 9/11, these elements take on a new and poignant dimension.

I ENTERED THE Jesuit Order in 1988 and was ordained as a priest in June of 1999. So on 9/11, I'd been a priest for two years, but I'd been a Jesuit for much longer.

Before all that, I lived and worked in New York. That was in the early eighties, after I graduated from the Wharton School of Business. I was a part of the financial world for six years. And in many ways, the World Trade Center was sort of a monument to that community.

Like most New Yorkers, I didn't find the Towers particularly attractive. Architecturally, that is. As buildings, they were pretty utilitarian. That part of the city was barren back then. Mostly people went down there for business or maybe to go to Windows on the World.

I would go down there occasionally for some meeting. But really, my primary use for the World Trade Center was orienting myself when I came up out of the subway. Downtown, you could look up, see the Towers, and say, "All right, that's south."

And it wasn't just when I was downtown. On 9/11, I was working for America Media on 56th and 6th. Even there, when you crossed the street, you could look still look south and see the Towers right down 6th Avenue.

I remember how disorienting it was—shocking, really—when I came up out of the subway for the first time after 9/11 and realized they were no longer there. It was like not seeing the Statue of Liberty. Or the Empire State Building. Or the sky, for that matter.

A lot of New Yorkers felt like that, I'm sure.

⇶⤙

On the morning of 9/11, I was at America House, our residence-slash-office. It was a Jesuit community and the office of *America* magazine together. Kind of unusual.

I was at my desk around 9:00 A.M. My mother called from Philadelphia and said, "A plane hit the World Trade Center."

My first thought was—I'm sure people told you this, too—of the pictures I'd seen of that World War Two airplane that hit the

Empire State Building.[108] And I said to my mom, "Well, I don't work anywhere near there. Why are you calling me?"

Then I turned on the television and saw the first Tower was hit. Obviously I thought it was an awful, tragic thing, and I thought of the people who were in there. I don't know if you remember, but at the time, people were unclear what was going on. It's just a terrible accident, that's what I thought.

A few weeks before, there'd been a fire in a tall office building in Center City, Philadelphia. A terrible mess. And I remember thinking, "Wow. They'll have to do the same thing here." You know, kind of dismantle the building.

We just weren't able to comprehend it. The scale hadn't hit me yet.

That morning, I had a doctor's appointment across town. On my way there, I started seeing all these people on the street checking their cell phones. This had to be within half an hour of the first plane hitting. I looked downtown and saw plumes of smoke pouring out of the building. I remember thinking it looked like a giant cigarette burning at the end of 6th Avenue.

When I came back from my doctor's appointment, the woman who's our receptionist said the Towers had collapsed. I got a bit nasty with her. I said, "What are you listening to? What kind of ridiculous radio program is that? What are you talking about?"

"No, no," she said. "They collapsed."

I got mad at her. I said, "Stop. Don't tell me that. It's crazy."

Then I went to my room and turned on the TV. I saw . . . and I couldn't believe it.

❯❯❯◀◀◀

That night, as you know, the whole city shut down. Our cook wasn't around, so I remember I cooked dinner for our community. Right after

---

108 On July 28, 1945, Lt. Colonel William F. Smith Jr. was flying a B-25 Mitchell bomber from Bedford Army Air Force Base in Massachusetts to Newark Metropolitan Airport in New Jersey. Disoriented in the thick fog, Smith made a wrong turn. His aircraft crashed into the north side of the Empire State Building, between floors 78 and 80. Smith and the other two soldiers aboard the B-25 were killed, along with eleven civilians in the building.

dinner, I walked from 6th Avenue all the way over to 9th, to St. Luke's Roosevelt Hospital. But they said, "No, no, we don't need you here."

So I headed to Chelsea Piers, because there was a rumor that that's where survivors were taken. I went to a triage center where there were all these priests and nurses and doctors. At that point, it was a very ad hoc situation. There was no guidance from the Archdiocese of New York or the Jesuits or anyone. Everyone was there on their own.

We waited a couple of hours. I expected at any moment that dozens of injured people would come in. But they didn't. No one came. Because, as we now know, there were no survivors.

I went back the next day, but it was the same thing. It was frightening.

>>>«<<

Now in those first few days, do you remember all the talk about missing people? Posters of the missing went up all over the city. Of course—again—there were no survivors. But we didn't know that then.

There was an article in the paper that said if you're a family member and you're looking for someone, you could check lists from all the hospitals. And there was a center set up at the New School, at one of their buildings. On 12th Street, I think it was. I went down there to help people, to counsel them. But there wasn't a lot to do.

The next day, I went back to Chelsea Piers. I was still looking for a way to contribute. And this is where the ministry kind of started.

A police cruiser came up to me. The police officer leaned out and said, "Do you want to go down there?"

I was wearing my Roman collar, so I was easy to recognize. I said yes.

"Get in," he said.

I'll never forget it. We drove from Chelsea Piers. I was in the backseat with a psychiatrist. I think the police officer had just sort of picked him up, too. We drove further and further south. That's when I started to see how things were.

See, if you were in Manhattan . . . say, near the 40s and 50s . . .

you couldn't really tell something was wrong. I mean, sure, there was less traffic. And there was the smell. Other than that, though, things seemed pretty normal.

But then we kept driving down past 14th Street. And you started to see, like . . . ash. We kept going south, and I saw fires burning all over the place. This was on September 13.

We pulled right up to the site. I got out. The psychiatrist said, "Good luck." The car drove away.

I was by myself at the Pile.

It was really overwhelming, like a scene from a war movie. Terrifying. The scale of it. These huge jagged remains of the building. And it was still on fire, still smoking. Other buildings nearby were still burning, too. And the smell was . . . well. You knew you were standing next to a grave.

I saw hundreds of uniformed personnel from every possible agency. Like an alphabet soup of initials: OSHA and CIA and FBI and army people. Policemen and firemen. This was before any sort of order had been imposed on the place. In a few weeks or a few days, maybe, there would be fences. But I just walked right in. Back then, even the term "Ground Zero" was new.

I remember looking around and wondering what I could possibly do. And here I thank my Jesuit training. Because, I thought, I cannot work in the morgue. I just didn't think I was capable of doing that. But I thought that at least I could minister to the rescue workers. So that's what I started to do.

When I say minister, I mean trying to help them. You listen to them. "How are you?" That sort of thing. Most of this is what we call a ministry of presence. In the same way as if you were a firehouse chaplain or a police chaplain, you help people to find God where they are. To know God's present among them.

But you know what was funny? The people I met were more solicitous of *me*. I kept hearing, "How are *you* doing, Father? Are *you* okay? Is this difficult for *you*?" It was so generous.

Everyone I saw was so other-directed. Other-centered. This was evidenced by their already being down there. I found it very moving.

So that's what I did for a couple of weeks. I was walking around, ministering, helping people. By that point, we knew there were no survivors. It was just rescue workers. Then I brought other Jesuits down and we celebrated Mass there, which was incredible.

I wrote about this in my book *Searching for God at Ground Zero*. Which, actually has reminiscences that are probably more accurate. Because, you know, it was twenty years ago.

Which I still can't believe. I just can't believe it.

⫸⫷

My experience of Ground Zero was one where the Holy Spirit was present. It was a place of generosity and love, community and union. Charity, concord, and service.

There were all these people working for others. And remember, you had people coming from all over the country. In those early days, anyone would come in. Firefighters, sure, but also . . . there were these women from the Midwest who'd set up a candy stand. I'll never forget that.

So while, for many, Ground Zero was a place of Good Friday— the suffering, dying, and burial of Christ—I saw a different aspect. I saw it as a place of Easter Sunday. Because there was a sense of new life there. Both these things present at the same site.

What do I mean by the term "Holy Spirit?" I mean God's presence. An active presence. And that's important. Because you could say that God's presence is everywhere, the idea that God's spirit pervades the world as a sort of benign presence. But I believe God's Spirit impelled those people to listen to their conscience. "Go and help," it said. And they listened. That's the active spirit I'm talking about. This sense of the Holy Spirit drawing people together.

⫸⫷

I'll never forget this. One day, there was sort of like a tourist boat docked at the river nearby. This was on a Sunday. And there was a ton of food down at the site because, if you remember, restaurants were donating all this food. And a lot of people working at the site would go and eat their meals on this boat.

So this Sunday, I was there. We had celebrated Mass outside. Like I said, an interesting, very moving experience. And after Mass it was lunchtime, so my fellow Jesuits and I lined up to go on this boat.

It had two floors, as I recall. Two levels for dining. And when I walked on, I saw this scene of, if you can imagine, nurses, doctors, police officers, firefighters, CIA, FBI, volunteers. Everyone eating together. And all I could think of was the Eucharist, the heavenly banquet. This beautiful image of everyone breaking bread together, which is a very Christian image. An image of unity and togetherness. For me, it was another experience of the Holy Spirit.

But get this. After I'd eaten, I got off the boat and looked back. What's the boat called? The Spirit Boat. Written on the side in big letters.

The Spirit Boat.

And I thought, well, of course.

>>><<<

Why did God let 9/11 happen? The answer to that question is, we don't know.

The deeper answer, of course, is free will.

The terrorists who flew those planes into the Twin Towers and into the Pentagon and in Pennsylvania . . . they had free will. Meaning they were able to choose between doing good and evil. And they chose evil. That's part of the world we live in.

But you know . . . "Why does evil happen?" is a question that saints and theologians have grappled with for 2,000 years. And there's still not a satisfactory answer.

When I talk to a person who self-identifies as a believer in Christ and they ask me that question, I ask them to give their own perspective on it first. Then I listen to where they're coming from. Because I think that's important. I'll ask them why they're asking that question.

Usually it has to do with some suffering in their own lives. And I see if I can help them to find God in the midst of the suffering. Then, only at the end do we talk about what's called the mystery of suffering.

The mystery of suffering is . . . well, let's put it like this. We have some propositions that don't match, am I right? God is supposed to be all good and all powerful. But if God is all good, why is there suffering? If there's suffering, maybe God isn't all powerful. Or if God is all powerful and there's suffering, then maybe God isn't good.

These things seem inconsistent and that's the mystery. It doesn't square. We have to face that.

The question of 9/11 is right up there with "Why does a little child get cancer and die?" Or the Holocaust. Any answer to these questions feels really unsatisfactory.

I mean, just think of all the answers we've been given over time. "God's testing us." "God's punishing us." "There's some hidden meaning that we're meant to find out."

These answers are all pretty monstrous when you think about it. And they're all about the same topic, which is suffering. Which we simply can't answer in a satisfying way.

In the end, I think the believer needs to come up with his or her own meaning. It's especially challenging during an event like 9/11, some terrible tragedy. Or when someone is sick. Or if you get sick. You really have to grapple with this.

For most people, the answer they come to is that God is *with us* in the suffering. And this enables them to continue. But some people find it a real challenge to their faith.

I personally believe that God is with us in our suffering. Also, that Jesus understands our suffering. Because he was—he *is*—both human and divine. So when we pray to Jesus, we can be sure that he understands all things. Not only because he's divine, but because he experienced all things as a human being.

＞＞＞＊＜＜＜

As a Jesuit, I got a sense that there were concentric waves of suffering that came from 9/11.

First, there was the inner wave: people who lost a loved one, family members, and friends. The most immediate damage. But there was also this secondary wave where you knew people who knew people.

The second wave wounds were tangential. They still hurt, but they weren't so immediate.

Another wave was the people who lived in that neighborhood whose lives and homes were affected. Then New Yorkers as a group. Then Americans. And so on.

The waves rolled out and, obviously, everyone had different responses.

But put yourself in the position of someone in that central group, someone who lost a loved one in a very public way. See, it wasn't just a terrible accident, sudden and awful. No, the added layer of the event being so *public* makes it even more difficult.

For those people, the meaning of 9/11 is probably going to be a lot different than it is for the people in all other circles.

I wouldn't want to say that people in that inner circle "missed anything." Meaning, they've probably gone through the whole grieving process. But I would say that we as a country sort of skipped some stages. And by doing that, we squandered the unity we'd gained. That, plus our ability to pick a more thoughtful response to what happened.

⟶⟫⟪⟵

Do you remember the very beginning—let's say the first month or two right after 9/11? The country was united. The whole world was saying, "We're all New Yorkers. We're all Americans. We're all with the United States."

There was this tremendous opportunity for us to build on that. But we didn't. After 9/11, some pretty abhorrent things happened.

I'm not a politician. But basically, things could have gone two ways. We could have said, "This is awful. A group of insane terrorists did this. We have to take a new look at terrorism." I mean, in another scenario, you could imagine President Bush saying, "This is a wakeup call for all nations. We're going to work together through the United Nations to beef up our security, fight this particular brand of terrorism where it started, and make sure this never happens again."

But we didn't do that. Instead, the government said, "We're going to war in Iraq." So now, instead of the global war against terror, we got a war in Iraq and Afghanistan. It shifted people's focus to "We have to kill Saddam Hussein."

Obviously, I hold no brief for Saddam Hussein. But this focus seemed off.

And you know, it's strange. A lot of people say we're a Christian nation. Well, Jesus said, "Love your enemies. Pray for those who persecute you." Jesus forgave his executioners on the cross. That's a pretty clear example of how forgiveness should work. But a lot of Christians, I think, find that countercultural. That is, they think it would be impractical as a matter of public policy.

Imagine what would have happened if George Bush had said, "I personally forgive the terrorists." I think he would have been impeached.

Again, I'm not a politician. But from what I understand, Saddam Hussein didn't have a whole lot to do with 9/11. If there was any connection at all, it was with Saudi Arabia.

Also, you read enough history, you'll see that a lot of people in the Bush administration were looking for an excuse to finish what George Bush's father didn't do. Look what Colin Powell was asked to do in front of the UN.

So we ended up going to war with Iraq. I strongly disagreed with that. So did the Vatican, by the way. I thought 9/11 was used as an excuse to invade Iraq. And by doing that, I think we lost a lot of that unity, peace, and concord, both globally and within the United States.

I was very disappointed by that. I thought it was a real tragedy. Still do.

Also, you could make the case that our invading Iraq completely destabilized the region. The effects of that situation have been lasting.

As Pope John Paul II said, "War is always a defeat for humanity."

For me, it was an example of how we can listen to the Holy Spirit or not. That's the whole point. We get to choose. It's up to us. So which will it be?

⋙⋘

The war was something I disagreed with on a large scale. On a smaller scale, I strongly disagreed with how they redeveloped Lower Manhattan.

It's a grave. And I thought it should have been left like that, the entire sixteen-acre campus. I wanted to see it left as an open field. But of course, people said, "You can't possibly do that."

The rush to rebuild was so total. It was as if we were saying, "We have to show that what happened here doesn't affect us."

Well, of course it affects you.

It's like saying, "Oh, my dad died today. But I'm going to show everybody how tough I am by going right back to work. I'm not even going to the funeral. No. Right back to work the next day."

What does that say? How does that show people anything?

But the speed with which the city, the state, and everything snapped into action was just breathtaking. We're going to rebuild! I thought, well, that's typical American arrogance. It's all about money. That's all it is.

The truth is, Ground Zero became a tourist attraction almost immediately. Within, like, a week there were people right outside the perimeter selling postcards with images of the explosion. The worst pictures you can imagine. It was so weird. It was disgusting. I found it offensive to the people who suffered that day

It's the monetization of tragedy. It's this statement that people can make a buck off of anything. What does that say about us as a culture?

Now, look. A lot of the people selling those postcards were poor people trying to make a living. Most of them didn't speak English. So you could assume they were recent immigrants who were struggling economically.

Still. They know what happened there. And you chose to do this? But I get it. It's complicated.

>>>«««

The way I see it, there were two groups of people who died at Ground Zero. There were the office workers, meaning those who were killed when the planes flew into the buildings and got trapped in the Towers when they collapsed. And there were the rescue workers who gave their lives trying to help the office workers escape. Rescue workers who continue to give their lives to this day, I would add.

Now, with the first group, that was murder pure and simple. It was an act of war. But the second group, there was a kind of selflessness involved. A sacrifice.

Members of that second group understood the risk, but they went in anyway. Firefighters, police officers, and rescue workers. They offered their lives. That's different.

That's what I wanted to see celebrated at the site. But it isn't.

In the memorial, when you go and look in those fountains, it's completely despairing. You look into that void. The water just goes into this black hole. How is that in any way a marker for the selfless sacrifice of the rescue workers? That's what I object to. It's nihilistic to me. It's more geared toward the sudden deaths of unwilling participants than the heroic sacrifice of first responders.

I also have problems with the new building, World Trade Center One. What do I want to say about it? It's banal. I don't think it's very distinguished. I mean, after a year of design contests, that's what they came up with? That's it? It's just a big glass-and-steel office building.

Yes, I've been down to the memorial. But I couldn't bring myself to go into the museum, though. I just . . . I have a hard time going down there.

I didn't lose any friends or family at the Trade Center, so I don't want to put myself on that level. But I don't want to go into that museum. I just don't want to.

>>><<<

Am I dissatisfied with parts of our culture? Sure. As a Christian, you should be dissatisfied.

We can't forget how parts of our society were impelled to help. Like I said, they came from all over the country. But then other parts were like, "We're gonna show them. Let's get something built down there as soon as possible!" So it's a mixed bag.

When I talk about turning within to find the Holy Spirit, letting it guide us . . . I'm assuming that you're a believer in Jesus Christ. If you're not, you could say instead that you're acting morally, rather than religiously.

So how do we get people to go there more? To really lean into the Holy Spirit? Basically, the question is: "Why do people choose bad things over good things? And how do we get them to choose good things over bad things?"

Jesus came and tried to help us figure that out. But a lot of people don't pay attention to him anymore, even in the church.

Still, I think there's a couple ways we can do it.

First, God says in the Old Testament, "Choose life."[109] And Jesus says, "Love your neighbor as yourself." And: "Do good to those who persecute you. Pray for the poor or the sick." So the first thing we can remind people is that these are things God asks us to do.

Second, we can urge people to act in ways that, ultimately, are for everyone's good.

Third, when you look within you, you can feel those two impulses, right? Selfless and selfish. Egocentric and charitable. Loving and not loving. You can feel that within you.

It's a kind of battle that goes on. It doesn't mean that we're all possessed by the devil. However, it does mean that we all have impulses. And we have choices to make.

This is a very Jesuit concept. One of the main insights of Jesuit spirituality is that God wants us to make good decisions. Not just

109 "I call heaven and earth to witness against you this day, that I have set before you life and death, the blessing and the curse: therefore choose life" (Deut. 30:19).

wants—he'll *help* us make good decisions.

So how do we do it? By paying attention to those feelings. In the Jesuits, we call this discernment. By looking at our feelings and by discerning them, by asking ourselves, "Why am I acting a certain way?" We can listen to God's voice, which essentially comes to us through our conscience.

Let's take a simple example. Someone cuts in front of you on the subway. You get angry. Now, you have two choices. You can punch this person in the face. You could. That could happen. That's how a lot of people feel. Or you can let it go.

Now, most people are smart enough to know—they also know in their conscience—that punching someone would be a bad thing to do, even though you feel it. So that's what I'm talking about.

Your interior life, your sense of right and wrong, can guide you. But very often, we don't pay attention. We punch the guy who cut in front of us on the subway when, really, that person had no idea he was stepping in front of us in the first place. We do that as individuals. But we discern even less as a country.

Obviously, 9/11 was directed at us. It wasn't an accident; it was a clear attack. Premeditated.

But look at what happened *after* 9/11. We wanted to punch someone, and we ended up punching the wrong person. That can happen when you're angry.

So again, I wish we'd dealt with what happened much better, in a more surgical way. Because, ultimately, our lack of discernment made the world less safe, not more safe.

Why don't people pay attention more? Go *within* more? Try to discern a bit more? Because, ultimately, God gave us free will. We're capable of giving in to our sinful nature. And sometimes we do.

Will that ever change? No. By which I mean, I don't think human nature's going to change. But I do think people can still get better and try to work with the good.

JILLIAN SUAREZ

While researching follow-up interviews, I began reading stories about the "Children of 9/11"—boys and girls who lost a parent or parents that day. Sadly, this list is long.

The average "9/11 kid" was nine years old when their father or mother was killed. Some were infants destined to grow up having no clear memory of their parents. In a handful of cases, the child had yet to be born when the planes struck the Towers.

Losing a loved one is always hard, but a child who loses a parent resides in a special sort of vacuum. The person you miss is always there. Always with you. Except that they're not.

There is no one to guide these children through the trials of being a teenager. No one to help them with math problems once the dinner plates have been cleared. No one to hug them after a graduation, or to walk them down the aisle.

Hearing "He's watching" or "She would have been proud of you" is never a substitute for the real thing.

For all these reasons and more, I was grateful when Jillian Suarez, twenty-eight, consented to be interviewed.

Jillian's father, Ramon, was an officer with the NYPD. On 9/11, Ramon and his partner, Mark Ellis, left their assigned posts to go down and help at the Towers. Both officers perished in the line of duty.

That in itself is a tale worth telling, a story of sacrifice worthy of men and women who wear their badges with honor. But what Jillian Suarez did with her life is more than a testament to her father's memory. It's a master class in alchemy, a lesson in turning lead into gold.

It turns out that there's a method for turning something bad into something good. And Jillian Suarez found it.

MY MOM SAID one of the reasons she fell in love with my dad was because of his great dimples. Every picture you see him in, he's smiling. He was just a ray of light. That's my memory of him. And not just me—that's how other people remember him, too.

All growing up, I knew he was a police officer. I knew he loved his job. He loved wearing the uniform. He loved helping people, being there for people. That's how I remember him. I was very proud of him for being a police officer.

I remember him being gone at different hours. Like, sometimes he'd be able to pick me up from school, and sometimes he wouldn't. But he was always there. He was very involved in my life.

At one point, he coached my elementary school track team. He was very dedicated. I mean, he wasn't like a half-assed coach. He was there for the kids. He always made sure, if the kids were having trouble, he was going to help them in every way possible.

This one time I remember, I had a track meet at St. John's University, and he had worked a double shift that day. But he didn't go home to get sleep. He just went straight to the track meet after work.

I remember this day so clearly because this was the day that I won my first gold medal. I was the smallest out of the group, and I ended up winning the gold medal.

I remember my dad was so happy, he fainted. He was happy, he hadn't got sleep, so it was all a combination of that. But he had that kind of happiness for everyone who won a medal. He was amazing with kids. It was remarkable.

He was sort of a health nut, too. Like, he was definitely a runner. He was a boxer. Always working out. Sometimes he worked out twice a day. There's never a time that he wasn't able to eat whatever he wanted, no problem. He was always healthy.

I read these stories about him later. Like, one of his old partners, Steve Rentas. He said my dad would see somebody, a colleague, eating a donut or drinking an energy drink. And my dad would say, "You know what? Why don't you have something healthier?"

Officer Rentas said my dad was a perfectionist about everything: His uniform. His appearance. His performance on the job.

That sounds like him. All of it does. It fits with my memory of him.

>>><<<

There's this family story about my dad. We were living in Ridgewood, Queens, in the top apartment, on top of a furniture store. I don't know how old I was but I know I'd been born. I was around when this happened.

So one day, my mom and my dad were all dressed up to go to a party. And I guess my dad looked out the window and he saw a few teenagers beating up a guy across the street. So my dad gave my mom one of those looks, you know? Then he ran downstairs and across the street. He chased these kids and he caught them.

My mom later said she didn't know how my dad used to do that stuff. She said he must've had wings.

He was a track guy. He ran, and he caught them and held them down until backup came. Like, minutes later, a patrol car came and the kids were arrested.

That was my dad.

>>><<<

So that day, this is what I remember.

I had just turned nine on the Sunday, two days before. On 9/11, I was at after-school with a close friend of mine at the time named Ashley. She was a year or two older than me and she lived, like, four blocks away from my house.

We sat down, but the moment I got up to pick up my books, the teachers told us, "Ashley and Jillian, your parents are here."

Ashley and I were, like, huh? We thought it was so weird. I mean, we didn't have a moment of after-school. We'd just sat down and automatically got picked up.

But then we thought, okay. This is cool. We're gonna leave earlier now.

I'm honestly not sure, but I think my dad was supposed to pick me up that day. But the way it happened, I remember my mom picked me up. I was wondering why my she was crying. I thought it was just, like, her and my dad had got in an argument or something. And I thought, you know, it was okay. Everything was going to be fine.

Ashley was going to come over because it was a nice day, as we all remember. And since we'd been picked up early from school, Ashley and I were going to go in the pool. We lived in a three-family home and we had an above-ground pool in the backyard.

I remember I wanted to call Ashley, because I was wondering why she was taking so long and she didn't live far at all. Then I heard my mom screaming on the phone and yelling and saying, "They can't find them!"

I didn't know what was going on. All I know is I ran to my bed, I just fell to my knees, and I prayed. I prayed and prayed. I prayed that my dad was gonna come home, because I'd heard that he was in trouble.

Ashley finally got to the house. We were so excited to go in the pool. We were splashing around and playing, but I kept wondering what was going on.

At the time, my uncle on my mom's side lived in the basement apartment. That's where everyone was. I think they were down there watching the news and trying to sort out what had happened.

I didn't understand the seriousness of what was happening because I wasn't allowed to watch it. I just knew that something was going on because the adults were acting very strangely. They didn't want me to see what was going on. They were trying to protect me, I guess.

I felt that, whatever it was, it involved my dad. But I thought, never mind. He's gonna come home.

Then Ashley said, "Didn't you hear?"

"Hear what?"

She said, "There was a terrorist attack. The World Trade Center got hit with planes."

"Oh my God. My dad is probably there. Because I heard my mom say that he hasn't been found."

But my friend said, "No, he's definitely gonna come home."

And I said, "Yeah, you're right. He's gonna come home."

And then we just enjoyed playing in the pool. We were laughing and playing, and everything was fine because I felt like he would come home.

>>><<<

Obviously, I was little at that time and I didn't know a lot of the details. I learned all this later on.

What happened . . . my dad was assigned to the transit system. Transit District 4, the Delancey Street/Essex Street subway station down on the Lower East Side. It's a little under two miles from the Trade Center. That was his normal assignment.

He was there that day with his partner, Officer Mark Ellis. And I guess they got word about what was happening over their radios. After that? I don't know.

You read some articles, they say my dad hailed a cab. Other articles say he "commandeered" a cab. I also heard that he hailed a cab, then he left it. Jumped right out and ran down there himself.

I assume that he and his partner left Delancey and Essex together and took the cab together. But I don't really know for sure. There's only two people who truly know—that's my dad and his partner.

After that? There's a photograph of my father. He's down at the Towers in the rubble of Tower 1, I guess it was, and he's helping an African American woman whose leg was hurt.

It's clearly my dad in the picture, and this woman is clearly in distress. He was helping her, which of course he would do.

I think that's the last recorded instance of anyone seeing him. People say he ran back into the building, I believe it was the second Tower, the South Tower. And that's where they found him three months later.

The day they found him, that's when it really hit me. He wasn't coming home.

>>><<<

This is what my mother tells me. She was working that day on 5th Avenue in Manhattan. She was an assistant supervisor for an Argentinian bank. She told me, later, she was walking to work. She was on the street, on the sidewalk. She looked at everyone and was wondering what was going on. They were all looking up. Looking south.

And that's when she saw the Tower get hit. The second Tower.

She told me she knew my dad would go there. She said she had, like, a gut feeling that he would be there. He wouldn't *not* help people. He would always be there.

Later that day, Steve Rentas's wife called my mom. She asked if my mom had heard from my dad.

"No," she said. "What happened?"

Mrs. Rentas said, "Carmen, he's not answering his radio. They're looking for him. They can't find him."

And my mom knew right then that something was wrong. She knew it in her heart, she said, and she almost fell to the ground because even then, she had an idea of what was going on.

⟫⟫⟪⟪

On December 4, 2001, President George W. Bush awarded my dad the New York City Police Department Medal of Honor. That's the highest award the agency bestows on its members.

My dad was also awarded the 9/11 Heroes Medal of Valor. There's a plaque with his name on it at the Transit District 4 precinct in Union Square.

But growing up, I didn't tell many people about my dad. For about ten years after it happened, I told people he passed away of a heart attack.

Obviously, people in my high school knew who I was and who my dad was . . . how he really passed away, and when. I mean, they named the intersection of Catalpa and Woodward Avenues after him.

But for people I'd just met? I didn't want them to know. I guess I didn't want people to look at me differently. Because not everyone knows somebody whose parent passed away on 9/11. I wanted to start over fresh.

It helped that I got to meet people who'd also lost family members that day. My mother and I are very active in the New York Police and Fire Widows and Children's Benefit Fund. They're a great organization. Amazing. Like, they're never not there for us.

They would take us to baseball games and hold dinners. We'd get to talk with other people who were like us. It meant a lot. It especially helped my mom. She met a lot of her best friends through the Fund.

But at the same time, I never spoke much about what had happened. I wasn't speaking to anyone, really.

It's not easy to constantly go through the memorials and hear your father's name on that list of people who passed away.

⟫⟪

All along, it was sort of made clear to me that my father's shield was there if I ever wanted to be on the job. They kept it for me. And I knew I always wanted to be a police officer. I always wanted to be like my dad.

When he passed away, I remember feeling, I'm going to be just like him.

So I went to St. John's University, got a BS in criminal justice. That was in 2015.

Right after graduation, I went straight into a program to get a master's degree in homeland security, criminal justice, and leadership. I got that in 2017. All told, I studied six years.

Then I went to work full-time in the forensics department for the NYPD. About a year later, I entered the New York City Police Academy. That was April 2018. That's a six-month program. It's like a full-time job. There's physical training, firearms training, procedural training. It's pretty intense.

I graduated with my class in October 2018. I remember getting my father's badge. It's badge number 12671, and it's mine now. That shield means everything to me.

At the swearing-in ceremony, the commissioner for the NYPD, James O'Neill, he said, "I know your dad is proud you're wearing his shield today, Jillian. And so are we."

When I felt the confetti coming down, I felt him hugging me. My dad was there.

⫸⫷

Yes, I like being a police officer. I always saw my dad's passion for his job and how he loved wearing that uniform. I want to be able to help others the way he did.

The whole thing is about helping people and being there for people. If people need me, I'll drop anything to help them. I don't care what it is. That's what gives me happiness.

But it's definitely tough. It's not a normal job. It's not about the nine to five. It's not about, this person will be home at this time. You don't always know what times you'll be home. Sometimes, you don't even know if you'll be able to make it home at all. You sleep at the precinct. It's a lifestyle the people around you have to adapt to.

There are times where you have to miss holidays, you have to miss birthdays. It's tough on people. Not every person's used to missing a holiday with their loved ones. I mean, now, with this generation, it's sort of easy to FaceTime people. But even then, it's hard to see your family together and know you're not there with them.

I remember my best friend had her baby gender reveal—and this is a best friend of mine of fifteen years. But I couldn't make it. I had to be at work. I was so sad, because my best friend was having twins. I was so excited to see her facial expression. And it killed me inside to see it through a FaceTime call and not be there and hug her and cry with her and be excited with her.

It just shows, you have to make sacrifices. This job is all about sacrifices.

But it's worth it. It's worth it. At the end of the day, you took that shield. You took it with honor. And with honor you will carry it.

I know my father is watching me. And I know I won't let him down.

GLENN GUZI

The Port Authority of New York and New Jersey (PANYNJ) is a bi-
state transportation agency created in 1921 by an interstate compact au-
thorized by the United States Congress. It oversees a zone known as the
Port District, defined as a circle whose radius extends twenty-five miles
from the Statue of Liberty.

Over its long and storied history, PANYNJ has built many iconic structures, including the George Washington Bridge, the Lincoln and
Holland Tunnels, the new Bayonne and Goethals Bridges, and the World
Trade Center. The agency owns and operates these infrastructure assets
along with a portfolio of others, including the three major airports most
iconic to New York City: JFK International, Newark Liberty International, and LaGuardia.

Known by some as the fifty-first state, PANYNJ has its own police
force (PAPD). The more than 2,200 officers of PAPD are sworn to protect the region's ports, airports, bridges, and tunnels. By doing so, they
protect America's gateway to commerce and travel on the northeast coast.

Under the terms of the 1921 compact, the governors of New York
and New Jersey run the Port Authority cooperatively.

Glenn Guzi, MBE, has worked for PANYNJ since 1998. He currently works on Major Capital Projects and GOCOR, the agency's Government and Community Relations department. GOCOR's primary
mission is to represent the Port Authority's interests and initiatives to its
government, community, and commercial stakeholders.

On September 11, 2001, Glenn, fifty-two, was the designated GO-
COR representative for the World Trade Center. His office was on the
68th floor of Tower 1, where the Port Authority was headquartered. The
agency lost eighty-seven employees in the terrorist attacks, including thir-
ty-seven members of the PAPD.

In the weeks, months, and years following 9/11, Glenn and his Port
Authority colleagues became instrumental in rebuilding the World Trade
Center site. The obvious work of clearing debris and putting up new struc-
tures was the least of their worries. As Glenn so ably points out, at the

core of all rebuilding efforts was the ongoing, compassionate, and skillful attempt to harmonize hundreds if not thousands of conflicting interests and viewpoints.

My interview with Glenn took place in late January 2021. Though it boggled my mind, he noted then that, nearly two decades after 9/11, certain aspects of rebuilding the World Trade Center were still underway.

I NEVER TOOK much vacation back then. On September 11, 2001, I think I'd only taken four days off the whole year. But I had this personal commitment come up, which required me to be home on the afternoon of 9/11.

Being me back then, I spent the better half of a week debating, "Should I take the whole day off? Or just take a half day? The whole day? A half day?" I couldn't decide. Something never felt right when I thought about going in.

At the time, our agency's executive director was a man named Neil Levin. He'd only been on the job a few months. That morning, he was scheduled to be at a breakfast function at Windows on the World, forty floors above our offices at the top of Tower 1. It was normal for people like me—meaning government affairs people—to attend those functions, especially if outside entities were involved.

Basically, I wasn't sure if I'd be asked to attend or not. That was part of my back-and-forth about taking a vacation day.

⇉⇇

So now it's Monday night, September 10. I live in Peekskill, right up the Hudson River in Westchester County, the northern suburbs of New York City. I was having a glass of wine with a friend and telling him how I was still on the fence.

He said, "What's wrong with you? Just take the day off!"

"You're right," I said. "This makes no sense. I'll do it."

As soon as I did that? This cloud of easiness came over me, and I felt completely comfortable. There was an energy taking place around this decision that I could not understand. Voices telling me not to go in. I felt an internal pull not to go into the office. That night, I felt completely safe. I'm not making that up.

But the next morning rolled around. It's Tuesday, September 11, 2001, and I second-guessed my decision. Immediately, the feelings of uneasiness came back.

I thought, "Okay, I've got this personal commitment in the afternoon, and I know I have to be home for that. But I'll just go into the office this morning in case something's needed. Then I'll come home."

I put my suit on. I was tying my tie when the phone rang. It was a volunteer for a local board I served on. Back then, I was on a bunch of boards—a historic foundation board, a parks conservation board, a performing arts center board, you name it. This volunteer was calling me because she was nervous about an upcoming function. I kept reassuring her. "Look, you've done this kind of work before. You'll do the right thing." Then I hung up the phone.

That conversation made me late for my train. And I said, "You know what? This is crazy. Something's intervening here again." I took my tie off. "Forget it. I'm not going in."

Quite literally, I thought to myself, "What's going to happen if I don't go into the office one day?"

Well, not much later, I got a call from my friend, Michael, who also lived in Peekskill. He was a commuter, like me, and that morning, he took the train to his office in SoHo, same as he always did.

When I picked up the phone, he was frantic. Michael said, "You've got to get out of the building!"

I was like, "What are you talking about?"

Michael knew where I worked, and his office faced south. He'd said he was looking right at the Towers and he'd seen the plane coming toward them. He was watching it live, and he's shouting, "Get out! You have to get out!"

He didn't know I hadn't gone into work yet.

I heard screaming in the background. That must have been his colleagues watching what happened.

>>><<<

Once I heard the screaming, I hung up the phone and called my office. I got through for a couple of seconds before the lines went down. That was it.

That day, tragedy struck. The unimaginable happened. Evil invaded our lives.

Now, in the case of extreme emergencies, back then there were necessary steps one would take. The most immediate thing was to reach out to leadership who would reach out to the governor of New York, because the situation happened at the World Trade Center. I had to make sure leadership had their emergency protocols in place. But the communication lines were down. It looked like the plane had hit almost precisely where our offices were located. And, of course, Neil was at Windows on the World.

All this was happening at a very quick pace. I mean, like, a matter of minutes.

I remember I was on the phone with Tim, the head of Battery Park City Authority—that's the organization that runs Battery Park City, directly across the street from the Trade Center. Tim had been in the New York governor's office before his appointment to Battery Park, and he told me his office had already had very quick communication with the governors of New York and New Jersey.

So picture this. I'm trying to contact everyone, make sure all channels of communication are open. But suddenly, most of the phone lines are overloaded and I'm home in Peekskill, right? I had no idea what was going on—not with the governments, not with our partners, not with the people I worked with.

When the second plane hit the South Tower, I was talking to Vinny, who was VP of the New York Power Authority. And I exclaimed right away, "This is terrorism, not an accident." The second plane's impact gave the whole event a different complexion.

You know, I stay calm and focused in situations. But this was a disaster.

Then, of course, it got worse.

※※※

One of the people I got through to was Bob Boyle. He'd just retired as our executive director, the man Neil Levin replaced. Even though he'd retired, Bob was still patched into the New York State apparatus.

I told Bob that Neil had been scheduled to attend a function that morning at Windows on the World and I couldn't reach him. I was advised to go to a regional office for the governor of New York in Westchester County. Bob was going to meet me there along with the head of the Battery Park City Authority. The idea was to assemble people who could communicate our knowledge and needs to the governor, who of course has ultimate say in the state of New York.

The office wasn't a far drive for me. I got ready to go.

I remember the South Tower collapsed before I left my house. At that point, I presumed every person in both towers, every person I worked with, was dead. I was devastated. My younger brother, Ed, was with me, and I told him, "They're all gone!"

※※※

My mom ended up driving, because I was too busy on the phone to steer.

We drove past the local election polling station. It was primary day in New York State, and we pulled in. This may seem corny but I said, "We have to vote now! I don't know if I'll have time to vote later!" In all seriousness, my thinking was, "We're under attack. It is supremely important to make sure I still vote."

So we voted.

By the time I arrived at the regional office, both towers were down. Basically, the whole World Trade Center campus had been destroyed. I presumed everyone was gone. I mean, what else could I think? Horrified.

Listen, if I choke up a bit here . . . I've never talked about this before. I mean, the thought of being there that day is horrible, you know? But the fact that I *wasn't* there is also bad, the weirdness of that. There were times in the past I've felt guilty.

Neil Levin died that day. Other people I worked with died. The relatives of friends and . . . sorry. This is hard to talk about.

>>>«««

At the regional office, the officials and I were trying to make some cohesive plan out of what was essentially the unthinkable. The mood was numb. I mean, total shock.

Very quickly it became clear that Governor Pataki had control of the situation, which was a comfort. At that point, it was a national issue and I was in a holding pattern. Things were in play *way* above my pay grade. For the moment, there was nothing to do but go home and wait. But for what? I mean, what was tomorrow going to be? The place where I worked was totally destroyed.

I remember walking out of the building and down the street to my car. I bumped into a married couple I knew, Eileen and Jorge. She was the chairman of the local Democratic Party; we were friends. He worked for a construction company that worked with the Port Authority, but mostly I knew him because we were both on the Paramount Center for the Arts board.

When they saw me on the sidewalk, they stopped their car in the middle of the road and jumped out. Faces in shock. Trying not to cry. They knew I worked in the Trade Center. They ran right up to me, and . . . no words spoken. They grabbed me, held me, broke down.

She whispered in my ear, "You're alive . . . you're alive."

I guess many people thought I was gone. Many people thought that. There were a lot of nervous calls and visits to my mom's house throughout the rest of the day.

Later that night, a guy we all knew and had nicknamed "Lucky" Chuck called me from California, where he had traveled for business. "I hear you're the lucky one," he said. He was all choked up.

But back on the street, the next thing I remember, there were these people—strangers standing around, dumbfounded, watching us. I guess they were thinking, "What's going on? Why are these people grabbing this person and crying in the middle of the road?"

Everyone knew what had happened downtown. But Eileen and Jorge explained where I worked and that, normally, I would have been there. Suddenly, I had strangers comforting me, being human, being one. It was powerful, but I just needed to go home. My head, my being was elsewhere, with my colleagues.

Later, I got together with friends. We had drinks. We had some ice cream at Ariane's house with Michael, the one who'd called me in the morning from his office to warn me. We tried to find Cookie, a friend who worked in Battery Park City. We weren't sure if she'd survived. It turns out she did, and so did our friend, Paulie. Still, I felt empty.

That evening, it hurt too much to sleep. I was elsewhere, I don't know where.

»»»«««

Frankly? If I'd gone in that day? Assuming I'd survived, I don't know if I'd have been mentally able to separate myself and do the work I had to do in the coming months and years. It was a very mind-numbing, body-numbing time.

How to do this? How to find the strength to go all the way through and get the work done? Strength was needed, deep from within. Strength, patience, love, dedication. Love was needed to be able to do this.

There was a lot happening all at once. We dove into our immediate response with laser focus and held engineering consultations to stabilize the site. Because, where the Towers had stood, there was now this big pile of rubble that burned while firefighters tried to stop it for something like forty days. That was going on even below street level. Depending on which part of the campus you stood on, we had ten to twelve stories of sub-level structure.

We also had to deal with the two PATH train tunnels that run under the Hudson, connecting the World Trade Center with Exchange Place in Jersey City. When the Towers collapsed, those tunnels filled with water. Not from the Hudson, but from the fire fighters working to extinguish the blaze. We had to figure out a way to plug the tunnels so Exchange Place wouldn't be flooded. Site stabilization, slurry wall stability.[110] Those were the first big pieces.

But of course, we didn't stop there. Moving forward, the number of players the agency had to deal with was . . . I'd call it voluminous.

The World Trade Center has always been a complex place. The Port Authority designed, engineered, built, and operated the complex. The agency owns the land, the buildings, and so on. But, technically, the Port Authority is a separate entity from the city and state of New York. So we had to meet with local, city, and state elected officials. We met with our neighbors, meaning Battery Park City Authority. We met with Manhattan Community Board 1, which represents residents who live near the World Trade Center. We met with representatives from the federal government.

To further complicate matters, shortly before 9/11, the Port Authority had entered into a ninety-nine-year net lease on roughly ten million square feet of commercial space throughout the World Trade Center campus. This was a long, drawn-out negotiation between many interested parties. Eventually the lease went to Silverstein Properties.[111]

The agreement included office space in Towers 1 and 2, plus the low-rise buildings we had on campus, World Trade 4 and 5. Silverstein's lease did not include retail space, like the mall beneath the Towers. It also didn't include the PATH systems or the parks that

---

110 The slurry wall is a three-foot-thick concrete structure that was constructed around the World Trade Center's below-ground area, to hold back the Hudson River and keep the buildings' basement levels from flooding. From a structural standpoint, the slurry wall is critical to the site's integrity.

111 Founded in 1957 by Chairman Larry Silverstein, Silverstein Properties (SPI) is a full-service real estate firm that specializes in developing, managing, and investing in properties spanning the gamut of office, residential, retail, hotel, and mixed-used designations.

were designated for PATH.[112] That all remained separate.

When I say we entered the lease "shortly before 9/11," I mean we'd literally held the signing ceremony out on the World Trade Center plaza something like six to eight weeks prior. We handed Larry Silverstein a ceremonial big set of keys. The governor was there. The ink wasn't totally dry on the papers, but the agreement was fully executed. Officially, Silverstein Properties was the prime tenant and operator of this vast commercial space for the next ninety-nine years. This gave them certain legal rights.

When 9/11 happened, SPI had moved some of their people into their new offices. They also lost people in the attacks.

I'm trying to say there were a lot of cooks in the kitchen, and nobody really knew what was going to be made once the stove got fired up.

⇶⇷

Early on, I remember talking with some of our commissioners—our vice chairman and some other people. Our position was that our agency had to be present in the local community more than ever. We couldn't shut the door, close ranks, and disappear. We had to be there and talk to people even when—plenty of times, especially early on—we didn't have new information to share.

I was the representative for the World Trade Center, and that's how I saw my job.

To this day, I tell people, "I don't work at an agency and then, at the end of the day, shut off the light and go to sleep under my desk. No, I go home to a community. And I know that, in my community, we have things that are very important to us."

So I understand there are things that are important to, for

---

112 Everyone has heard of the famous New York City subway system. Less known to out-of-towners is the Port Authority Trans-Hudson rapid-transit system, which connects Lower and Midtown Manhattan with cities like Newark, Hoboken, Harrison, and Jersey City across the river in northeastern New Jersey. Like the subway, Long Island Railroad, New Jersey Transit, and Amtrak train systems, PATH plays a vital role in New York City commerce, and therefore the commerce of the United States.

instance, the community of Lower Manhattan.

Some time after the towers came down, I was at a meeting with Community Board 1. Their members had come to discuss what they thought should happen with the site at some point down the road. And people got very upset.

We heard things like, "Those buildings wouldn't have collapsed if you'd built them better!"

Not true. In retrospect, those buildings did precisely what they were engineered to do in the case of a catastrophic breach. Instead of toppling over and taking out large swaths of the city, they pancaked down. That behavior was engineered. And the fact is, that outcome saved thousands and thousands of lives as well as countless properties.

9/11 was also the most successful evacuation ever conducted. For instance, PATH trains were used to move people out to the safety of New Jersey. And the wedge of light that cut through the cloud of darkness on the east side of the plaza helped guide people to safety.

But there was an individual present at this meeting whose son had been a firefighter killed on 9/11. He was very emotional. Very upset, angry. Rightfully so. There were others present who picked up on his emotion and shouted, "You guys are murderers!"

That term was thrown at us multiple times.

Our chief engineer was with me that day, a true gentleman named Frank Lombardi. He's since retired, but Frank had been with us forever and he was very upset by that accusation. I mean, he's an engineer. This was a direct affront to him.

I remember touching his arm and telling him, "Frank, it's okay. It's not personal."

They weren't really shouting at us. These people were just so upset, devastated and angry. We needed to let them show their emotions.

Personally, I was getting, you know . . . I was getting barraged quite a bit. The man whose son had died was very upset and confronting us.

When it was our time to respond, people turned to me, like, "Okay, what's he gonna do now? How's he gonna respond to that?"

There was nothing an organization, a government, an elected official . . . nothing anyone, really, could say that was appropriate. So I got up, walked over to this man, and I hugged him. We cried together in front of everybody.

The room was quiet. Totally quiet. And the tide began to shift.

What I think is that a lot of people needed someone tangible to blame. The idea of Osama bin Laden or al-Qaeda—that was something very foreign, not understood by people. But the Port Authority owned the World Trade Center. And owners? Well, that was something people could understand.

My gesture didn't change what happened. But it kind of let everyone know we're all human. The pain was shared. Different pain, different losses, but everyone felt it. We were all hurting.

Divisiveness continued throughout the next months and years, especially in certain legal negotiations. But from a human standpoint? That closeness and being together was clearly a better way to be.

That man I hugged? Pre-pandemic, we'd bump into each other downtown here and there, now and then, at functions and so on. He put his energy into something very productive and we developed a good working relationship. Every single time we see each other, we automatically hug each other. We still have a valued relationship.

>>><<<

As time went on, we dealt a lot with FEMA. The president had declared that the U.S. government would stand beside us. He kept his word. The federal government approved $4.55 billion in disaster recovery money.

Those funds were received by a public-benefit corporation called Empire State Development. The governor of New York State and mayor of New York City set up another state/city entity within EST called the Lower Manhattan Development Corporation, which dispersed the funds for very specific rebuilding projects. LMDC was also charged to come up with a plan for rebuilding the area.

So now we had more entities to talk to, deal with, work with. It was a complicated process. Plus, the global community was watching everything we did, jumping in with thoughts and opinions. I mean, this was a global issue. In fact, over the years, as part of my outreach and communications plan, we briefed world leaders whenever they would come to pay their respects, as well as elected officials at all levels of government from all across the United States.

>>><<<

In fairness, the situation was new for everyone. It was a case where the owners of a property, which had been destroyed, were working with a new partner to determine what ultimately was going to be rebuilt on the site. On top of all that, there were more than a few lawsuits thrown in.

The first and maybe the biggest was an insurance dispute brought from Silverstein Properties. It wasn't against the Port Authority, although it eventually involved us.

See, from an insurance standpoint, there were going to be payouts. But the insurance companies decided that 9/11 represented one terrorist incident. Silverstein claimed it had suffered two attacks, one when the first plane hit Tower 1, a second when the second plane hit Tower 2.

The lawsuits went on and on, the negotiations, the court hearings, all of it. Eventually, it was determined that 9/11 represented more than one terrorist incident but less than two. I think they put the final figure at something like 1.5 or 1.6 occurrences.

I mentioned that our agency was involved. This was because we also had insurance claims pending, and the precedent set in the Silverstein case would affect our own insurance payout. Which, in turn, would affect the scope of rebuilding.

The court finding for the Silverstein case adjusted how much money the Port Authority recovered from our insurers. At which point, we had to renegotiate our lease with SPI.

>>><<<

Larry's initial lease had a proviso that said, should the facilities suffer a complete loss, he had the right to rebuild in kind.

Now, I want to state this up front. There was no foreshadowing here. No conspiracy theory. Provisos like this are something you normally do in insurance, just like with a homeowner's policy. There's language in there for a complete loss of the structure. Very normal.

But the right to rebuild in kind meant the World Trade Center would be rebuilt precisely as it was. A Tower 1, a Tower 2, and so on. Each tower exactly the same height as before. You would just replicate them. That wasn't feasible.

Again, there was literally a global outcry about what should be done at the site. Some people thought nothing should ever be built there again. Some people thought a park should be built. Or a memorial. Just let it be a final resting ground, they said. Other people had strong beliefs that the World Trade Center should be rebuilt precisely as it had been before the attacks.

For as many people you spoke to, there were that many opinions on what should happen.

But almost right away, we knew that rebuilding in kind was impossible. We couldn't just put up new towers and call it a day. There would have to be a memorial. Back then, we didn't know what form it would take. But we knew there would have to be something.

So, we had to renegotiate that lease. Which led to another renegotiation. Which set the stage for another. Three renegotiations in all, all hashing out multiple angles that were developing while we worked.

Since Larry had net leased roughly ten million square feet from us, we had to come up with some way to give him that. Precisely how we'd distribute that space wasn't necessarily spelled out early on. You know, like in two towers, two low-rise office buildings, that kind of thing. It was just too soon for all that.

We still had to go through the design competition. LMDC set up listening sessions held at the Javits Center where people could come, take a look at the concepts being proposed, and comment on them.

They put these sessions online so people all over the world could participate.

We knew that, whatever design was chosen for the campus, it would have to take certain program elements into account. The Silverstein lease being one of them.

Ultimately, a jury selected the design by architect Daniel Libeskind for the master plan and Michael Arad's memorial design called *Reflecting Absence*. This jury included LMDC, the city, and the state. But when I say "the state," I mean both New York and New Jersey.

See, back in the day, the process was in fact very participatory. The governor of New York made it clear that New Jersey and the Port Authority, which is kind of co-owned by both states, would always have a seat at the table. So that's what happened.

You may have read there's sometimes a pull-and-tug kind of relationship between the states, where the Port Authority is concerned. That didn't happen here. Remember, we'd lost Neil. But when it came to appointing a new executive director for the agency, the governor of New York waited until a new governor was seated in New Jersey. That was done as a courtesy. It was very respectful.

I'm saying that people were being sensitive to everyone's needs and interests. Collaboration after a national disaster; I think we all found that very refreshing. And this spirit of collaboration lasted for quite some time. Politicians and public servants from both states maintained an honest working relationship.

Let's be clear. An honest working relationship doesn't mean you always agree. In this case, what it meant was we were able to hold conversations, even on issues where there wasn't agreement. And to do so in ways that were productive.

>>><<<

I don't mind telling you there were days when I thought, "I don't know how we're going to do this." Everything happening downtown was so Herculean. And tiring.

Had anyone taken me aside at the very beginning and painted

an accurate picture of the work that would be required, or said that, "Hey, twenty years later, you'll still be working on elements of re-building the World Trade Center," I might have run the other way. Well, okay. That's not true. I was in it to finish it! I always said, "We need to fix what happened to downtown."

But I can recall plenty of difficult situations. Like, there was a time—this was years down the road—when the site was under con-struction. And one of our people here at the Port Authority is Steve Plate. He's now our chief of major capital projects.

Steve was in charge of rebuilding the entire new World Trade Center. Everything inside the construction fence was his purview. My piece of the puzzle was everything outside the fence, the GOCOR piece—like working with media, networking with our partners, local businesses, and residents. But I strategized often with the folks at World Trade Center Construction. Steve and Alan Reiss, they were the guys in charge. Guys I still work with on other major capital proj-ects today.

Now, Steve's a tenacious, smart, dedicated guy. He knows how important it is to keep a project moving forward, and what it takes to get it done. But there were times I'd have to go in and say to him, "Look, we can't keep building at 2:00 A.M."

Steve would listen. He'd digest and find an accommodation. He always found balance and common ground. Having partners in re-building the Trade Center campus was important.

Why was I telling Steve we couldn't build at 2:00 A.M.? Because there's a woman named Pat, a very vocal and active member of Community Board 1. At the time, she was chair of the Quality of Life Committee. She lived directly across from the World Trade Center site, and I'd arranged with Pat that if she were awakened at night by anything we did, she could call me and wake me up, too. That was only fair, right? And she did. I'm not joking.

Pat is patient, understanding, strong, and smart. A lot of fun. She kept me on my toes, as did Catherine, who chaired CB1 for years.

We forged a very productive partnership for the benefit of Lower

Manhattan, along with the late Liz Berger, who led the Downtown Alliance during the really difficult periods. And many more on CB1, some of whom are no longer with us after so many years. Bloomberg, Patty, Nanette, Nancy—what a great team from the city. These people . . . we worked *together*, do you see? By working together, we produced results. And we became friends.

That's the point I'm trying to make. The story of rebuilding downtown is a story of cooperation. Doesn't mean it was easy or that we were always on the same page for every issue. We all had a job to do. But that journey led me to create friendships with people who, normally, I wouldn't be in alignment with. We all pulled together. It was that kind of effort.

Thinking of partners, I have to mention my work partner. One of the best working relationships and friendships I've ever had. Sandra Dixon.

We lost Sandra a couple of years ago. Sandra was one of my greatest strengths at work throughout all this. She would always listen, advise, and share. She always allowed me to breathe and laugh, clear my head. We had such different backgrounds, but we were such great friends. I miss her. She contributed so much to rebuilding the World Trade Center, and she contributed so much to me. Her family needs to know that.

≫≪

Now it's twenty years later, and I see a country that's forgotten how to pull together. I don't know if we've lost our way or if maybe we've just forgotten how strong we can be. Even with tremendous political ideological differences, we can be strong and unified.

When people think of 9/11, they often say, "Never forget." Well, clearly we haven't forgotten what happened that day. But I'd like to think we could, maybe on the twentieth anniversary, start to remember what we *became* that day. More unified. More one.

Remember those people I told you about who stopped me on the street? The ones who jumped out of their car and left it parked in the middle of the road? How those strangers gathered around me? How moving and powerful that was?

Some of those people didn't know me from a hole in the wall. And some, you know . . . I'm sure we had different politics. Different viewpoints. But we were all human beings, all Americans. Our differences didn't matter. And I think we may have forgotten that simple message.

This has become a theme of mine when I think about 9/11. On occasion, I've spoken about it: from darkness comes light.

Remember? It was such a beautiful day. Then it got dark. Dark emotionally, yeah, but the sky literally became dark downtown. Still, there was so much beauty and good that came out of it. You saw people coming together, helping strangers they may never, ever have seen again.

On that day we saw what evil was capable of. But also on that day and in the time that followed, we saw the power and beauty of humanity when good people come together. I remember how people cared for each other, stranger or friend.

We were a very strong community back then. I'd like to see us become that again.

⟫⟪

I guess after all this work, I'm still trying to figure out what it all means. Not sure. But I'll tell you this.

On September 10, 2001, there were still plenty of New Yorkers who would say the World Trade Center was ugly. Architecturally, I mean. That the idea of a superblock was a bad idea, from a public planning perspective.

And look. I know that now, twenty years later, there's still a lot of conversation about what was rebuilt down there. But I think what we did was perfect. And right. And wonderful.

Think about this. Roughly half the sixteen acres is now a beautiful, tranquil memorial that preserves the original locations of Towers 1 and 2. Personally, I think having the names engraved on the parapets of those footprints is fitting. I also like that the museum is largely below ground. Working with Alice Greenwald, the CEO of the 9/11 Memorial and Museum, and our steering committee with Jon Stewart, John Feal, Cathy Blaney, Michael Arad, and so many more—we created a beautiful and appropriate addition to the memorial plaza, to recognize and pay tribute to those first responders who'd succumbed to 9/11-related illness.

That includes my cousin, Charlie Wassil.

Now, think of the new buildings we put up to flank those structures. I think it was absolutely the right choice. There was criticism about the Transportation Hub, the cost of it, the architecture. Well, I absolutely love the Transportation Hub. That dramatic spine and wings of the Oculus. It helps us remember by positioning a "Wedge of Light" on the site. Plus, the passages below grade serve and connect all of Lower Manhattan. It's such a spectacular space.[113]

If you look for it, there's a lot of meaning that went into everything that was done. I'm proud that we took a tragedy and created a place where the general public, someone who's not a millionaire or a billionaire, can go and enjoy astounding architecture. And that's the word for it, really. Astounding. They can go and reflect. They can work. They can live. That's the whole point, isn't it? Living.

Back in the day, I used to say, "Given what happened, shame on us if we do anything less than something magnificent with this site." Something compelling, something extraordinary. That's what the global outcry required of us, and I'm glad both the governors in New York and New Jersey saw it the same way. The Port Authority, too. Plus all those who came along in the years that followed.

---

113 Designed by Spanish architect Santiago Calatrava, the World Trade Center Transportation Hub station house, better known as "the Oculus" or "the Hub," was opened to the public in March 2016. The $4 billion project provides entry to PATH lines and other modes of transport, such the New York City subway system, by linking with Fulton Center to the east of the World Trade Center campus and with the Battery Park City Ferry Terminal to the west. The Oculus also plays home to the Westfield World Trade Center mall. From street level, the World Trade Center Transportation Hub presents as an angled cage of interlocked white metal ribs that towers over downtown traffic and looks markedly different than any other structure in Lower Manhattan.

Had we listened to criticism, even our own internal criticisms, certain things would never have happened.

Did you know that, back in the day, the project to make Central Park was way over budget and way behind schedule? It was. But what would have happened if they'd cut that project in half? We wouldn't have Central Park the way it is today.

I'm glad we had the backbone to stick things out. That we had the vision and strength, despite opposition, to do the things we did. Nothing was easy.

But now we have beautiful buildings and a beautiful World Trade Center. We'll have a couple more buildings to come. It's a space that delicately balances what happened on 9/11 with living today and in the future.

When I reflect on all that, I feel incredibly proud and honored to have been a small part of something so huge.

CONTRIBUTING PHOTOGRAPHERS

The photographs in this edition of the book have all been donated by gracious photographers, both amateur and professional alike:

Abby Bullock
Frank Cutler
Damon DiMarco
Dick Duane
Rob Epstein
Fred George
Edward Hillel
R. Andrew Lepley
Bob London
Jessica Murrow
Drew Nederpelt
Steve Olsen
Michael Raab
Bobbie-Jo Randolph
Robert Ripps
Sheperd Sherbell
Scott Slater
Roger Smyth
Andrew Walker

WITH THANKS TO . . .

Martha Kaplan
Jeffrey Goldman
Kate Murray
Charles Goforth
William F. Brandt Jr.
Stephen Adly Guirgis
Carmen Suarez
John Liantonio
Glenn Guzi
Michael Z. Jody
Louis and Darleen DiMarco
Ethan Sky DiMarco

AND WITH SPECIAL THANKS TO . . .

This book's contributors.

Compiling *Tower Stories* was not easy. Many contributors exposed fresh wounds by sharing their stories and artwork so recently after the attack on the World Trade Center.

We offer this page as a place for you, the reader, to pause and reflect on the events of September 11, 2001.